CANADA'S
LEGAL PASTS

UNIVERSITY OF CALGARY Press

Canada's Legal Pasts

LOOKING FORWARD, LOOKING BACK

Edited by
LYNDSAY CAMPBELL,
TED McCOY, AND
MÉLANIE MÉTHOT

© 2020 Lyndsay Campbell, Ted McCoy, and Mélanie Méthot

University of Calgary Press
2500 University Drive NW
Calgary, Alberta
Canada T2N 1N4
press.ucalgary.ca

This book is available as an ebook which is licensed under a Creative Commons license. The publisher should be contacted for any commercial use which falls outside the terms of that license.

LIBRARY AND ARCHIVES CANADA CATALOGUING IN PUBLICATION

Title: Canada's legal pasts : looking forward, looking back / edited by Lyndsay Campbell, Ted McCoy, and Mélanie Méthot.
Names: Campbell, Lyndsay, editor. | McCoy, Ted, 1978- editor. | Méthot, Mélanie, 1970- editor.
Description: Includes bibliographical references and index. | Text in English; includes one chapter in French.
Identifiers: Canadiana (print) 20200182692 | Canadiana (ebook) 20200182749 | ISBN 9781773851167 (softcover) | ISBN 9781773851518 (hardcover) | ISBN 9781773851174 (Open access PDF) | ISBN 9781773851181 (PDF) | ISBN 9781773851198 (EPUB) | ISBN 9781773851204 (Kindle)
Subjects: LCSH: Law—Canada—History. | LCSH: Law—History—Research—Methodology. | LCSH: Law—Canada—Sources.
Classification: LCC KE394 .C36 2020 | LCC KF345 .C36 2020 kfmod | DDC 349.7109—dc23

The University of Calgary Press acknowledges the support of the Government of Alberta through the Alberta Media Fund for our publications. We acknowledge the financial support of the Government of Canada. We acknowledge the financial support of the Canada Council for the Arts for our publishing program.

Printed and bound in Canada by Marquis
This book is printed on Enviro paper

Copyediting by Francine Michaud
Cover image: "Group of Bloods at Fort Calgary, Alberta," 1878, NA-354-23.
  Image courtesy of the Glenbow Archives, Archives and Special Collections, University of Calgary.
Cover design, page design, and typesetting by Melina Cusano

For Louis A. Knafla, who inspires us all.

CONTENTS

Foreword: A Student's Take on Canada's Legal Pasts   IX
    Nick Austin

Introduction: Canada's Legal Pasts: Looking Forward,   1
Looking Back
    Ted McCoy, Lyndsay Campbell, and Mélanie Méthot

Section I: Illuminating Cases

1   Family Defamation in the Quebec Civil Courts: 11
    The View from the Archives
    Eric H. Reiter

2   Writing Penitentiary History   31
    Ted McCoy

3   Analyzing Bigamy Cases without Going to the Archives: 37
    It Is Possible
    Mélanie Méthot

4   Trial Pamphlets and Newspaper Accounts   45
    Lyndsay Campbell

5   The Last Voyage of the *Frederick Gerring, Jr.*   51
    Christopher Shorey

6   The Text Book Edition of James Kent's *Commentaries* Used   83
    in *Canada v. Gerring*
    Angela Fernandez

Section II: Exploring Systems

7 Empire's Law: Archives and the Judicial Committee of the Privy Council   103
     Catharine MacMillan

8 Practising Law in the "Lawyerless" Colony of New France   115
     Alexandra Havrylyshyn

9 Poursuivre son mari en justice: femmes mariées et coutume de Paris devant la Cour du banc du roi de Montréal (1795–1830)   149
     Jean-Philippe Garneau

10 Getting Their Man: The NWMP as Accused in the Territorial Criminal Court in the Canadian North-West, 1876–1903   179
     Shelley A.M. Gavigan

Section III: Writing Legal History: Past, Present, and Future

11 Sex Discrimination in Canadian Law: From Equal Citizenship to Human Rights Law   241
     Dominique Clément

12 Legal-Historical Writing for the Canadian Prairies: Past, Present, Future   271
     Louis A. Knafla

Bibliography
     Primary Sources by Chapter   297
     Secondary Source Bibliography   319

Contributors   343
Index   347

A Student's Take on Canada's Legal Pasts

Nick Austin

In July 2017, I immersed myself in the Canada's Legal Past conference at the University of Calgary. This was my first introduction to Canadian legal history, a field that I came to see as central to my own interests, learning, and understanding as a law student. The pieces in this collection are a marker of what students in multiple fields can learn through attention to the legal histories of Canada's past.

Both at the conference and in reading the volume, I have been most taken with what one might call the "mythology building." As a young nation, we are still searching for the moments and individuals that define our collective Canadian "mythos." Where will Canadian legal historians find their totemic figures—their heroes and villains? Should we reject the totemic figures of previous generations—the John Beverley Robinsons and William Osgoodes—in favour of unknown figures? Could these be the mounted police recruits brought to life by Shelley Gavigan? The enterprising legal professionals examined by Alexandra Havrylyshyn, who challenges the myth that there were no lawyers in New France? Or perhaps, like me, one may be struck by the detail and charm of "The Last Voyage of the *Frederick Gerring, Jr.*," by Christopher Shorey, an exploration of a possible Canadian *Pierson v. Post* analogue with enough narrative finesse to tap into the latent maritime nostalgia that I did not suspect I had. If I were unafraid of writing in hackneyed grade-school clichés, I might say that it "makes history come alive." Or, perhaps Albertans like myself will find it enlightening to peek behind our cultivated sense of identity and unravel the mythology with Louis A. Knafla's examination of the writing of prairie history. Speaking of ingrained social praxis, Dominique Clément and Jean-Philippe Garneau's explorations of gender may help readers better understand the unique place of women in our legal past and present: Clément examines the incremental and imperfect development of sex discrimination law in Canada, while Garneau analyses 250 civil cases of married women asking for a *séparation de biens* in Montreal judicial district between 1795–1827.

I am also struck by the great variety of methodological approaches (the "how" as opposed to the "what"). Eric Reiter looks to Quebec's civil court archives (gleaning unpublished details, litigation strategies, and allegations from case files) in his writing on early defamation cases. Catharine MacMillan describes untapped archival resources about the Judicial Committee of the Privy Council in London, England, resources that may help enhance our understanding of how this body influenced the development of Canadian law beyond the constitutional sphere. Lyndsay Campbell discusses her use of newspaper accounts and pamphlets in her work on mid-nineteenth century libel cases and the controversies they reveal. Ted McCoy addresses historiographical concerns when approaching the vast Kingston Penitentiary archives, and by extension the lives of the workers and the women prisoners who resided there. Angela Fernandez examines the role of legal publishing in determining which text a judge had at hand. Regardless of the specific approaches taken by the authors, embedded in these pieces are countless moments of hard-fought discovery, understanding and, undoubtedly, gratification. Mélanie Méthot, for example, acknowledges the visceral thrill of leafing through time-worn paper ephemera in her work on bigamy cases. Most importantly, this collection is both inspired and inspiring, and I am excited to consider where the field may go next.

Canada's Legal Pasts: Looking Forward, Looking Back

Ted McCoy, Lyndsay Campbell, and Mélanie Méthot

In 1977 a group of historians met at Laval University to consider the emergence of Canadian legal history as a distinct and worthy field of study. Although legal history in Britain and the United States enjoyed a longer and more established tradition, in Canada it was in its formative stages in the 1970s. It emerged alongside a growing interest in fields of Canadian studies, gender studies, and social history—all fields that the study of law would eventually touch upon and incorporate into its own development. Over forty years have passed since that first conference, eventful decades in which the field has matured and absorbed theoretical and methodological developments in scholarship, while profiting from the tremendous improvement in the availability of sources that has come with digitization projects now widely accessible on the internet. In this introduction to *Canada's Legal Pasts: Looking Forward, Looking Back*, we outline some key moments. By foregrounding Canadian legal history's rich array of sources, methodologies, and questions, this book not only marks the maturity of the field but also aims to welcome new scholars and new contributions.[1]

The 1977 Laval conference led to a collection of essays edited by Louis A. Knafla. Each chapter in the Laval proceedings was loosely oriented around topics relating to crime in Canadian society. This in itself was methodologically different, providing evidence that the proceedings at Laval sought to reorient views of Canadian history into new areas of research involving the law. In his preface, Knafla described how the papers illustrated the potential for seeing our society through an appreciation of legal problems in their social, cultural, and economic settings.[2] What these first papers indicate is the intertwining of legal and social history as a route forward for understanding not just crime, but all areas of Canadian society.

Shortly after the meeting at Laval, the field's momentum increased with the founding of the Osgoode Society for Canadian Legal History. Two years later, the Osgoode Society published the first volume of its *Essays in the History of Canadian Law* series, edited by David H. Flaherty. Flaherty proposed a model for legal history in Canada that would explore the relationship between law and society in terms roughly connected to those of the "Wisconsin School," employing the method of Willard Hurst.[3] Knafla noted in a subsequent review that this approach, with its focus on the state's intervention in the industrializing economy, was simultaneously rather too Ontarian and too American to serve as a model for the young field. Furthermore, its instrumentalism largely sidelined important methodologies that might incorporate histories of crime, among other topics, in an understanding of the law,[4] methodologies that were actually anticipated in R.C.B. Risk's prospectus for Canadian legal history, which Flaherty commended as "Hurstian in the best sense of the term." For Risk, legal history could be considered "the study of the history of legal processes in three overlapping elements: the influences of societal values on the law, the effect of law itself on the minds and events of the society, and the structures, procedures, and functions of such institutions as the legislature, the courts, and the legal profession."[5] Risk's agenda included the analysis of French and American, as well as English influences on Canadian law and explorations of crime, the family, and law's role in contributing to a sense of Canadian identity. Subsequent scholarship has wrestled to come to grips with the ways in which Hurst's approach, as well as approaches advanced by Risk, E.P. Thompson, Douglas Hay, and others, have by turns opened and limited lines of analysis in Canadian legal-historical scholarship.[6] Indeed, Knafla's own scholarship on Western Canada has contributed greatly to one vital element of Canadian legal history that escaped Flaherty and Risk: the colonial violence imposed through law, among other forces, on Indigenous people.

The field of Canadian legal history got another push in 1985 with the creation of a multidisciplinary scholarly association devoted to the study of law and society. Law professor John McLaren was elected the first president of the *Association canadienne droit et société / Canadian Law and Society Association*. A year later, the Association published the first volume of the *Canadian Journal of Law and Society / Revue Canadienne Droit et Société*, edited by Rainer Knopff.[7] Knafla, McLaren, Knopff, and others applied their western Canadian energies to the field.

A decade after the first meeting at Laval, Canadian legal history could claim that the project initiated there was firmly underway. In 1987 Canadian legal historians met again, this time at Carleton University, where nearly fifty papers were presented. The social history of law was the predominant theme. This was social history broadly conceived, addressing—among many other topics—histories of sex crime, "common sense" in railway regulation, political and legal culture, debt, obscenity, and morality. The multitude of research interests was evidence of an expanding rigour in the field. It represented not only the growing number of researchers using legal history to understand Canadian society, but a widening conception of what the contours of that society included. Perhaps the biggest development signaled by the 1987 conference was the theoretical and political enrichment of Canadian legal history through the addition of the broader theoretical perspectives added by Marxism and feminism. The influence of E.P. Thompson's and Douglas Hay's work on the ideological basis of law was apparent in essays that considered Marxist theorizations of punishment, and Greg Marquis addressed the place of "British justice" in Canadian history. Marquis's work, in particular, added insight into the possibilities of cultural history in our understanding of the Canadian legal culture and disrupted, as Thompson did in England, older notions of how the nineteenth-century working-class understood, responded to, and used the law to their own purposes.[8]

The introduction of feminist perspectives to Canadian legal history was a welcome consequence of the changing gender balance of Canadian academe and the growing influence of gendered analysis in all areas of social history. Eight different papers illustrated the possibilities of feminist analysis in Canadian legal history, among them considerations of patriarchy and the state by Jane Ursel, who theorized about production and reproduction in the sexual division of labour in Canadian society. Ursel sought to theorize the place of law in the organization of power and authority in nineteenth-century Canadian society in a paper that joined together the possibilities of Marxist and feminist analysis. As David Flaherty had anticipated in 1981, "major interpreters of the Canadian past" had ceased to assume the legal system to be "secondary and passive rather than an instrumental and dynamic aspect of historical development."[9]

Other papers at the Carleton conference hinted at the changing landscape of Canadian scholarship about the law. Among them were two essays that began to consider Indigenous rights in Canada. D.R. Williams discussed land claims litigation in a piece that presciently asked questions about the rule of law, legal history, and reconciliation, though not in the language that defines our contemporary debate on these issues.[10] A second essay, by Tom Flanagan, questioned the meaning of Indigenous rights—a relatively new topic in 1987—by considering the long history of international law on these questions.[11] Although post-colonial scholarship swiftly moved past both of these interpretations, they represent early attempts to grapple with the legal implications of Canadian colonial history. In the larger sense, these essays hinted, too, at the influence of social history in our field, revealing the dawn of anti-colonial scholarship and race theory that would come to influence all areas of scholarship about Indigenous people in Canada.

Post-colonial scholarship and legal history in Canada were significantly strengthened by the founding of UBC Press's Law and Society book series, edited by W. Wesley Pue, which published its first title in 2002.[12] Processes of colonization, expropriation, and other uses and abuses of power have been central preoccupations of that series. Legal history now shows its merits both as a topic of study and as a historical methodology in unpacking these processes. The essays in this volume reflect both longstanding concerns and newer ones, well-known kind of sources and some that have only really become available with digitization and the internet. In addition to the UBC Law and Society book series and Osgoode Society for Canadian Legal History, legal historians have presented their research at the annual ACDS/CLSA conferences and published their work in the scholarly journal of the association. Perhaps because scholars found so many venues for their research, it took another thirty years before a third

Canadian legal history conference was held. In July 2017, the University of Calgary, under the leadership of Lyndsay Campbell and Ted McCoy, hosted sixty-five scholars identifying as legal historians. The papers reflected both continuities and discontinuities with past scholarship. The effects of colonization on Indigenous peoples in northern North America was a major thread, with papers by Jean-François Lozier, Nicole O'Byrne, Jacqueline Briggs, Robert Hamilton, David G. Bell, Genevieve Painter, Sarah P. Pike, and Shaunnagh Dorsett (providing a point of Māori comparison) all contributing to the conversation. Still, the absence of Indigenous historians themselves from this debate is in itself evidence of a field that must expand its efforts to incorporate voices from beyond the traditional power structures of the academy. Just as legal history expanded to include class and gender in its understanding of the law, the challenge ahead will be to move beyond Indigenous people as a topic of study and welcome Indigenous perspectives.

At the 2017 conference, the legal history of Quebec was well represented, especially by a number of scholars exploring the ways in which women navigated family issues in civil courts in the nineteenth century.[13] Other papers explored aspects of Canadian constitutionalism, the law's relation to ethnicity and race, judicial biography and histories of lawyering, legal ideologies and geographies, dimensions of the history of tort, property, municipal, administrative and human rights law, gender and sexuality, transboundary legal problems, the institutions of colonialism, and the challenges of writing about crime and punishment.[14]

The papers presented in Calgary provide evidence of a field that has outgrown its traditional definitions. Legal history is not only a topic of study, but the basis of an expansive historical methodology that enriches multiple areas of historical analysis. Just as social history explores more than merely society, as though it could be separated from everything it encompasses, legal history in Canada has become a method of inquiry and research that incorporates the law into understandings of historical processes and change of every kind. This moment did not arrive overnight. The methodological maturity of legal history in Canada is the product of four decades of historical research and writing on every aspect of the law and how it affects Canadian society. It also speaks to the deepening political commitment of scholars who seek to challenge the structures of inequality in Canadian society by investigating legal history as one avenue toward change.

The essays in this volume explore a variety of topics with a particular eye to methodology, on the one hand because we wish to emphasize the possibilities inherent in thinking about legal history as a methodology and, on the other, because we hope to welcome to the field scholars who may be unfamiliar with legal sources and arguments. The book has three parts: the first focuses on writing about specific cases; the second interrogates the workings of legal systems and their participants; and the third offers historiographical scope, looking forward and back. We include five short pieces about particular kinds of sources and how they can be used in legal history research: Mélanie Méthot's chapter on finding bigamy cases using archival and non-archival sources; Ted McCoy's essay on the rich offerings of prison records; Catharine MacMillan's chapter on the largely unexplored treasure-trove of the records of the Judicial Committee of the Privy Council; Angela Fernandez's chapter on the history of a particular, low-cost law book used in the *Gerring* case, which Christopher Shorey discusses in his chapter; and Lyndsay Campbell's essay on finding and interpreting the accounts of trials contained in pamphlets and newspapers.

The chapter by Christopher Shorey is a case study of the interplay of legal and political pressures on the fate of an American fishing schooner whose crew were caught packing up fish on the wrong side of the international boundary off Nova Scotia. In writing about a "hard case"—the kind that lawyers know make "bad law"—Shorey offers a novel contribution to Canadian legal history by venturing into admiralty law, a much-neglected area for a country with so much coastline. Consistent with Risk's and Flaherty's calls for research on the profession itself,[15] we include Alexandra Havrylyshyn's chapter on lawyering in New France, where the professional hierarchy and social status of those who represented others in court were markedly different from those of France. Also exploring aspects of legal systems is Shelley Gavigan's chapter on the strangely hybrid disciplinary and criminal proceedings brought against mostly young North-West Mounted Police officers before Alberta and Saskatchewan became provinces. Gavigan shows the vulnerability of these young men who went West in the name of a colonial vision of social order, but whose troubling encounters with the justice system demonstrated its highly personal, fluid lines of authority.

Canadian legal historians have long been interested in the relationship between gender and law. Jean-Philippe Garneau's chapter on how married women navigated civil law before the Court of King's Bench in Quebec between 1795 and 1830 takes up this historiographical thread. To describe the history of women's activism in Canada and its contribution to the dramatic changes in equality law, Dominique Clément, in his essay, pulls together a vast amount of secondary scholarship amassed by historians of women's history and connects it with his own research on legal reform.

We begin the book with Eric Reiter's "Family Defamation in the Quebec Civil Courts: The View from the Archives," an essay that puts methodology at its centre and masterfully demonstrates how the actual physicality of the archive can inform us about how real people used law. We conclude with a forward-looking historiography of the prairies presented by Lou Knafla, the editor of the 1977 conference proceedings, now Professor Emeritus of History at the University of Calgary. Knafla's essay underlines both what we know and what we have yet to learn, as scholars—perhaps including some of the newcomers we hope to welcome to our field through this volume—bring new insights into the histories of Indigenous peoples and settlers in Canada. Lou has for decades been a driving force in Canadian legal history; his career was once described as "charted by a restless mind driven forward by a genuine curiosity about the world in which he lives."[16] Lou remains an inspiring, gently towering figure in our field, and it is to him that we dedicate this book.

NOTES

1. We are grateful to the Social Sciences and Humanities Research Council of Canada for its support of this project.
2. Louis A. Knafla, "Preface," in *Canadian Society for Legal History. Proceedings 1977*, ed. Louis A. Knafla (Toronto: Canadian Society for Legal History by the York University Law Library, 1977), ii.
3. David H. Flaherty, "Writing Canadian Legal History: An Introduction," in *Essays in the History of Canadian Law*, vol. 1, ed. David H. Flaherty (Toronto: University of Toronto Press for the Osgoode Society, 1981), 7–8.
4. Knafla, Review of *Essays in the History of Canadian Law*, vol. I, ed. David H. Flaherty, *American Journal of Legal History* 27, no. 4 (1983): 389–90.

5   Flaherty, "Writing Canadian Legal History," 7–8.

6   See particularly W. Wesley Pue, "Locating Hurst," *Law & History Review* 18, no. 1 (2000): 187–95; David Sugarman, "Reassessing Hurst: A Transatlantic Perspective," *Law & History Review* 18, no. 1 (2000): 215–21; and the other essays in volume 18, number 1 of the *Law & History Review*.

7   http://www.acds-clsa.org/?q=en/content/short-history-canadian-law-and-society-association.

8   Greg Marquis, "Doing Justice to 'British Justice': Law, Ideology and Canadian Historiography," in *Papers Presented at the 1987 Canadian Law in History Conference Held at Carleton University, Ottawa, June 8–10, 1987*, vol. 1 (Ottawa: Carleton University, 1987), also published as Greg Marquis, "Doing Justice to 'British Justice': Law, Ideology and Canadian Historiography," in *Canadian Perspectives on Law and Society: Issues in Legal History*, ed. W. Wesley Pue and Barry Wright (Ottawa: Carleton University Press, 1988).

9   Jane Ursel "The State and the Maintenance of Patriarchy: A Case Study of Family, Labour and Welfare Legislation in Canada," in *Gender and Society: Creating a Canadian Women's Sociology*, ed. Arlene Tigar McLaren (Toronto: Copp Clark Pitman, 1988), reprinted in *Papers Presented at the 1987 Canadian Law in History Conference*, vol. 1.

10 David R. Williams, "Native Land Claims – Rule of History or Rule of Law?" in *Papers Presented at the 1987 Canadian Law in History Conference*, vol. 2.

11 Thomas Flanagan, "Francisco de Vitoria and the Meaning of Aboriginal Rights," in *Papers Presented at the 1987 Canadian Law in History Conference*, vol. 2.

12 A full list of the Osgoode Society's publications is available on its website, at www.osgoodesociety.ca/books/. The catalogue of UBC Press's Law and Society series is available at www.ubcpress.ca/law-and-society.

13 Serge Dauchy, Donald Fyson, Jean-Philippe Garneau, Peter Gossage, Marie-Neige Laperrière, Michel Morin, Thierry Nootens, Darren Pacione, Eric Reiter and Brian Young all presented papers on the legal history of Quebec.

14 These contributors were Constance Backhouse, David G. Bell, Blake Brown, Michael Boudreau, Andrew Buck, Lyndsay Campbell, Erika Chamberlain, Lori Chambers, Dominique Clément, Angela Fernandez, Shelley Gavigan, Philip Girard, Claire Gjertsen, Sarah Hamill, Douglas C. Harris, Ian Holloway, Lou Knafla, Rande Kostal, Catharine MacMillan, Greg Marquis, Ted McCoy, John McLaren (presenting a paper authored by himself and Pooja Parmar), Jeffrey L. McNairn, Mélanie Méthot, Bradley Miller, James Muir, Nicole O'Byrne, Stefan Parker, Karen Pearlston, Jim Phillips, Graham Price, Christopher Shorey, Mary Stokes, Carolyn Strange, Jonathan Swainger, and Barrington Walker.

15 Flaherty, "Writing Canadian Legal History," 16.

16 Jonathan Swainger, "Prologue: Louis Knafla and Canadian Legal History," in *People and Place: Historical Influences on Legal Culture*, ed. Jonathan Swainger and Constance Backhouse (Vancouver: UBC Press, 2003), vii.

SECTION I
ILLUMINATING CASES

Family Defamation in the Quebec Civil Courts: The View from the Archives

*Eric H. Reiter**

Introduction

In October 1912 in Montreal, Joseph Robert started defamation proceedings against Jean-Baptiste Barbeau, the brother of his deceased first wife. Robert alleged that a month earlier, Barbeau had come into his home, accompanied by one of Robert's sons from the first marriage, and said to his current wife, "I dare say there's a sore throat here, syphilis if you really want to know. . . . There wasn't anything like that in the house when my sister was alive."[1] Robert claimed the exorbitant sum of $5,000 in damages on behalf of both himself and his second wife, Hélène Brunet. About a month and a half later, in December, Barbeau filed his defence, in which he admitted going to Robert's home out of concern for his nieces still living there, but denied everything else. He also added, among other things, that if he had said anything (which he denied), it was strictly within the family, and outsiders had heard nothing of it.[2] There the matter stood until five months later, in May, when the next documents were added to the case file: a notice by Robert that he was discontinuing his case, and a judgment formally dismissing the action with costs.[3]

The case of *Robert v. Barbeau*—ordinary in many respects, unusual in others—illustrates some of the ways in which judicial archives provide a particular picture of the workings of a legal system, different from what published case reports provide. By shedding light on the procedural side of litigation, the materials contained in the judicial archives complement the substantive issues on which legal historians usually focus. They record hints about strategy and motivation, nuances that show litigants using the courts in instrumental ways. We cannot say for sure what motivated Joseph Robert to drop his case and pay the costs six months after he initiated it. But the exaggerated damages claim (in similar cases at the time the high end of the scale was between $500 and $1,000, while many plaintiffs demanded far less), the unenthusiastic pursuit of the case, and the relationship between the parties all suggest that sending a message was more important than receiving a final judicial resolution.

The case files and registers that make up the Quebec judicial archives can be read as texts in their own right, texts that shed light on the motivations and strategies of litigants. Reading archives of various kinds as texts has been the subject of numerous influential studies, and legal archives are no exception.[4] Legal archives, however, present distinct problems and promises due to the nature of the legal process that produced them. As Carolyn Strange has noted about a particular legal archive, the capital case files compiled by the Canadian government in order to determine whether or not to commute a death sentence, the archive and the files that make it up can be analyzed "not only as material artefacts but as a discursive means of organizing knowledge and producing meaning."[5] My focus is not on how the judicial archive itself structured knowledge and meaning (an interesting question outside the scope of this chapter), but instead on how the submission, recording, and archiving of documents, the literal archival remains, actualized litigants' strategies and choices within developing litigation. To this end, I will look at the case files and court registers not as completed and closed records of litigation, but rather as narratives of the development of legal actions over time. The documents in the files and the dated entries in the registers record the progress of a case: the long pauses and periodic flurries of activity reveal the ebb and flow of litigation as it proceeded. This diachronic picture of cases offers historians valuable, and oftentimes the only evidence of the parties' commitment to the case and their reasons for pursuing it as they did.

This chapter is based on a subset of cases drawn from a larger project that sampled the Quebec judicial archives between 1840 and 1920 for cases relating to family matters. Overall, our team identified, photographed, and compiled into a database some 1,836 civil and criminal cases from the judicial districts of Montreal, Quebec City, and Trois-Rivières, at both the Superior Court (civil matters) and the Court of Queen's (King's) Bench (criminal matters).[6] Broadly speaking, the identified cases cover sexual infractions, intra-familial violence, matrimonial and parental difficulties, and conflicts concerning the patrimonial or moral status of the family. My focus here will be on the last group: cases of family defamation, that is slander, insult, and libel (Quebec law did not distinguish as the common law did) in which the victim or the defamer was a member of the plaintiff's family or in which the nature of the insult was family-related.[7] I will begin with a brief discussion of the compilation and content of the Quebec judicial archives, and then present an overview of the family defamation cases found in our sample, before offering some conclusions about the insights gained by the view from the archives.

Litigation's Archival Traces

Quebec's civil court archives—much more voluminous than the criminal side, in mass of paper produced, if not in number of cases—have been relatively underutilized by historians despite the riches they preserve.[8] The archives comprise a series of registers of all cases, along with case files containing the documents submitted to and produced by the judicial process. Compared to the published reports of decided cases, the archives present a strikingly different view of litigation, particularly with respect to defamation actions. Unlike the reports, the archives preserve the fine grain of litigation: the arguments the parties raised, factual allegations—whether or not the court accepted them in the end— and, in many cases, the words of witnesses recorded in their depositions. The archives are also much wider in scope than the fraction of cases included in the published reports of the period, which were produced for the profession, and so their editors selected for inclusion those cases that illustrated important legal points.[9]

The Quebec reports published in the period of our study unsurprisingly presented almost exclusively cases that reached formal and final judicial resolution, and more particularly those cases that made novel legal points. Incidentally, of course, the published reports also provide a wealth of information about the conflicts that drove litigants to court and the ways in which those social conflicts were legalized and resolved by the courts. The archives, however, while structured by the state and reflecting its governance priorities, were left unfiltered by the assessments of editors, by the criterion of final resolution, or even, for the most part, by the needs of the legal profession. They thus provide at least a modicum of information on every case for which proceedings were instituted, not just those that made it to judgment. Viewed from the perspective of the users of the system, the archives preserve an overview of the triggers that pushed plaintiffs over the brink of tolerance, sending them to a lawyer to get things rolling.

A case entered the archive as soon as the plaintiff instituted proceedings by asking (and paying) for the issuance of a writ summoning the defendant. (The cost was not trivial: in 1912, for example, Joseph Robert's writ and declaration cost him $10.60, which included the bailiff's fees to serve it on the defendant.) The first administrative steps in constructing the archive involved assigning the case a number, inscribing it in certain registers, and opening a file for it. This file expanded according to two forces: the requirements and deadlines imposed by law and court practice on the one hand, and the strategic decisions of the parties and their lawyers on the other. The latter is my subject here, but a brief outline of the former will be useful.

Compiling and organizing the judicial archive was the responsibility of the prothonotary (clerk of the court) of the district in question, who issued writs and received documents from the parties.[10] The prothonotary was also required to keep four registers of proceedings: a register of writs of summons (excepting subpoenas); a register of writs of execution; a register of orders, decisions, and judgments; and a *plumitif* in which was entered "a concise note of all that shall have been done in each cause."[11] The case file itself, linked by number to the registers, was to contain all procedural documents filed in the case, put into chronological order, and consecutively numbered by the prothonotary (although these last steps were not always carried out).[12]

Typically, a case that went to trial would produce at least the following documents, supported by summonses, appearances, notices, and affidavits: a writ instituting proceedings by summoning the defendant, with an attached declaration stating the plaintiff's case; a defence or plea; the plaintiff's answer to the defence; the defendant's reply to the plaintiff's answer (and sometimes further back-and-forth); any exhibits (evidence) mentioned in the parties' submissions; and an inscription for proof and hearing, indicating that all issues had been joined between the parties and the case was ready to go to trial. Alongside these basic elements, various other documents could of course be added, particularly motions that could range from simple requests for continuance to interlocutory matters raising complex legal issues. Not all cases went this far, however, as we will see. Finally, many, though not all, files included transcribed witness depositions, an invaluable resource for historians. As a general rule, witness testimony at trial was taken stenographically and, as the *Code of Civil Procedure* put it, those transcripts "constitute and shall be considered as the evidence of the witness."[13] Witnesses could also be deposed on discovery before trial, and those depositions, too, formed part of the case file.[14]

In theory, then, the registers plus the original case files gave a comprehensive chronological overview of the proceedings, and assuming they are intact, they still do. Lacunae crept into the archive, however, and created gaps. The most significant gap in many cases involved the judgment. Draft final judgments were sometimes filed, but not always. The judges submitted their drafts to the prothonotary who was responsible for transcribing them into the register of judgments,[15] but the register contained the *dispositif* only—the formal terms of judgment of the court, usually in the form "Considering that . . . ; For these reasons, the Court . . . ," and so forth. The discursive reasons for judgment that in many cases the judge read out in court were not entered into the register, and did not always make it into the case file. Printed case reports (and, for big cases, occasionally newspapers) sometimes included both, sometimes only the discursive reasons, and sometimes only the *dispositif*.[16] A good example is the case of *Mell v. Middleton*, which is discussed below. The case file includes a two-page *dispositif* of the trial judgment, which would have been entered into the register. The case was appealed, however, and by chance the respondent's factum (the document containing their arguments and other submissions to the appellate court) transcribed in its entirety the judge's detailed eleven-page discursive reasons, which would otherwise have been absent from the file. The working of time, of course, also resulted in gaps that compromised the integrity of some case files. Parts or even whole files could be misfiled, lawyers preparing cases sometimes borrowed the originals and failed to return them, and the predations of dampness, insects, rodents, and other destructive forces led to losses as well. Occasionally the files preserve indications of the alarmingly haphazard state of contemporary archival practices, such as a voluminous 1889 Montreal Superior Court case file, which contains a slip of paper with the handwritten note "the Couillard file is on the other side at the foot of the armoire."[17]

In this way, the archive provides both an overview of the procedural steps of each case and a sense of strategic give-and-take and human decision-making that shaped the litigation over time. The files show that once the plaintiff had initiated an action and the duly-summoned defendant had formally filed an appearance, various progressions could ensue, which can be roughly grouped as follows:

- Some actions were filed, but little else was done. These cases seem to have been fairly quickly abandoned: the case file typically contains the plaintiff's declaration, the returned writ, and usually the defendant's appearance, but nothing further.
- Some actions stalled further into the process: after the defence was filed, after the plaintiff replied to the defence, or after a motion raised an interlocutory matter. Again, these cases seem to have been informally abandoned.
- Some actions were formally discontinued by the plaintiff or perempted by the defendant (which was possible after two years of inaction on the part of the plaintiff).[18]
- Some actions settled out of court, with the settlement ratified by the judge.
- Some actions went to final judgment on the merits or beyond, to appeal.[19]

The archives thus turn a flat, teleological outcome into a textured narrative that unfolded over time. Tracing the proceedings as they developed is a way to uncover the strategic choices and responses litigants made—in short, to see how plaintiffs used the court system when they felt their family name and honour were threatened. If we abandon the assumption that a final judgment was the norm—or even the goal—rather than the relatively small tip of a large litigation iceberg, we can start asking what it means that certain cases stalled, discontinued, or settled out of court. What we find is that litigation was being used for instrumental purposes, in many cases without any real expectation that the matter would reach a final judgment. Family defamation cases form a revealing subset in which to explore these issues.

Family Defamation—Intra and Extra

Among the sampled cases are sixty-eight family defamation actions (as defined above). Some cases touching defamation more obliquely were left aside, which calls for a brief explanation. First, since my focus is on how litigants responded to insults to their family, I limited the analysis to cases in which defamation was the main action, rather than an incidental or supplemental part of a more general complaint. This meant excluding cases of separation from bed and board in which "grievous insult" was one of the grounds alleged, as well as cases of alienation of affection, in which a husband sued his wife's lover and alleged injury to his honour as part of the damage claimed. In both of those types of cases, defamation was one part of a broader slate of complaints, and so it is impossible to determine the extent to which the alleged reputational injury drove the litigation or affected whatever resolution resulted from it. Second, I also excluded those defamation cases in which a wife sued for non-family-related insults directed at her personally, and in which the only family element was the participation of the husband to authorize his wife to institute the action. The defamation in those cases was individual rather than collective, and was distinct from others in which the husband sued to avenge both his own and his wife's honour.

The cases included in the analysis illustrate a range of situations. Most were actions taken by the male head of household against insults to family members, mostly to his wife, but also his children, deceased relatives, or the family name generally. Some were actions by widows on behalf of their children; one involved children suing over defamation of their elderly mother. In these cases, the plaintiff claimed damages for more than his or her personal violated honour. Typical are cases in which a husband sued for violation of both his own and his wife's honour and reputation, or in which the husband stated that he was suing on his wife's behalf since he was the guardian of her honour. Of particular interest are a group of cases in which the defamation came from within the family rather than from outside. Thirteen such cases, which I call intra-family defamation, appear among the files, a subset wholly absent from the published case reports.[20] In those cases, while the substance of the alleged defamation was not necessarily family-related, the family relationship between the parties calls for their inclusion.[21] The thirteen intra-family defamation cases are likely an undercounting, since family relationships between the parties are not always evident on the face of the record.[22] What are we to make, for example, of cases such as one in which insults were alleged to have been expressed while the defendant was visiting the plaintiff's home on New Year's Day? Was the defendant a relative? A close friend? A neighbour? Since it is impossible to specify a relationship without further digging in other sources, such cases have been classed as extra-family defamation for the time being. The idea of family is also fluid, as social historians well know, and the boundaries of "family" would differ according to whether we focus on legal, affective, or economic ties between kin—and indeed others—within a household.[23] Acknowledging that this research is a starting point only, what can we say about the litigational dynamics of family defamation cases? We can start with some statistics, with the caveat that our numbers are small (Table 1.1).

Among the sixty-eight family defamation files under study, thirteen were intra-family cases, including the *Robert v. Barbeau* case that introduced this chapter.[24] Of those thirteen cases, only one went to judgment (it was dismissed), and interestingly it featured the most tenuous family connection (tutorship rather than blood or marriage relationships). Of the others, five settled out of court, one was formally discontinued, and

TABLE 1.1 Outcomes of intra- and extra-family defamation cases (percentages rounded)

	INTRA-FAMILY CASES		EXTRA-FAMILY CASES	
Stalled:	6	46%	20	36%
Discontinued:	1	8%	2	4%
Settled:	5	38%	4	7%
Total of stalled, discontinued, settled:	12	92%	26	47%
Judgment for plaintiff:	0	0%	13	24%
Judgment for defendant:	1	8%	16	29%
Total of judgments:	1	8%	29	53%
Total cases:	13		55	

the others stalled, all of them early in the process (an average of thirty-nine days after the action was instituted). Two of the stalled files contain nothing after the plaintiff's declaration and the writ, two nothing after the defendant's appearance, and two nothing after the defence. In other words, only 8 percent of the small sample went to judgment, while about 92 percent were settled, discontinued, or stalled.

While the intra- and extra-family defamation cases as I have defined them are not strictly comparable, the contrast between the two groups is intriguing in several respects. I will develop some of these contrasts further below. Of the fifty-five extra-family cases, more than half went to judgment (slightly favouring defendants[25]), while less than half settled, were discontinued, or stalled. Among those that stalled, moreover, the extra-family cases stalled further along in the process. In terms of procedural stage, more than half of the extra-family cases stalled at some point after the defence was filed, while only one-third of the intra-family cases stalled at that stage. In duration, the extra-family cases stalled an average of 183 days after they were instituted, compared to thirty-nine days for the intra-family cases.

The contrast in settlement rates between the two groups of cases is particularly striking, a point I will develop below. Even if the adage "most cases settle" is more characteristic of the contemporary Canadian legal system than the comparatively more accessible courts of this earlier period, it is noteworthy that 38 percent of the intra-family cases settled, while only 7 percent of the extra-family cases did. The case files are mostly silent on the terms of the settlements, though a few of the intra-family cases offer some information. A 1906 Quebec City case, for example, in which the plaintiff sued his brother-in-law for $150 for allegedly calling him a drunkard, a good-for-nothing, and a coward, settled for $10 six weeks after the action was instituted.[26] In an 1890 case from Yamachiche, in which the parties were the respective parents of a young couple, the plaintiffs sued for $195 over various insults, but claimed that their purpose was not to fleece the defendant but only to have their "violated reputation, character, and honour" avenged in a public way.[27] To this end, they made clear that while monetary damages would do the trick, "if the defendant preferred to make an honourable retraction to the plaintiffs at the door of the parish church of Yamachiche, after mass ended on a Sunday to be determined by the court," the plaintiffs would drop the damages claim and take costs only.[28] This was presumably what happened, since the case settled, though the final terms were left undisclosed.

Two Family Defamation Actions

Two other family defamation cases—one extra-family, the other intra-family—are worth looking at more closely. While they should not be taken as representative of a diverse set of cases, they do serve to illustrate the points about strategy and motivation that I have so far outlined in general terms only.

The first is an extra-family case from Montreal in 1902.[29] The plaintiff was Alfred Mell, whose daughter Helen was engaged to be married to Charles Arnold. The alleged defamation arose during an altercation between Arnold and his former employer, Thomas Middleton, who ran a burglar alarm and messenger service. Middleton said he had been angry after receiving an anonymous letter, which he believed to be from Arnold and the plaintiff's wife (details of the letter are sketchy, since Middleton never produced it in evidence). Laying into Arnold, with whom he already had a strained relationship, he said "he would show Mrs. Mell who she was to talk about anybody; he said she had a different man for each of her children and that she had sold her own daughter [the aforementioned Helen] to her father."[30] Alfred Mell, as head of household, sued Middleton for $500 for the injury to the reputation, feelings, and honour of himself and his family.

Mell instituted his action right away—eleven days after the incident, one of the shortest intervals among the family defamation cases. This in itself is a strong indication of the effects of the slander on the family. Moreover, since Mell and Middleton had no prior relationship, Mell would have had little to gain and potentially much to lose in seeking to resolve the matter extra-judicially. Middleton seems to have had other ideas. At some point after the action was instituted, Arnold, his mother, and Helen had an apparently chance encounter with Middleton at a restaurant. Though details of the meeting were contested, Middleton was, according to the trial judge, "all sweetness and honey, cajolery and enticement" in trying to get the Mells to settle the case, offering to pay their costs if they dropped the suit. The offer—if indeed it had ever been made—was rejected, and Alfred Mell pursued his action expeditiously through to trial, where he produced twelve witnesses and key documentary evidence. Judgment came eight months after the action was instituted, and Justice Siméon Pagnuelo awarded Mell $200 and costs. In his judgment, Justice Pagnuelo also confirmed the Mells' honour and strongly reproached Middleton's "abominable" conduct, which he saw as gratuitously attacking the Mells, Helen in particular, in order to settle a score with Arnold. The judge condemned the slander as "most atrocious when used against honest people and altogether unprovoked." Middleton's appeal to the Court of Review, alleging excessive damages, was dismissed.[31] The damages—40 percent of the demand—were rather steep, though not unusually so, and were explained by the defendant's evident malice and mendacity.

The second example comes from Montreal in 1893 and involved two siblings squabbling over their mother's future succession (she was at the time still very much alive and residing with the plaintiff). The plaintiff, Alexandre Andegrave *dit* Champagne, claimed that his sister Octavie Andegrave *dit* Champagne and her husband Séraphin Taillefer had accused him of taking some of their mother's things. He alleged that his sister had said, before an audience of other family members, "The dishes, where are they? The knives, where are they? The hand towels, where are they? The soap, where is it? They used to be here, now you've taken them away and kept them hidden."[32] In monetary terms this was hardly a high-stakes (pre-)succession battle, though on an emotional level nerves were plainly raw. The plaintiff also claimed the defendants had accused him of starving his mother in violation of the terms of a *donation entre vifs* by which he had undertaken to provide her with room and board. Finally, he pointed to a gratuitous insult, stating that one of them had called him "a happy cuckold" (*un cocu content*). The defendants denied making the comments about starving the mother, but admitted they might have suggested the brother was not taking the best care of her. They also denied the accusation of theft of the housewares, but said they might have casually wondered where things were. The sister countered with her own claim that the plaintiff had levelled at her a list of many of the usual insults against women during this period, calling her a bitch, sharp-tongued, a thief, a sow, and a good-for-nothing.[33] The respective allegations suggest a family spat, though we should never discount the feelings involved.

The plaintiff sued for $1,000 for having been wounded and humiliated by the defendants' words, one of the highest demands among the intra-family defamation cases. Despite the large amount of money ostensibly in play, the action meandered along in a leisurely fashion—this was no scorched-earth flurry of motions and counter-motions. The better part of a year elapsed between the alleged insult and the filing of the action. The time limit for bringing a defamation case was one year counting from knowledge of the insult, so the plaintiff was well within that deadline, but many other plaintiffs hustled to a lawyer and fired off an action within weeks, sometimes even days like Alfred Mell did, so the slow pace here is noteworthy. Once instituted, the action itself lasted more than 500 days—almost a year and a half. This included close to six months before the plaintiff responded to the defence, and almost a year before he had the case inscribed on the roll for hearing. At the hearing, after the plaintiff had deposed eight witnesses (the last of whom was the defendant husband), but before the defendants began presenting their case, the plaintiff withdrew his action and the case settled, even later than on the proverbial courthouse steps. The file includes the terms whereby the parties would pay their own costs, but "upon declaration by the defendants that they never intended to violate the honour of the plaintiff or his spouse..., having always considered them to be honest and respectable."[34] And with that the file closed, a conciliatory ending indeed, if the terms of the settlement were in fact carried out.[35]

Conclusions

What conclusions does this view from the archives allow us to draw about family defamation litigation? What can we learn about litigants' motivations, strategies, and goals as they went to court to protect or avenge their family honour? The two groups of family defamation cases each involved threats to the honour of the family and its members, some originating from outside the family, others from inside. In some ways they reveal similar concerns at work, but in other ways they are strikingly different from one another.

The extra-family defamation cases show clear urgency about repelling the threat to the family. Plaintiffs tended to resort relatively promptly to formal law, with the time between the incident and institution of proceedings being on average about half that of the intra-family cases. This was followed in most cases, as we have seen, by vigorous pursuit of the action, carrying it to judgment or, if not that far, then at least deep into proceedings. Several factors might explain this general profile of extra-family defamation litigation. First, the absence of close affective relationships in most cases would make plaintiffs less hesitant to adopt impersonal means of dealing with the threat to honour, by taking the conflict to the courts rather than trying face-to-face negotiation. In most cases we do not know what went on before institution of proceedings, but the short delay in many extra-family cases would have left little time for serious informal dispute resolution. Second, as in all moral injury cases, while the monetary demands were effectively punitive rather than compensatory, plaintiffs were generally realistic in their punitive expectations. Amounts demanded were high, but not excessively so (despite what defendants like Thomas Middleton said). Judges in successful actions rarely awarded the whole claim, but they did often award a quarter or a third of it, provided that the initial demand was not outrageous. This degree of restraint by many plaintiffs, coupled with their commitment to pursue the case to the end, suggests that plaintiffs in the extra-family cases were actually looking to make the defendant pay. Third, alongside the punitive goals, moral redress was also a factor. Without a relationship to heal, public vindication became more important to counter slander or injurious falsehoods from neighbours, employers, or the press. Judges at the time had a keen sense of honour and the boundaries of propriety, and they tended to see it as self-evident that it was a compensable injury to call someone's spouse "a damned disgusting streetwalker, a cow, a sow, a bitch" (to cite just one example from a successful action).[36] Plaintiffs who could make a reasonable case without exaggeration stood to receive a judgment that was a public acknowledgement of the family's honour and the defendant's transgression. All this suggests that in the extra-family cases, family honour was a vital asset to be protected vigorously.

Turning to the intra-family cases, we find some of these same characteristics but some important differences as well. In those cases, public vindication was again evidently a key goal, as we see for example in the terms of settlement in the Andegrave *dit* Champagne affair and in the case of the insulting in-laws from Yamachiche. But public vindication had its limits—the desultory pursuit of many of these cases suggests that the point was less the outcome than the process, and public vindication seems often to have taken a back seat to private pressure within an ongoing relationship. Other differences reflect similar concerns. First, the amounts demanded in some of these cases were outlandishly excessive, far more than any court would ever award, and the parties' lawyers would certainly have made known to them the unlikelihood of receiving more than a tiny fraction of such huge amounts. The average demand in the intra-family cases was more than twice that of the extra-family cases ($1,107 compared to $490), while the medians were closer ($450 and $275 respectively). This difference is explained by the presence of a number of astronomical claims at the top end of the intra-family cases, such as Joseph Robert's $5,000 demand or several others over $1,000, amounts more akin to what defamed politicians demanded from newspapers at the time. Rather than a realistic claim for compensation, these amounts were rhetorical (and emotional) positions designed to underscore the severity of the situation. Second, the actions within families took about twice as long as extra-family cases to come to court, suggesting less urgency to proceed and perhaps the exploration of informal means of redress before resorting to the courts when those failed. Finally, as already mentioned, the much higher rate of settled, stalled, and discontinued cases, as well as the failure in any of those cases to proceed much beyond the initial salvo commencing the litigation, further indicate that instituting proceedings was the point, not bringing them to a prompt and public formal resolution. As mentioned, judges tended to be sympathetic to reasonable plaintiffs, making it even more striking that almost none of the intra-family cases were pursued to judgment. In most of those cases, however, judgment was likely never the point. Intra-family defamation litigation was symbolic: it was less about mulcting relatives for their intemperate remarks, than about rhetorically chastising people with whom one would usually have to resume some kind of ongoing relationship. Plaintiffs, fed up with their relatives' conduct, sought the threat of judicial authority to bring them into line and restore some semblance of family harmony. Rather than repelling a threat to family honour from outside, those cases were about making a point to difficult relatives, or about escalating private internal family conflicts that had crossed lines of tolerance. Dragging one's insulting sister or uncle or nephew into court, forcing them to retain counsel and to address allegations made against them, and in general making them suffer the financial and emotional toll of litigation, at least for a short while, was a powerful way to express displeasure, presumably after more personal means had gone nowhere. This was often enough to make one's point, and indeed settling a case or declining to carry it forward might have salvaged a relationship (if that was desired), when pursuing the case to judgment and a damages award would have destroyed it irreparably.

This picture of the procedural life of litigation has little to do with the substantive legal arguments raised and adjudicated in the cases; it comes from reading the registers and case files that make up the judicial archives as texts in their own right, rather than simply as repositories of information. As Mariana Valverde has argued, legal case files are different from those produced in other disciplines such as psychiatry: "legal cases are specific problems or conflicts, as documented and presented by authorized parties in very specific formats. Legal formats are designed not to build up knowledge for the sake of knowing . . . but rather to generate a highly formatted resolution."[37] The material in legal case files, as we have seen, was compiled and archived for purposes mandated by the legal process, but it was also in large part produced with explicitly argumentative and strategic aims in mind. In other words, it reflected not reality but rather opposed argumentative positions about a highly contested reality. The archival case file is more than an encapsulation of a conflict, however. It is also a record of the development of a litigation over time, a diachronic picture of a developing process rather than a static product. As such, the documents a case file preserves provide valuable insights into the parties' motivations, degree of commitment, and emotional engagement with their conflict.

NOTES

* This chapter draws on a project entitled "Familles, droit et justice au Québec, 1840–1920," undertaken by Peter Gossage (principal investigator), Donald Fyson, Thierry Nootens, and myself, and funded by the Social Sciences and Humanities Research Council of Canada. In addition to my collaborators, I would like to acknowledge the invaluable work of our research assistants Marilyne Caouette, Myriam Cyr, Giselle Giral, Aude Maltais, Frédéric Mercier, Lisa Moore, Anne-France Morin, and Megan Wierda as well as of Julie Perrone, my research assistant for an earlier project funded by the Fonds de recherche du Québec – société et culture

1 Robert et ux v Barbeau, [1912] no. 2500 (Sup. Ct. Montreal), cont. 1987-10-014/1126, SSS1, SS2, S2, TP11, Bibliothèque et Archives nationales du Québec—Vieux-Montréal (BAnQ, V-M), Bref et déclaration (filed 25 October 1912), 1: "J'oserais dire qu'il y a ici-dedans ... un mal de gorge, la syphilis, si vous voulez le savoir.... Il n'y a jamais eu de ça dans la maison du temps de ma défunte sœur."

2 Robert et ux v Barbeau, Défense du défendeur (filed 5 December 1912), 1–2.

3 Robert et ux v Barbeau, Désistement (15 May 1913); Jugement renvoyant action du demandeur avec dépens suivant désistement (16 May 1913, Justice Charles Archer).

4 Important works include Natalie Zemon Davis, *Fiction in the Archives: Pardon Tales and Their Tellers in Sixteenth-Century France* (Stanford: Stanford University Press, 1977); Carolyn Steedman, *Dust: The Archive and Cultural History* (New Brunswick, NJ: Rutgers University Press, 2002); Antoinette Burton, ed., *Archive Stories: Facts, Fictions and the Writing of History* (Durham, NC; Duke University Press, 2005); Ann Laura Stoler, *Along the Archival Grain: Epistemic Anxieties and Colonial Common Sense* (Princeton: Princeton University Press, 2009). On legal case files in particular, see Carolyn Strange, "Stories of Their Lives: The Historian and the Capital Case File," in *On the Case: Explorations in Social History*, ed. Franca Iacovetta and Wendy Mitchinson (Toronto: University of Toronto Press, 1998) and Mariana Valverde's contributions to "On the Case: Explorations in Social History: A Roundtable Discussion," *Canadian Historical Review* 81 (2000): 272–78.

5   Strange, "Stories of Their Lives," 33.

6   Among the civil cases, the sampling rate varied according to the volume of cases in each district. At Trois-Rivières and Quebec City, one year in ten during the period was sampled, and five percent of files were selected within those years. At Montreal, the much larger volume, particularly in the twentieth century, necessitated a reduced sampling rate of 2.5 percent of files. This information is provided by Peter Gossage, "Familles, droit et justice au Québec, 1840–1920: aperçu global et bilan provisoire," paper presented at the Séminaire CIÉQ-CERHIO, Angers, France, 19–20 May 2016.

7   Surprisingly little has been published on defamation in Quebec. See André Lachance, "Une étude de mentalité: les injures verbales au Canada au XVIIIe siècle (1712–1748)," *Revue d'histoire de l'Amérique française* 31 (1977): 229–38; Joseph Kary, "The Constitutionalization of Quebec Libel Law, 1848–2004," *Osgoode Hall Law Journal* 42 (2004): 229–70; Ollivier Hubert, "Injures verbales et langage de l'honneur en Nouvelle-France," in *Une histoire de la politesse au Québec: normes et déviances, XVIIe–XXe siècles*, ed. Laurent Turcot and Thierry Nootens (Quebec City: Septentrion, 2015). For our period outside Quebec, see Rosemary J. Coombe, "Contesting the Self: Negotiating Subjectivities in Nineteenth-Century Ontario Defamation Trials," *Studies in Law, Politics and Society* 11 (1991): 3–40; Andrew King, "Constructing Gender: Sexual Slander in Nineteenth-Century America," *Law and History Review* 13 (1995): 63–110; S.M. Waddams, *Sexual Slander in Nineteenth-Century England: Defamation in the Ecclesiastical Courts, 1815–1855* (Toronto: University of Toronto Press, 2000); Lisa R. Pruitt, "'On the Chastity of Women All Property in the World Depends': Injury from Sexual Slander in the Nineteenth Century," *Indiana Law Journal* 78 (2003): 965–1018.

8   For most of the period covered by this project (after the earliest years), Quebec's civil courts comprised principally the Circuit Court (the lowest level of trial court), the Superior Court, and, for appeals, the Court of Queen's (King's) Bench. This chapter focuses on the Superior Court, the main trial court of general civil jurisdiction.

9   Raymonde Crête, Sylvio Normand, and Thomas Copeland, "Law Reporting in Nineteenth-Century Quebec," *Journal of Legal History* 16 (1995): 147–71.

10 What follows draws on the applicable laws and regulations, in particular the *Code of Civil Procedure* (*CCP*) and the *Rules of Practice of the Superior Court* (*Sup. Ct. Rules*). The period of this project, 1840 to 1920, saw significant changes to this legislative framework, especially the initial codification of civil procedure in 1867 and several fundamental revisions of the *CCP* subsequently. This overview is based on the state of the rules circa 1900, as set out in R. Stanley Weir, ed., *The Code of Civil Procedure of the Province of Quebec* (Montreal: C. Théoret, 1900), which includes the *Sup. Ct. Rules*. See also Jean-Maurice Brisson, *La formation d'un droit mixte: l'évolution de la procédure civile de 1774–1867* (Montreal: Thémis, 1986) and Evelyn Kolish, *Guide des archives judiciaires* (Quebec City: Bibliothèque et Archives nationales, rev. ed. and online 2017), 27–28.

11 *Sup. Ct. Rules*, rules 18–20.

12 *Sup. Ct. Rules*, rule 22.

13 *CCP*, arts. 345 and 350 (quotation). This had been introduced as an option for the parties in 1871 (SQ 1871, c 6, ss 10–11): the rule was strengthened in 1884, so that in the

14   main judicial districts the judge or either party could require it (SQ 1884, c 8, s 4), and broadened further in 1890 to include most courts in the province (SQ 1890, c 46).

14   *CCP*, art. 288.

15   *CCP*, art. 544.

16   Crête, Normand, and Copeland, "Law Reporting," 161–62.

17   Couillard v Jeannotte, [1889] no. 1912 (Sup. Ct. Montreal), BAnQ-VM, TP11, S2, SS2, SSS1, cont. 1987-05-007/2301, "Le dossier de Couillard est vis-à-vis au pied de l'armoire."

18   *CCP*, arts. 275–78 (discontinuance) and 279–85 (peremption).

19   Until 1920, a first level of review was available before three judges of the Superior Court sitting as a Court of Review (*CCP*, arts. 1189ff). For those who were still unsatisfied with the review judgment and who had the means to pursue the matter, a further appeal could be brought to the Court of Queen's (King's) Bench (*CCP*, arts. 1209ff).

20   An exhaustive search of published case reports turned up, unsurprisingly, large numbers of defamation cases, many of which involved insults directed at family members, but none in which it was clear that the defendant was a relative of the plaintiff. I thank Julie Perrone for undertaking most of this search.

21   An example is Théoret v Letang, [1896] no. 1400 (Sup. Ct. Montreal), BAnQ-VM, TP11, S2, SS2, SSS1, cont. 1987-05-007/2988, in which a notary sued his uncle for allegedly casting aspersions on his practice and professional abilities. "Ordinary" defamation cases like this were excluded from the extra-family list, since those cases had nothing to do with family.

22   Not all of the case files include depositions, which sometimes reveal relationships between the parties that are otherwise hidden. Genealogical research might shed further light on relationships, but is beyond the scope of this chapter.

23   On the "elasticity" of Quebec families and households, see Sherry Olson and Patricia A. Thornton, *Peopling the North American City: Montreal 1840–1900* (Montreal: McGill-Queen's University Press, 2011), 214–42.

24   Two of the cases are tentatively included because the parties have the same surname, though the file does not permit further precision about their relationship. I have also included one case involving a tutorship relationship (akin to guardianship in the common law) and five cases involving in-laws.

25   Judgments for defendants include one case of peremption by the defendant under *CCP* 279, the effect of which was to enter a judgment dismissing the suit.

26   Hamel v Buteau, [1906] no. 1700 (Sup. Ct. Quebec City), BAnQ-Québec [BAnQ-Q], TP11, S1, SS2, SSS1, cont. 1960-01-353/1016, Bref d'assignation et déclaration (filed 6 November 1906), 1: "d'ivrogne, de vaurien, de lâche et autres appellations semblables."

27   Bellemare et ux v Bellemare, [1890] no. 216 (Sup. Ct. Trois-Rivières), BAnQ-Trois-Rivières [BAnQ-TR], TP11, S3, SS2, SSS1, cont. 1983-11-001/120, Bref et déclaration (filed 27 August 1890), 2: "venger leur réputation, leur caractère et leur honneur outragés par une réparation publique."

28 Bellemare et ux v Bellemare, Bref et déclaration, 2–3: "si mieux n'aime le dit Défendeur faire réparation d'honneur au dit Demandeur et à la dite Demanderesse, à la porte de l'Eglise de la Paroisse de Yamachiche, le dimanche, à l'issue du service divin du matin, à la date fixée par cette Honorable Cour, et dans ce cas à ne payer que les frais des présentes."

29 Mell v Middleton, [1902] no. 1880 (Sup. Ct. and Sup. Ct. Rev. Montreal), BAnQ-VM, TP11, S2, SS2, SSS1, cont. 1987-05-007/2172.

30 The plaintiff's factum in review consists mostly of a transcription of the judge's discursive reasons for judgment, from which this and the following quotations are taken. Mell v Middleton, Factum du demandeur (filed 11 December 1902).

31 The review judgment was simply a printed form dismissing the appeal: Mell v Middleton, Jugement rendu en révision (Sup. Ct. Rev., 31 March 1903, Loranger, Archibald, St-Pierre JJ.). Unusually, however, the file contains the draft rough notes of one of the review judges (likely Justice Archibald since they are in English), which indicate that this one justice at least strongly agreed with the findings of the trial judge.

32 Andegrave dit Champagne v Andegrave dit Champagne et vir, [1893] no. 600 (Sup. Ct. Montreal), BAnQ-VM, TP11, S2, SS2, SSS1, cont. 1987-05-007/2761, Bref et déclaration (filed 21 April 1893), 2: "'La vaisselle, où est-elle? les couteaux, où sont-ils? les essuie-mains, où sont-ils? le savon, où est-il? il y en avait, vous l'avez soustrait, caché, gardé'."

33 Andegrave dit Champagne v Andegrave dit Champagne et vir, Défenses de la défenderesse (filed 5 May 1893), 3: "la traitant de salope, de mauvaise langue, de voleuse, de truie, de vaut-rien etc."

34 Andegrave dit Champagne v Andegrave dit Champagne et vir, Procédés à l'enquête et mérite (filed 5 October 1894), 1: "Le demandeur retire son action, chaque partie payant ses frais sur déclaration des défendeurs qu'ils n'ont jamais entendus [sic] attenter à l'honneur du demandeur et de son épouse Dame Philomine Gohier, les ayant toujours considéré[s] pour honnêtes et respectables. Parties mise[s] hors de cour."

35 It is worth pointing out that while this action closed, there may have been other actions between these same parties, a far from rare occurrence, but something we have not yet been able to trace.

36 Thomas v Robinson, [1904] no. 2540 (Sup. Ct. Montreal), BAnQ-VM, TP11, S2, SS2, SSS1, cont. 1987-05-007/1829, Bref et déclaration (filed 1 August 1904), 1: "maudite écœurante, traîneuse de rue, vache, truie, salope."

37 Valverde in "On the Case," 270.

Writing Penitentiary History

Ted McCoy

In 2013, Kingston Penitentiary shut down as a maximum security federal prison after 178 years of operation. The prison is now a historical site and has become part of the heritage industry celebrating old Upper Canadian attractions. Aside from touring the structures of the penitentiary, legal researchers will find a vast archive of historical material connected to the first century of penitentiary history in Canada.[1] It is not an easy repository of records to navigate or understand, which may speak in part to the relative scarcity of legal history that incorporates the historical penitentiary into its narrative. But the records connected to Canada's penitentiaries represent a relatively untapped resource for legal historians to understand criminal justice, in addition to intersecting histories of poverty, class formation, gender, and race. New researchers will also want to confront questions about what they hope to uncover in penitentiary records. What is visible and obscured in records created by institutions like penitentiaries? Can we see prisoners as well as prisons?

A brief note on historiography will add to an exploration of penitentiary sources in Canada. Scholars should locate two fundamental sources as a shortcut through the maze of primary material stemming from Canadian penitentiary history. The first is J.M. Beattie's *Attitudes Towards Crime and Punishment in Upper Canada, 1830–1850*.[2] This is a documentary study published in 1977 by the Centre of Criminology at the University of Toronto. In this extraordinary working paper, Beattie not only writes one of the clearest explanations for the rise of the Canadian penitentiary, but he also provides future scholars with a roadmap to the essential documents for understanding his narrative. This includes excerpts from legislative reports that detail the ongoing debates over incarceration in Upper Canada between 1835 and 1845. Beattie offers samples of some records from the penitentiary itself, so that scholars can get a sense of what is important in the massive volume of records connected to Kingston Penitentiary. These include wardens' reports, penitentiary regulations, and the essential documents connected to the 1849 Brown Commission that brought an end to the first brutal years of Kingston Penitentiary.

The second key historical work is Peter Oliver's 1998 *"Terror to Evil-Doers": Prisons and Punishment in Nineteenth-Century Ontario*.[3] If Beattie's documentary study is an elementary overview of the available source material, Oliver's book is a master's class on navigating the archive of prison records, and the depth of his research into the workings of Kingston Penitentiary history is invaluable. One of Oliver's great talents was working out the precise mechanisms by which power and influence operated in the penitentiary and tracking these through the archival record. Beattie and Oliver together provide a rich resource for any study of punishment in Canada.

New prison historians will want to sort out some methodological questions as they embark on this research. What kind of prison history do you want to write? Government records about the penitentiary—in the form of the *Sessional Papers of the Dominion of Canada* (a source Shelley Gavigan also relies on in her essay in this volume), Department of Justice annual reports, Royal Commission reports, and legislation—are abundant and easy to access. These will help you to reconstruct an "official" history of the penitentiary, the institution as it was seen by its political masters and makers. Of course, there are analytical possibilities in the scores of pages written about penitentiaries in Canada by these figures, and they reveal much about how officialdom viewed this institution in its formative stages. But the official record is imperfect when it comes to understanding the experience of imprisonment. Who lived and breathed in penal spaces, as wardens, guards, and prisoners? To delve deeper into this story, records that are closer to the penitentiary itself are essential and can be found in the archival collections connected to the Department of Justice in Canada.

Until recently, these records were only accessible on reels housed at Library and Archives Canada (LAC), necessitating long hours in the dark scanning barely legible microfiche reproductions of the original records. The LAC is Canada's national repository of historical documents. It is located in Ottawa and houses original documents and reproductions connected to most activities of the federal government of Canada, including penitentiaries. It is the historian's lab—the spot where new discoveries are made and new interpretations initiated. Fortunately for prison researchers, the entire collection of penitentiary reels is now digitized and available online, which should allow for researchers to make both more extensive and more careful examinations of this tremendous resource.[4] The collection contains a fairly complete record of the operation of Kingston Penitentiary between 1835 and 1900. The reels include inmate history description ledgers, wardens' letter books and daily journals, inspectors' minute books and letter books, punishment ledgers, and medical registers. Researchers should also note that the Kingston Penitentiary reels are not the sum total of penitentiary records held at LAC. Record Group 73 (Penitentiaries) is a repository with a vast number of penitentiary files related to penitentiary governance in Canada. Finally, a strange archival anomaly is that records for other federal penitentiaries from the nineteenth and early-twentieth century are spread across the country and housed in various federal records centres. These are more difficult to access. Some records centres have no public reading rooms or staff resources to provide archival services. Still, researchers who can trek to Winnipeg or Burnaby will find their way to viewing original records from Manitoba Penitentiary and the New Westminster Penitentiary, both dating to the 1880s. Some of these records are mundane papers, and some are remarkable relics of the nineteenth century. For example, the Federal Record Centre in Winnipeg holds original registry, punishment, and medical books from Manitoba Penitentiary. To view these enormous registers is to physically trace the pencil and pen strokes of the subjects of your research. These marks record the rhythms of prison life. They are recorded in ways that will convey to researchers the numbing routines that characterized these institutions as well as the punctuation of violence, tragedy, and pain.

Some brief examples will illustrate the value of seeing these records in their original form. In 1849 Liberal newspaper publisher George Brown investigated abuse and misconduct occurring at Kingston Penitentiary under its original warden, Henry Smith. One of the central issues revolved around the excessive use of corporal punishment. Under investigation, Warden Smith claimed that he routinely "ordered" punishment but subsequently "cancelled" such punishments. Several staff members corroborated this practice, while other members of the staff testified to the punishments taking place. How were investigators to know whether punishments were ever truly delivered? How can legal historians work out their own version of the truth? Commissioners in 1849 carefully examined Warden Smith's punishment registers and determined that he falsified the records by "cancelling" the punishments after they had already taken place. This they concluded on the basis of the style of writing and the fact that the punishments were ordered in pen and cancelled in pencil. Researchers can support this finding by examining the same records and noting the different styles of handwriting. Similar notes of emphasis are possible for legal historians to locate throughout different historical prison records, illustrating that the historical data itself can live and breathe in the same way that the past did.

On questions of tragedy, pain, living, and breathing, researchers will want to get closer still. How can we understand the men and women who are not prominently featured in archival records, and yet are still inexorably the *subject* of much that they record? Seeing prisoners is a difficult task for the legal historian who will be confronted with two extremes. At one end are those prisoners who make a very large mark in the archival record. These are the offenders who stood out for the wrong reasons. Some crimes were extreme and resulted in notoriety which persisted behind prison walls. The best example of this visibility is found in the case of Grace Marks, the convicted murderer imprisoned in 1843 who became the subject of Margaret Atwood's *Alias Grace*. Atwood brought Grace Marks to life, but she first constructed a skeleton of her real prison life by researching her years at Kingston Penitentiary in records at LAC.[5] At the other end, some prisoners stood out for their notoriety or involvement in extreme political turmoil. In the aftermath of the North-West Rebellion in 1885, Canada incarcerated forty-four First Nations men at Manitoba Penitentiary. Among them were Cree Chiefs Poundmaker and Big Bear. Their incarceration was the source of political debate in the penitentiary, the Department of Justice, and the Parliament of Canada. Researchers will find documents detailing these men's imprisonment that reveal the sensitive political negotiations that underlay these prison sentences as well as the chiefs' eventual release. As with many Indigenous prisoners, pardon did not signal victory as both Cree leaders would die of tuberculosis shortly after their release.

Other prisoners appear disproportionately in prison records for failing to conform to the demands of prison life. They were punished more often and their behaviour generated disciplinary reports and commentary. Such examples give researchers an opportunity to understand penal responses to incorrigibility and nonconformity, and also ideas about criminality and moral reform as they operated in penitentiaries and prison reform debates. The ways the penitentiary responded to some prisoners will also force legal researchers to stretch beyond the legal realm if they are to understand the totality of the prison experience. Within prison walls a complex network of power and class relations unfolded on terrains of moral regulation, evangelical and educational reform, and medicine. This requires a different reading of archival records that are explicitly non-legal, yet necessary to understanding the larger question of punishment.

The disproportionate examples can also distort. Many prisoners experienced the penitentiary in ways that generated nothing beyond the barest biographical or administrative detail. Their stories are more difficult to tell and require a legal history that seeks answers from areas of absence or obscurity. For example, the long history of women's incarceration in Canada remains relatively unexplored, particularly in the realm of federal penitentiaries. For more than a century after 1835, women were incarcerated alongside men in federal prisons but remained marginal figures within those institutions. A deep and palpable silence about how women lived is evident in official records, their experiences often obscured by euphemisms or endless optimism. Similar absences characterize records about people of colour or Indigenous prisoners: they both experienced imprisonment in different ways than the predominantly white, male, working-class population of inmates. The answer to the original question of this short essay is that researchers can certainly see prisoners, but some are harder to see than others. Thus, to counter the marginalization of the penitentiary some experienced, researchers can employ methods that combine legal history with distinctly non-legal approaches such as microhistory or biography.

Both raise the possibility that understanding one life, or a small group of prisoners, can help speak to the composite whole. In those cases where an individual appears in the mist of obscurity—for instance, one woman who appears far more prominently in records than others—the example can speak to larger structural or social elements that might constrain many prisoners who cannot be seen.[6]

Finally, the penitentiary provides an opportunity for a research subject with great intersectional potential. Researchers approaching it from the perspective of legal history can look forward to using the broad canvas of penitentiary history to talk to multiple analytical concerns about the nineteenth and twentieth centuries. The penitentiary is a legal institution, but it also touches on multiple areas of Canadian society. It links local histories of crime and poverty together with federal justice policies and bears the influence of international currents of ideological reform, republicanism, and liberalism. The potential for writing compelling history based in penitentiary research is vast, yet ultimately accessible to the newest legal history researcher.

NOTES

1 While this piece discusses penitentiaries, researchers should note that this is just one of a vast network of nineteenth- and twentieth-century institutions used to incarcerate individuals. Penitentiaries were operated by the government of Canada (and its colonial antecedents) from 1835 onwards. Alongside these institutions were: local gaols, for pre-trial detention and short sentences; provincial prisons, such as the Mercer Reformatory in Toronto and the Fort Gary Jail in Manitoba; and later, youth-prisons or reformatories. There was also a connected network of non-legal institutions including insane asylums, orphanages, and emigrant asylums.

2 J.M. Beattie, *Attitudes Towards Crime and Punishment in Upper Canada, 1830–1850: A Documentary Study* (Toronto: University of Toronto Centre of Criminology, 1977).

3 Peter Oliver, *"Terror to Evil-Doers": Prisons and Punishment in Nineteenth-Century Ontario* (Toronto: University of Toronto Press, 1998).

4 See Kingston Penitentiary records, Héritage website, http://heritage.canadiana.ca/view/oocihm.lac_mikan_134807.

5 Atwood discusses her research process in Margaret Atwood, "In Search of Alias Grace: On Writing Canadian Historical Fiction," *American Historical Review* 103, no. 5 (December 1998): 1503–16.

6 This approach is drawn from the notion of the "exceptional typical" introduced by Italian historian Edoardo Grendi, "Micro-analisi e storia sociale," *Quaderni storici* 35 (1977): 506–20.

Analyzing Bigamy Cases without Going to the Archives: It is Possible

Mélanie Méthot

After nearly thirty years in the field, I still feel my heart racing when my fingers touch old yellowed court documents. Sometimes filled with spidery scrawls, these documents often reveal the waved-like calligraphy of a person who spent his life (for most of the eighteenth, nineteenth, and early twentieth centuries, court employees were men) transcribing countless items of precious information. And what to say about the times I realize I am the first researcher to peruse those centennial documents, not yet unfolded or unstapled, requiring the delicate touch of the historian? Leafing through archival material is definitively exhilarating. I am thankful, however, for the technological advances of the twenty-first century. It took me years to read through microfilmed newspapers during my doctoral research: I can only wonder how many times my tired eyes skipped over valuable information. Now researching the prosecution of bigamy in both Canada and in Australia, I again use archival data and newspapers but I retrieve the data differently.

Digitalization has revolutionized the way we conduct research. One can now read from the comfort of one's home any issue of *The Globe* (from 1844) or the *Toronto Star* (from 1894), to name only two important Canadian newspapers. Historians can sometimes search historical newspapers databases by keywords, such as *Peel's Prairie Provinces* which has a modest holding of newspapers from the region (http://peel.library.

ualberta.ca/newspapers/), while Bibliothèque et Archives nationales du Québec [BAnQ], which holds a substantial number of magazines and newspapers searchable online, cannot always be investigated by keywords (http://numerique.banq.qc.ca/ressources/details/RJQ). As for Library and Archives Canada, it will perhaps follow the Australian path and digitize every newspaper in its possession.[1] Until our public institutions invest in this technology, we can check diverse online archives to access freely rich historical data. Institutions constantly add to their holdings and refine their digital tools, although, as Donald Fyson pointed out many years ago about Early Canadiana Online (now canadiana.ca), a digital historical library holds "ultimately (a) selective collection of the primary sources."[2] Carolyn Strange made the same argument even earlier about archival court documents, warning legal historians that it was the keepers of court records who decided what each *case file*[3] would contain.[4] Regardless of the kind of research we do, we have to remind ourselves constantly how we often have access to only some of the information, something easily forgotten when a new piece of the puzzle emerges.

The slenderness of the case files produced in bigamy prosecutions—when these files exist at all—often leads to frustration. For instance, when I encountered on the pages of a Montreal prison's ledger Philomène Déry who was serving a term of five months of hard labour for bigamy,[5] I did not locate any corresponding court documents related to her case. I remember my excitement when I came across newspaper articles providing some of the missing information. At least three Montreal newspapers mentioned the case. I even found out who informed the authorities: a priest, as the *Montreal Star* reported.[6] I chose the Déry case to introduce one of my recent publications on "Marriage Norms and Bigamy in Canada."[7] Too happy to have found more details on the case, I had forgotten to take into account the nature of the source disclosing the information. In 1870, the *Montreal Star* was a very sensationalist paper. The four historians working on the "Famille, Droit et Justice au Québec, 1840–1920" project discovered the Déry court file.[8] According to their documents, Déry's illegitimate husband was the one who lodged the complaint. This example serves as a good reminder to always place the sources we use in their historical context. Considering today's concerns about "fake news," one may ask if historians should rely on newspaper accounts to get accurate facts. My research on bigamy in Australia reveals that Australian newspapers have had a real appetite for everything that deals with the offence; specific cases could easily be mentioned in dozens of articles, even more. For instance, the Lily May Strike case was reported in forty-three articles. However, details about the case vary greatly from one article to the other, sometimes contradicting each other. As Lyndsay Campbell discusses in her piece on pamphlets in this volume, "learning to sift the facts from the slant" is "[o]ne of the great challenges and joys of history." Campbell also mentions how one can glean the discourses of the time on specific issues. Historical newspapers are definitely worth turning to in order to find some details on criminal cases, which can then be verified through other types of sources such as civil records and court files. Analyzing the articles as narratives, not only for what they include or leave out, but for their tone also serves to shed light on society.

Let me turn to a specific example to illustrate how one can go about doing legal history research without spending much time at the archives (although I highly recommend going to any archives!). Just as with Philomène Déry, I first encountered Julie Morin on the pages of a prison ledger. I leafed through the massive, red Quebec City gaol register,[9] although one can search some of the registries online, in the database of the BAnQ, between 1813–1866 for men and up to 1899 for women. It is possible to search by family or given name, country or ethnic origin, date of imprisonment, offence, sentence or grounds for discharge (http://www.banq.qc.ca/archives/genealogie_histoire_familiale/ressources/bd/instr_prisons/prisonniers/index.html). Morin was jailed briefly twice: on 12 November 1879, before she pleaded not guilty, and on 28 April 1880, the night before her trial. I was able to locate a very slim case file containing four documents related to her preliminary inquiry: (1) the testimony of Édouard Robitaille confirming he was the legal husband of Julie Morin, (2) the testimony of Reverend James Sexton who celebrated the union between the Widow Morin and William Russell in 1877, (3), papers providing information about the two individuals who posted her bail, and (4) a writ of assignment. In sum, beyond the names of the two husbands, the names of two witnesses confirming Morin was Robitaille's legal wife, the identity of the two men who posted bail, the dates of the two marriages, and the dates of the court proceedings, the file disclosed nothing on any informant, motivations, or outcome. Fortunately, dates mentioned in these documents and those from the prison ledger allowed me to narrow further my research to Quebec City newspapers, which yielded a total of twenty-four articles from six different papers. Some papers followed every step of the legal procedure, from the first accusation, through the postponement of trial, to the actual trial and verdict, while others chimed in at intervals. All six papers covered the April 1880 trial, a few reporting the examinations, cross- and re-cross examinations of some of the fourteen witnesses. No single paper covered the trial exhaustively. From these accounts, I could somewhat reconstruct the trial—at the very least establish who participated in it—and ascertain the defense's strategy and the newspapers' different outlooks.

The Morning Chronicle devoted space to the judge's explanation of the nature of the offence:

> That crime is committed by those who being married contract another marriage while their first wife or their first husband is still living. To constitute this offence, proof must be adduced of the first marriage, and that, at the time of the celebration of the second marriage, of which also proof must be produced, the first wife, or the first husband, as the case may be, was still alive.[10]

The inclusion of the judge's explanation in the newspaper cited above suggests that the common citizen would not have known much about the nature of the offence. It also seems that the Crown assigned one specific function to each of its witnesses. For instance, Father Sexton had to prove that the two marriages took place, something he did easily. He damaged the Crown's case, however, when he testified that "[h]e did not put any questions to the prisoner before marrying her because she was recognized by the people of St-Roch as widow of Robitaille who had been prayed for some years previously as dead in St-Roch's Church": evidently, he and the neighbours believed Morin a widow.[11] Charles Fitzpatrick, a young criminal lawyer who later became Chief Justice of Canada and lieutenant-governor of Quebec, organized Morin's defense around two main pieces of evidence. He opened with an official record of the circuit court dated from

1873 in which the prisoner was a party in an unrelated suit and was styled, "Julie Morin, widow of Édouard Robitaille." The document had established the legal recognition of Morin as a widow. Fitzpatrick concluded his case with another document, an 1871 letter received by Morin and seen by Robitaille's father stating that Édouard Robitaille had died after receiving the last sacraments of the Church and had made the author of the letter, a co-worker, promise to inform his wife of his death.

Without great surprise, all the newspapers announced the following day that Julie Morin had been acquitted. The Canadian law on bigamy provided exceptions such as "any person marrying a second time whose husband or wife has been continually absent from such a person for the space of seven years then last past, and was not known by such person to be living within that time."[12] The jury deliberated less than ten minutes. The newspapers portrayed Fitzpatrick as a much better lawyer than the Crown prosecutor who only produced five witnesses, one of whom even turned out to be a powerful ally for Morin's cause. By contrast, Fitzpatrick brought nine people to vouch for the defendant and adopted the astute strategy of starting and finishing his case with documents. Regardless of the sincerity of witnesses, in a court of law tangible documents often weigh more heavily than personal recollections.

I could have stopped the research there, but instead my curiosity was awakened by some of the testimonies of the witnesses, especially the niece of the illegitimate husband, Ellen Russell. She had mentioned how her uncle had made a will making her the sole heir, but had subsequently modified it to the benefit of his wife. I checked Canadian censuses (http://www.bac-lac.gc.ca/eng/census/Pages/census.aspx), trying to understand what happened to the main actors of the saga. I found a Julie Russell, a widow living with her sister in 1881, 1891, and 1901. I was also able to check online the 1877 marriage contract between William Russell and Morin, as well as the different wills Russell had executed (http://bibnum2.banq.qc.ca/bna/notaires/index.html). One can also consult the parish registries online to find out details about marriages (http://bibnum2.banq.qc.ca/bna/ecivil/). In the United States, and I suspect in many other countries, genealogical websites are some of the most visited. As such, private companies are developing great tools to conduct genealogical research; for instance, without having to subscribe to them, one can navigate through the Church of Jesus Christ of Latter-day Saints' FamilySearch database for free (https://www.familysearch.org/). These databases allow researchers to find more personal information about the people involved in their case studies.

From newspapers to genealogical searches, I decided to do what any respectable twenty-first century individual would do: I googled "Julie Morin" and "Bigamy." With great excitement, I found the *Queen's Bench Reports* and discovered that Russell's niece contested the validity of his last will, which opened up a completely new avenue for this intriguing case.[13] In the end, historical research is about ingenuity, curiosity, and open minds. No one should hesitate to use the ever-growing online resources, archival or not, and everyone should remember to situate the sources in their historical context.

NOTES

1. As its website states, TROVE "helps you find and use resources relating to Australia. It is more than a search engine. Trove brings together content from libraries, museums, archives, repositories and other research and collecting organisations big and small": https://trove.nla.gov.au/general/about. Searching with keywords such as "bigamy" or "bigamists," I get more than 100,000 hits. My research team has already identified nearly eight hundred cases by going through the Trove database. Furthermore, under the direction of Mark Finnane at Griffith University, *The Prosecution Project*, which is investigating the history of the criminal trial in Australia and digitizing the registers of all courts, provided a preliminary lists of bigamy trials: https://prosecutionproject.griffith.edu.au/. Interestingly, there are very few discrepancies between the accused bigamists of the PP data set and my data retrieved from TROVE.

2. Donald Fyson, "À la recherche de l'histoire dans les bibliothèques numériques: les leçons de *Notre mémoire en ligne*," Érudit 59, no. 1–2 (été/automne 2005): 95–113.

3. A case file is a dossier that encloses some or all documents used by the court to assess the guilt or innocence of a defendant. It may contain the information/complaint, crown solicitor correspondence, subpoena, bail, recognizance to give evidence, police reports, personal letters, list of exhibits, exhibits, depositions, and very rarely judgments.

4. Carolyn Strange, "Stories of Their Lives: The Historian and the Capital Case File," in *On the Case: Explorations in Social History*, ed. Franca Iacovetta and Wendy Mitchinson (Toronto: University of Toronto Press, 1998), 29.

5. Prison registries 1870, #478, SS1, S1, E17, Centre d'archives de Montréal, BAnQ Montréal.

6. "A Romish Clergyman Lodged the Information," *Montreal Star*, 23 February 1870.

7   Méthot, "Finding the Ordinary in the Extraordinary: Marriage Norms and Bigamy in Canada," in *Marriage, Law and Modernity: Global Histories*, ed. Julia Moses (London: Bloomsbury Academic, 2017).

8   Donald Fyson, Peter Gossage, Thierry Nootens, and Eric Reiter. Eric Reiter's chapter in this volume reflects his work on this project.

9   A jail (formerly "gaol") was a local lock-up for short sentences and pre-trial detention, which duration was usually no more than three months. The term "prison" is generally used to refer to a penitentiary. The penitentiary is an invention of the late eighteenth century, aimed at the reform of the offender and normally providing for both solitary and congregated confinement. The labour of inmates could be employed to financially support penitentiaries. In these institutions, generally larger than jails, sentences tended to be longer. As the nineteenth century unfolded, penitentiaries came to gradually replace other corporal methods of punishment (whipping, stocks, banishment, and so forth).

10 "Court of Queen's Bench – Crown Side," *Morning Chronicle* (Quebec), 28 April 1880.

11 "Court of Queen's Bench – Crown Side," *Morning Chronicle* (Quebec), 29 April 1880.

12 *An Act Respecting Offences against the Person*, SC 1869, c 20, s 58, available on http://eco.canadiana.ca/.

13 I am currently writing a monograph on the Morin-Russell saga.

Trial Pamphlets and Newspaper Accounts

Lyndsay Campbell

Writing history involves a lot of detective work. Among my favorite sources of information about trials are accounts written by the parties and their supporters before, during, or, most often, after their trials. Publishing these accounts was common in the nineteenth-century Anglo-Atlantic world, at least where newspaper presses were numerous and energetic. Often you learn a lot about not only the trial but also the various participants' lives before the trial took place, especially if what they had been up to was somehow relevant to what happened during the trial. In libel law—a central area of research for me—competing versions of the past are often part of the dispute. For example, a man brought a criminal libel action against a newspaper in Boston in 1833 over allegations he had wrongfully escaped his creditors. In a sixty-four-page pamphlet meant to set the record straight, he described being an unpopular opponent of freemasonry in upstate New York before moving to Boston, still pursued by freemasons. The freemasons were dedicated to making his life miserable for revealing their conspiracy to murder a certain William Morgan in 1826, possibly by pushing him over Niagara Falls when he threatened to disclose masonic secrets.[1] The persecuted antimason, Samuel Greene, was now promoting the Antimasonic party, the first "third party" in American political life.

You can often discover the existence of a pamphlet simply by doing an internet search for the names of the participants in the case.

Occasionally, finding one pamphlet may lead you to one or more other pamphlets, all written to correct the "errors" in earlier accounts. When Joseph T. Buckingham suggested that an itinerant Methodist preacher named John N. Maffitt was not really devoted to his religious beliefs, but actually just liked the access it provided to the private quarters of young women, a pamphlet war accompanied Maffitt's unsuccessful libel prosecution.[2] Arguments about freedom of the press and the importance of character are intertwined with details about what it was like, in early nineteenth-century America, to be a poor but aspiring printer, or a young Irishman with religious inspiration but little education.

The American Antiquarian Society, in Worcester, Massachusetts holds a treasure-trove of pamphlets. Even if you will not be travelling to Worcester, you can use their search engine to discover the existence of pamphlets, which can often be found elsewhere. Some of their collection is digitized as well. The Internet Archive, archive.org, is another excellent source of pamphlets—and actually of pretty much any text now out of copyright. Hathi Trust's website also has an immense amount of material, as does Google Books. If you are fortunate enough to have access to the database The Making of Modern Law: Trials, 1600–1926 or the Gale Primary Sources database, definitely use them. It is also worth checking the catalogs of local archives and libraries in the places where the events that interest you took place, as well as the catalogs of the Toronto Public Library and the Fisher Rare Books library at the University of Toronto to find out what kinds of texts exist. Even if you cannot immediately get access to the text, the first step is finding out that it exists and getting the author's name and the title. If you have a pamphlet, note the publisher: if it is the name of a newspaper or of someone who also published a newspaper, it is a good bet that the newspaper reported on the trial as well. Quite likely a rival newspaper also covered it.

Accounts of trials that appeared in newspapers are generally harder to find than pamphlets. You usually have to know when the trial took place and then find local newspapers and search them. A wonderful database called Worldcat attempts to archive all the surviving holdings of every text ever published, meaning that it can tell you, for example, that a certain library has all the issues of a given magazine from November 1955 to June 1957, followed perhaps by a gap, and then all the holdings from March

1960 to October 1963. It can also give you the names of all the newspapers and other periodicals published in a certain city from year X to year Y, as long as copies of at least some of the issues survive. Once you learn the names of the papers, you can figure out where to look for them.

Although digital databases of newspapers exist (such as the *Globe and Mail* Online, Nineteenth Century US Newspapers, Paper of Record, and the Early Alberta Newspapers Collection), they are not all reliably searchable because optical character recognition does not always work well on old documents that have been microfilmed. As well, many if not most newspapers still await digitization, so you may have to look for them on microforms (microfilm or microfiche). University libraries often have microform collections, and you can also order microforms—and books and periodicals—through a service called interlibrary loan. You can do this through public libraries as well. Your library borrows what you need from another library and then lends it to you. Once you receive the film or fiche that covers the date range you need, you have to look through it, page by page, to find coverage of the trial that interests you. It is often a good idea to read a few months before and after the trial as well, to unearth any pre-existing controversies and to discover how the opinions and arguments diverged once it was over. William J. Snelling, for instance, was successfully prosecuted in Boston for a libel against a police magistrate called Benjamin Whitman. Snelling alleged that Whitman did his job badly and was drunk on the bench. However, even though Whitman and the Commonwealth won the libel prosecution, Whitman resigned his position shortly afterward, a development that hints that his reputation was not thoroughly redeemed through his victory in court.[3]

What do you do with a pamphlet once you have it in your hands or on your screen? First, you have to imagine that you have wandered into a room full of people you have never met before having a heated conversation about a matter you only dimly recall. It is important to begin with the assumption that you really know very little. Even if you think you know how it ended, you may still be wrong. There may have been a second act to the play. Be humble but highly attentive. Pamphlets and newspaper articles can be extremely useful about structural matters that were understood by everyone at the time but that we may now wonder about. For example, pamphlets from Massachusetts libel cases in the 1820s and

1830s will reveal how a trial actually operated: who spoke first, who testified, and so forth. They make it clear that many people accused of libel had legal counsel (evidently lawyers were not forbidden), but many other people conducted their own cases. This was because they could not testify under oath. The complainant in a criminal case could give sworn testimony, but a defendant who retained a lawyer to conduct the proceedings could only sit anxiously and listen. In a civil case neither party could testify. The results of these strategic decisions become clear from pamphlets and news articles. The political fortunes of Nova Scotia's Joseph Howe, for example, rose when he successfully defended himself on libel charges in 1835. According to him, the jury that freed him thereby brought freedom of the press to Nova Scotia; being a central figure in the history of freedom of the press in your own jurisdiction is not a bad claim for an aspiring politician, and it served Howe well.[4]

Pamphlets and newspaper descriptions of trials also reveal women, racialized minorities, servants, and other non-famous people living their lives, criticizing their neighbours, and making their arguments, both in and out of court. For example, Boston police magistrate Benjamin Whitman's ex-daughter-in-law testified that Whitman was frequently drunk and abusive to herself and her children (his grandchildren). Whitman supported the children, but, she said, "[t]hey are not well treated; they often go lousy, and with their knees out."[5] From this you get a glimpse of parenting norms and the sorts of criticisms made about them in the time period, not to mention a hint about the prevalence of lice. It is not enough for formal conclusions, but it is a snippet of evidence, to be combined with other snippets.

You may also, of course, interpret a pamphlet or an article in order to find out what happened. Occasionally a pamphlet provides vital information about how some long-gone institution functioned. The Halifax Court of Commissioners, for example, heard a huge volume of small debt cases in the 1820s and 1830s, but almost no records survive. Joseph Howe's criticisms of the court—delivered as part of his explanation for printing what he had about Halifax's governing magistrates—amount to one of the few accounts of what that court did. Of course, often you are able to correlate and cross-match references to details—what people said and when, and what they meant—to other records that have survived, such as reported versions of legal cases and notes judges left in the files. Like lawyers, judges, and all the other participants, pamphleteers and journalists are almost always biased but in interesting ways. They may skip over substantial parts of one party's case and give loving regard to the other's, especially if it is their own. One of the great challenges and joys of history is learning to sift the facts from the slant.

Pamphlets can teach us not only about people and institutions, but also about what ideas and arguments people thought would be persuasive or unpersuasive. In 1829, when a Boston man named Origen Bacheler tried to have witnesses from a Christian sect called the Universalists barred from testifying on the grounds that they did not believe God would judge them in the afterlife (even if they lied on the witness stand), the judge was clearly uncomfortable about the effect that excluding relevant testimony would have on the trial, and he refused to prevent the witnesses from testifying.[6] A few years later, however, the same judge barred a witness who was a "Free Inquirer," who, if he believed in anything, believed that God was only embodied in the material universe.[7] We have to be careful about leaping too quickly to the conclusion that the judge was prejudiced against one group but not the other. We make sense of these events through practices of interpretation that involve, first, understanding what the Universalists, the Free Inquirers, and the other courtroom actors believed and how their various views collided. We also need to understand the religious politics of the period: who was influential in society, whose influence was growing, and what threats to the public good were perceived in these different religious causes. We would want to bear in mind as well that Massachusetts prided itself on its freedom of religion. We would look outside the courtroom to see what else these different groups were doing. The Universalists, as it happens, were lobbying hard to end state financial support for religion, and they and others succeeded in having the state constitution changed, effective in 1834. Some won and some lost with this change. The Free Inquirers were mounting an even larger challenge to society: they criticized capitalism, women's oppression in marriage, what they saw as the absurdities of Christianity, and slavery. They advocated birth control and a form of marriage that could be ended at will by either partner. Their opponents saw the edifice of civilized, God-fearing society collapsing all around. Understanding these movements requires us to realize that our interpretive horizons (in Hans-Georg Gadamer's terms) are bounded, and to work to extend them so that they merge, as far as possible, with those whose mental frameworks we are trying to understand. Working with pamphlets—and other primary sources—calls for a suspension of judgment, a respect for those who came before us, and a willingness to set today's frameworks and assumptions aside in order to appreciate yesterday's. The rewards are rich.

NOTES

1. Samuel D. Greene, *Appeal of Samuel D. Greene, in Vindication of Himself against the False Swearing of Johnson Goodwill, a Morgan Conspirator, in the Case of Commonwealth v Moore & Sevey, Editors of the Masonic Mirror, for a Libel on Said Greene* (Boston, 1834), online: Making of Modern Law: Trials database.

2. See *A Correct Statement and Review of the Trial of Joseph T. Buckingham, for an Alledged [sic] Libel on the Rev. John N. Maffit, Before the Hon. Josiah Quincy, Judge of the Municipal Court, Dec. 16, 1822* (Boston: William S. Spear, 1822), online: hathitrust.org; *Report of the Trial of Mr. John N. Maffitt, before a Council of Ministers, of the Methodist Episcopal Church. Convened in Boston, December 26, 1822* (Boston: True & Greene, 1823), online: hathitrust.org; *A Vindication of Publick Justice and of Private Character, Against the Attacks of a "Council of Ministers" of the "Methodist Episcopal Church"* (Providence, RI: John Miller, 1823), online: Gale Primary Sources (Sabin Americana, 1500–1926); *An Exposure of the Misrepresentations Contained in a Professed Report of the Trial of Mr. John N. Maffitt, before a Council of Ministers of the Methodist Episcopal Church, Convened in Boston, December 26, 1822* (Boston, 1832); *Maffit's [sic] Trial; or, Buckingham Acquitted, on a Charge of Slander against the Character of John N. Maffit, Preacher in the Methodist Episcopal Society* (New York: C.N. Baldwin, 1831).

3. "Judge Whitman," *Boston Masonic Mirror*, 11 January 1834.

4. See Joseph Howe, *Trial for Libel, on the Magistrates of Halifax, the King v Joseph Howe, Before the Chief Justice and a Special Jury, Supreme Court—Hilary Term* (Halifax, NS: 1835), online: hathitrust.org.

5. *Trial of William J. Snelling for a Libel on the Honorable Benjamin Whitman, Senior Judge of the Police Court. Commonwealth vs. Snelling. Supreme Judicial Court of Massachusetts, December 27th, 1833. Before the Hon. Samuel Putnam, Justice* (Boston, 1834), online: Gale Primary Sources (Sabin Americana, 1500–1926).

6. See John W. Whitman, *Trial of the Commonwealth, versus Origen Bacheler, for a Libel on the Character of George B. Beals, Deceased, at the Municipal Court, Boston, March Term, A. D. 1829. Before Hon. P. O. Thacher, Judge* (Boston: John H. Belcher, 1829), online: http://lawcollections.library.cornell.edu/trial/catalog/sat:0105; Origen Bacheler, *Review of the Trial of Origen Bacheler, Editor of the Anti-Universalist, for an Alleged Libel; And of the Report of that Trial* (Boston Whitcomb & Page, 1829), online: Making of Modern Law: Trials, 1600–1926 (Gale).

7. E.H.W., Untitled letter to the editor, *Boston Investigator*, 2 October 1835.

The Last Voyage of the *Frederick Gerring, Jr.*

Christopher Shorey[*]

Twenty-fifth of May 1896. It was late in the afternoon, on a calm day, off the southern coast of Nova Scotia. The Canadian Dominion cruiser *Aberdeen* steamed alongside the American fishing schooner, the *Frederick Gerring, Jr.* The *Gerring*'s crew were busy bailing fish from the purse seine into waiting barrels on deck. The ship's master, Captain Daniel Doren, stepped to the gunnel to speak to the *Aberdeen*'s master, Captain Charles Knowlton. Knowlton told Doren that he was seizing the *Gerring* for fishing in Canadian waters within three miles of the coast, contrary to the treaty of 1818 that established the boundary between the United States and British North America, as implemented through British and Canadian statutes that prohibited foreign ships from fishing in Canadian waters. The *Gerring* would never fish again.

At the admiralty court trial in Halifax, the parties focused on whether the *Gerring* had indeed been within three miles of land when apprehended by the *Aberdeen*. Chief Justice McDonald found that it was. Specifically, the ship was within three miles of a small Canadian island named Gull Ledge and therefore in violation of the treaty.[1]

The owner of the *Gerring*, Captain Edward Morris, appealed the admiralty court's decision to the Supreme Court of Canada. On appeal, the parties assumed the fish had entered the nets in international waters. The parties focused on the legal question of whether the *Gerring* was still

51

actually "fishing" when it was found in Canadian waters and was therefore in violation of the 1818 treaty, UK legislation, and Canada's *Act Respecting Fishing by Foreign Vessels*, none of which contained a definition of fishing.[2] This issue was tied to a determination of the point at which the *Gerring* had taken possession of the fish. Once possession was complete, the fish legally were no longer wild animals but became the ship's property—at which point the *Gerring* was no longer fishing.[3] The relevant questions were: (a) were the fish captured once secured by the seine, in which case they were caught in international waters and the crew *were not* "fishing" when approached by the *Aberdeen*; or (b) were the fish only captured once secured in barrels on the deck of the *Gerring*, in which case the crew *were* still fishing when the *Aberdeen* arrived?

The Supreme Court favoured the latter interpretation and, on 1 May 1897, upheld Chief Justice McDonald's judgment against the *Gerring*.[4] Undeterred, Morris sought a political solution and pleaded for help from his congressmen and senators. It seemed to work. The Canadian government immediately offered to return the vessel in exchange for a nominal fine. However, Morris rejected the offer, causing significant political embarrassment, the reverberations of which lasted for decades.

After an impasse and many years of delay, the case was included in an international arbitration of outstanding claims between the United States and Great Britain. In May 1914, after eighteen years, it finally seemed that the matter had settled. However, for the second time in the case's history, the perceived resolution failed to materialize. Despite reports in newspapers and legal journals that the case was over, Canada refused to recognize the settlement. The last record of the *Gerring v. Canada* is from 16 October 1924, when Canada, while agreeing to pay the other awards from the international claims arbitration, reaffirmed that it would not pay for the *Gerring*.[5]

Justice Désiré Girouard's concurring reasons for judgment at the Supreme Court of Canada cite and reproduce large sections of a famous New York case about fox hunting from 1805, *Pierson v. Post*.[6] Despite being over two hundred years old, the *Pierson* case is still widely cited in legal academia and taught in Canadian law schools as establishing the rule that one must capture a wild animal in order to possess it. However, the application of the rule is not restricted to wild animal cases. Its use in law school classrooms and legal literature helps shape our understanding of property law, the legitimacy of claims to possession of all kinds of wild or "fugitive" resources, and even the concept of ownership itself.[7] However, despite the case's importance in legal academia, there has been no academic comment on its prominent link to the Supreme Court's decision in *Gerring v. Canada*, which remains the only case that includes an extensive judicial consideration of *Pierson*.[8]

As a foundational decision for generations of North American lawyers, *Pierson*'s uptake and incorporation in Girouard's judgment warrants greater scrutiny for *Gerring v. Canada*. This is especially so considering the aftermath of the case, which suggests that Canadian political and economic needs, rather than abstract legal concepts, were the ultimate driving force behind the *Gerring*'s fate. The case sparked international scandal, was a thorn in the side of the Minister of Fisheries and Oceans for over a decade, came across the Prime Minister's desk more than once, was energetically covered by the press, and singlehandedly delayed international arbitration proceedings between Great Britain and the United States. More than twenty-five years after the Supreme Court's decision, the controversy was still, unbelievably, live. The extent of Canada's boundaries, its ability to enforce them, and Canada's recent independence from Britain were all at stake in this case and were probably more significant for Canada than whether the *Gerring* took a net or a barrel to catch a fish.

Gerring v. Canada is *the* case that incorporated *Pierson*-style first possession principles into Canadian law. Whether it is only recognized as such, or whether it also sparks further conversation about the legitimacy of these principles in Canadian law, depends on the legal community. Regardless of its legacy, the extraordinary history of the case should be a part of the conversation.

The primary sources for this chapter are the British and American "memorials" that were assembled for the international claims arbitration. These memorials include the transcripts from trial, the factums filed with the Supreme Court, and exhibits from trial such as copies of the chart showing the *Gerring*'s location. Most of the information from the time period after arbitration came from Canadian government correspondence retrieved from the National Archives.[9]

The Arrest of the *Frederick Gerring, Jr.*

The story begins in the late spring of 1896, in the bustling seaport of Gloucester, Massachusetts. Gloucester was renowned for its fishing schooners. Thousands of its handsome wooden sailing ships plied their trade on the east coast and throughout the Maritimes. Every Canadian knows what a fishing schooner looks like, as the famous *Bluenose* is on the face of the dime.

The life of a fisherman was exceedingly dangerous. Between 1860 and 1906, over six hundred fishing vessels were lost at sea from Gloucester alone, either to heavy weather or wrecked on shoals and islands.[10] A schooner like the *Gerring* was not itself used for fishing. Once the ship arrived at the fishing grounds it launched its dories, small, open boats that were rowed into position. From the dories, the dorymen netted the fish, encircling whole schools of fish in large nets called purse seines.

The *Gerring* was built in 1870 in Essex, a few miles west of Gloucester.[11] Edward Morris purchased the ship in November 1892 for approximately $3,000.[12] The *Gerring* was 73'7" in length, with a 21'1" beam, a draft of 7'8, and a displacement of 67 tons.[13] Unlike the coal-powered *Aberdeen*, which towed it away, the *Gerring* recalled an earlier age, being powered only by sail.

Morris was originally from Guysboro, Nova Scotia, but became an American citizen on 20 July 1866, and made his home in Gloucester.[14] He was a fisherman-turned-ship owner.[15] The loss of the *Gerring* and the costs of litigation were ruinous to Morris. According to a sympathetic *Washington Post* report, "It broke the old man completely. Everything he had was tied in that vessel."[16]

The *Gerring* operated with a crew of nine: three Canadians, five Americans, and one Frenchman.[17] Although Morris owned the *Gerring*, he was not on board when it was seized. The master operating the ship at the time was Daniel Doren. Doren had been master of the *Gerring* for only four days when they left Gloucester on 13 May 1896, headed for the White Islands, off of Guysboro County, Nova Scotia.[18]

The *Gerring* arrived at the fishing grounds off the south shore of Nova Scotia at about 3:00 pm on Monday, May 25, joining at least a dozen other

American schooners. The winds were calm and the mackerel were "playing about" on the surface of the water.[19]

The *Vigilant* was also sailing the area. The *Vigilant* was a "Dominion cruiser" that belonged to the precursor of the Canadian Coast Guard, which was not formally created until 1962. Commanded by Hector MacKenzie, the *Vigilant* was a former fishing schooner, previously called the *Highland Light*, which had been seized a few years earlier for fishing within the three-mile limit and bought by the federal government.[20] Charles Hardy, the captain of another American fishing schooner, the *Marguerite Haskins*, called out to MacKenzie to ask if they were outside the three-mile limit. MacKenzie replied, "you are all right, go ahead."[21] Hearing this, the crew of the *Gerring* launched their dories, cast their nets, and started fishing.

The *Gerring* was purse seine fishing. With this type of fishing, a large rectangular net (the *Gerring*'s net was approximately one thousand feet long and one hundred and eighty feet deep)[22] was lowered into the water. The net had floats on the top and weights at the bottom so that it floated vertically. The dorymen would encircle a school of fish with the net so that it formed a large cylinder. The bottom of the cylinder was then drawn closed or "pursed up." When pursed, the net was shallower but still about ninety feet deep.[23] The top ends of the net were then secured to either end of the schooner. The result was a net full of fish attached to the side of the ship. The crew would then bail the fish into barrels on the schooner with a "dip net."[24] The ship would be allowed to drift during the bailing, as the net would foul if the ship were anchored.

The crew of the *Gerring* had finished netting the fish and were bailing them onto the ship when another Dominion cruiser, the *Aberdeen*, arrived.[25] Its captain, Charles Knowlton, had his chief officer take a bearing, and he determined the *Gerring* to be within three miles of Nova Scotia. More specifically, he calculated that they were just less than two miles from a small island called Gull Ledge. Knowlton seized the *Gerring* for fishing within the three-mile limit and towed it to Liscombe Harbour for the night and then on to Halifax for trial in admiralty court five days later, on Saturday, 30 May 1896.[26]

The Trial

The Nova Scotia Court of Vice-Admiralty, Nova Scotia's original admiralty court and the second admiralty court in what would eventually become Canada, had existed since 9 September 1720, when Daniel Henry received his commission and was appointed the judge at Annapolis.[27] One of the court's principal functions was to regulate trade among the North American colonies and Great Britain.[28] Barristers of the Supreme Court of Nova Scotia were permitted to appear at the Court of Vice-Admiralty.[29] British acts of Parliament gave authority to these colonial courts. However, after Confederation in 1867, the provinces started asking for their own home-grown admiralty courts, citing excessive litigation costs, procedural issues, and the general disconnect between local problems and far-away British administration.[30]

The Exchequer and Supreme Courts of Canada were established in 1875[31] and, in 1891, the Exchequer Court acquired admiralty jurisdiction.[32] The vice-admiralty court in Halifax became the "Exchequer Court of Canada, Nova Scotia Admiralty District." The chief justice of the Supreme Court of Nova Scotia, James McDonald, who had been the judge of vice-admiralty since 1881, became the new judge of the Nova Scotia admiralty district.[33] It was McDonald who heard the *Gerring* trial.

The *Gerring* was represented by local lawyer William F. MacCoy, Q.C. of MacCoy, MacCoy & Grant.[34] Morris paid MacCoy $808.11 for representation at trial, $250 for representation at appeal, $80 for transcripts, and $50 for security for court costs he might be required to pay if he lost.[35] For Morris, already suffering the loss of his ship, the total amount—almost $1,200—was a significant sum of money, approximately a third of the cost of a new sailing ship.

Canada was represented by William Bruce Almon Ritchie. Ritchie was a third-generation member of a prominent Nova Scotia legal family.[36] Ritchie's uncle, Sir William Johnstone Ritchie, was one of the first six Supreme Court of Canada judges and chief justice from 1879 to 1892. W.B.A. Ritchie's son, Roland Almon Ritchie, would go on to become a Supreme Court of Canada judge as well, from 1959 to 1984.

W.B.A. Ritchie, educated at Harvard University in 1881 and 1882, was part of a new generation of Canadian lawyers educated in the American,

Harvard style of law rather than traditional British models of legal education.[37] In 1889, he joined Robert Borden, future prime minister of Canada, in forming the firm of Borden, Ritchie, Parker, and Chisholm. Ritchie and Borden were both very successful and sought-after appellate-level barristers.[38] Ritchie was still with Borden in 1896 when he argued the *Gerring* case on behalf of the attorney general of Canada.[39]

The *Gerring* trial began on Saturday, 30 May, and continued on 1 June, 29 June, and 5 August 1896.[40] Procedure was as in any other common law court, and trial proceeded by judge alone, as was always the case in the admiralty court. Although the trial took five days and twenty witnesses were called, the issues in dispute were relatively straightforward.[41] First, where was the *Gerring* when seized by the *Aberdeen*, and second, was the *Gerring*, in law, "fishing" at the time?

The *Gerring* began fishing outside the three-mile territorial limit. As well as telling the master of the *Marguerite Haskins* that they were "all right" to fish, MacKenzie of the *Vigilant* took a bearing of the *Gerring* and determined it was a "good half mile" outside the limit, presumably as measured from Gull Ledge.[42] The real factual dispute came when determining how far the *Gerring* had drifted after an hour or two of bailing fish. Knowlton of the *Aberdeen* testified that the *Gerring* was apprehended "less than a mile and three quarters" from Gull Ledge.[43] If this was correct, the ship had drifted nearly two miles to the northwest.

MacCoy called four witnesses, including Morris, who testified that, given the direction of the wind, to travel northwest towards Gull Ledge would have been impossible.[44] So long as the net was in the water attached to the *Gerring*, it would have acted as a sea anchor, and the swell should not have carried the ship that far. The problem for the *Gerring* was that Knowlton of the *Aberdeen* was the only one who had actually measured the *Gerring*'s final position. Despite the testimony of experienced sailors that they could not see how the *Gerring* could have moved from where MacKenzie thought it had been to where Knowlton said it had ended up, Knowlton's measurement carried the day. For Justice McDonald, it was "immaterial to inquire how the vessel reached that position."[45] Unless Knowlton was dishonest or incompetent, of which McDonald found there was no evidence, the *Gerring* was in fact within three miles of Gull Ledge.[46]

But was Gull Ledge a landform from which the three-mile limit could be drawn? The parties spent significant time at trial determining the nature of Gull Ledge. If it was too small to be considered part of the coast of Canada, then the *Gerring* would have been safely outside the limit. However, MacCoy probably recognized that this was a losing argument and abandoned it before making final submissions, as there is no discussion regarding the size of Gull Ledge in Justice McDonald's decision. While Gull Ledge is a small, barren island, it is not some partially submerged wash rock or "a sunken reef several miles seaward," as described in the American press.[47] Ritchie produced witnesses at trial who testified that a half acre of the island was covered in long grass and that it even held the remnants of an old wooden shanty.[48]

Was the *Gerring* fishing when apprehended? The Court found that the *Gerring* had netted the fish in international waters, but was bailing them in Canadian waters. Whether the bailing of the fish, or simply netting the fish, constituted "fishing" was a legal question, not an evidentiary one. However, Mackenzie, who had originally said that the schooners were "all right" to fish, thought that the seizure was wrong. He gave the following testimony at trial while being cross-examined by MacCoy:

> Q. Where were you when [the *Gerring*] was seized?
>
> A. I was a mile or a mile and a half away.
>
> Q. Why did you not bear down and seize her yourself?
>
> A. I did not feel myself justified in doing so, because I know that she had taken the fish outside.[49]

MacCoy argued that the act of fishing was complete once the fish were trapped in the pursed up seine; however, Justice McDonald did not agree:

> I cannot accept [MacCoy's] contention that the "fishing" and the "catching" of the fish was complete when the seine was successfully thrown. Further labour is required to save the fish from the sea, and reduce the property to useful pos-

session, and until that be completed the act of fishing and "catching" fish is not in my opinion completed.[50]

Justice McDonald ordered the *Gerring* and its catch forfeited with costs. This was the only penalty available for a foreign vessel caught fishing in Canadian waters.[51]

The Supreme Court of Canada

After the trial, Morris met with US Secretary of State Richard Olney, who was a prominent Boston lawyer before being appointed by President Cleveland and also reportedly an avid fisher. Olney advised Morris to appeal to Canada's Supreme Court.[52] In October 1896, Olney wrote to the American ambassador in London, Thomas Bayard, for help.[53] Olney relied on the following passage from McDonald's decision, which Olney interpreted as supporting the view that this was "a proper case for the exercise of executive clemency":

> It would, I apprehend, be difficult, if not impossible, to enforce these Fishery laws, to which our people attach supreme importance, if those American subjects who so eagerly seek to compete with our people along our shores in this industry, and who are not, I fear, overscrupulous in the observance of laws of which they have ample notice, should be permitted to plead accident or ignorance to a charge of infraction of such laws. *Such a plea, however effective it may be to the executive authority of the country, cannot avail in this court.*[54]

However, London advised that there could be no political intervention until after the decision of the Supreme Court.[55]

At the Supreme Court, MacCoy focused his submissions on where the *Gerring* was apprehended, arguing that Knowlton must have been wrong that the ship was within the three-mile limit, and, in any event, that the *Gerring* was not, at law, "fishing" when it was apprehended by the *Aberdeen*. He argued that the fish had been "taken" once they had been secured in the seine and that therefore the act of fishing had been completed.[56]

Although the lawyers for Canada addressed the issue of where the *Gerring* was caught, their focus was on the definition of fishing.[57] The crux of their argument was that, whatever property right the *Gerring* might have earned through netting the fish, the act of fishing was not yet complete, because it could still be frustrated by the escape of some or all of the fish:

> It was contended that the act of fishing is complete when in line fishing the fish is hooked, or in net fishing, is surrounded by a net. According to this contention, a fish would be caught as soon as it is hooked, which would, I think, be found to be contrary to experience.
>
> It is submitted that fish caught in a net on the high seas and still in the water are not in the possession in any sense of the fisherman; but assuming that they are to be so regarded, and that property in them is thereby vested in the fisherman his title is qualified, a special interest liable to be divested before they are killed by the escape of the fish.
>
> See Blackstone's Commentaries, 15th edition, page 403.
Kent's Commentaries Text Book Series, page 348.[58]
>
> It is submitted that the acquiring of this special and very precarious right is not, in the ordinary use of language, the completion of the act of fishing, but that something more remains to be done before the fishing is completed and the fish finally taken.[59]

In May 1897, a panel of five Supreme Court judges released their decisions. Although Chief Justice Sir Henry Strong and Justice John Gwynne would have allowed Morris's appeal, they were in the minority. By a 3:2 majority, Justices Robert Sedgewick, George Edwin King, and Désiré Girouard agreed with Justice McDonald that the *Gerring*'s crew were still "fishing" when they were bailing the fish into barrels. Sedgewick defined fishing as follows:

> The act of fishing is a pursuit consisting, not of a single but of many acts according to the nature of the fishing. It is not the isolated act alone either of surrounding the fish by the net, or by taking them out of the water and obtaining manual custody of them. It is a continuous process beginning from the time when the preliminary preparations are being made for the taking of the fish and extending down to the moment when they are finally reduced to actual and certain possession. That, at least, is the idea of what "fishing," according to the ordinary acceptation of the word, means, and that, I think, is the meaning which we must give to the word in the statutes and treaty.[60]

There are currently over sixty cases citing to the Supreme Court case, and Sedgewick's definition of fishing as a "continuous process" is still quoted to this day.[61] For example, the above quotation has been reproduced, exactly, by the Nova Scotia Court of Appeal in 1994,[62] the New Brunswick Court of Queen's Bench in 2003,[63] the Newfoundland Court of Appeal in 2006,[64] the British Columbia Supreme Court in 2008,[65] and the PEI Court of Appeal in 2009.[66] The Federal Court of Canada cited the decision in 2003[67] and the Tax Court of Canada in 2008.[68] The Supreme Court has cited *Gerring v. Canada* three times: in 1914,[69] 1917,[70] and 1931.[71]

Although Sedgewick's judgment is often cited, Justices King's and Girouard's concurring decisions have received little attention.[72] For example, of the over sixty cases that cite *Gerring v. Canada*, only two cite King's or Girouard's decisions.[73] King and Girouard were also the only judges to refer to James Kent's *Commentaries on American Law*, and Girouard is the only judge to cite *Pierson* directly. However, despite *Pierson*'s evident importance to Girouard, none of the cases that reference *Gerring v. Canada* also reference *Pierson*. This is an unfortunate omission, because, for over one hundred and twenty years now, the link between Canadian law and *Pierson*, the foundational American property law case so many American and Canadian lawyers were raised on, has been missed.

Pierson v. Post

Pierson is a very well-known case. It has been referenced in almost eight hundred law journal articles and other secondary sources since it was decided some two hundred years ago[74] and has been a mainstay in American property law casebooks since the early twentieth century.[75] However, despite its incredible uptake into legal academia, *Pierson* has only been cited in reported cases thirty-three times.[76] Until very recently, *Gerring v. Canada* was the only Canadian decision to reference it. There has been no commentary on this Canadian link to *Pierson*.[77]

Pierson was included in Girouard's decision because Ritchie cited it. And Ritchie cited it because, like William Blackstone's *Commentaries on the Laws of England*, James Kent's *Commentaries on American Law* was a staple text both inside and outside the United States. Kent's work was first published in 1827, and in it he discussed *Pierson* (a case he heard as a judge) at length. Kent also mentioned *Buster v. Newkirk*, an 1822 New York case that cited *Pierson*.[78] The cases were in a chapter on qualified property rights and wild animals.[79] Kent's *Commentaries* was hugely influential on American lawyers and was largely responsible for plucking *Pierson* out of obscurity and sending it on its path to rockstar-case status.[80]

W.B.A. Ritchie may have become familiar with *Pierson* during the time he studied at Harvard University in 1881–82, given that 1881 was the year when Oliver Wendell Holmes Jr. published his famous lectures *The Common Law*. In Lecture VI, "Possession," Holmes discussed at length whether the impossibility of escape was the true test for the possession of wild animals. He discussed the facts of *Pierson*, citing it and Kent's discussion of it in the *Commentaries*.[81] As he prepared the Government of Canada's factum for *Gerring*, Ritchie turned to one of the editions of Kent's *Commentaries* published between 1873 and 1896. The most famous 12th edition (1873) was edited by Holmes, and other editions appeared in print as well.[82] The references to *Pierson* in these editions remained essentially the same as they had since the first edition.

As noted above, Ritchie included the reference to Kent's *Commentaries* in his factum, which was relied on by the Supreme Court. Justices Girouard and King both picked up on the reference to Kent's *Commentaries* and included it in their own judgments. Justice King more or less paraphrased Ritchie's factum:

> It may well be that the "Gerring" people had sufficient control and dominion to have acquired a qualified property in the fish; *Young* v. *Hichens* [6 Q.B. 106]; Pollock & Wright on Possession 37; 2 Kent's Com. 348; but an operation at sea of taking several hundred, or one hundred barrels (as here) of loose and live fish from a bag net, is attended with such obvious chances of some of them at least regaining their natural liberty, that the act of fishing cannot be said to be entirely at an end in a useful sense until the fish are reduced into actual possession.[83]

Girouard took his decision to a loftier scholarly level, citing to famous, if not antiquated, French, German, Dutch, and ancient Roman legal scholars to support his view on whether the crew of the *Gerring* were still fishing.[84] Rather than just citing Kent, he mentioned that "Chancellor Kent" cited two American cases "with approbation," and then proceeded to reproduce large sections of Justice Daniel Tompkins's majority judgment from *Pierson* within his own reasons.[85]

As a final quirk, it is not clear that the *Pierson* case or Kent's *Commentaries* actually fully support the conclusions that Chief Justice McDonald and then Justices Girouard, King, and Sedgewick drew from them. In *Pierson*, Tompkins wrote that,

> [E]ncompassing and *securing such animals with nets* and toils, or otherwise intercepting them in such a manner as to deprive them of their natural liberty, and render escape impossible, *may justly be deemed to give possession of them* . . .[86]

Here the fish were in the purse seine net. While a few fish might get out, not many would. In fact, fish would sometimes stay in the seine for days if the crew wished to carefully pack and salt the fish while still at sea.[87]

Would the possibility of a few fish escaping mean that the fish, generally, are not caught?

State v. Shaw, an American case from 1902, concerned fish in Lake Erie caught in a "pound," basically a large net with a one-way entrance.[88] Fish could escape the net, especially when heavy weather caused waves to roll over the top of it. Shaw was charged with larceny for stealing the fish out of the pound, but argued that unowned property cannot be stolen. Citing a number of cases as well as Kent's *Commentaries* as authority, he argued that the owner of the pound had only a qualified possessory right in the fish, as escape from the pound was not impossible. The Supreme Court of Ohio disagreed:

> We think that this doctrine is both unnecessarily technical and erroneous. . . .
>
> They were confined in nets, from which it was not absolutely impossible for them to escape, yet it was practically so impossible; for it seems that under ordinary circumstances few, if any, of the fish escape.[89]

This case, aside from being another example of the pervasiveness of Kent's *Commentaries* at the turn of the century, also shows that the *Gerring* case could have been decided differently. That it was not suggests that the driving force behind the decision was the policy reason behind the Treaty of 1818, that is, the enforcement of Canada's borders and sovereignty, rather than what was *necessarily* so in property law. Clearly this political concern was on McDonald's mind in the Nova Scotia admiralty court, as he reasoned that it would "be difficult, if not impossible" to enforce Canada's fishery laws if American ships could claim that they accidentally drifted over while engaged in lawful fishing under the treaty.[90]

Failed Diplomacy after the Supreme Court's Decision

In June 1897, soon after the Supreme Court's decision, Morris wrote to the US Secretary of State, John Sherman, for assistance with the case.[91] Rather than dealing with Canada directly, Sherman wrote to the British ambassador, Lord Julian Pauncefote. Sherman explained to Pauncefote that the violation of the treaty was unintentional and asked for the *Gerring*'s return.[92]

The Canadian Minister of Marine and Fisheries, Louis Henry Davies, sympathized with the plight of the *Gerring* and recommended that the ship be returned to Morris:

> [The minister] is convinced that notwithstanding the fact that the vessel was found actually taking fish from the seine within the three-mile limit, that these fish had been practically taken, to all intents and purposes, so far as the actual netting is concerned, outside the prohibited zone. . . . "[93]

On 15 July 1897, the British happily reported to Sherman that the "Government of the Dominion" was prepared to return the ship, less a nominal fine ($1) and litigation costs.[94] On 19 July, the Acting Secretary of State, William Day, wrote to Morris with the good news.[95] Day also wrote to the British Chargé d'Affaires, Frederick Adam, warmly thanking the British government for the positive outcome.[96] It seemed that, despite the Supreme Court's decision against Morris, just over two months later the parties had come to an amicable conclusion. However, on 7 September 1897, Morris wrote back to Sherman, explaining that the *Gerring* had been left in terrible condition by the Canadians and was not worth the cost to recover.[97] He had good reason to believe this as, in July that year, his insurance agent from the Mutual Fishing Insurance Company had inspected the *Gerring* and, Morris asserted, reported that it had deteriorated to a near worthless condition. The seine was ruined, the boats had lain in the water and one had "split to pieces," the stores and provisions had spoiled, the sails had been put away wet, and other equipment had rusted. The whole thing was now worthless, Morris said.[98]

On 25 November 1897, Prime Minister Wilfrid Laurier wrote to Davies, asking about the *Gerring*.[99] Laurier had read a letter from Morris (probably the letter he wrote to Sherman) that had alleged that the *Gerring* was in poor condition. Davies assured Laurier that the *Gerring* had been well taken care of and the "innuendos" from Morris were unfounded.[100]

On 1 March 1898, Sherman wrote an apologetic letter to the British ambassador Pauncefote, explaining that, despite the apparent agreement made with Acting Secretary Day, Morris had rejected the Canadian offer. Sherman acknowledged that it was exceptional to reopen a matter after a diplomatic settlement had been reached.[101]

In April 1898, Pauncefote wrote back to Sherman. He appended a 31 March 1898 report from the Privy Council of Canada about the *Gerring*. The report explained that while the Canadian government was originally sympathetic with Morris's plight after the trial decision, they had waited for the Supreme Court's decision in case it allowed the appeal.[102] When the Supreme Court upheld the trial decision, Canada "voluntarily offered to exert Executive clemency, and remitted the penalty of forfeiture, substituting a fine of one dollar," and about $600 in costs.[103] The Privy Council thought this was a generous offer and that the *Gerring* was in good shape; the Minister was "unable to see what further relief Canada could afford."[104] They also made a point of stating that they were not under orders from Britain.

By July 1898, the Canadian government was unsure about how to proceed. The *Gerring* was incurring holding costs and they were not sure whether the offer to return the vessel had been squarely rejected or not.[105] The Americans suggested that, in order to resolve the matter, representatives from both the United States and Canada go to inspect the vessel's condition.[106] However, Minister Davies objected, saying that there should be no survey of the *Gerring*:

> The offer for the return of the vessel was an offer purely as a matter of grace and favor on the part of the Crown, and whether the vessel had deteriorated or not could not in any possible way affect the offer, though it might affect the determination of the owners to receive her.[107]

The Privy Council authorized the sale of the *Gerring* at public auction and the ship was sold by James Duggan & Sons at Halifax on 31 May 1899.[108] Morris had sworn that the vessel and gear together were worth $5,251.50.[109] Three other affidavits, from Gloucester-based ship owners and a purse seine manufacturer, supported his valuation of the *Gerring*.[110] However, the federal government ultimately purchased the *Gerring* and its gear for only $870.

The *Gerring*'s low selling price indicates that it probably was in bad condition. Moreover, it was never again used as a proper sailing ship. The federal government converted the *Gerring* into a lightship (a floating lighthouse), stripping its rigging and anchoring it to the floor of Miramichi Bay, New Brunswick, to guide mariners in fog and darkness.[111] The *Gerring* was the Miramichi lightship until at least 1904.[112] Captain Robert McLean received his salary as the lightkeeper of the "Miramichi lightship"—quite possibly still the *Gerring*—from 1902 until at least 1916.[113]

Although the *Gerring* sold at auction in 1899, the matter was not over. On 6 December 1900, the American ambassador, Joseph Choate, wrote a lengthy letter to Lord Lansdowne, a former Governor General of Canada and the British Secretary of State for Foreign Affairs. Choate wrote a detailed history of the matter and requested "payment of a just and reasonable indemnity."[114] Included in his letter were memoranda from Senator George Hoar and Congressman William H. Moody, both of Massachusetts. Moody, who chaired the Appropriations Committee in the House of Representatives, stated that Morris was seeking $11,549.11 from the Canadian government.[115]

Moody's letter, aside from disagreeing with the judge's concept of fishing, addressed the issue of the three-mile boundary. The Treaty of 1818 demarcated a boundary "within three marine miles of any of the coasts, bays, creeks, or harbours" of what had become Canada.[116] According to the American ambassador, senator, and representative, Gull Ledge was such a minor and "isolated piece of rock" that it should not be considered part of Nova Scotia's coast from which to extend the three-mile boundary.

The following spring, in May 1901, Minister Davies outlined the ministry's position to the Canadian cabinet.[117] Davies disagreed with the Americans that the three-mile boundary could not be drawn from Gull Ledge.[118] Davies quoted Thomas Bayard himself—the American ambassador who began the dialogue with London—who, while Secretary of State, wrote,

> [T]he sovereignty of the shore does not, so far as territorial authority is concerned, extend beyond three miles from low water mark, and that the seaward boundary of this zone of territorial waters follows the coast of the mainland, extending where there are islands, so as to place around such islands the same belt.[119]

Davies also referenced a British admiralty case from 1805, the *Anna*, in which an American ship was seized by a British privateer within a mile and a half of islands formed from "temporary deposits of logs and drift" off the mouth of the Mississippi River. In that case, the High Court of Admiralty in London proclaimed that islands must form a part of the territory, or else they could be "'embanked and fortified'" by foreign powers, creating hostile bases just offshore.[120] Also, Morris had not brought a further appeal to the Privy Council in England, apparently on the advice of then-Secretary of State Olney. Davies thought it "inconceivable" that Olney would have advised *against* bringing the appeal so long as there was any doubt about the legal basis for the decision because, in the past, the US had prohibited any diplomatic efforts before judicial options were exhausted.[121] Finally, Davies addressed the fact that America and Canada had each released ships to each other in the past when they had accidentally drifted into foreign waters in similar circumstances. In each case the ships were returned without compensation, the same offer that Morris rejected.[122] Davies advised Lansdowne that, in short, the request for compensation could not be entertained. Lansdowne, in turn, paraphrased Davies's report, editing out some of the less diplomatic turns of phrase, in a letter to the American ambassador Joseph Choate on 12 August 1901.[123] Congressman William Moody relayed the bad news to Morris.[124]

However, although three years passed, the matter of the *Gerring* was not over. On 16 June 1904, the American Secretary of State, John Hay, proposed that the British and American governments come to "'an arrangement for the adjustment of all claims of citizens of the United States against the British Government and of all claims of British subjects against the Government of the United States by a mixed claims Commission.'"[125]

On 5 January 1906, the British foreign secretary, Sir Edward Grey, instructed the British ambassador to the United States, Sir Mortimer Durand, that an independent arbitration at The Hague would be preferable, and that Britain and the United States should exchange a preliminary list of claims that they would like included in the arbitration.[126] However, American Secretary of State Elihu Root, who replaced Hay, doubted that Congress would agree to the expense associated with arbitration at the Hague, which had the potential to eclipse the amount of the claims at issue; Root would have favoured a mixed-claims commission.[127] Britain preferred to discuss costs after "the value of the claims and the form of procedure" had been agreed to.[128]

On 20 February 1906, Durand spoke with Root.[129] Already, the *Gerring* was getting in the way. Root told Durand that "certain Senators" still thought "the Gerring case involved 'gross injustice'" and asked Durand whether they "could not get the case 'out of the way'."[130] At Britain's request, Canada reluctantly agreed that the *Gerring* claim "would not be excluded from the scope of the proposed arbitration."[131]

By January 1907, further pressure was mounting on Canada. Britain's Chargé d'Affaires in Washington, Esme Howard (standing in for the ambassador), sent a confidential dispatch to Canada's Governor General, Albert Grey.[132] Howard advised that there were several British claims that the Americans recognized as payable but for which Congress had not ratified payment. Senator Henry Cabot Lodge of Massachusetts was preventing any payments until the *Gerring* case was settled:

> [T]here are only three or four American claims outstanding against His Majesty's Government, and of these the claim of the "Frederick Gerring Junior" is the most important.... Mr. Lodge, from his place in the Senate, has said that they are just, and ought to be paid, but that they will not be paid until the British Government settle the American claims.[133]

In February 1907, Prime Minister Laurier demanded a full report on the *Gerring* and an explanation for why the claim could not be paid.[134]

On 6 July 6 1911, the Americans and British agreed to a schedule of claims that included the *Gerring*, and in August they agreed to establish an arbitral tribunal to hear these claims.[135] In September 1911, the *Washington Post* reported,

> No redress was obtainable for the Captain. So Senator Lodge planted himself on the floor of the Senate against allowing the payment of any claims of British subjects against the United States. This held up the pecuniary claims of both countries. The agreement to include the Frederick Gerring claim among those to be adjudicated in the forthcoming arbitration loosened the key-log and claimants on both sides now have a chance, of adjudication at least, although even after that it may take years to get the money from Congress for such damages as may be awarded the Americans.[136]

The Americans and the British prepared and submitted the detailed memorials that contain much of the information supplied in this chapter. The parties argued their case in Washington in the spring of 1914.[137] Instead of imposing an arbitrated resolution, the president of the tribunal, Henri Fromageot, suggested that Canada settle the matter by paying out the value of the ship, minus the costs of prosecution and a nominal fine—nominally identical to their original offer to return the ship.[138] On 1 May 1914, it appeared that Canada had agreed to pay $9,000, more than ten times what the *Gerring* sold for at public auction, and the settlement was put on the record of the tribunal.[139]

Unfortunately, for the second time, the reported settlement was premature, although this time it was the Canadians who were backing out. What Canada had meant to agree to was for the arbitrator to make a "recommendation" that they pay approximately $7,000, with the understanding that the Canadian government would then implement that recommendation.[140] However, the idea that the issue had been "settled" for payment of $9,000 was unacceptable to Canada, and it refused to ratify the settlement. World War I would break out in a matter of months and the problem was left unresolved.

After the war, the parties were arranging to have their respective awards paid, and Britain contacted Canada to see if it was prepared to pay the awards made against it. On 16 October 1924, Canada advised that it concurred that "provisions should be made ... for immediate payment of the awards," but that it was "unable to regard the F. Gerring Jr. claim as the subject of any award or liability."[141] Canada remained steadfast that it had not settled the case for $9,000, and it appears the claim was never paid.[142]

The Legacy of the *Frederick Gerring, Jr.*

There is a divergence between what a judge orders and what actually happens after a trial.[143] The *Frederick Gerring, Jr.* case is a good example of how different those outcomes can be. The decision itself nowhere reveals (and could not have revealed) that the Supreme Court's judgment was only a prelude to over two decades of diplomatic efforts. Had the case been included in Canadian law school property law casebooks in the standard way, this long and complicated after-life of the case would very likely have gone untold.

After the Supreme Court's decision, the Canadian government was quick to offer to return the *Gerring*, although they had just spent a year and great expense litigating over the validity of the seizure. Perhaps the government was concerned with establishing a principle? The Minister of Marine and Fisheries, Davies, at least at first, questioned the legal principle regarding fishing, arguing that for "all intents and purposes" the act of fishing had been complete before the *Gerring* was apprehended by the *Aberdeen*.[144] Given the initial offer to return the ship, albeit spurned, and given that Canada was later prepared to pay $7,000, if recommended by the arbitrator, what do such concessions mean for *Gerring v. Canada* as a piece of legal doctrine and as a precedent? Should it matter that the seemingly correct result at law is treated as impractical, harsh, and unworkable by nearly all parties involved? *Gerring v. Canada* is the leading case on the definition of fishing under the *Fisheries Act*, although the diplomacy, arbitration, settlement, and connections to *Pierson v. Post* and Kent's *Commentaries* are all but forgotten. With how much reverence ought we to treat the decision when the federal government was ultimately prepared to fully compensate Morris for seizing his ship? If the majority of the

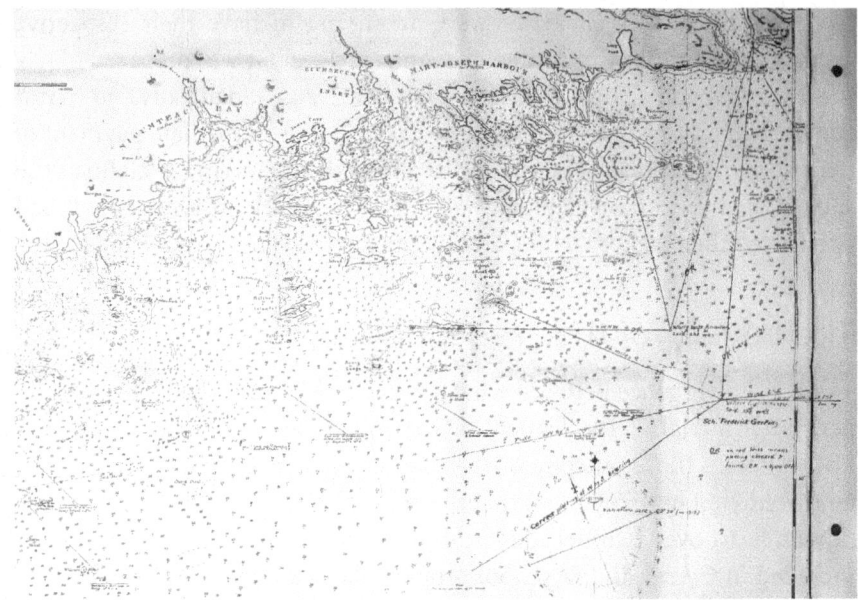

FIGURE 5.1 Detail of the chart of Nova Scotia's south east coast included in the *US Memorial* showing the location and bearing of the *Frederick Gerring, Jr.*

Supreme Court of Canada judges were politically motivated in deciding to adopt the capture rule, how confident can we be that the correct definition of fishing was adopted?

Regardless of the case's extrajudicial history, as a matter of law, the legal principle remains suspect: the Supreme Court was split on the matter, and the majority judges' reasons included references to Kent's *Commentaries* and *Pierson*. Both of these authorities specifically contemplate possession by way of catching wild animals in nets and lean towards a standard of impossible escape.[145] However, was it truly significant that a few fish, out of thousands, might escape?

Whether the *Gerring* case continues as a throw-away reference in fishing cases or becomes part of a broader discussion about how we treat possession cases in Canada is up to the legal community. As a first step, *Gerring v. Canada* should be recognized not simply as a fishing case but as the case that incorporated *Pierson*-style first possession principles into Canadian law. The next step, given what we know about the history of the case, would be to consider whether we should rethink our understanding of those principles. Generally, I hope that this chapter shows how important and interesting it can be to look beyond the reported decision of a case.

Lastly, I hope the reader feels some sympathy for Captain Morris and his ship. Whatever the merits of the case, it seems wrong for a once proud wooden schooner to spend its final years with its sails cut, chained to the bottom of a harbour. The legacy of the *Frederick Gerring, Jr.* should be more than that.

NOTES

* This essay began as a paper for "Legal Archaeology: Study of Cases in Context," a course taught by Angela Fernandez at the University of Toronto Faculty of Law in 2015. She and I are currently working with Bradley Miller of the University of British Columbia Department of History on a longer book project, to be published with UBC Press in the Landmark Cases in Canadian Law series. The book is tentatively entitled *The Frederick Gerring, Canada's Twenty-First Century* Pierson v Post.

1 *Canada v Frederick Gerring, Jr. (The)* (1896), 5 Ex CR 164 ["*Canada v Gerring*"].

2 *Convention Respecting Fisheries, Boundary, and Restoration of Slaves*, United States and United Kingdom, 20 October 1818, TS 112, 8 Stat 248 (entered into force on 20 October 1818) ["Treaty of 1818"]; *An Act to Enable His Majesty to Make Regulations with Respect to the Taking and Curing Fish on Certain Parts of the Coasts of Newfoundland, Labrador, and His Majesty's Other Possessions in North America, According to a Convention Made between His Majesty and the United States of America*, 59 Geo. III (1819), c 38 (UK); *An Act Respecting Fishing by Foreign Vessels*, RSC 1886, c 94, s 3, stipulating that any vessel "found fishing or preparing to fish" within three miles of the coast "shall be forfeited." Miles were "marine miles" (nautical miles), equal to 1.852 km.

3 Ships are treated like legal "persons" in maritime law.

4 *Frederick Gerring Jr. (The) v Canada* (1897), 27 SCR 271 ["*Gerring v Canada*"].

5 Public Archives Canada / Governor General's Office, RG 7, G21, vol. 103, File/Dossier 192G, pt. 5a. (Copy of Telegram from the Governor General [Julian Byng] to the Secretary of State for the Colonies [James Thomas], 15 October 1924).

6 *Pierson v Post*, 3 Cai R 175 (NY SC 1805) ["*Pierson*"].

7 See Angela Fernandez, *Pierson v Post, the Hunt for the Fox: Law and Professionalization in American Legal Culture* (New York: Cambridge University Press, 2018).

8 Two recent cases mention *Pierson*, the first really as an aside: *R v Hamm*, 2018 NSPC 17 at para 6 and *Association for the Protection of Fur-Bearing Animals v British Columbia (Minister of Environment and Climate Change Strategy)*, 2017 BCSC 2296 at para 35.

9 Details are in the primary source bibliography.

10   Gordon Thomas, *Fast and Able, Life Stories of Great Gloucester Fishing Vessels*, 50th anniversary ed. (Beverly, MA: Commonwealth Editions, 2002), 301.

11   United States. *American and British Claims Arbitration: Frederick Gerring, Jr. Memorial of the United States in Support of the Claim* (Washington, G.P.O., 1913), 11 ["*US Memorial*"].

12   Swearing an affidavit about his damages, Morris set the value of the ship and its seine, dories, and other gear at more than twice this amount: *US Memorial*, 102, 197.

13   *US Memorial*, 11, 102.

14   *US Memorial*, 12.

15   Morris described having to go back to fishing to earn a living: *US Memorial*, 109.

16   "Claims Against Government: Some Famous Cases in Which Efforts Were Made to Get Damages from Uncle Sam," *Washington Post*, 10 September 1911, MS3 ["Some Famous Cases"].

17   In the order in which they testified, they were Daniel Doren (master—Gloucester, Massachusetts); James Gracie (crew—Nova Scotia); Harvey L. Bailey (crew—Le Havre, France); Henry Burhester/Burmeister (crew—American); John Gough/Goff (crew—St. John's, Newfoundland); Leander Gaudet (crew—Weymouth, Nova Scotia); John R. Gammett (crew—Gloucester, Massachusetts); Joseph Carpenter (crew—Gloucester, Massachusetts); and Alfred Deane (cook—Connecticut). See *US Memorial*, 13, 31-37.

18   *US Memorial*, 20.

19   *US Memorial*, 20.

20   The *Highland Light* was seized on 1 September 1886, off of East Point, PEI. The ship was tried in the vice-admiralty court at Charlottetown, but the master, J.H. Ryder, admitted the offence and offered no defence, thus surrendering the ship to the federal government. The ship was sold at auction in Georgetown, PEI, on December 14 when the "Dominion Govt" picked it up for $5,800 and put it to use: Henry James Morgan ed., *The Dominion Annual Register and Review for the Twentieth Year of the Canadian Union, 1886* (Montreal: Eusèbe Senécal & fils, Printers, 1887) at 125, 322-23; Brian Payne, *Fishing a Borderless Sea: Environmental Territorialism in the North Atlantic, 1818–1910* (East Lansing: Michigan State University Press, 2010), 42. Note that Morris ended up claiming a similar amount, $5,251, for the *Gerring* and its gear.

21   *US Memorial*, 71.

22   *US Memorial*, 87.

23   *US Memorial*.

24   *US Memorial*, 46.

25   *US Memorial*, 24.

26   *US Memorial*, supra note 6 at 3.

27   *The Admiralty Act, 1891*, SC 1891, c 29, s 3 ["*Admiralty Act*"].

28　Arthur Stone, "The Admiralty Court in Colonial Nova Scotia," *Dalhousie Law Journal* 17, no. 2 (1994): 366.

29　Stone, "The Admiralty Court in Colonial Nova Scotia," 373.

30　Stone, "The Admiralty Court in Colonial Nova Scotia," 418–19.

31　Stone, "The Admiralty Court in Colonial Nova Scotia," 424; *An Act to Establish a Supreme Court, and a Court of Exchequer, for the Dominion of Canada*, SC 1875, c 11.

32　*Admiralty Act*.

33　Stone, "Admiralty Court in Colonial Nova Scotia," 427.

34　William MacCoy to Mr. Cassels, 7 November 1896. In "Schooner Frederick Gerring Jr. v The Queen (1896)," file 1597, vol. 144, R927, RG125-A, Library and Archives Canada ("LAC").

35　*US Memorial*, 101 and 198.

36　Philip Girard, "Ritchie, William Bruce Almon," in *Dictionary of Canadian Biography*, vol. 14, University of Toronto/Université Laval, 2003–, http://www.biographi.ca/en/bio/ritchie_william_bruce_almon_14E.html.

37　Girard, "Ritchie."

38　Girard, "Ritchie."

39　*US Memorial*, 19. Ritchie also has the dubious distinction of having represented Canada in a notorious immigration decision, the case of the *Komagata Maru*, or *Canada v Singh* (1914), 6 WWR 1347, 20 BCR 243 (CA). The *Komagata Maru* was a ship commissioned by immigrants from British India, bound for Canada. Canada's "continuous voyage" law (*The Immigration Act*, SC 1910, c 27, s 38) required immigrants to arrive in Canada via a non-stop voyage. The voyage of the *Komagata Maru* became the test case to challenge this piece of legislation. On 23 May 1914, 376 weary and mostly Sikh immigrants arrived in Vancouver, but the federal government denied them admission. Although the immigrants challenged the decision, Ritchie won the case for Canada and the vast majority of immigrants, that is, 352, were turned away. I invite the reader to visit http://komagatamarujourney.ca for more information. The *Komagata Maru* was escorted out of Vancouver Harbour on 23 July 1914. See also Janet Mary Nicol, "'Not to Be Bought, Nor for Sale': The Trials of Joseph Edward Bird," *Labour / Le Travail* 78 (fall 2016): 219–36, regarding one of the lawyers for the *Komagatu Maru*.

40　*US Memorial*.

41　*US Memorial*, 102.

42　*US Memorial*, 67.

43　*US Memorial*, 46.

44　*US Memorial*, 81, 87, 91, 93.

45　*Canada v Gerring*, 172.

46　*Canada v Gerring*, 172–73.

47　"Some Famous Cases."

48   *US Memorial*, 76, 77. The reader can see Gull Ledge on Google Maps at 44°54'37.8"N 62°01'54.4"W.

49   *US Memorial*, 71.

50   *Canada v Gerring*, 173.

51   *Canada v Gerring*, 173.

52   *US Memorial*, 108; "Richard Olney Dies; Veteran Statesman," *New York Times*, 10 April 1917, 13.

53   *US Memorial*, 104, 14 October 1896.

54   *Canada v Gerring*, 173 (emphasis added), quoted in Richard Olney to Thomas F. Bayard, 14 October 1896. In *US Memorial*, 104–5.

55   Lord Salisbury to Thomas Bayard, 20 February 1897. In *US Memorial*, 107–8.

56   Great Britain, *Arbitration of Outstanding Pecuniary Claims between Great Britain and the United States of America: The Frederick Gerring, Jr.* (Ottawa: Government Printing Bureau, 1913), 14–24 ["*British Memorial*"].

57   The Supreme Court decision identifies "Newcombe Q.C." as representing Canada and W.B.A. Ritchie as the solicitor. Edmund Leslie Newcombe was deputy minister of justice and deputy attorney general of Canada and was therefore nominally responsible for all crown lawsuits. He also appeared personally at most Supreme Court hearings, including, it would seem, *Gerring v Canada*. He was appointed to the Supreme Court in 1924: Girard, "Newcombe, Edmund Leslie."

58   Ritchie was likely referring to James Kent, *Commentaries on American Law*, new and revised edition, ed. William M. Lacy, vol. 2 (Philadelphia: Blackstone Publishing Co., 1889), *348–50; and William Blackstone, *Commentaries on the Laws of England*, 15th ed., ed. Edward Christian (London: A. Strahan, 1809), 2:*403, wherein Blackstone writes that everyone has a right to "take" wild animals unless he is otherwise restrained by municipal law, and "they become while living his qualified property, or, if dead, are absolutely his own: so that to steal them, or otherwise invade this property, is, according to the respective values sometimes a criminal offence, sometimes only a civil injury." See in this volume Angela Fernandez, "The Text Book Edition of James Kent's *Commentaries* Used in *Canada v Gerring*." Many editions of Blackstone's and Kent's respective *Commentaries* have been published, with lengthy notes added by later editors. The asterisks refer to Blackstone's or Kent's original pagination. Later editions will of course have their own pagination, but they also note the original page numbers, so if you open a later edition, you will find that you are on Blackstone's or Kent's page *101, when in fact you are on perhaps page 114 of the edition you hold in your hands. This practice allows for the easy tracking of text added by later commentators.

59   *British Memorial*, 31.

60   *Gerring v Canada*, 280–81.

61   See e.g., *R v Steer*, 2013 BCPC 163, para 56.

62   *R v Morash* (1994), 129 NSR (2d) 34, 37 (NSCA).

63   *R v Kelly*, 2003 NBQB 148 at paras 17, 20.

64   *Canada v White*, 2006 NLCA 71 at para 11.

65   *R v Aleck*, 2008 BCSC 1096 at para 107.

66   *R v Gavin*, 2009 PECA 23 at para 19.

67   *Kwicksutaineuk/Ah-kwa-mish Tribes v Canada (Minister of Fisheries and Oceans)*, 2003 FCT 30 at para 23 (to argue that fishing is complete once possession of the fish is obtained).

68   *Chon v Canada (Minister of National Revenue)*, 2008 TCC 622 at para 9 (to argue that oyster farming is not fishing because the oysters have no possibility of escape).

69   *Carlson v Canada*, [1914] 49 SCR 180, 192.

70   *John J. Fallon (The) v Canada*, [1917] 55 SCR 348, 351.

71   *R v Krakowec* (1931), [1932] SCR 134, 142.

72   Girouard was an academic and well-read lawyer. He studied law at McGill, graduating in 1860, the same year that he published a notable legal text (Désiré Girouard, *Essai sur les lettres de change et les billets promissoires* [Montreal: J. Lovell, 1860]). Although politically conservative, he declined Conservative cabinet positions in 1891 and 1895, and in 1895 he accepted appointment to the Supreme Court of Canada where he stayed for ten years: Michael Lawrence Smith, "Girouard, Désiré," in *Dictionary of Canadian Biography*, vol. 14, University of Toronto/Université Laval, 2003–, accessed October 2, 2019, http://www.biographi.ca/en/bio/girouard_desire_14E.html.

73   *R v Johnson and Wilson* (1987), 78 NBR (2d) 411, 427, 198 APR 411 (NBPC) & *R v Weir* (1993), 110 Nfld & PEIR 121, 128–29, 346 APR 121 (NLSCTD).

74   See Fernandez, *Pierson v Post, the Hunt for the Fox*, 1 (using the online database HeinOnline).

75   For a discussion that traces the way *Pierson* was included in American property law casebooks starting in 1915, see Fernandez, *Pierson v Post, the Hunt for the Fox*, 274–86. On Canada, see e.g. *R v Hamm*, 2018 NSPC 17 at para. 6, where Justice Scovil observes, "The first lesson taught in our class in Property Law at then Dalhousie Law School in the late 1970s was the case of *Pierson v Post* from Massachusetts in 1802." Scovil mistook New York for Massachusetts, and the appellate report is dated 1805, not 1802. Ironically, though, the dispute actually did happen in December 1802, a fact that was unknown until Angela Fernandez discovered the judgment roll in the *Pierson* case and publicized it in 2009. See Fernandez, "The Lost Record of *Pierson v Post*, the Famous Fox Case," *Law and History Review* 27, no. 1 (2009): 149–78. A transcript of the roll is reproduced in Fernandez, *Pierson v Post, the Hunt for the Fox*, Appendix B, 336–57.

76   See Fernandez, *Pierson v Post, the Hunt for the Fox*, Appendix A, 331–35, which provides names, citations, a brief statement of what the case was about, and a division of the citations into animal and non-animal cases.

77   Apart from Fernandez, *Pierson v Post, the Hunt for the Fox*, the book project upon which I was working when I discovered that *Gerring v Canada* considered *Pierson* extensively (which led to the book's discussion of the connection between the cases), I have located two other texts that cite both cases but fail to mention the connection between them: William Mack, *Cyclopedia of Law and Procedure*, vol. 19 (New York:

American Law Book Company, 1905), 988 (*Pierson*), and 1006, 1026 (*Gerring*), and Bruce Ziff, "The Law of Capture, Newfoundland-Style," *University of Toronto Law Journal* 63, no. 1 (2013): 54 (*Pierson*) and note 11 (*Gerring*).

78   *Buster v Newkirk*, 20 Johns Rep 75 (1822).

79   James Kent, *Commentaries on American Law*, vol. 2 (New York: O. Halsted, 1827), 281–83, citing *Pierson* at 282 and *Buster v Newkirk* at 283.

80   See Fernandez, *Pierson v Post, the Hunt for the Fox*, 14–23, 26–31, 252–57.

81   Oliver Wendell Holmes Jr., *The Common Law* (Boston: Little, Brown and Company, 1871), 216–18.

82   See Fernandez, *Pierson v Post, the Hunt for the Fox*, 257–63 (discussing Holmes' work on possession and the connections to *Pierson* and his edition of Kent's *Commentaries*).

83   *Gerring v Canada*, 298.

84   Girouard cites Pufendorf, Trebatius (as cited by Justinian), Domat, Savigny, Heineccius, and Grotius, among others.

85   *Gerring v Canada*, 305–7.

86   *Pierson*, 178 (emphasis added).

87   *US Memorial*, 184.

88   *State v Shaw*, 67 Ohio St 157 (1902).

89   *State v Shaw*, 164–65.

90   See above. Interestingly, Ritchie argued in his factum that even if the *Gerring* were not "fishing," Canada was still permitted to seize the ship for being within its waters without lawful purpose: *British Memorial*, 33, 34.

91   *US Memorial*, 143.

92   *US Memorial*, 149.

93   L.H. Davies to Governor General in Council, 21 June 1897. In Privy Council Office, "Seizure of fishing vessel FREDERICK GERRING JR., that same be released and returned to owners on payt [payment] of costs and copy of report be forwarded to Col Secy [Colonial Secretary]—Min M and F [Minister of Marine and Fisheries] 1897/06/21 recs," Privy Council Minutes, Jun. 28–30, 1897, Series A-1-a, RG2, LAC ["Privy Council Minutes"].

94   *US Memorial*, 152.

95   *US Memorial*.

96   *US Memorial*, 153.

97   *US Memorial*, 155.

98   *US Memorial*, 145–46.

99   Davies to Laurier, 6 December 1897. In Sir Wilfrid Laurier fonds. Political papers. General correspondence (20 December 1897), C-752, vol. 59, MG26-G, LAC ["Davies Letter"].

100 Davies Letter.

101 *US Memorial*, 159–60.

102 *US Memorial*, 163.

103 *US Memorial*, originally $1,200, less $600 for the sale of the fish.

104 *US Memorial*, 165.

105 *US Memorial*, 165–66.

106 *US Memorial*, 167–68.

107 *US Memorial*, 171.

108 *US Memorial*, 210.

109 *US Memorial*, 197.

110 *US Memorial*, 200–3.

111 *US Memorial*, 209; W. Bell Dawson, "Annual Report of the Chief Engineer of the Department of Marine and Fisheries," in *Thirty-Third Annual Report of the Department of Marine and Fisheries 1900: Marine*, 22–81 (*Sessional Papers of the Dominion of Canada* [*CSP*] 1901, vol. 9, no. 21), 55.

112 William P. Anderson, "Annual Report of the Chief Engineer of the Department of Marine and Fisheries," in *Thirty-Sixth Annual Report of the Department of Marine and Fisheries 1900: Marine*, 35–77 (*CSP* 1904, vol. 8, no. 21), 65.

113 J.G. MacPhail, "Report of the Commissioner of Lights," Appendix 2 to "Report of the Deputy Minister of Marine and Fisheries," in *Forty-Eighth Annual Report of the Department of Marine and Fisheries for the Fiscal Year 1914–15: Marine*, 64–94 (*CSP* 1901, vol. 17, no. 21), 67. After 1916, the *Sessional Papers* stopped recording the names and salaries of the lightkeepers, and merely recorded the number of lightships per province. At least one lightship was operating in New Brunswick until 1925, when the *Sessional Papers* ceased publication. Beyond that, I cannot say what became of the *Frederick Gerring, Jr.*

114 *US Memorial*, 179.

115 *US Memorial*, 187, 197–99.

116 Treaty of 1818, article I.

117 L.H. Davies to Governor General in Council, 25 May 1901. In "Claim of United States Government for compensation for seizure of schooner FREDERICK GERRING JR.—For breach of the fishery laws—From Marine Department," files 1901-320 and 1901-69, vol. 2306, RG13-A-2, LAC.

118 Davies to Governor General in Council, 25 May 1901, 8.

119 *US Memorial*, 192.

120 Christopher Robinson, *Reports of Cases Argued and Determined in the High Court of Admiralty; Commencing with the Judgments of the Right Hon. Sir William Scott, Michaelmas Term 1798*, vol. 5, 373–385d (London: A. Strahan, 1806), 376, 385d. See also *The "Anna"* (1805), 165 ER 809.

121 Davies to Governor General in Council, 25 May 1901, 10, 11.

122 Davies, to Governor General in Council, 25 May 1901, 12.

123 *US Memorial*, 188.

124 *US Memorial*, 195.

125 Quoted by F.H. Villiers, in Villiers (for Sir Edward Grey) to Sir Mortimer Durand, 5 January 1906. In Privy Council Office, Proposal for settlement of outstanding claims U.S. [United States] and Canada by arbitration—Tribunal at The Hague—following claims will be considered: COQUITLAM, KATE, and FAVOURITE and possibly, FREDERICK GERRING JR—Col Sec [Colonial Secretary], Order-in-Council 1906–0923M, Series A-1-a, RG2, LAC ["Settlement Proposal Letters"].

126 Villiers to Durand, 5 January 1906.

127 Durand to Grey, 22 January 1906. In Settlement Proposal Letters.

128 Grey to Durand, 31 January 1906. In Settlement Proposal Letters.

129 Durand to Grey, 21 February 1906. In Settlement Proposal Letters.

130 Durand to Grey, 21 February 1906.

131 Extract from a Report to Council, 29 March 1906. In The British Ambassador at Washington—Respecting the claims of the Canadian Electric Light Company and Radcliffe and Eastry against the United States Government—Also seizure of the United States fishing vessel FREDERICK GERRING JR., 1907, Secretary of State of Canada general correspondence, file 967, vol. 128, RG6-A-1, R174-26-2-E, LAC. ["1907 Files"].

132 Howard to Grey, 16 February 1907. In 1907 Files.

133 Howard to Grey, 16 February 1907.

134 J. Pope to Mr. Venning, 21 February 1907. In 1907 Files.

135 37 Stat. 1627–30 (1911–13); Chandler P. Anderson, "American and British Claims Arbitration Tribunal," *American Journal of International Law* 15, no. 2 (April 1921): 266–68.

136 "Some Famous Cases."

137 37 Stat. 1627–30 (1911–13); Anderson, "American and British Claims Arbitration Tribunal."

138 "Tribunal Has Awarded $9,000 To Captain Morris," *Gloucester Daily Times*, 2 May 1914.

139 "Award in the Matter of the Frederick Gerring, Jr," *American Journal of International Law* 8, no. 3 (1914): 655.

140 C.J.B. Hurst to Edward Grey, 4 June 1914. In Foreign Office, Settlement of Questions between the United States, Canada and Newfoundland. Further Correspondence Part XV, 1914–15, Confidential Print: North America, FO 414/243, National Archives, UK.

141 Governor General Julian Byng to Secretary of State for the Colonies James Henry Thomas, 16 October 1924. Office of the Governor General of Canada fonds, file 192G, pt. 5a, vol. 103, G21, RG 7, LAC.

142 I have not found any more recent correspondence than this 1924 letter.

143 Richard Danzig describes this as a version of "the capability problem": Richard Danzig, *The Capability Problem in Contract Law: Further Readings on Well-Known Cases* (Mineola, NY: Foundation Press, 1978), 2–3.

144 L.H. Davies to Governor in Council, 21 June 1897. In Privy Council Minutes.

145 See discussion above. Both Kent and the majority in *Pierson* understood the issue in terms of the insufficiency of mere pursuit. This fine parsing was lost on subsequent commentators, including Holmes, who put aside his doubts about impossible escape owing to Kent's equivocation on the issue and failure to make it clear in *Buster v Newkirk*. On this issue, see Fernandez, *Pierson v Post, the Hunt for the Fox*, 17–21, 258–64.

The Text Book Edition of James Kent's *Commentaries* Used in *Canada v. Gerring*

Angela Fernandez[*]

Nova Scotia judge Alexander Stewart wrote to American judge and jurist James Kent in 1847, the year Kent died: "[y]our Commentaries are the textbook we put into our students' hands and next to Blackstone . . . are our most esteemed works."[1] As if to prove the point was still true nearly fifty years later, the Nova Scotian lawyer who argued the *Gerring* case for the government, W.B.A. Ritchie, cited both famous works in his factum when arguing that the fish caught by the *Gerring* were "qualified property" and hence her captain and crew were indeed fishing inside the three-mile limit when the ship was apprehended by the Canadian authorities. In his factum, submitted in 1896 to the Supreme Court of Canada defending the government's action, Ritchie wrote:

> It is submitted that fish caught in a net on the high seas and still in the water are not in the possession in any sense of the fisherman; but assuming that they are to be so regarded, and that property in them is thereby vested in the fisherman his title is qualified, a special interest liable to be divested before they are killed by the escape of the fish.
>
> See Blackstone's Commentaries, 15th edition, page 403.
> Kent's Commentaries Text Book Series, page 348.[2]

Both sets of Commentaries used a version of the "institutes" form derived from the Roman legal thinker Gaius, who divided everything into three fundamental social categories: persons (subjects), things (objects), and actions (the interrelation between subjects and objects), creating a system of ordering reality and of perceiving and constructing the world probably rivalled only by Aristotle's.[3] In doing so, "Gaius formulated (if he did not create) one of the most distinctive enduring systems of thought in Western history," imitated in influential legal works by the Roman Emperor Justinian and much later the German jurist and historian Friedrich Carl von Savigny.[4] Civil law countries such as France and Spain, where formal state law was used in order to solidify the nation state in the seventeenth and eighteenth centuries, employed versions of the tripartite Gaian arrangement, e.g., in the order and structure of the civil code and in choosing how to organize the study of national law in their universities and the attendant text book commentary.[5]

In the 1760s, William Blackstone created a very influential four-volume version for English common law, *Commentaries on the Laws of England*, in an environment in which Roman and civil law had dominated university-taught legal education (as opposed to the Inns of Court, where teaching the common law prevailed).[6] Blackstone was widely used in the United States (and Canada) even after James Kent produced a home-grown American version in the 1820s, *Commentaries on American Law*, which itself became an influential contributor to variations on the Institute theme.[7] Both were common law works patterned on the Gaian dialectical method and arrangement, aimed at bringing clarity, order, and elegance to the chaos of the common law by presenting its elemental (i.e., foundational) aspects in a format that—unlike the formerly used institute-work for the common law, *Coke Upon Littleton*—was easy to read.[8]

Blackstone's discussion of qualified property occurs in the second (1766) volume on property in a section on acquiring "title to things personal by occupancy," and specifically how occupancy is established in wild animals (*ferae naturae*).[9] He wrote that unless restrained by some municipal law, all mankind has the right to pursue and take wild animals and "when a man has so seized them, they become while living his *qualified* property, or, if dead, are absolutely his own."[10] Kent, who was providing an American version of Blackstone's text, wrote, in a section entitled

"Property in chattels personal is either absolute or qualified," that like air, light, and water, which "are the subjects of qualified property by occupancy," animals *ferae naturae* "are also the subject of a qualified property."[11] The fish in the *Gerring* were still alive in the purse seine net and so were not absolute property, which according to Blackstone required that they be dead. The fish had not yet been reduced to possession. They were still qualified property that could escape because they were still alive, or so the argument went according to these two august and regularly relied upon authorities.

Kent's text was originally published in 1827. The nineteenth century saw multiple editions of the text, the first five in Kent's lifetime and then, after he died in 1847, his son William published the following three editions.[12] The publisher changed to Little, Brown in the ninth edition in 1858.[13] By the last quarter of the nineteenth century, the most famous edition was undoubtedly the twelfth, completed by Oliver Wendell Holmes Jr., then a practising lawyer and legal scholar.[14] Yet Ritchie used something called the "Text Book Series" edition in his *Gerring* factum.[15] What was this edition and why was a lawyer as eminent as Ritchie using it, rather than the fancier Holmes edition? This short essay seeks to answer these questions.

According to Philip Girard, Ritchie was a "member of . . . Nova Scotia's best-known legal dynasty."[16] His uncle, Sir William Johnstone Ritchie, was one of the first six Supreme Court of Canada judges appointed in 1875 and chief justice from 1879–1892;[17] W.B.A.'s son, Roland Almon Ritchie, Oxford educated, would go on to sit on the Supreme Court of Canada from 1959–1984. W.B.A. attended Harvard Law School in 1881–82 (following in the footsteps of an older brother who received a Harvard LL.B. in 1877 and four cousins who also studied there).[18] W.B.A. Ritchie returned to Nova Scotia where he was called to the bar in June 1882.[19] In 1889, future Canadian Prime Minister Robert Borden asked him to join his law firm. As Girard puts it, W.B.A. Ritchie was "an exemplar of the Maritime lawyers who in the 1890–1920 period migrated to the western provinces, where they soon rose to positions of power and influence."[20] Indeed, "he and Borden were two of the most sought-after counsel in Nova Scotia appeals before the Supreme Court of Canada in the years 1890–1905."[21] The *Gerring* in 1897 falls squarely in this period.[22]

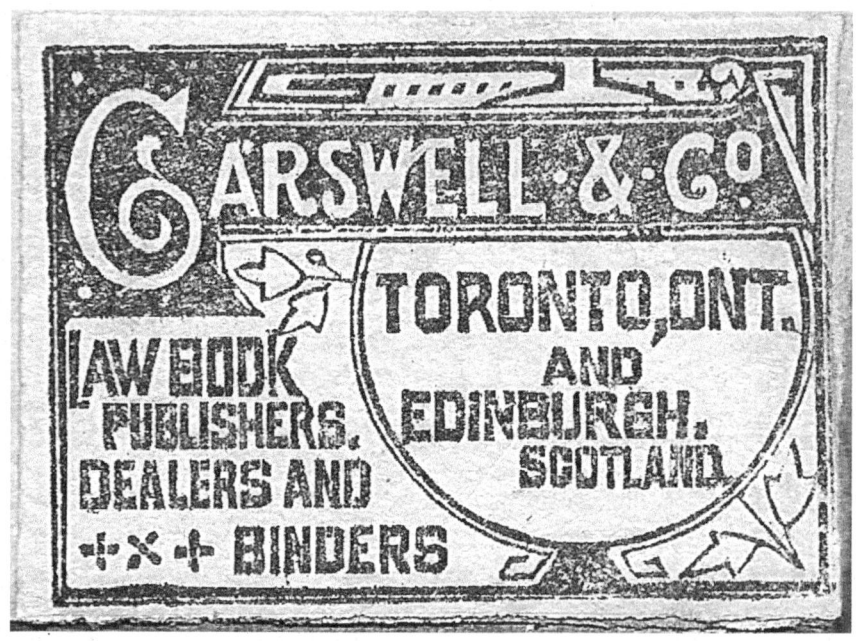

Figure 6.1 Small sticker from inside the front cover (bottom right-hand corner) of volume 2, from James Kent, *Commentaries on American Law*, edited by William M. Lacy, vol. 2 (Philadelphia: Blackstone Publishing Company, 1889) of the copy "presented to the Library of the University of Toronto by the Executors of the Estate of the Late George Tate Blackstock, Esq., K.C." George Tate Blackstock was a prominent Toronto lawyer, who practised with the law firm that became Faskens. See Wilson, "Blackstock, George Tate." (Image provided by Sufei Xu, Infoexpress Librarian and Access Services Coordinator at the Bora Laskin Law Library.)

The "Text Book Series" was a book-reprinting and selling initiative spearheaded by an American company named "the Blackstone Publishing Company," a business located at 19 South Ninth Street in Philadelphia, Pennsylvania.[23] The series provided pirated editions of classic English works to Americans and those in other countries at a fraction of the regular price, one book per month for a set subscription fee of $15 per year.[24] Single volumes could be purchased for $1.25 each.[25] Their agents in Canada were "Carswell and Co."[26]

Book notices touted the Blackstone Text Book series as an excellent way for students to obtain valuable treatises at extremely reasonable prices. For example, the *Kansas City Law Reporter* contained an advertisement from the company which described the system as a way to get a "working library" at a moderate price. This advertisement appeared among others for things that were useful to lawyers such as legal blanks, typewriters, and fireproof safes.[27] The first volume in the series (Smith on Master and Servant) was issued on 1 December 1886.

The *Canada Law Journal* listed the books in the series to date, describing the "prices [as] so absurdly low, as to enable even every student who enters an office to secure a good law library by the time he is ready to begin practicing."[28] A month later, in May 1887, it stated, "We presume most of our readers are subscribers to this series by this time. If not they had better begin at once."[29] A South African law journal reprinting of the *Canada Law Journal* note demonstrates that the series was marketed beyond North America.[30]

British commentators (predictably) frowned upon this system of "absorbing the brains of English law authors without paying [them] a penny."[31] Editors of the *Canada Law Journal* objected to the use of the term "pirated" in connection with the Blackstone Text Book series, pointing out that it was legally permissible to reprint in places where the copyright did not extend.[32] Some called for an international law of copyright.[33] Meanwhile the *Railway and Corporation Law Journal* reported that the series (5,738 printed pages to date in early 1888) "met the approval of a large class of American lawyers" grateful for these "English treatises of exceptional excellence and value."[34] The reviewer did, however, note that the encouragement and commendation of the series left aside "the question of piracy."[35] Such reprints were very common in the United States because they were so much cheaper than the originals.[36] There was no American copyright protection for foreign authors.[37] One estimate put the price at about 1/10 the cost of imported versions of these books.[38] Editions ranged from straight reprints to those that involved an editor, who would be paid for adding American notes and cases.[39]

The editor, who would have been hired and paid for this express purpose by the Blackstone Publishing Company, was a lawyer named William M. Lacy of the Philadelphia Bar.[40] Kent's work was "a perennial bestseller" and so it made sense for the Blackstone Publishing Company to want to reissue it.[41] However, Kent's *Commentaries* were a domestic, not a foreign work.

Perhaps this is why, when the Text Book series edition appeared in 1889, it earned the Blackstone Publishing Company the accolade that it was "revolutionizing the law book business."[42] The practice of hiring an in-house editor who would be paid a fixed fee for their work and then reproducing "unauthorized," but just-as-good *and* much cheaper editions, was a winning strategy for foreign books. Could it also be used for domestic ones? Were a new editor's additions and changes to the notes enough to protect the Text Book edition from infringing the copyright Kent's heirs or publishers of the *Commentaries* held inside the United States? What did Kent himself have to say about the matter?

In his *Commentaries*, Kent wrote quite extensively about the "original acquisition, by intellectual labour" (in the same part coincidentally where he discussed "original acquisition, by occupancy") and specifically copyright.[43] He did not discuss the point about editors' notes in particular, at least not initially. He did write that "[a] copyright may exist in part of a work, without having an exclusive right to the whole," words that could be interpreted to give an editor protection.[44] In the second edition (1832), Kent discussed amendments made to the *Copyright Act* in 1831, which extended protection from fourteen to twenty-eight years with a possible renewal for another fourteen years.[45] Unlike the fourteen-year renewal provided under the 1790 act, an author no longer needed to be alive to renew. Noah Webster, the chief architect of the 1831 act, secured the renewal right for the widow and children of the author.[46] Kent emphasized the "personal benefit" this change in the law bestowed on the author's wife and children, and their "entitlement."[47] Ironically, however, it was the fifth edition of his text, published in 1844, shortly before he died, that introduced a note, relying on the famous copyright dispute between reporters for the United States Supreme Court *Wheaton v. Peters* (1832), that stated "[a]n editor may have a copyright in his own marginal notes."[48]

Kent died in 1847. He had re-registered the copyright twice, in 1832 (six years after the initial registration on 25 November 1826 and one year after the law changed in 1831) and 1840 (fourteen years after the initial registration). William Kent re-registered the 6th, 7th, 8th, and 9th editions in 1848, 1851, 1854, and 1858, the year the publisher changed to Little, Brown.[49] William was still the name on the copyright on the 10th edition in 1860.[50] However, the 11th edition in 1866, which featured a new editor, one George Comstock, changed to "Mrs. William Kent" (presumably William's widow). The 12th and 13th editions in 1873 and 1884 reverted back to "James Kent" (edited by Oliver Wendell Holmes Jr. and Charles Barnes, respectively) with the last, 14th edition (edited by John Gould) naming the copyright registrant as "Estate of James Kent."[51]

How would the law have treated these registrations if they had been contested, and exactly whose interests in what text would they have protected? Well, twenty-eight years after Kent's original registration in 1826 would bring the protection to 1854, which, when renewed by his heirs for another fourteen years, would have extended the protection until 1868, only ten years after the publisher changed from Kent's son to Little, Brown. Yet Little, Brown carried on for almost thirty more years, until 1896, with no direct competitors, at least until the Blackstone Publishing Company came along.[52]

Little, Brown might have argued against any such interlopers that each new edition restarted the forty-two year clock, especially if significant enough changes were made by the editor. In the 12th edition, in his summary of the 1870 congressional consolidation of the copyright statutes, Holmes noted that "[t]he subject of a book need not be new, nor the materials original, in order to entitle an author to copyright, provided he has made a new arrangement and combination of materials."[53] But were new notes, even those as elegant as Holmes's, really "a new arrangement and combination of materials"? Holmes himself seemed to understand that, however great he might become and however important his work on the edition was to him, "the owners of the copyright" were Kent's heirs and the estate.[54]

Acknowledging in his treatise on intellectual property that new editions "present questions of extreme nicety and great difficulty in determining whether this is a basis for a new copyright," Eaton Drone did think there was a "general rule," namely,

> that each successive edition, which is substantially different from the preceding ones, or which contains new matter of substantial amount or value, becomes entitled to copyright as a new work. It is immaterial whether the new edition is

produced by condensing, expanding, correcting, rewriting, or otherwise altering the original, *or by adding notes, citations, &c.*[55]

The question, as Drone put it, was whether the work was "substantially different."[56] It seems pretty clear that none of the texts of Kent's *Commentaries* would have been considered different enough to be the basis for an entirely new copyright. The notes, even Kent's, did not change the text that much. It was still Kent's work. If the copyright on the original text and notes had expired, then it was fair game. Drone wrote that "anyone may revise or annotate and republish a book not protected by copyright, and obtain a valid copyright for the new edition,"[57] although "the new copyright, as a general rule, will cover only what is new."[58] The Text Book Series edition had a different publisher with a different editor and its own notes. For example, Lacy did not include the note, which appeared in the 5th through 14th editions, about the possibility that an editor could hold a copyright in his own marginal notes (the note with the *Wheaton v. Peters* citation). The copyright on Kent's main text and notes had likely expired. The law is not very clear, but we probably can safely say that new notes by other editors did not extend the copyright on the original material and its notes because they did not make the text different enough. Given Drone's views, it is possible that a court might have found that the Blackstone Publishing Company's copyright only extended to protect Lacy's new notes. At the end of the day, even if the notes were valuable and distinctive enough to be protected, what would they be without the text they commented upon? That out-of-copyright text would have to accompany the new material in order for it to make any sense, whether published by Little Brown, Blackstone Publishing, or someone else.

When Lacy's edition appeared, the *Virginia Law Journal* announced that the volumes would be in "the usual style" of the Blackstone Publishing Company Text Book series, namely, "well printed and cheap."[59] After volume one, volumes two, three, and four would follow, one a month.[60] Not everyone was happy about this, specifically Little, Brown. The *American Law Review*, published by Little, Brown, charged that the Text Book Series edition was not as good in terms of print and paper as the Little, Brown edition.[61] This review also reported that Kent's heirs were willing to offer

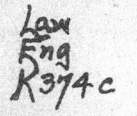

COMMENTARIES

ON

AMERICAN LAW.

BY

JAMES KENT.

IN FOUR VOLUMES.

VOLUME II.

NEW AND THOROUGHLY REVISED EDITION

BY

WILLIAM M. LACY,
OF THE PHILADELPHIA BAR.

PHILADELPHIA:
THE BLACKSTONE PUBLISHING CO.
1889.

FIGURE 6.2 Title page of James Kent, *Commentaries on American Law*, edited by William M. Lacy, vol. 2 (Philadelphia: Blackstone Publishing Company, 1889) from the same copy identified in Figure 6.1. (Image provided by Sufei Xu, Infoexpress Librarian and Access Services Coordinator at the Bora Laskin Law Library.)

the 13th edition, "retain[ing] the valuable notes of Judge Holmes," in "Law Sheep," for $12[62]—nice, but subscribers to the Blackstone series obtained eight more books throughout the year for their $15. The claim about problems with the print and paper did not appear in other reviews. The *Green Bag* said "type and paper are satisfactory in every respect."[63] And the *Legal News* said it was "on good paper."[64] However, the *Railway and Corporation Law Journal* did note that it fell "below the high standard of Mr. Justice Holmes' elegant edition."[65] And the *Central Law Journal* described the leatherette binding as "very unsatisfactory."[66] The *Canada Law Journal* showed no hesitation endorsing the volumes, which it said were "of considerable interest and value to Canadians."[67] The review in the *Railway and Corporation Law Journal*, when volumes 2 through 4 appeared, pretty much sums up the situation. First, Lacy's edition "of course suffers in comparison with the elegant edition of Judge Holmes."[68] And, second, although it was "well printed, on good paper," it did need to be better bound, which when done would still keep the price lower than the set from Little, Brown.

Important to note here is the wider context of books being offered using the "subscription method." Michael Hoeflich explains that this was a common and important publishing scheme in nineteenth-century America.[69] It was the way the first American edition of Blackstone's *Commentaries* was sold in the late eighteenth century.[70] "Forced" or guaranteed sales were a way, as Hoeflich puts it, to offer "substantial risk reduction to printers and booksellers and often substantial price savings to buyers."[71] Philadelphia was an old player in the book publishing and book printing trade.[72] Hoeflich identifies the most important and longest-lived law subscription publishing scheme in antebellum America as "The Law Library" initiated by John S. Littel of Philadelphia in 1833.[73] Subscribers were asked to pay $10 a year for one book a month.[74] It ran for twenty-six years and reprinted more than one hundred English legal texts.[75] It would have been a model for the Blackstone Publishing Company's Text Book Series.

In terms of understanding legal publishing and law-book habits, Hoeflich has emphasized "the importance of the mundane necessities of life without which high theory can come to nothing.... [G]reat doctrinal developments in the law may be advanced or impeded by nothing more glamorous than a decent postal route."[76] Decent postal routes and cheap editions are not the things of grand theory, but they did determine what editions of what books lawyers in the nineteenth century had access to, and were using, at any particular time and place; they also influenced which ideas lawyers would formulate. The fact that the Text Book edition of this volume of Kent's *Commentaries* cost $1.25 is highly significant and provides pretty much all the explanation one needs in order to understand why Ritchie was using it, especially when there was scarcely any difference in quality between it and the authorized edition, with the exception of notes. However fancy a lawyer Ritchie was, $1.25 is pretty difficult to argue with. And it might be that differences over something rather esoteric like the authorship of the notes was less meaningful the further away one was from Boston, the stomping grounds for Holmes and his elite Brahmin community.[77]

We do not know where or how Ritchie acquired his copy of the Text Book series edition of Kent's *Commentaries*. However, Ritchie's use of the book did not necessarily mean that he subscribed to the whole series, as it was common practice for local book agents to obtain multiple copies as subscribers, which they would offer for resale.[78] Ritchie might have obtained it as a solitary set or even a stand-alone volume from a book shop or law book agent in Halifax, Boston, Philadelphia, or New York at any point between 1889 (when it was published) and 1896 (when he used it in Halifax for his factum in the *Gerring*).

The fact that Ritchie was located in British North America, specifically Halifax, meant that he would have been part of a legal culture that long benefited from pirated texts from the United States, whether the authors were English or American. The *Canada Law Journal*, at least, consistently showed no hesitation in touting the strengths of the Text Book Series, including its reproduction of English works. Belonging to this culture would have meant Ritchie had little concern about using an allegedly "pirated" edition, which, once shipping costs were taken into consideration and any mark-up from resale was added, likely cost him more than the bargain basement price of $1.25. He probably would not have been thinking in terms of "piracy" at all, being very used to editions that were straight reprints, as well as those with variations that ranged from slight to significant, especially for legal texts where updates were required given changes in the law.

Little, Brown issued the last edition of the *Commentaries* in 1896, highlighting its key strength and competitive advantage, namely, that it had been edited by Holmes.[79] The 13th edition in 1884 had not included Holmes' name, suggesting that experience with the Blackstone Publishing Company edition in 1889 spurred Kent's heirs and Little, Brown on to competitive action.[80] The 14th edition only listed the copyrights going back to the Holmes 12th edition, perhaps to dissuade anyone who could count to forty-two from wondering how, when the initial registration by Kent was in 1826, the heirs could still claim to be in possession of the copyright in 1896. Yet all of this skirmishing appears to have been end-of-life activity, as the 14th edition was the last edition of Kent's *Commentaries* that anyone published. The Blackstone Publishing Company's edition in 1889 also appears to have been its last imprint.[81]

The 1891 *International Copyright Act* (or Chace Act) gave some copyright protection to non-US authors so long as the work was manufactured on US soil.[82] The express permission to reproduce the works of foreign authors that had existed in US law until this time was finally removed.[83] This meant that the Blackstone Publishing Company could no longer boldly republish British works. Yet domestic works were also legally risky, since, as we have seen, uncertainties existed over what was or was not a substantially different or substantially similar work that might either entitle a publisher to a new copyright or render them in violation of another's copyright. Authors' heirs and estates (and their lawyers) could be keen to argue over copyright ownership issues, especially for famous law books (as was evident from the dueling court reporters in *Wheaton v. Peters*). American judges and juries were likely to be more sympathetic to American authors than to British ones, should legal contests arise. All of these factors would have created a hostile environment for the Blackstone Publishing Company to continue doing in the 1890s what it had been doing in the 1880s.

As for Kent's *Commentaries*, perhaps the substantially cheaper (and probably still available) Text Book Series absorbed the extant market of readers for such a text at home and abroad, and Little, Brown simply gave up on making money out of it. Moreover, the size of the market for that particular text would have been shrinking, as Kent's style of cosmopolitan learning (drawing on natural law, Roman law, and civil law) was on the wane in the United States and was coming to an end, at least in Upper Canada, by the 1890s.[84] This feature—namely, the Roman and civilian orientation to the old question of how one acquires possession in a wild animal—more than any other explains why the *Gerring* did not experience the uptake one might have expected in the twentieth century, at least in Ontario, despite the fact that it did become a leading case on the definition of "fishing" in Canada under the *Fisheries Act*.[85] However, that is a story for another day.[86]

NOTES

* This chapter is from research for a book-length study under contract with the UBC Press in the Landmark Cases in Canadian Law series, tentatively titled *The Frederick Gerring, Canada's Twenty-First Century* Pierson v Post (to be co-authored with Christopher Shorey and Bradley Miller).

1 Quoted in Philip Girard, "'Of Institutes and Treatises': Blackstone's *Commentaries*, Kent's *Commentaries* and Murdoch's *Epitome of the Laws of Nova-Scotia*," in *Law Books in Action: Essays on the Anglo-American Legal Treatise*, ed. Angela Fernandez and Markus D. Dubber (Oxford: Hart Publishing, 2012), 60, citing Stewart to Kent, 28 April 1847, James Kent Papers, reel 5, Library of Congress. Kent died on 12 December 1847.

2 W.B.A. Ritchie, "Filed in the Registry of the Supreme Court. Respondents Factum. In the Supreme Court of Canada, 1896," in Great Britain, *Arbitration of Outstanding Pecuniary Claims Between Great Britain and the United States of America: The Frederick Gerring, Jr.*, Appendix, Annex 5, 25–34 (Ottawa: Government Printing Bureau, 1913), 31 ["Respondent's Factum"].

3 See Donald R. Kelley, "Gaius Noster: Substructures of Western Social Thought," *American Historical Review* 84, no. 3 (1979), 621.

4 Kelley, "Gaius Noster: Substructures of Western Social Thought," 620.

5 See John W. Cairns, "Blackstone, an English Institutist: Legal Literature and the Rise of the Nation State," *Oxford Journal of Legal Studies* 4, no. 3 (1984): 322.

6 John Cairns argues that Blackstone's departure from the *Institute* form of Justinian (e.g., treating the English system of government in the first book) should not exclude his work from the institutionalist tradition. See "Blackstone, an English Institutist," 350.

7 Philip Girard argues that it is incorrect to view the institute form as giving way to stand-alone legal treatises on specialized topics, as for instance John Langbein has argued was true of Kent's *Commentaries* and as Brian Simpson generally supposed when he wrote about treatises. See Girard, "Of Institutes and Treatises," 44–46.

8 See Girard, "Of Institutes and Treatises," 45.

9   See William Blackstone, *Commentaries on the Laws of England*, vol. 2 (Oxford: Clarendon Press, 1766), 400, 403. Institutes, treatises, and other old law books are widely available in databases such as Hathi Trust, Google Books, Hein Online, and the Making of Modern Law. An excellent electronic version of Blackstone's *Commentaries* is available at http://avalon.law.yale.edu/subject_menus/blackstone.asp.

10   Blackstone, *Commentaries on the Laws of England*, 2: 403.

11   James Kent, *Commentaries on American Law*, vol. 2 (New York: O. Halsted, 1827), 281.

12   See James Kent, *Commentaries on American Law*, 6th ed., 4 vols. (New York: W. Kent, 1848). William Kent published the seventh edition in 1851 and the eighth in 1854.

13   James Kent, *Commentaries on American Law*, 9th ed., 4 vols. (Boston, MA: Little, Brown, 1858).

14   James Kent, *Commentaries on American Law*, 12th ed., ed. Oliver Wendell Holmes Jr., 4 vols. (Boston, MA: Little, Brown, 1873). Holmes spent three years working on the project, updating the English and American case law. See Michael I. Swygert and Jon W. Bruce, "The Historical Origins, Founding, and Early Development of Student-Edited Law Reviews," *Hastings Law Journal* 36, no. 5 (1985): 745.

15   James Kent, *Commentaries on American Law*, ed. William M. Lacy, 4 vols. (Philadelphia: Blackstone Publishing Company, 1889).

16   Philip Girard, "Ritchie, William Bruce Almon," in *Dictionary of Canadian Biography*, vol. 14, University of Toronto/Université Laval, 2003–, http://www.biographi.ca/en/bio/ritchie_william_bruce_almon_14E.html.

17   Gordon Bale and E. Bruce Mellett, "Ritchie, Sir William Johnston," in *Dictionary of Canadian Biography*, vol. 12, University of Toronto/Université Laval, 2003–, http://www.biographi.ca/en/bio/ritchie_william_johnston_12E.html.

18   Girard, "Ritchie, William Bruce Almon."

19   Girard, "Ritchie, William Bruce Almon."

20   Girard, "Ritchie, William Bruce Almon."

21   Girard, "Ritchie, William Bruce Almon."

22   Ritchie was the solicitor of record for the respondent, the Dominion government (see *Frederick Gerring, Jr. (The) v Canada* (1897), 27 SCR 271 at 308). He also wrote the factum: Ritchie, Respondent's factum, 34. However, the barrister who argued the case was a Queen's Counsel named Newcombe (see *Gerring*, 273). This was certainly Edmund Leslie Newcombe, also from Nova Scotia, who succeeded Robert Sedgewick as Deputy Minister of Justice and Deputy Attorney General in 1893, and served in this role until his 1924 appointment to the Supreme Court of Canada: Philip Girard, "Newcombe, Edmund Leslie," in *Dictionary of Canadian Biography*, vol. 16, University of Toronto/Université Laval, 2003–, http://www.biographi.ca/en/bio/newcombe_edmund_leslie_16E.html

23   "Law. 12 vols. for $15," *Kansas City Law Reporter* 1, no. 7 (10 August 1888): vii.

24   The $15 price was for volumes bound in "limp leatherette." Binding in "Law Sheep" cost $20 for the year: "Law. 12 vols. for $15." "Sheep" was "the common binding for

law books"; "calf" was leather and usually more expensive; and deluxe editions would features things like "calf with gilt decoration": M.H. Hoeflich, *Legal Publishing in Antebellum America* (New York: Cambridge University Press, 2010), 71, 65, 76, 86. Offering binding in "limp leatherette" and "sheep" (as the fancy option) indicates that the volumes in the Text Book series were meant to be working rather than "display" items. Books bound more expensively in "calf" or even "calf with gilt decoration" tended to be aimed at more affluent members of the profession who might want to display their learning, not merely read. On the "prestige" versus "working" value of law books, see Hoeflich, *Legal Publishing in Antebellum America*, 87, 123, 112 n. 23.

25 "Book Notices," *Green Bag* 1, no. 9 (September 1889): 412.

26 See "New Law Books," *Canada Law Journal* 23, no. 6 (15 March 1887): 116.

27 See the advertising pages in *Kansas City Law Reporter* 1, no. 7 (10 August 1888).

28 "Law Books," *Canada Law Journal* 23, no. 8 (15 April 1887): 141.

29 Untitled, *Canada Law Journal* 23, no. 10 (15 May 1887): 181.

30 "Law Books," *Cape Law Journal* 4, no. 3 (1887): 183–84.

31 Untitled, *Law Journal*, 22 (12 November 1887): 597.

32 "Copyright and Piracy," *Canada Law Journal* 24, no. 2 (1 February 1888): 35–36. The first use of the term "pirated" appears in an untitled note in the *Law Quarterly Review* 4, no. 1 (January 1888): 121. A follow-up, explaining that the term was used with "full deliberation," appears in "Notes," *Law Quarterly Review* 4, no. 2 (April 1888): 225.

33 "The Blackstone Text-Book Series," *Scottish Law Review and Sheriff Court Reports* 5, no. 58 (October 1889): 251–52.

34 "New Books," *Railway and Corporation Law Journal* 3 (7 January 1888): 24.

35 "New Books," 24.

36 See Hoeflich, *Legal Publishing in Antebellum America*, 59, 81.

37 Hoeflich, *Legal Publishing in Antebellum America*, 82, 58.

38 See "New Books and New Editions: Blackstone Publishing Company's Text-Book Series," *Albany Law Journal* 37, no. 20 (9 May 1888): 404.

39 Hoeflich, *Legal Publishing in Antebellum America*, 46–47 (on publishers paying American authors and editors), 60 (on the legal and competitive advantage of adding notes). See "New Publications," *American Law Record* 15, no. 10 (April 1887): 633–34, advertising a series in which the first two installments were straight reprints.

40 "Book Notices," *Green Bag* 1, no. 9 (September 1889): 412.

41 Hoeflich, *Legal Publishing in Antebellum America*, 87. See also Philip Girard's discussion of the longevity of the "institute" and its co-existence with treatises in "Of Institutes and Treatises," 43–45.

42 "Kent's Commentaries," *Copp's Land-Owner* 1, no. 11 (1 September 1889): 121.

43 See Kent, *Commentaries*, 2: 298–99, 306–15 (1st edition, 1827).

44 Kent, *Commentaries*, 2: 313.

45 4 Stat. 436. See e.g. James Kent, *Commentaries on American Law*, 2nd ed., vol. 2 (New York: O. Halsted, 1832), 383.

46 Bracha, "Commentary on the Copyright Act 1831."

47 Kent, *Commentaries*, 2nd ed., 2: 384.

48 James Kent, *Commentaries on American Law*, 5th ed., vol. 2 (New York: printed for the author, 1844), 382 n (c). See *Wheaton v Peters*, 33 US (8 Pet) 591 (1834).

49 The copyright history is recorded on the opening pages of the first volume of James Kent, *Commentaries on American Law*, 9th ed., 4 vols. (Boston, MA: Little, Brown, 1858).

50 James Kent, *Commentaries on American Law*, 10th ed., 4 vols. (Boston, MA: Little, Brown, 1860).

51 James Kent, *Commentaries on American Law*, 11th ed., ed. George F. Comstock, 4 vols. (Boston, MA: Little, Brown, 1866); James Kent, *Commentaries on American Law*, 12th ed., ed. Oliver Wendell Holmes, Jr., 4 vols. (Boston: Little, Brown, 1873); James Kent, *Commentaries on American Law*, 13th ed., ed. Charles M. Barnes, 4 vols. (Boston: Little, Brown, 1884); James Kent, *Commentaries on American Law*, 14th ed., ed. John M. Gould, 4 vols. (Boston: Little, Brown, 1896).

52 Question-and-answer editions were introduced over the years, the first, by Asa Kinne, initially appearing in 1838 with Kent's approval. John C. Devereaux similarly secured the permission of William Kent when publishing his question-and-answer edition started in the 1860s. See Asa Kinne, *The Most Important Parts of Kent's Commentaries Reduced to Questions and Answers*, 2nd ed. (NY: W.E. Dean, 1840); John C. Devereux, *The Most Material Parts of Kent's Commentaries Reduced to Questions and Answers* (NY: Lewis & Blood, 1860). These were very different works than the original, and while they may have competed they were certainly separate new works for copyright purposes. I have not examined the original's resemblance to the following two works, an 1886 abridgement or an 1875 "analysis." See Eben Francis Thompson, *The Student's Kent: An Abridgement of Kent's Commentaries on American Law* (Boston: Houghton, Mifflin, 1886); Frederick S. Dickson, *An Analysis of Kent's Commentaries* (Philadelphia: Rees Welsh, 1875).

53 Kent, *Commentaries on American Law*, 12th ed., 2: 373 n. 1(b).

54 Kent, "Preface." Holmes was thirty-two in 1873. He expressed the belief that greatness had to be achieved before forty, if it were to be achieved at all. Holmes wrote, "'I remember that I hurried to get it [*The Common Law*] out before March 8 [1881], because then I should be 40 and it was said that if a man was to do anything he must do it before 40'": see Mark DeWolfe Howe, *Justice Oliver Wendell Holmes, vol. 2: The Proving Years, 1870-1882* (Cambridge MA: Belknap Press of Harvard University Press, 1963), 135. For a sense of the importance of the *Commentaries* project to him, see the anecdote related in Angela Fernandez, *Pierson v Post, the Hunt for the Fox: Law and Professionalization in American Legal Culture* (New York: Cambridge University Press, 2018), 257–58.

55 Eaton S. Drone, *A Treatise on the Law of Property in Intellectual Productions in Britain and the United States: Embracing Copyright in Works of Literature and Art, and*

Playright in Dramatic and Musical Compositions (Boston, MA: Little, Brown, 1879), 146 (emphasis added).

56   Drone, *A Treatise on the Law of Property in Intellectual Productions in Britain and the United States*, 147.

57   Drone, *A Treatise on the Law of Property in Intellectual Productions in Britain and the United States*, 148.

58   Drone, *A Treatise on the Law of Property in Intellectual Productions in Britain and the United States*, 149.

59   "Book Notices," *Virginia Law Journal* 13, no. 7 (July 1889): 619.

60   "Book Notices," 619.

61   "Book Reviews," *American Law Review* 23, no. 5 (September–October 1889): 850–51. See Michael I. Swygert and Jon W. Bruce, "The Historical Origins, Founding, and Early Development of Student-Edited Law Reviews," *Hastings Law Journal* 36, no. 5 (1985): 757 (identifying Little, Brown as the publisher of the *American Law Review*).

62   "Book Reviews," *American Law Review* 23, no. 5 (September–October 1889): 851.

63   "Book Notices," *Green Bag* 1, no. 9 (September 1889): 412.

64   "New Publications," *Legal News* 12, no. 41 (12 October 1889): 321.

65   "Kent's Commentaries," *Railway and Corporation Law Journal* 6 (24 August 1889): 160.

66   "Recent Publications," *Central Law Journal* 29, no.15 (18 October 1889): 295–96.

67   "Commentaries on American Law," *Canada Law Journal* 25, no. 14 (2 September 1889): 437.

68   "New Books," *Railway and Corporation Law Journal* 6 (21 December 1889): 500.

69   Hoeflich, *Legal Publishing in Antebellum America*, 126–43.

70   Hoeflich, *Legal Publishing in Antebellum America*, 128, 131–34.

71   Hoeflich, *Legal Publishing in Antebellum America*, 143 and 127, n. 8, citing Rosalind Remer, *Printers and Men of Capital: Philadelphia Book Publishers in the New Republic* (Philadelphia: University of Pennsylvania Press, 1996), 125–30, says that the term "forced sales" was used for subscription sales and other mechanisms that guaranteed a market for the text.

72   See Edwin Wolf II, *The Book Culture of a Colonial American City* (Oxford: Clarendon Press, 1988).

73   Hoeflich, *Legal Publishing in Antebellum America*, 142.

74   Hoeflich, $10 was apparently also supposed to be the price of the Blackstone Publishing Company series. See "New Publications," *American Law Record* 15, no. 10 (April 1887): 633–34. This might have been wishful thinking or a confusion based on the earlier Law Library series.

75   Hoeflich, *Legal Publishing in Antebellum America*, 142–43.

76   Hoeflich, *Legal Publishing in Antebellum America*, 171.

77 See Menand, *The Metaphysical Club: A Story of Ideas in America* (New York: Farrar, Straus and Giroux, 2002). Holmes belonged to the Metaphysical Club, an informal discussion group that met in Cambridge, Massachusetts for nine months in 1872 and included the important moral philosopher William James and founder of semiotics Charles Sanders Peirce. The term the "Brahmin Caste of New England" was used in the title of an 1860 story published in *The Atlantic*: "The Professor's Story: Chapter 1: The Brahmin Caste of New England," *Atlantic Monthly*, January 1, 1860, 91-93. Webster's dictionary says, as an alternate meaning of Brahmin, "a person of high social standing and cultivated intellect and taste <Boston ~s>." See *Webster's Ninth New Collegiate Dictionary* (Springfield, MA: Merriam-Webster, 1986).

78 Hoeflich, *Legal Publishing in Antebellum America*, 134, 138.

79 James Kent, *Commentaries on American Law*, 12th ed., ed. Oliver Wendell Holmes, Jr., 4 vols. (Boston: Little, Brown, 1873); James Kent, *Commentaries on American Law*, 14th ed., ed. John M. Gould, 4 vols. (Boston: Little, Brown, 1896).

80 James Kent, *Commentaries on American Law*, 13th ed., ed. Charles M. Barnes, 4 vols. (Boston: Little, Brown, 1884).

81 A publishing company with the same name operated in the 1940s from an office at 455 Spadina Road, Toronto, Ontario. See Drummond, "Supplement to List of American and British Law Book Dealers and Publishers," 342.

82 See Robert E. Spoo, "Courtesy Paratexts, Informal Publishing Norms and the Copyright Vacuum in Nineteenth-Century America," *Stanford Law Review* 69, no. 3 (2017): 645–46.

83 See Thorvald Solberg, "Copyright Law Reform," *Yale Law Journal* 35, no. 1 (1925): 50.

84 See G. Blaine Baker, "The Reconstruction of Upper Canadian Legal Thought in the Late-Victorian Empire," *Law and History Review* 3, no. 2 (1985): 267–69.

85 This point is elaborated on in Angela Fernandez, "Fish, Colony, and Nation" in a forthcoming collection of essays in honour of G. Blaine Baker to be published by the Osgoode Society for Canadian Legal History and McGill-Queen's University Press.

86 For its beginnings, see in this volume Christopher Shorey, "The Last Voyage of the *Frederick Gerring, Jr.*"

SECTION II

EXPLORING SYSTEMS

Empire's Law: Archives and the Judicial Committee of the Privy Council

Catharine MacMillan

Canada, as an independent political nation, was largely a product of evolution, rather than revolution, from its British colonial origins. Nowhere is the nature of this evolutionary process clearer than in the development of Canadian law and legal institutions. While the Dominion created by the 1867 *British North America Act*[1] soon had its own Supreme Court sitting in Ottawa, the final appellate court was the Judicial Committee of the Privy Council sitting in London, England. As the British constitutional theorist A.V. Dicey drily observed, the Judicial Committee was the "true Supreme Court of the Dominion."[2] While Canadian scholars have long studied the decisions of the Judicial Committee in relation to the Canadian constitutional structure, legal historians have examined the role of the Judicial Committee in relation to particular cases. However, there has been little systematic study of the broader impact of the Judicial Committee on the development of Canadian law beyond constitutional law. This fits into what could be seen as an even broader pattern of neglect, for there has been little detailed consideration of the functioning of the Judicial Committee as a whole.[3] There are many reasons for this, a prominent one being the physical disconnection between prospective scholars (generally located outside London) and the historical records (generally located in

London) which would form the basis for their study. This chapter attempts to bridge this disconnection by describing the records available in London and shedding light on how they may be approached from a distance. It presents an explanation of what the Judicial Committee was (and to some extent still is), how it functioned, and where scholars can locate its records in public archives in London. As will become apparent, these records are important for a range of different research projects: while some may be interested in the functioning of the Judicial Committee, which ran as a form of global court, others will be interested in how the Judicial Committee shaped the law of particular jurisdictions. The records also contain material of use to political, social, economic, and cultural historians.

What was the Judicial Committee of the Privy Council?

While the jurisdiction of the Judicial Committee is originally derived from medieval custom with the *Curia Regis* (the court of the king's counsellors who did the business of state of whatever kind), the Judicial Committee was created in the modern period by the Judicial Committee Act, 1833.[4] That this fount of colonial justice grew from an ancient crown prerogative is only one of the many oddities of the Judicial Committee. The 1833 Act came about as a result of the work of the reforming Whig Henry Brougham as a part of his much more wide-ranging plans in 1828 to reform the administration of justice. By that point the Judicial Committee was struggling to make its way through the growing numbers of colonial appeals. This growth in numbers was exacerbated by imperial expansion, which produced a greater and increasing range of legal systems, both European and non-European, which required adjudication—and also only a modicum of suitable legal talent in London to decide these appeals.[5] The Judicial Committee was given appellate jurisdiction over all of the colonies in the British Empire, along with consular courts and protectorates. It was, in short, the world's first global court. It adjudicated these appeals according to the legal system of the jurisdiction from which the appeal came, a development that gave it a unique diversity in its jurisprudence. The judges of this court were privy counsellors; in 1871 legislation allowed the appointment of two former Indian judges and two former judges of English superior courts.[6] The 1871 Act was designed to overcome the backlog of Indian appeals. Indian appeals presented their own complexity in that they were decided according to the legal system of the litigant. In 1876 the *Appellate Jurisdiction Act* authorized the appointment of the first Lords of Appeal in Ordinary and, for the first time, requirements for legal qualifications were put in place.[7] The *Judicial Committee Amendment Act, 1895* permitted a select group of judges from dominions and colonies to sit as members of the Judicial Committee[8]: eventually Canada sent more judges than did any other colony or dominion. In addition to what was referred to as Indian and colonial appeals, the Judicial Committee also had a domestic jurisdiction. As envisioned by Brougham, this encompassed ecclesiastical cases, admiralty,[9] and appeals from the Prize Court. To Brougham's vision was added (until 1907) the power to extend the life of a patent, a more limited role in copyright, and appeals under the *Endowed Schools Amendment Act, 1873*.[10] In short, this was a court that heard cases without a natural home elsewhere in English courts. The homeless nature of the Judicial Committee is also apparent in the fact that its imperial functioning was largely ignored by English contemporaries. The little public awareness that arose in England regarding the court was in relation to its ecclesiastical jurisdiction which involved the Church of England. The contemporary view of the relative importance of ecclesiastical cases and the colonial litigants before the Judicial Committee is summed up by a "correspondent" to the satirical weekly *Punch* in a "letter" to the editor:

> SIR,
>
> Why can't the Judicial Committee of the Privy Council stick to one thing at a time, and finish that off, instead of muddling themselves with all sorts of cases, running into one another?
> For instance, I am fond of Ecclesiastical squabbles, and therefore I look with pleasure for the continuation of those Ritualistic Causes which were only partly heard.

Well, Sir, say on Monday I read MARTIN v MACHONOCHIE, it reaches an interesting point, and is to be continued in to-morrow's paper.

I take up to-morrow's paper, and turn to Judicial Committee Privy Council. Instead of MARTIN v MACHONOCHIE, I find EMILY ANNE v AMELIA JANE, which turns out to be not a question of people utterly at sea about lights, but of people not having lights at sea. After this is THE BOOMERSUND V ALLEN BAY, a dispute about a collision, unworthy of the Great Judicial Privy Council! The next day I again turn to the Judicial Committee and expect MARTIN v MACHONOCHIE or some such serious ecclesiastical trial, which is more befitting the J.C.P.C.'s consideration than the horrid swearings and counter-swearings of a lot of reckless mariners. No, Sir, I read that the Court was occupied in investigating whether RUMTUM JELLY BAG of Badhapoorlooror was right in appealing against a decision of a Judge in Calcutta who had directed a verdict in favour of BABOO BRODLECURT TUBAHOY BHOY. A thoroughly heathen case is allowed to put the Christian out of Court. Collisions are taken the next day, and BARRY LULLABY LALLA RHOO has his turn next day. I believe they've forgotten all about the important Ecclesiastical questions awaiting their Lordships' final decision.

I am, Sir, your obedient servant,
A MAN
(Clerk to St. Simon's Without.)[11]

Since 1833, a number of procedural treatises have been written which have explained to contemporary lawyers the functioning of the Judicial Committee.[12] Inevitably, these have become useful guides to the legal historian. We are not concerned here with an examination of the different rules applicable to different jurisdictions as to how an appeal could be brought before the Judicial Committee of the Privy Council, but with the procedural requirements applicable once the appeal was brought, for these tell us what can be found in the archives. The appellant and respondent were required to agree upon a record, an inclusion of all that was necessary to consider the disputed question before the Judicial Committee. This could include not only procedural records but also transcripts of lower court proceedings and judgments, copies of exhibits given in evidence in the lower courts, and documents filed before these lower courts. For some appeals copious materials went into the record. Each party also submitted a case as a pre-condition to the hearing of the appeal. The case was to consist of numbered paragraphs stating concisely the circumstances out of which the appeal arose, the contentions to be urged by the particular party, and the reasons for appeal. While similar to a Canadian factum, the case rarely contained extensive legal arguments or many references to law for this was not the practice of the Judicial Committee. The cases, of course, provide insight into how the litigants, or more aptly the litigants' counsel, saw their cases. It was the appellant's responsibility to bind together, "in cloth or half leather," ten copies[13] of both parties' cases, the record, and any supplemental record for the use of the Judicial Committee at the hearing.[14] It is undoubtedly the production of such a comparatively large number of copies of the cases and records which ensured the survival of so many of these into the twenty-first century.

The records form a rich trove of information about each case.[15] Few Canadian lawyers or political scientists are unaware that Canada's constitution is a "living tree" and that women are persons; the papers filed before the Judicial Committee provide a unique understanding of the arguments of counsel in the "Persons Case."[16] Taken as a whole, these records explain the workings of the Judicial Committee and its role in the development of Canadian law, both common law and civil law. The records give the best available knowledge of the workings of this global, imperial court. And the materials contained within the reports provide a rich source of information not easily available elsewhere for historians concerned with matters beyond legal history. Within the records of the proceedings, one finds copies of the sworn testimony of witnesses and the documentary exhibits produced at trial, and these give insights into a huge range of areas: cultural and familial practices of birth, death, marriage, and inheritance. Corporate records provide information into the business and mercantile practices across the centuries and around the globe. Scientific reports and testimony furnish fascinating insights into the state of knowledge employed in particular cases. That they are largely unstudied makes them all the more alluring. We turn now to consider where the records of the Judicial Committee can be found, both in their original sources and in online digitizations.

The London Records

A number of publicly accessible sources in London hold records from the Judicial Committee. Because our focus is on Canadian legal history, this chapter will consider the Indian and colonial appeals to the Judicial Committee. At the time of writing, none of these archives held a complete set of the records available to the public. The records of the Judicial Committee of the Privy Council were kept onsite at 12 Downing Street, where the Judicial Committee sat, as a part of its registry until the Judicial Committee was moved to the Middlesex Guildhall in 2009, the result of a wider program of constitutional and judicial reform in the United Kingdom. Since that time the records have been held in storage controlled by the Ministry of Justice; some of these records have been released to the National Archives in London, where they are available for research. While there are plans to transfer the entirety of the records to the National Archives, the time line for this transfer remains uncertain.

At present, the National Archives have only a small number of the total records available for public use, but these are unique because the Judicial Committee itself created them. The most significant of these records—the minutes of its proceedings between 1830 and 2005—became available in September 2016.[17] These are an invaluable starting point for anyone concerned to gain an overview of the functioning of the Judicial Committee. The minutes contain a day-by-day record of when the Judicial Committee sat, the judges who made up the panels, the parties' names, the origins of the cases, and the cases the panels heard. Announcements made to the Judicial Committee were also recorded and it is in this way that one learns of the appointment of new members to the panel, the death of previous members and counsel, the appointment of new registrars, new procedural announcements, and so forth. While there is much one would have liked to see in the minutes, such as the names of counsel, information that was only introduced well into the twentieth century, there is no other overall record of such detail currently available. An index exists at the front of each volume listing appeals according to jurisdiction and, within each jurisdiction, in the chronological order by which each appeal or petition was first heard.

The National Archives also contain a record of the petitions brought to the Judicial Committee for leave to appeal since 1917. These petition books record a summary of the details of applications to process appeal actions. From these records one can ascertain the year of the petition, the identity of the petitioner, the respondent and their solicitors, the subject of the petition, and various related observations.

What was not available at the National Archives at the time of writing were the printed cases and records from the appeals to the Judicial Committee.[18] The printed cases and records make up the materials filed by the parties in their presentation of the appeal. As noted earlier, they generally contain a wealth of material not readily available elsewhere and form a significant source of information not only for legal historians but also for economic, social, and political historians. While the broad overview of the proceedings before the Judicial Committee can be ascertained from the holdings at the National Archives, a detailed study of particular case papers and judgments currently needs to be undertaken in other archives. To undertake that study, the researcher needs to board the Tube and travel from leafy Kew in southwest suburbia to the bustle of Russell Square and Euston Road in central London.

Because multiple copies of cases had to be filed with the Judicial Committee's registry, multiple copies continue to exist: another important archive for these records is the British Library on Euston Road in London. The British Library holds the printed cases of appellants and respondents from 1861–2009.[19] Also included in these holdings are the judgments and associated orders in council, combined with the printed records of the proceedings in the courts in which the case originated. Privy Council Registers from the sixteenth to the eighteenth centuries can be consulted electronically from the Reading Rooms (but not yet online). The British Library also holds the records of the India Office and thus, the detailed background to the numerous Indian Appeals to the Judicial Committee.

The Institute for Advanced Legal Studies on Russell Square—part of the University of London—holds a partial set of printed cases and related materials filed by litigants between 1866 and 2008. These materials are to be found in its library. By a happy accident the founding of the Institute coincided with the end of Canadian appeals to the Judicial Committee in 1949 and the Institute purchased a Canadian law library in London which was no longer needed by Canadians. The result is that the holdings of Canadian materials are particularly strong, including not only the materials filed by litigants but also the treatises and legal authorities consulted by the Canadian barristers who travelled to London as they prepared to argue their cases. Intriguingly, the annotations within some of the printed cases appear to be those of the judges who heard the appeals, a matter which provides a unique insight into the basis of the resulting judgments.[20]

Online Resources

Few online sources of Judicial Committee material exist. A prominent exception, though, is the Institute for Advanced Legal Studies' digitization project. The Institute has digitized many of the materials it holds and made these available on the British and Irish Legal Information Institute (BAILLI).[21] Thousands of searchable PDFs of case papers have thus been made available online. In addition, BAILLI contains a complete set of judgments for the Judicial Committee taken from the original records.[22] A number of online articles on the website explain the significance of the Institute's records to the history of the Judicial Committee.

The Privy Council Papers, a research project undertaken by Dr. Nandini Chatterjee and Dr. Charlotte Smith, consists of the case papers for six cases decided between 1869 and 1939.[23] Also included on their online website is a catalogue of metadata for appeals decided between 1792 and 1998. As well, the site comprises a number of significant research articles concerned with the Judicial Committee and its records.

Various other websites offer smaller "snapshots" of portions of the records. These include the first fifty appeals from the East India Company Territories to the Privy Council (1679–1774).[24] In addition, McQuarrie University has posted material pertaining to Australian appeals to the Judicial Committee between 1809 and 1850.[25] Materials regarding the appeals from the thirteen colonies which became the United States are available through the Ames Foundation at Harvard University.[26] The website also contains a wealth of information about the functioning of the Judicial Committee with regard to pre-revolutionary America.

The current state of online sources provides a useful and productive starting point for scholars interested in both the functioning of the Judicial Committee of the Privy Council and the individual cases which appeared before the Judicial Committee. The high quality PDFs of documents available on BAILLI through the Institute of Advanced Legal Studies' digitization project are particularly significant. And there is every indication that the online sources will continue to expand in the next few years. For the impatient, though, the temptation of archival research in London beckons. The records that await her will more than compensate for the length of the journey.

NOTES

1. *British North America Act*, 1867 (UK), 30–31 Vict c 3. In 1982, as a part of the patriation of the constitution, the *British North America Act* was renamed the *Constitution Act, 1867*.

2. A.V. Dicey, *Lectures Introductory to the Study of the Law of the Constitution* (London: Macmillan and Co, 1885), 155.

3. Two prominent exceptions to this pattern of neglect are P.A. Howell, *The Judicial Committee of the Privy Council 1833–1876: Its Origins, Structure, and Development* (Cambridge: Cambridge University Press, 1979), and D.B. Swinfen, *Imperial Appeal: The Debate on the Appeal to the Privy Council, 1833–1986* (Manchester: Manchester University Press, 1987). On the functioning of the modern Judicial Committee, see Jonathan Mance and Jacob Turner, *Privy Council Practice* (Oxford: Oxford University Press, 2017).

4. *Act for the Better Administration of Justice in His Majesty's Privy Council*, 1833 (UK), 3 & 4 Wm IV, c 41.

5. Howell, *Judicial Committee of the Privy Council 1833–1876*, 9–12.

6. *Judicial Committee Act*, 1871 (UK), 34 & 35 Vict, c 91.

7. *Appellate Jurisdiction Act, 1876*, 1876 (UK), 39 & 40 Vict, c 59.

8. *Judicial Committee Amendment Act, 1895*, 1895 (UK), 58 & 59 Vict, c 44.

9. Admiralty was removed in 1876.

10. *Endowed Schools Act, 1873*, 1873 (UK), 36 & 37 Vict, c 87.

11. A Man [F.C. Burnand], "The Judicial Committee," *Punch*, 19 December 1868, 259.

12. Prominent examples are: John Macqueen, *A Practical Treatise on the Appellate Jurisdiction of the House of Lords and the Privy Council* (London: A. Maxwell & Son,

1842); William Macpherson, *The Practice of the Judicial Committee of Her Majesty's Most Honorable Privy Council* (London: Henry Sweet, 1860); William Macpherson, *The Practice of the Judicial Committee of Her Majesty's Most Honorable Privy Council*, 2nd ed (London: Henry Sweet, 1873, available on hathitrust.org); Frank Safford and George Wheeler, *The Practice of the Privy Council in Judicial Matters* [etc.] (London: Sweet and Maxwell, 1901, available on hathitrust.org); Norman Bentwich, *The Practice of the Privy Council in Judicial Matters* [etc.] (London: Sweet & Maxwell, 1912, available on hathitrust.org).

13   The number was reduced to ten after 1908, while it had been greater earlier. Macqueen reports that forty copies had been required for the use of the Judicial Committee in the nineteenth century: Macqueen, *Practical Treatise on the Appellate Jurisdiction of the House of Lords and the Privy Council*, 712.

14   Rule 68, the Judicial Committee Rules 1908, a copy of which can be found in Bentwich, *Practice of the Privy Council*, n. 11.

15   See Catharine MacMillan, "Canadian Cases before the Judicial Committee of the Privy Council," Institute of Advanced Legal Studies, School of Advanced Study, University of London, http://ials.sas.ac.uk/sites/default/files/files/IALS%20Digital/Digitisation%20 projects/JCPC/Canadian_Constitutional_Cases_Comment.pdf.

16   *Edwards v AG of Canada*, [1930] AC 124 (JCPC). The Judicial Committee materials can be viewed on the Judicial Committee of the Privy Council (JCPC) database on BAILII, at http://www.bailii.org/uk/cases/UKPC/1929/1929_86.html.

17   Judicial Committee of the Privy Council, Minutes, PCAP 9, National Archives.

18   Once released, these records will be within the National Archives in Judicial Committee of the Privy Council, Printed Cases in Indian and Colonial Appeals, and Printed Papers in Appeals, PCAP 6. At present, they are held in storage by the Ministry of Justice, following their removal from the original Downing Street registry and are not available for public inspection (if at all).

19   Judicial Committee of the Privy Council Appeal Cases, British Library website, at https://www.bl.uk/collection-guides/judicial-committee-of-the-privy-council-appeal-cases.

20   The annotations thus explain what appears inexplicable in the law reports. See, for example, MacMillan, "The Mystery of Privity: *Grand Trunk Railway Company of Canada* v *Robinson* (1915)," *University of Toronto Law Journal* 65, no. 2 (2015): 1–36. In this case it would appear from the notations and marginal characters that the writer (presumably a panel member) was sufficiently impressed with the importance of Canadian railway capitalism to disregard the rules of privity of contract.

21   See http://ials.sas.ac.uk/digital/digitisation-projects/judicial-committee-privy-council-case-papers/advanced-search and http://www.bailii.org. The Institute has also begun creating a searchable database of the cases it holds—the Privy Council Decisions Documents Directory—available at http://193.62.18.232/dbtw-wpd/textbase/PCDDDsearch.htm.

22   The actual cases were often reported, through the nineteenth century, under titles that vary somewhat, but of which the first volume is *Reports of Cases Argued and*

Determined before the Committees of His Majesty's Most Honourable Privy Council, Appointed to Hear Appeals and Petitions. The first two volumes were compiled by Jerome William Knapp, who was succeeded by Edmund F. Moore after whom the colloquial name, Moore's Privy Council Reports, began to be applied to the series. The Indian cases had their own series, known by titles such as *Reports of Cases Heard and Determined by the Judicial Committee and the Lords of Her Majesty's Most Honourable Privy Council, on Appeal from the Sudder Dewanny Adawlut and High Courts of Judicature in the East Indies.* These volumes, or most of them, can be found online, if enough energy is employed in the hunt, through archive.org, hathitrust.org and Googlebooks. As well, various authors have published collections of JCPC cases from Canada.

23 Privy Council Papers, http://privycouncilpapers.exeter.ac.uk .

24 Privy Council Appeals Data, Anglo-Indian Legal History website, http://angloindianlaw.blogspot.com/p/privy-council-cases-from-india-before.html#data.

25 Decisions of the Superior Courts of New South Wales, 1788–1899, Macquarrie University website, http://www.law.mq.edu.au/research/colonial_case_law/nsw/site/scnsw_home/.

26 Appeals to the Privy Council from the American Colonies: An Annotated Digital Catalogue: Part 1, Ames Foundation, Harvard University, at http://amesfoundation.law.harvard.edu/ColonialAppeals/index.php.

Practising Law in the "Lawyerless" Colony of New France

Alexandra Havrylyshyn

For more than a century, historians have, to varying degrees, clung to the myth that there were no lawyers in New France. This chapter investigates that claim specifically as it applies to early Canada, or the French colony centering around the Saint Lawrence River Valley. The French monarchy laid claim to this geographic space between 1534, when Jacques Cartier first began exploring the Saint Lawrence River, to 1763, when King Louis XV ceded the colony of Canada to Britain as part of the Treaty of Paris to end the Seven Years' War. Today, early Canada is known as the province of Québec. Although French speakers had also settled in the places we now call Maine, New Brunswick, Nova Scotia, and Prince Edward Island, the French monarchy referred to that region as "Acadia," to distinguish it from "Canada."

One of the first historians of the Canadian legal profession confidently declared in 1897 that under the French regime, "il n'y avait pas d'avocats."[1] This historian, indeed, argued that the Canadian legal profession only began to exist with the transition to British rule in 1763.[2] A recent study, published in 1997, dates the origin of the Québec Bar Association to 1779, and fails to explicitly reject the claim that there were no lawyers in New France.[3]

The assertion that there were no lawyers in early Canada, however, rests on a misreading of primary sources. First, the myth depends upon a narrow and anachronistic definition of the lawyer as a university-educated legal expert who belongs to a professional bar association. It is true that in 1678, three members of the colony's highest court, or Sovereign Council, reported that "in this country neither advocates, attorneys, nor practitioners are to be found."[4] Advocates (*avocats*), attorneys (*procureurs*), and practitioners (*praticiens*) might today all be known as lawyers, but in early Canada and in Ancien Régime France they constituted three distinct categories of professional legal representatives. Professional here means both experienced in and paid for one's services. To clump advocates, attorneys, and practitioners all together into the modern Anglo-American category of "lawyer" obscures cultural and historical differences. Indeed, one goal set in this chapter is to elaborate on the meanings of these terms within their socio-historical context and ensure that we impose neither early modern English nor modern categories of legal practice.[5]

To understand what the members of the Québec Sovereign Council meant by the categories of advocate, attorney, and practitioner, I first consult Ancien Régime French legal dictionaries. University-educated advocates ranked above formally-trained attorneys, who in turn ranked above informally-trained legal practitioners. Appreciating the variety of legal representatives in Ancien Régime France expands the definition of "lawyer," thereby helping to dispel the myth that there were no lawyers in New France. Just as historians have identified many legalities in colonial North America, we can identify many modalities of legal representation in New France, where a mixture of paid and unpaid, trained and untrained individuals did the work of representing people in court.[6] This is not to say that the categories of advocate, attorney, and practitioner functioned the same way on the books as they did on the ground, or that they operated in Canada the same way as they did in France. Disentangling these terms, however, allows us to begin to describe more precisely the hierarchy of legal representation in the French colony of Canada.

The myth that there were no lawyers in New France further springs from a misreading of the Sovereign Councillors' remark, in 1678, that "it is even to the advantage of the colony not to allow any [advocates, attorneys, or practitioners]."[7] Historians have wrongly extrapolated from these words that the administration of New France officially banned French lawyers from immigrating to the colony of Canada. However, the primary source merely states a policy recommendation, and should not be taken as evidence of a policy that was actually implemented. The councillors reasoned that the colony would be better off without these various kinds of Ancien Régime legal representatives, not only because of the inexperience of judges and process-servers, but also because of the difficulty of travelling during winter months. As in other colonial spaces, this suggests that judges travelled from place to place to perform their duties.[8] Furthermore, the councillors described the colonial inhabitants as both ignorant and impoverished.[9] Greedy lawyers, the councillors insinuated, could easily persuade colonial inhabitants to undertake frivolous lawsuits, and this would increase the cost of justice in a colony whose administrative resources were already scarce.[10]

In the end, the councillors never did ban advocates, attorneys, or practitioners from the colony.[11] Thus Canada differs from French Caribbean colonies such as Martinique and Saint Domingue, where royal ordinances and colonial decrees explicitly prohibited advocates and attorneys from even making the transatlantic journey.[12] In fact, Canadian authorities explicitly recognized the profession of the attorney in 1693 and 1732.[13] Furthermore, the claim that there were no lawyers in New France fails to account for change over time. Although advocates, attorneys, and practitioners may have been scarce or even absent in 1678, this changed with time. By 1740, one-third of claimants hired someone who identified himself as an attorney or legal practitioner to represent them before the Québec Provost Court.[14]

This chapter, finally, dispels the myth that there were no lawyers in New France by looking beyond the official regime of licensing that operated in France, and instead at what individuals actually did in their communities. While emerging literature on the legal profession sheds light on notaries and attorneys, I focus on the Ancien Régime's lowest-ranking representatives: legal practitioners (*praticiens de droit*).[15] Trial records, notarial records, and sacramental records reveal that at least seventy-six men in early Canada identified as professional, but informally-trained legal practitioners before 1764, the first full year of British rule. Although these lowest-ranking representatives lacked formal training, they professed proficiency in legal practice and were paid for their services. The names of these seventy-six men present further evidence weighing against the claim that lawyers emerged in Canada only with the British Regime. Perhaps the history of early Canadian legal practitioners has been underwritten because many did not settle or die in the colony. Telling their full life stories will require conducting research beyond Canada, whether in the former French Empire or elsewhere. Attorneys and legal practitioners are worth studying because they facilitated access to justice for the ordinary people of early Canada.

The Hierarchy of Ancien Régime Legal Representatives

We must first seek to understand what the Sovereign Council members meant when they referred to the three categories of legal representatives: barristers, attorneys, and practitioners. The Ancien Régime lexicography (or dictionary-writing) movement provides an introduction to this question.[16] Precursors to encyclopedias, Ancien Régime dictionaries described the fundamental elements of various fields of study.[17] Although more encyclopedic than modern dictionaries, Ancien Régime dictionaries are by no means exhaustive.[18] Other sources, such as Jean Imbert's *Institutes de practique en matiere civile et criminelle* (1547), Laurent Bouchel's *Bibliothéque* [sic] *ou Thrésor du droict français* (1615), and Pierre Jacques Brillon's *Dictionnaire des arrests, ou Jurisprudence des Parlemens de France, et autres tribunaux* (1711), more closely resemble textbooks, providing more comprehensive explorations of Ancien Régime jurisprudence and legal practice.[19] Lexicographers, in contrast, intended their works either as starting points for novices, or as reference manuals for experts. Claude-Joseph de Ferrière, for instance, described his dictionary as a "key to law and to practice."[20] His dictionary, therefore, offers an entry point into historical debates surrounding the practice of law in early Canada.

This is not to say that dictionaries should be viewed uncritically. Lexicographers claimed to describe rather than to prescribe; to explain rather than critique; to inform rather than reform.[21] However, it is in their descriptions of the way "the world was" that we can see their biases and, in turn, learn much about the hierarchy of legal representatives in the Ancien Régime. The subjectivities of dictionaries make them rich historical sources—whether for understanding society, norms, or legal institutions and procedures.[22]

I analyze three dictionaries, all of which were widely circulated and frequently reprinted. Containing entries on law as well as many other fields of study, *Le Dictionnaire universel françois et latin* covers the widest breadth of material. Ten editions printed between 1704 and 1771 reflect the dictionary's popularity as a general reference source.[23] Although this dictionary reached the most general audience, it still excluded the largely illiterate public. Because this dictionary synthesized three predecessors, Ancien Régime historians prefer it to other general dictionaries.[24] It emerged out of a fraught political conflict between Catholics and Protestants. When the dictionary's first editor, Abbot Antoine Furetière, died, the Protestant Henri Basnage de Bauval revised the religious entries and republished the dictionary in the Netherlands. Incensed by the changes, certain French Jesuits sought to reclaim the dictionary, restoring the religious entries to fall back in line with Catholicism. For the most part Jesuit authors retained anonymity, but historians know that Robert Simon and Etienne Souciet took leading roles in the first and second editions, respectively. Many laypeople also collaborated.[25] The first two editions of the dictionary were published in the French town of Trévoux, in the province of Ain, near Lyon.[26] The dictionary thus became colloquially known as the *Dictionnaire de Trévoux* and is the only dictionary of the period to bear the name of a place.[27] This dictionary reveals how lettered non-specialists understood the hierarchy of Ancien Régime legal representatives.

A more specialized legal dictionary, Claude-Joseph de Ferrière's *Dictionnaire de droit et de pratique* was published eleven times between 1734 and 1787.[28] The son of an advocate in the Parlement of Paris, Claude-Joseph was a jurist and legal scholar.[29] From such a highly-educated member of the legal profession, we might expect a bias against lower-ranking members. Intending a more specialized audience than did the authors of the Trévoux dictionary, de Ferrière wrote for both the law student and the seasoned advocate.[30] When de Ferrière died in 1747, Antoine-Gaspard Boucher d'Argis took over editing duties. D'Argis also collaborated with the century's two most famous encyclopedists, Denis Diderot and Jean le Rond d'Alembert, on over four thousand entries concerning jurisprudence. The dictionary attained an even more encyclopedic quality.[31]

Finally, I consult one dictionary that postdates the French regime in Canada, Joseph-Nicolas Guyot's *Répertoire universel et raisonné de jurisprudence civile, criminelle, canonique et bénéficiale*, which was first published between 1775 and 1783 and republished in 1784–85. Like Boucher d'Argis, Guyot participated in the encyclopedia movement, for instance publishing the *Encyclopédie méthodique* in 1782. Although published after the British Conquest, the dictionary still signals an Ancien Régime barrister's subjective views of attorneys and practitioners, as Guyot became a barrister in 1748 and gained his professional experience during the Ancien Régime period.[32]

When seeking to understand the rise of the early Canadian legal profession, it makes most sense to consult the editions that appeared as closely as possible to 1740, when the number of litigants who hired professionals to represent them at the Québec Provost Court rose to one in three.[33] Therefore, I rely on the fifth edition of the *Dictionnaire de Trévoux* (1740), the third edition of de Ferrière's *Dictionnaire de droit et de pratique* (1749), and the first edition of Guyot's *Répertoire universel et raisonné* (1775–1783).[34]

In the highly stratified society of France during the Ancien Régime France, the practice of law was a very attractive—if not always successful—means of social mobility. Of course, in an absolutist regime, the king claimed a position at the very top of society's pyramid-like structure. He granted privileges, or private legal agreements, to various subjects. Justice emanated from him; judges and magistrates merely administered justice in his name. Below judges and magistrates, the highest-ranking legal representatives (advocates) could hope to gain honour, dignity, and personal nobility as a result of their profession.[35] Attorneys occupied the next rank down, enjoying comparatively less honour and dignity.[36] Practitioners enjoyed very little status, thus occupying the bottom rung of the hierarchy.[37] A close reading of the dictionaries demonstrates that as we move down the status ladder, levels of education, social prestige, and political power diminish.

Advocates studied law (*droit*) at university. De Ferrière writes, "in order to become an Advocate, one must have obtained a Bachelor's degree in Letters and a License in a Faculty of Law."[38] In response to corrupt law faculties that sold licenses to students, Parisian advocates in 1693 further required that any aspiring advocate complete an apprenticeship (*stage*) of two years and obtain the approval of six senior advocates before beginning legal practice.[39]

Following the medieval Bologna law school model, French universities initially taught only Roman and canon law.[40] This began to change with the Edict of Saint-Germain-en-Laye in April 1679, which required the appointment of professors specializing in French ordinances and customs. This edict required law students to complete five hours of training in French customs each week during the third year of study.[41]

Among legal representatives, barristers claimed exclusive expertise in law, which the *Dictionnaire de Trévoux* defined as a "a principal of that which is just and unjust."[42] We might think of this as substantive, as opposed to procedural, law. Like English barristers, French advocates did not interact directly with clients.[43] Rather, a prospective client first approached an attorney, who in turn consulted with an advocate for substantive legal advice if necessary.[44] Advocates wrote legal briefs and made oral arguments in court.[45] They claimed the exclusive right to orally argue certain kinds of cases, such as appeals, civil requests, royal cases, and questions of the state.[46]

By operating in the domain of "high law," in the language of Shelley Gavigan (chapter 10 of this volume), advocates enjoyed social prestige. The elite sub-stratum of the Third Estate, Parisian advocates were united in their desire to achieve upward social mobility through the practice of law.[47] Ancien Régime lexicographers, similarly, esteemed individuals who had been educated at law schools. Guyot adulated the excellence of the "profession of the Advocate." "In order to merit such a distinguished title," he confidently declared, "one must have talents and qualities which do not at all belong to common men."[48] De Ferrière similarly praised barristers. He warned that young men should not pursue the demanding profession of the advocate unless they knew themselves to be full of genius, probity, and honesty.[49]

Throughout the Ancien Régime period, advocates successfully resisted venality, or the sale of public offices.[50] In this way, advocates differed from attorneys, who needed to either purchase or inherit a venal office before being able to practice law.[51] Under the venal system, the crown monetized the total value of each office. A buyer advanced a partial sum of money to the king in exchange for an office, which was a form of immovable property that could be bequeathed, sold, or even rented out. Three main advantages accompanied the purchase of an office: 1) the right to perform specific governmental functions in the name of the king; 2) a promise by the king to make a payment of 1 percent to 12 percent of the value of the buyer's initial investment if the office-holder ever chose to sell the office; and 3) privileges such as tax exemptions, honour, and dignity. The latter, in particular, led to elevated social status.[52]

Integral to the Ancien Régime socio-economic system, venality was well-established by the sixteenth century.[53] The number of offices for sale ballooned under the reign of King Louis XIV, as the king found himself embroiled in war and desperate for revenue.[54] Near the end of the eighteenth century, the price of offices skyrocketed.[55] Although revolutionaries abolished offices in 1789, the French state today continues to sell some public offices, such as those of notary and process-server.[56] Ancien Régime French aristocrats abhorred venality since it jeopardized a social system in which blood and birth determined status.[57] Historians today appreciate the opportunities for social mobility that venality offered to those not lucky enough to be born into the nobility.[58] As royal officers, nevertheless, attorneys had a duty to represent the French state and were subject to discipline if they failed to do so. The sale of offices to individuals who became attorneys meant they never could enjoy the degree of political autonomy that advocates did.[59]

In a country with a highly censored press, furthermore, legal briefs (*mémoires* and *factums*) produced by advocates were one of the few forms of printed material to evade censorship laws.[60] Advocates not only submitted briefs to the court but circulated them widely, contributing to the birth of a public sphere where opposition to monarchical absolutism could be challenged. High-profile lawsuits or *causes célèbres* soon became as popular as novels.[61] In this way, law courts "were the only part of a free people's education furnished by the old regime."[62] Beginning in 1730, advocates increasingly saw themselves as the spokespersons of the public, becoming the vanguard of reform in the two decades leading up to the French Revolution.[63]

While the three lexicographers explained the superior status of advocates, they made clear that attorneys did not enjoy the same prestige.[64]

Claire Dolan finds in her study of attorneys in the South of France that like advocates, this class of legal representatives used their legal practice as a source of economic and social mobility.[65] However, attorneys occupied significantly lower social positions than advocates. A myriad of ritual acts reflected this professional distinction. For instance, legal procedure required attorneys to bend one knee in court while a barrister was speaking.[66] An edict of 1549 forbade wives of attorneys from wearing the velvet hoods that signified the status of an advocate's wife.[67] Although an attorney traditionally wore a black robe to distinguish himself from laypeople, he tended to own only one. Extremely worn, it had often been passed down from office-holder to office-holder.[68]

Unlike an advocate, an attorney had not necessarily studied law at a university. Guyot explained that "because of his rank, the attorney is not at all obliged to study law."[69] Nevertheless, the state required a professional attorney to be at least twenty-five years old and to have trained with a more senior professional attorney for at least ten years.[70] An aspiring attorney could therefore begin his training at the age of fifteen.

While an advocate specialized in law, an attorney specialized in practice. Ancien Régime lexicographers distinguished law (*droit*) from legal practice (*pratique*). The title of Claude-Joseph de Ferrière's *Dictionnaire de droit et de pratique* implies this distinction, as does the following definition:

> PRACTICE. In Palace terms, the science of preparing a trial according to the forms prescribed by Ordinance, the Customs of the country, & relevant regulations. In this way [Practice] is opposed to Law. An attorney must know practice well, and a Barrister the law.[71]

With an emphasis on legal forms, this excerpt demonstrates that an attorney specialized in legal procedure, while a barrister excelled in knowing legal substance or jurisprudence.

De Ferrière, likewise, described attorneys as "masters of procedure," tasked with guiding barristers on all the legal formalities that differed from jurisdiction to jurisdiction.[72] Under a regulatory *arrêt* of the Parlement de Paris, the state forbade attorneys from making oral arguments in appeal cases and other comparable cases of high law. Attorneys could only defend parties in civil cases where the legal question hinged more around fact and procedure than around jurisprudence.[73] Similarly, the state forbade attorneys from arguing about the guilt or innocence of the accused in criminal trials.[74] However, the state required attorneys to intervene if a procedural question arose during a criminal trial.[75]

Some lexicographers derided attorneys as manipulative and conniving. For instance, Guyot wrote,

> [T]he Advocate, who necessarily holds honour and public esteem in light of his work, would almost never make use of the chicaneries and subtleties characteristic of the Attorney's science. For their profit and for the ruin of their parties, Attorneys assiduously multiply acts and make trials last eternally.[76]

Of course, as an advocate Guyot had an interest in elevating his professional rank. But culturally, he was not alone in ridiculing attorneys for their purported chicanery, as the 1678 Sovereign Council quotation demonstrates. Guyot may have been trying to differentiate himself from members of other, purportedly dishonest, members of his profession. De Ferrière, likewise, warned that attorneys must remember their lower rank within the legal profession: "[An Attorney] must never forget that his function does not at all extend to that which belongs to Advocates. His share is ample enough that he should content himself with it."[77]

The lower rank of attorneys helps explain why early Canadian authorities ultimately tolerated the growth of the legal profession's lower branches.[78] If they were simply paper-pushers, they would be unlikely to disrupt the colony's order. Of course, even procedure is political, but more subtly so than substantive law. Perhaps it was precisely through masquerading as masters of procedure that attorneys proliferated, despite the regime's initial antipathy towards them. In France, attorneys continued to buy and sell offices until the Revolution, at which time they refashioned themselves as *avoués*.[79]

French categories illuminate the social and professional significance of the terms advocate, attorney, and practitioner, but these categories did not apply precisely in Canada because the king prohibited the sale of venal offices in the colony. Nor could French office-holding attorneys import their offices (which were forms of immovable property) to the colony.[80] It is not entirely clear what process replaced the purchase or importation of an attorney's office. Perhaps attorneys and legal practitioners claimed their professional titles in much the same way that individuals in New France claimed noble status: by acting in a way that made their rank believable to the people around them. Perhaps, like the esquires (*écuyers*) and knights (*chevaliers*) who carried around folders of the various legal acts evincing their noble status, attorneys and practitioners clutched these valuable papers as they moved through their daily lives.[81]

Since attorneys and practitioners in New France did not hold offices, the king did not pay them or hold them accountable for representing his interests. Rather, ordinary members of the public paid attorneys and practitioners in New France to represent their interests.[82] In this way, the colony may have been a sort of laboratory for a new, liberal conception of the profession, based not on status or allegiance to a monarch, but on merit and performance in a market economy.[83]

In France, office-holding attorneys received pay from clients for their work, unless they chose to work without compensation for friends or family.[84] Using a legal device called a *procuration*, clients and family members could grant an attorney power to act on their behalf in all legal affairs, or only in one particular legal matter.[85] The *Dictionnaire de Trévoux* explained that the *procuration*, "by which one gives charge to someone or something... makes it as valid, as if one were doing it in person."[86] A good translation for *procuration*, therefore, is power of attorney agreement.

Ordinary members of the public could also empower amateurs to act on their behalf, whether in courts of law or in commercial transactions. Lacking legal training, a one-time attorney was simply a person who, by virtue of a power of attorney agreement, acted on behalf of another, usually a friend or family member. Parties could orally agree on a power of attorney but often agreed in writing. A power of attorney could extend for an unlimited or a limited time period, whether the duration of a person's absence or of a particular legal dispute.[87] Although not office-holding attorneys, ordinary members of the public who held power of attorney agreements performed legal work by representing others in legal disputes.

By looking beyond venal office-holding as a marker of legal representation, we can see that in the colony of New France, a mixture of paid and unpaid, trained and untrained individuals did the work of representing others at law.

Ancien Régime lexicographers observed, perhaps with some surprise, that "even women" could act as attorneys.[88] In the colonial setting of New France, power of attorney agreements were an early form of women's empowerment.[89] Following the Custom of Paris, the law in New France typically deprived a married woman of independent legal capacity, essentially treating her as a minor. With a power of attorney agreement, however, a married woman could temporarily escape these limitations.[90] Exceptionally mobile, men from the town of Québec might sojourn for months or even years at a time. Men travelled east to Louisbourg and across the Atlantic Ocean to France, west to the fur trading Great Lakes region, or south to Louisiana and the French Caribbean. In such instances, men had the option to empower another person to act on their behalf in commerce and at law.[91]

For the period 1700 to 1765 in the town of Québec and its environs, 265 power of attorney agreements with women survive.[92] *Procuratrices* generally represented their husbands, but 20 percent represented their sons, brothers, or even fathers. On rare occasions, men entered into power of attorney agreements with women outside their families.[93] Usually members of the bourgeoisie, *procuratrices* performed a variety of legal and commercial tasks, such as recovering debts, buying and selling real estate, executing wills, and (should it become necessary) representing the absentee in a dispute before a court of law.[94] Although not paid directly, *procuratrices* benefited from power of attorney agreements, which in the patriarch's absence allowed these women to control the family's enterprise, worldly assets, and legal affairs.

The lexicographer de Ferrière claimed that one-time attorneys were especially prevalent in the colonies, which he labeled "subaltern jurisdictions."[95] Because they lacked formal legal training, one-time attorneys were less well-equipped than advocates to challenge the monarchy. This further explains why early Canadian authorities tolerated amateur attorneys while successfully preventing the growth of a vibrant community of advocates.

Legal practitioners occupied the lowest rank of the legal profession.[96] Unlike one-time attorneys, legal practitioners were trained, but informally. The *Dictionnaire de Trévoux* explained that a practitioner, "knows style and usage, the forms, procedures and regulations of the court [and] knows how to draft a contract, to prepare a trial for judgment."[97] De Ferrière and Guyot provided almost identical definitions. Through frequenting legal spaces, practitioners acquired enough familiarity with legal style, usage, procedure, forms, and regulations to claim professional legal knowledge.[98] Advocate-lexicographers deemed practitioners capable of preparing legal papers such as acts and summons.[99] Practitioners faced no explicit requirement to obtain a license or even train under another practitioner for a certain period of time. Many regulations forbade practitioners from signing civil requests and legal briefs. Barristers claimed exclusive ownership over these duties.[100] The law on the books forbade practitioners from acting at law in the name of clients.[101]

Because of their lowly status, practitioners stood to gain from venturing outside of continental France to its newly claimed colonies, where formally trained legal professionals were scarce. In general, the state appointed only highly-educated men as judges. Under the Ordinance of April 1667, practitioners could only step in to judge a case if a jurisdiction lacked both advocates and office-holding attorneys.[102] As Miranda Spieler remarks, "under the monarchy the colonies were extensions of France in a legal sense but governed by protocols distinct from those that applied to domestic territory."[103] Advancing in the legal profession might therefore mean crossing the Atlantic Ocean. Far from the metropole with its rigid on-the-books distinctions among advocates, attorneys, and practitioners, early Canada provided some men with opportunities to achieve upward social mobility through the practice of law.

Early Canadian Legal Practitioners

Legal professionals in colonial Canada indeed followed a different protocol from that of France. Advocates occasionally ventured to the colony to assume senior judicial positions, but for the most part they did not represent clients, either by writing legal briefs or orally arguing cases.[104] Louis-Guillaume Verrier, for instance, studied law in Paris, worked as a barrister in the Parlement of Paris beginning in 1712, and left for Canada in 1728 when an opportunity arose to join the Superior Council.[105] As one of the only advocates in the colony, Verrier offered free lectures on the basics of French jurisprudence to colonial officials and members of the Superior Council, who did not necessarily possess a deep knowledge of the law.[106]

Québec archives provide a promising means to learn much more about legal practitioners. Not only is this the group of Ancien Régime legal representatives that historians understand least well, but they are also a more discrete group than attorneys. Whereas a search for the word *procureur* will mix in instances of the king's attorney, the fiscal attorney, commercial attorneys, and one-time attorneys, the term *praticien de droit* clearly refers to a professional legal representative. First, *Pistard* digitally catalogues records held in the *Bibliothèque et Archives nationales du Québec* ("BAnQ"). First-instance tribunals exercising jurisdiction over towns and seigneuries created records that eventually ended up in BAnQ's TL group. The records of appellate tribunals are found in BAnQ's TP group. During a given legal proceeding, court clerks collected petitions and summons. If a case reached the trial stage, they transcribed oral arguments and testimony. Generally, judges did not issue reasoned judgments but rather ordinances and decrees. In an absolutist regime, judges were less motivated by justifying their opinion than they were by resolving a particular legal dispute. BAnQ archivists have meticulously catalogued the primary sources, including the names of professional attorneys and legal practitioners who appear in the record. We can therefore identify the legal representatives who, some historians have argued, did not "exist" at all in this time period.

Second, notarial records preserve the names of attorneys and practitioners. In both their private and professional lives, attorneys and practitioners visited notaries to record contracts such as marriages, land sales, and power of attorney agreements. In fact, a notarial act was "among the most common forms of the written word that early modern urban populations came into contact with."[107] Notaries did not represent clients in litigation but did review, verify, and record legal agreements. In an era before credit reporting agencies existed, notaries wielded power because they provided potential lenders with information on the creditworthiness of potential borrowers.[108] The state charged notaries with the task of record-keeping, while private clients paid them.[109] In this way, notaries mediated relations between state and society, between literate king and his often illiterate subjects.[110] Notaries kept contracts within their own office (*étude*), but today the province of Québec holds their papers as part of the public record. Archivists initially organized this collection of papers according to the notary who recorded the act, not according to the parties to the contract. This can make research in notarial records cumbersome, for unless one happens to know the name of the notary who recorded the marriage of Jean and Marie, one cannot easily find their marriage contract. To address this problem, the group *Société de recherche historique Archiv-Histo* created a database called *Parchemin*, which organizes notarial records between 1626 and 1801 by the names of the parties. The *Parchemin* database includes various identifiers which the original record uses to describe the parties. Hence, by simply searching for the term *praticien de droit*, we can uncover more names to counter the myth that there were no lawyers in early Canada.

Third, church records provide a glimpse into the social lives of attorneys and practitioners. In a heavily Catholic society, clergy recorded life events such as births, marriages, and deaths. The names of attorneys and practitioners appear when they were involved in baptisms (as parents or godparents), marriages, and deaths. Although produced as religious records, these documents are also rich sources for social historians. The *Programme de recherche en démographie historique* (PRDH), initiated by the *Université de Montréal*, indexes Catholic parish records of baptism, marriage, and burial between 1621–1849. In using this catalogue, of course, we must take into consideration what groups it excludes. First, it generally excludes non-Catholics who did not participate in the sacraments, although PRDH has recently added Protestant marriages for this entire period. Second, the catalogue excludes any individual who did not stay in the colony long enough to partake in such ceremonies. We may tend to imagine societies of long ago as being rather stationary, but Atlantic literature demonstrates that the early Canadian population was indeed quite mobile.[111] Legal practitioners itinerated not only throughout the French Atlantic world, but also dabbled in various occupations within the legal profession, as discussed below.

Together, all of these archives provide evidence weighing against the argument that professional legal representatives arose only with the

British regime. As French lexicographers instructed their readers, the law forbade lowly practitioners from performing the functions of advocates or office-holding attorneys. In early Canada, however, men who identified as legal practitioners frequently entered into power of attorney agreements, gave clients legal advice, and represented them in court when civil disputes arose.[112]

The humblest of legal representatives, practitioners were also the least threatening to an absolutist regime, which helps to explain their growth as a community in a colony whose administrators had initially expressed antipathy towards legal representatives. The appended table (8.1) presents the names of seventy-six men who identified as practitioners of law well before the end of the Seven Years' War. Their names, along with the denotation "praticien de droit," appear in records held either in *Pistard*, *Parchemin*, or PRDH. These seventy-six names alone present powerful evidence to rebut the claim that there were no lawyers in New France. Widening the lens of inquiry illuminates a longer, more francophone history of the practice of law in Canada.

One of the most striking features of this group is their permeability among ranks and roles. Ancien Régime lexicographers distinguished attorneys from practitioners in terms of their social rank and day-to-day tasks, but Québec's archival sources demonstrate a different reality. In the absence of venal offices, the distinctions between attorneys and practitioners blurred. When a practitioner entered into a power of attorney agreement, he became known as the attorney of that person. Although not an office-holding attorney, the practitioner differed from a one-time attorney in that he was a repeat player. In the 1740s, when the number of litigants hiring a legal representative grew rapidly, men like Jacques Nouette de la Poufellerie, Pierre Poirier, and Jean-Claude Panet frequently entered the record as "praticien, son procureur."[113] Court clerks identified them as practitioners, sometimes also specifying whose attorney they were at that time. As shown in the appended table below, at least twenty legal practitioners at some point bore the title of attorney not by buying a royal office, but by entering into a power of attorney agreement with an ordinary person in New France.

As in early Louisiana, where anyone with a smattering of legal knowledge might flex their skills to practise legal representation, individuals in early Canada also floated among different kinds of legal roles.[114] For instance, notaries (*notaires*), process-servers (*huissiers*), and court clerks (*greffiers*) at times put themselves forward as practitioners. Pierre Cabzie even acted as a judge in Montréal in 1703, yet still identified three years later as a practitioner. This permeability complicates the hierarchy that Ancien Régime lexicographers dictated.

Although Ancien Régime lexicographers purported to describe clear delineations among advocates, attorneys, and practitioners, they did not acknowledge gradations among legal practitioners. In the absence of a rigid line between attorneys and legal practitioners, the colony developed distinctions among legal practitioners. While some men merely called themselves practitioners, others claimed the titles of senior practitioner (*ancien praticien*) or master practitioner (*maître praticien*). As Table 8.1 shows, at least eight men were designated senior practitioners. Because the title "master practitioner" appeared only once in this search, this was probably the highest rank.[115] Ancien Régime protocol dictated that the most experienced practitioners could fill the roles of even higher legal officials.[116] For instance, the senior practitioner Jean-Baptiste Adhémar of Montréal (who was also a notary) acted as a substitute for the Royal Prosecutor in a 1743 criminal trial.[117] Similarly, the senior practitioner of the town of Québec, Christophe-Hilarion Dulaurent, rendered a judgment in a 1750 civil dispute between Germain Chalifou and Jean-Baptiste Savard, two inhabitants of the seigneurie Notre-Dame-des-Anges.[118] Early Canada provided an escape from certain Ancien Régime rigidities, but not without recreating its own distinct hierarchy of legal representatives. The importance of rank and status persisted, even in the colony.[119]

Practitioners did not enjoy the elite status of colonial administrators or magistrates, but practising law helped them secure a social rank above the general population. In a largely illiterate society, legal practitioners' literacy alone distinguished them from most inhabitants. In 1750, only 43 percent of residents in the town of Québec could sign their names. An even smaller proportion of inhabitants would have been able to use written words to communicate ideas.[120] Combining written words with technical legal knowledge, practitioners wielded powerful tools.

Neither practitioners nor attorneys generally belonged to the nobility. First, members of the nobility enjoyed a higher social rank. Second, the crown exempted members of the nobility from taxation.[121] In New France, the second advantage was meaningless, because the crown exempted all colonists from taxation.[122] In France, one could prove nobility by producing a letter from the king granting noble status, by exercising a certain public function for a prescribed period, or simply by belonging to a family that had been known as noble for such a long time that no one would dare question it.[123]

Individuals could and did claim noble status without actually possessing any of these three means of proof. Because all colonists were exempt from taxation, however, colonial administrators had little incentive to clamp down on the *faux-noble* problem.[124] In practice, consistent designation as an *écuyer* or *chevalier* sufficed to secure the social advantages of noble status in early Canada.[125] For example, when the senior practitioner Jean-Baptiste Decoste de Letancour's son married in 1759, the notary recognized both him and his son as noble when he followed both of their names with the term *écuyer* (literally meaning esquire) in the marriage contract.[126] This designation was rare among practitioners, but not unheard of.

Other practitioners probably integrated themselves into the bourgeois class through marriage and land purchase. For instance, the practitioner Pierre Panet married a daughter of the bourgeois family, Trefflet dit Rautot.[127] The son of a bourgeois gentleman himself, the practitioner Jacques Bourdon bought a piece of land from his father-in-law one year after marrying.[128]

In addition to shifting upwards through social ranks, practitioners relocated more than one would have expected given the difficulty of travel in this period. PRDH records provide a window into the geographic mobility of legal practitioners. At least forty-seven practitioners migrated to the colony from France, and no less than fifteen were from Paris. One practitioner even found his way to Canada from his homeland in Portugal.

An Atlantic perspective, furthermore, raises the question as to where these legal practitioners died. The historiography of early Canada has largely privileged the study of those who came and stayed, over the study of those who came and left. Many practitioners did marry and have children in the colony, signifying their rootedness there. However, limiting our study of practitioners to founding families would be a mistake, because the itinerary of leaving France to settle and procreate in Québec was not necessarily typical of legal practitioners. At present, we can only determine that forty-six of seventy-six practitioners died in the colony. The others may have died in France, in other French colonies, or elsewhere altogether. In a new setting, they might have performed different legal work. Gabriel Lambert, for example, refashioned himself as a notary and royal surveyor in Guadeloupe, where he likely died.[129]

Long before the formal establishment of the Québec bar association, legal practitioners in the French colony along the Saint Lawrence River Valley represented individuals in their civil disputes. A critical examination of Ancien Régime dictionaries first disentangles the terms advocate, attorney, and practitioner, helping us grasp the many modalities of legal practice in the early modern world. The superior status of the advocate helps explain why colonial authorities tolerated the development of the legal profession's lower branches, whose members were less well-equipped in terms of legal knowledge, social prestige, and political power to overtly challenge an absolutist regime. Second, Québec's archives—whether trial records, notarial records, or parish registers—present powerful evidence against the claim that there were no lawyers in early Canada. In addition to providing the names of seventy-six men who identified as legal practitioners before 1764, this chapter shows that legal practitioners were more mobile, both professionally and geographically, than we might expect. Finally, the mobility of members of this group explains why their history has been underwritten.

TABLE 8.1 Practitioners of Law in New France, 1670–1763

YEAR	NAME	ALTERNATIVE PROFESSIONAL IDENTIFIER	BIRTHPLACE	CHILDREN BORN IN COLONY	DIED IN THE COLONY
1670	Gosset Buisson, Jean-Baptiste	Huissier au Conseil souverain	France	Yes	Unknown
1672	Bourdon, Jacques		France	Yes	Yes
1678	Marnay, Jean		Unknown	Unknown	Unknown
1681	Genaple (Belfond), François	Huissier et procureur (1681), notaire, procureur général (1707)	France (Paris)	Yes	Yes
1681	Hubert, René	Huissier au Conseil souverain et procureur fiscal (1684), greffier et procureur (1701)	France (Paris)	Yes	Yes
1681	Métru, Nicolas	Huissier de la Prévôté de Québec (1691)	Unknown	Unknown	Unknown
1681	Roger, Guillaume	Procureur (1680), juge de la seigneurie Notre-Dame-des-Anges (1688)	France (Paris)	Yes	Yes
1682	Marquis, Charles	Huissier et procureur (1694), procureur (1697)	France	Yes	Yes
1683	Petit, Jean	Huissier de Montréal (1712)	Unknown	Unknown	Yes
1688	Dupuis, Guillaume		Unknown	Unknown	Unknown
1688	Prieur (dit Cusson), Joseph	Huissier (1702), procureur du Roi (1704)	France	Yes	Yes
1689	De Lamarre, Jean		Unknown	Unknown	Unknown
1689	Perrot (Perrault), Charles		Unknown	Unknown	Unknown
1693	Quesnevillé, Jean		France	Yes	Yes
1694	Pruneau, Georges	Huissier (1700), commis procureur du roi (1703)	Unknown	Unknown	Unknown
1695	Barbel, Jacques	Procureur (1711), notaire en la Prévôté de Québec (1714)	France	Yes	Yes
1697	Galipau (Galipeau on PRDH), Antoine		France	Yes	Yes

TABLE 8.1 (*continued*)

YEAR	NAME	ALTERNATIVE PROFESSIONAL IDENTIFIER	BIRTHPLACE	CHILDREN BORN IN COLONY	DIED IN THE COLONY
1699	Barette (Baret), Guillaume		France	Unknown	Yes
1699	Corda, Jérôme		France (Paris)	Yes	Unknown
1699	Rivét (Rivet Cavelier), Pierre	*Procureur* (1701), *notaire royal en la Prévôté de* Québec (1710), *greffier en chef de la Prévôté de Québec* (1714)	France	Yes	Yes
1700	Genouzeau (Genouseau, Jenouzeau), Michel		Unknown	Unknown	Yes
1701	Lepailleur, Michel	*Procureur* (1699), *juge prévôt* (1702), *notaire royal de l'île de Montréal* (1711),	France (Paris)	Yes	Yes
1702	Meschin, Jean	Huissier audiencier de la *Prévôté de Québec* (1711)	France	Unknown	Yes
1703	Cognet (Coignet), Jean (-Baptiste)	*Huissier au Conseil supérieur de Québec* (1723)	France	Yes	Yes
1703	L'aperche (Laperche), Jean	*Procureur* (1702)	France	Yes	Yes
1703	Huyet (Huguet), Pierre	*Procureur* (1705)	Unknown	Unknown	Unknown
1704	Rageot (de Beaurivage?), François	*Protonotaire* (1704)	Québec	Yes	Yes
1705	Fillieu (Filleul) (Fily), Pierre		France (Paris)	Yes	No
1706	Cabzie (Cabazié), Pierre	*Juge de Montréal* (1703) *huissier de Montréal* (1712), *ancien praticien* (1717)	France	Yes	Yes
1706	Lefebvre, Edmond		France	Yes	Yes
1707	De La Cettière (LaCetière), Florent	*Procureur* (1703)	Unknown	Unknown	Unknown
1707	Lambert, Gabriel (*fils*)	*Procureur* (1719)	Québec	Unknown	No
1708	Bega (Bégat), Jacques		France (Paris)	Yes	No

TABLE 8.1 (*continued*)

YEAR	NAME	ALTERNATIVE PROFESSIONAL IDENTIFIER	BIRTHPLACE	CHILDREN BORN IN COLONY	DIED IN THE COLONY
1710	Gaillard, Guillaume	*Conseiller* (1713), *Procureur* (1719)	France	Yes	Yes
1711	Adhémar (St-Martin), Jean-Baptiste	*Notaire royal de Montréal* (1743)	Unknown	Yes	Yes
1715	(De) Dessalines, Jean-Baptiste	*Procureur fiscal* (1730)	France	Yes	Yes
1716	De Bled, Charles	*Procureur* (1712)	Unknown	Unknown	Unknown
1718	David, Jacques		Québec	Yes	Yes
1725	Dulaurent, Christophe-Hilarion	*Procureur et notaire* (1734), *protonotaire* (1734–1759), *notaire* (1750)	France	Unknown	Yes
1727	Chetivau de Rouselle (Chetinau de Roussel), Claude		Unknown	Unknown	Unknown
1728	Jacquet, Pierre		France	Unknown	Yes
1730	Balthazar Pollet (Paulet), Arnould	*Notaire royal en la Prévôté de Québec* (1734)	Unknown	Unknown	Unknown
1735	Mercier, Pierre-Simon		France (Paris)	Yes	Yes
1739	Girouard (Giroire), Antoine	*Ancien praticien* (1746)	France	Yes	Yes
1739	Simonet (Simonnet), François	*Protonotaire* (1737-1778), *ancien praticien* (1757)	France	Yes	Yes
1740	Thibault, François		Unknown	Unknown	Unknown
1740	Nouette, Jacques de la Poufellerie	*Procureur* (1741)	France (Paris)	Unknown	Unknown
1741	Canac, Marc-Antoine (*père*)		Québec	Yes	Yes
1741	Poirier, Pierre	*Procureur* (1741)	France	Yes	Unknown
1743	Ferrand (Ferrant), Jacques		Unknown	Unknown	Unknown
1743	Panet, (Jean)-Claude	*Procureur* (1741)	France (Paris)	Yes	Yes

TABLE 8.1 (*continued*)

YEAR	NAME	ALTERNATIVE PROFESSIONAL IDENTIFIER	BIRTHPLACE	CHILDREN BORN IN COLONY	DIED IN THE COLONY
1745	Esnard, Jean		Unknown	Unknown	Yes
1745	Guillet (dit Chaumont), Nicolas-Auguste	Notaire royal et ancien praticien de la juridiction royale de Montréal (1745)	France	Yes	Yes
1745	Guyard (Guyart), Jean-Baptiste (de Fleury?)	Ancien praticien (1765)	France	Yes	Yes
1745	Pinguet (dit Bellevue) Nicolas		Unknown	Unknown	Unknown
1746	Leproust (Le Proust-Prou-Leproulx), Jean	Notaire (1746)	France	Yes	No
1748	Lanoullier des Granges, Paul-Antoine-François	Juge prévôt (1758)	France (Paris)	Yes	No
1748	Laurent Lortie Coquot, Jean-Baptiste	Maître praticien et procureur fiscal de la Prévôté de Notre-Dame-des-Anges (1748)	Québec	Yes	Yes
1748	Turpin, (Antoine)-Charles	Ancien praticien (1748)	France (Paris)	Yes	Unknown
1749	Saulquin (Solquin St-Joseph), Joseph	Huissier royal et praticien de la juridiction royale de Montréal (1749)	France	Yes	Unknown
1750	Decharnay (De Charnay), Jean-Baptiste	Procureur (1750), procureur et notaire royal (1759)	France	Yes	Yes
1751	Hastier (dit Desnoyers), Pierre		Unknown	Unknown	Unknown
1752	Cassegrain (Casgrain), Jean		France	Unknown	Yes
1752	Lévesque, Nicolas-Charles-Louis		France	Yes	Yes
1752	Masson, François		France	Unknown	Yes
1753	Merle, Jean		Unknown	Unknown	Unknown
1754	Panet, Pierre	Notaire et procureur (1755)	France (Paris)	Yes	Yes

TABLE 8.1 (*continued*)

YEAR	NAME	ALTERNATIVE PROFESSIONAL IDENTIFIER	BIRTHPLACE	CHILDREN BORN IN COLONY	DIED IN THE COLONY
1754	Saillant, Antoine (Jean)	*Notaire et procureur* (1753)	France (Paris)	Yes	Yes
1757	Hianveu (Hyianveu) (Lafrance), Mathieu	*Greffier de la juridiction de Notre-Dame-des-Anges* (1759)	France	Yes	Yes
1758	Daunay (Daunais), Nicolas-Charles	*Substitut du procureur fiscal* (1758)	France	Unknown	Yes
1758	Giniée, François		Unknown	Unknown	Unknown
1759	Decoste (de Letancour) (De Moussel), Jean-Baptiste	*Huissier audiancier au siège de la juridiction royale de Montréal* (1742); *ancien praticien* (1759)	France (Paris)	Yes	Yes
1759	L'hoste, Laurent-Vincent		Unknown	Unknown	Unknown
1762	Amiot (Villeneuve), Jean-Baptiste	*Ancien praticien* (1749)	Québec	Yes	Yes
1763	Dumergue, François	*Huissier au Conseil supérieur de Québec* (1758)	France	Unknown	Yes
1763	Perrot (Perrault), François		Unknown	Unknown	Unknown
(1670–1763)	**Total: Seventy-six**	**At least forty-six fulfilled alternative professional roles**	**At least forty-seven migrated from France**	**At least forty-four had children in the colony**	**Forty-six for certain died in the colony**

NOTES

I would like to thank Guillaume Aubert, Lyndsay Campbell, Catherine Desbarats, Philip Girard, Allan Greer, Julia Lewandoski, Mélanie Méthot, Ted McCoy, and Christopher Tomlins for their valuable feedback on earlier drafts, and Jessie Sherwood for archival help.

1   Joseph-Edmond Roy, *L'ancien Barreau au Canada* (Montréal: C. Théoret, 1897), 20.

2   Roy, *L'ancien Barreau*, 28.

3   Christine Veilleux, *Aux origines du Barreau québécois, 1779–1849* (Sillery, QC: Septentrion, 1997), 16–17.

4   *Édits, ordonnances royaux, déclarations et arrêts du Conseil d'État du Roi concernant le Canada*, 95. All translations are my own. Established in 1663, the Québec Sovereign Council recorded royal ordinances and issued regulatory rulings (*arrêts* or decrees). The Québec Sovereign Council controlled finances, the fur trade, and commerce, and appointed judges, judicial officers, and notaries. See André Vachon, *The Administration of New France, 1627–1760* (Toronto: University of Toronto Press, 1970), http://admin.biographi.ca/en/special.php?project_id=49&p-16. For sovereign councils in France, see Serge Dauchy and Véronique Demars-Sion, *La justice dans le Nord: trois siècles d'histoire, 1667–1967* (Lille: Centre d'histoire judiciaire, 2001).

5   Translating the three terms *avocat*, *procureur*, and *praticien* into English is not a simple task. A standard translation for *avocat* within French legal history is barrister. To be sure, there were similarities between French *avocats* and English barristers, who did not busy themselves with procedural paperwork leading up to trial. However, newer literature reveals inadequacies with this translation. To modern ears, the term "barrister" might imply membership in a national bar association, but Hervé Leuwers demonstrates that the term *barreau français* only emerged in the 1760s, and that the regional *ordres d'avocats* were distinct from what eventually became the national French bar association: Hervé Leuwers, *L'invention du barreau français, 1660-1830: la construction nationale d'un groupe professionnel* (Paris: École des hautes études en sciences sociales, 2006). The translation of *avocat* as barrister is especially problematic in the Canadian context, as both primary and secondary sources reveal. The best reference point is an early Canadian translation of the word *avocat* into English. When Governor James Murray encountered legal representatives in Québec at the very beginning of the British regime in 1764, he recognized a difference between the barristers of England and the *avocats* of Québec. In the same document, Murray referred to advocates and barristers as two distinct groups. "Ordinance of September 17, 1764, establishing Civil Courts," in Adam Shortt and Arthur G. Doughty, eds., *Documents Relating to the Constitutional History of Canada, 1759-1791* (Ottawa: Dawson, 1907), 149–50. Staying close to the primary source, authoritative sources within Canadian legal history translate *avocat* as advocate and not as barrister: Philip Girard, Jim Phillips, and R. Blake Brown, *A History of Law in Canada*, vol. 1: *Beginnings to 1866* (Toronto: University of Toronto Press, 2018), 267–74; Vachon, *The Administration of New France*. These secondary sources also translate *procureur* as attorney and *praticien* as practitioner. Although the English legal system distinguished between an attorney who practised in common law courts and a solicitor who practised

in chancery courts, the absence of chancery courts in early French Canada makes attorney a better alternative than solicitor as a translation for *procureur*.

6   In "Many Legalities of Colonization: A Manifesto of Destiny for Early American Legal History," in *The Many Legalities of Early America*, ed. Christopher L. Tomlins and Bruce H. Mann (Chapel Hill: University of North Carolina Press for the Omohundro Institute of Early American History and Culture, 2001), Christopher Tomlins reconceives of law not as narrowly defined doctrine, but as more encompassing legality. His essay inspired a generation of colonial historians to move away from traditional sources of legal history (such as printed sources and appellate cases) towards sources of law in action (such as trial manuscripts and local records). At the local level, historians have found legality where law was absent or inchoate.

7   *Édits, ordonnances royaux, déclarations et arrêts du Conseil d'État du Roi concernant le Canada*, 95.

8   As Martha McNamara has shown, purpose-built structures devoted exclusively to judicial proceedings did not emerge in Massachusetts until the late eighteenth-century. These buildings, in turn, enhanced the standing of the legal profession: *From Tavern to Courthouse: Architecture and Ritual in American Law* (Baltimore: Johns Hopkins University Press, 2004). Similarly, Laura Edwards finds that in the post-revolutionary Carolinas, there was still "no single location for law": *The People and their Peace: Legal Culture and the Transformation of Inequality in the Post-Revolutionary South* (Chapel Hill: University of North Carolina Press, 2009), 67. Rather, judges travelled to litigants who gathered in multi-purpose public buildings such as taverns. William Eccles dates the construction of a purpose-built *Palais de Justice* in the town of Québec to 1689: *Government of New France* (Ottawa: Canadian Historical Association, 1971), 11. Perhaps this much earlier date helps explain the relatively early appearance of professional legal representatives in early Canada.

9   *Édits, ordonnances royaux, déclarations et arrêts du Conseil d'État du Roi concernant le Canada*, 95.

10   On the scarcity of administrative resources, see Eccles, *Government of New France*. Eccles, who accepted the myth that lawyers were forbidden from practicing in the colony, viewed the ban as a good thing because of the "rapacity of the legal profession" (15).

11   Jean-Philippe Garneau draws this conclusion based on a thorough reading of the royal edicts, ordinances, declarations, and decrees in, "Devenir porte-parole durant l'ère des révolutions: le lent et (parfois) difficile parcours des avocats du Québec colonial," *Criminocorpus: revue hypermédia* (novembre 2016), 2–3, http://journals.openedition.org/criminocorpus/3391.

12   For citations to the relevant decrees of 1713, 1766, and 1776, see Charles Bataillard and Ernest Nusse, *Histoire des procureurs et des avoués, 1483–1816*, vol. 2 (Paris: Librairie Hachette et Cie, 1882), 92. This is not to say that this ban was followed. A class of legal representatives emerged in response to popular demand, especially by local merchants: Bataillard and Nusse, *Histoire des procureurs et des avoués*, 92–93.

13   Garneau, "Devenir porte-parole durant l'ère des révolutions," 3, 22.

14   John Dickinson, *Justice et justiciables: la procédure civile à la Prévôté de Québec, 1667-1759* (Québec: Les Presses de l'Université Laval, 1982), 84. Dickinson bases this conclusion on his sample study of civil records from the Québec Provost Court, which served as a court of first instance for the town of Québec and an appeals court for surrounding seigneurial courts in the colony.

15   The best examinations of legal professionals in early Canadian courts include Claire Dolan, "Regards croisés sur les auxiliaires de justice, du Moyen Âge au XXe siècle," in *Entre justice et justiciables : les auxiliaires de justice du Moyen Âge au XXe siècle*, ed. Claire Dolan (Québec: Presses de l'Université Laval, 2005), 15-32; Donald Fyson, "Judicial Auxiliaries Across Legal Regimes: From New France to Lower Canada," in Dolan, *Entre justice et justiciables*, 383-403; Garneau, "Devenir porte-parole durant l'ère des révolutions"; Jean-Philippe Garneau, "Appartenance ethnique, culture juridique et représentation devant la justice civile de Québec à la fin du XVIIIe siècle," in Dolan, *Entre justice et justiciables*, 405-24; David Gilles, "Le notariat canadien face à la Conquête anglaise: l'exemple des Panet," in *Les praticiens du droit du Moyen Âge à l'époque contemporaine: approches prosopographiques (Belgique, Canada, France, Italie, Prusse)*, ed. Vincent Bernaudeau (Rennes: Presses universitaires de Rennes, 2014), 189-207; Girard, Phillips, and Brown, *History of Law in Canada*, 112-16; Louis Lavallée, "La vie et la pratique d'un notaire rural sous le régime français: le cas de Guillaume Barette, notaire à La Prairie entre 1709-1744," *Revue d'histoire de l'Amérique française* 47, no. 4 (1994) : 499-519; André Vachon, *Histoire du notariat canadien, 1621-1960* (Québec: Presses de l'Université Laval, 1962).

16   The classic background source on this movement is Bernard Quemada, *Les Dictionnaires du français moderne, 1539-1863* (Paris: Dider, 1968).

17   On dictionaries as precursors to encyclopedias, see Luigi Delia, "L'encyclopédisme du *Dictionnaire de droit et de pratique* de Ferrière," in *Les Encyclopédies: construction et circulation du savoir de l'Antiquité à Wikipédia*, ed. Martine Groult (Paris: L'Harmattan, 2011), 331. On the ambitions of lexicographers, see Isabelle Turcan, "Les panneaux de l'exposition 'Trésors de la Principauté de Dombes' à Trévoux du 18 au 25 septembre 2004," in *Quand le* Dictionnaire de Trévoux *rayonne sur l'Europe des Lumières*, ed. Isabelle Turcan (Paris: Harmattan, 2009), 81.

18   Turcan, "Les panneaux de l'exposition 'Trésors de la Principauté de Dombes,'" 82.

19   Jean Imbert, *Les institutes de practique en matiere civile et criminelle* [etc.] (Paris: Jean Ruelle, 1547); Laurent Bouchel, *La Bibliothéque ou Thrésor du droict français* (Paris: D. Langlois, 1615); Pierre Jacques Brillon, *Dictionnaire des arrests, ou Jurisprudence universelle des Parlemens de France, et autres tribunaux* [etc.] (Paris: G. Cavelier, 1711); Delia, "L'encyclopédisme du *Dictionnaire de droit et de pratique* de Ferrière," 336. As these dictionary titles make clear, seventeenth- and eighteenth-century authors did not share uniform practices around spelling or capitalization. In this chapter, I have not updated orthography or capitalization to modern standards, preferring instead to preserve the authenticity of the primary sources.

20   Delia, "L'encyclopédisme du *Dictionnaire de droit et de pratique* de Ferrière," 333.

21   Delia, "L'encyclopédisme du *Dictionnaire de droit et de pratique* de Ferrière," 335.

22   Delia, "L'encyclopédisme du *Dictionnaire de droit et de pratique* de Ferrière," 329-30.

23   Turcan, "Les panneaux de l'exposition 'Trésors de la Principauté de Dombes,'" 74.

24   The predecessors are: Pierre Richelet's *Dictionnaire François* (1679–1680), Antoine Furetière's *Dictionnaire Universel* (1690), and the *Dictionnaire de l'Académie française* (1694): Wionet, "L'esprit des langues dans le *Dictionnaire universel de Trévoux* (1704–1771)," 284; Turcan, "Les panneaux de l'exposition 'Trésors de la Principauté de Dombes,'" 72.

25   Turcan, "Les panneaux de l'exposition 'Trésors de la Principauté de Dombes,'" 73.

26   Turcan, "Les panneaux de l'exposition 'Trésors de la Principauté de Dombes,'" 71.

27   Michel Raymond, "Le mot du président de l'association Astrid et maire de la ville de Trévoux," in Turcan, *Quand le* Dictionnaire de Trévoux *rayonne*, 5.

28   Delia, "L'encyclopédisme du *Dictionnaire de droit et de pratique* de Ferrière," 343.

29   Delia, "L'encyclopédisme du *Dictionnaire de droit et de pratique* de Ferrière," 330–31.

30   Delia, "L'encyclopédisme du *Dictionnaire de droit et de pratique* de Ferrière," 333.

31   Delia, "L'encyclopédisme du *Dictionnaire de droit et de pratique* de Ferrière," 333.

32   Von Schulte, "Guyot, Joseph-Nicolas," in *Die Geschichte der Quellen und Literatur des canonischen Rechts von Gratian bis auf die Gegenwart*, vol. 3 (Graz: Akademische Druck- und Verlagsanstalt, 1956, originally published in 1875), 650.

33   Dickinson, *Justice et justiciables*, 84.

34   *Dictionnaire universel françois et latin, vulgairement appellé Dictionnaire de Trévoux* (Nancy: P. Antoine, 1740) [hereafter *Dictionnaire de Trévoux*]; Claude-Joseph de Ferrière, ed. *Dictionnaire de droit et de pratique, contenant l'explication des termes de droit, d'ordonnances, de coutumes & de pratique* (Paris: Brunet, 1749) [hereafter *Dictionnaire de droit et de pratique*]; Joseph-Nicolas Guyot, ed. *Répertoire universel et raisonné de jurisprudence civile, criminelle, canonique et bénéficiale* (Paris: J. D. Dorez, 1775–1783) [hereafter *Répertoire universel et raisonné*]. Although the *Dictionnaire de droit et de pratique* was published in Paris in 1740, this edition has not been fully digitized and therefore is not easily accessible.

35   Personal nobility did not transfer inter-generationally. Leuwers, *L'invention du barreau français, 1660–1830*, 160.

36   There is some confusion among the works reviewed here as to whether attorneys enjoyed dignity or honour, but all of them agree that attorneys held less social and economic status than advocates. Referring to a "ladder of honorabilities" (échelle des honorabilités), Robert Descimon writes that exercising the office of a *procureur* in the Châtelet de Paris from the sixteenth to the eighteenth centuries could eventually lead to honour but never to dignity: Robert Descimon, "Les auxiliaires de justice du Châtelet de Paris: aperçus sur l'économie du monde des offices ministériels (XVIe-XVIIIe siècles)," in Dolan, *Entre justice et justiciables*, 324. In contrast, Claire Dolan refers to a "dignity ladder" (échelle de dignité), emphasizing that when an attorney sold his office, he would lose whatever temporary dignity he had gained by buying it. However, she stresses that in reality having practised law as an attorney would promote that individual's status within the community: Claire Dolan, *Les procureurs du Midi dans l'Ancien Régime* (Rennes: Presses universitaires de Rennes, 2012), 259–60.

37 Dolan, *Les procureurs du Midi*, 39.

38 De Ferrière, *Dictionnaire de droit et de pratique*, I: 197.

39 David Bell, *Lawyers and Citizens: The Making of a Political Elite in Old Regime France* (New York: Oxford University Press, 1994), 34.

40 Marie Seong-Hak Kim, "Civil Law and Civil War: Michel de l'Hôpital and the Ideals of Legal Unification in Sixteenth-Century France," *Law and History Review* 28, no. 3 (2010): 792. For a general background on the dissemination of the eleventh-century Bologna law school model throughout western Europe, see Manlio Bellomo, *The Common Legal Past of Europe: 1000–1800*, trans. Lydia G. Cochrane (Washington, D.C.: Catholic University of America Press, 1995), 55–71 and Franz Wieacker, *A History of Private Law in Europe with Particular Reference to Germany*, trans. Tony Weir (New York: Oxford University Press, 1995).

41 Jean-Louis Thireau, *Introduction historique au droit*, 3rd ed. (Paris : Flammarion, 2009), 251–52.

42 *Dictionnaire de Trévoux*, II: 1583.

43 Girard, Phillips, and Brown, *History of Law in Canada*, 272.

44 David Bell, *Lawyers and Citizens*, 30.

45 De Ferrière, *Dictionnaire de droit et de pratique*, I: 197.

46 De Ferrière, *Dictionnaire de droit et de pratique*, I: 197; II: 590.

47 Bell, *Lawyers and Citizens*, 29–38.

48 Guyot, *Répertoire universel et raisonné*, IV: 53.

49 De Ferrière, *Dictionnaire de droit et de pratique*, I: 200.

50 Bell, *Lawyers and Citizens*, 38–40.

51 This became a formal requirement under the Edict of 1620. See Bataillard and Nusse, *Histoire des procureurs et des avoués*, 92.

52 David Bien, "Les offices, les corps et le crédit d'État: l'utilisation des privilèges sous l'Ancien Régime," *Annales: Histoire, Sciences Sociales* 43, no. 2 (March-April 1988): 379–404.

53 William Doyle, *Venality: The Sale of Offices in Eighteenth-Century France* (New York: Oxford University Press, 1996), 3.

54 Doyle, *Venality: The Sale of Offices in Eighteenth-Century France*, 26–57.

55 Doyle, *Venality: The Sale of Offices in Eighteenth-Century France*, 221–38.

56 Doyle, *Venality: The Sale of Offices in Eighteenth-Century France*, 312.

57 Bien, "Les offices, les corps et le crédit d'état," 382; Doyle, *Venality: The Sale of Offices in Eighteenth-Century France*, 90.

58 Ralph E. Giesey, "Rules of Inheritance and Strategies of Mobility in Prerevolutionary France," *American Historical Review* 82, no. 2 (April 1977): 271–89; Jean Nagle, *Un orgueil français: la vénalité des offices sous l'Ancien Régime* (Paris: Odile Jacob, 2008).

59   Bell, *Lawyers and Citizens*, 39–40.

60   Bell, *Lawyers and Citizens*, 15, 31.

61   Bell, *Lawyers and Citizens*, 163–74; Sarah Maza, *Private Lives and Public Affairs: The Causes Célèbres of Prerevolutionary France* (Berkeley: University of California Press, 1993), 1–17.

62   Bell, *Lawyers and Citizens*, 21 (quoting Alexandre de Tocqueville, *The Old Regime and the Revolution*, originally published in 1856).

63   Bell, *Lawyers and Citizens*, 164–215.

64   This paper focuses on legal attorneys (*procureurs "ad lites"*), who represented people in court. In contrast, *procureurs "ad negotia"* represented people in business transactions. On this distinction, see de Ferrière, *Dictionnaire de droit et de pratique*, II: 590.

65   Dolan, *Les procureurs du Midi*, 128.

66   Dolan, *Les procureurs du Midi*, 71.

67   Dolan, *Les procureurs du Midi*, 75.

68   Dolan, *Les procureurs du Midi*, 187.

69   Guyot, *Répertoire universel et raisonné*, XLVIII: 431.

70   De Ferrière, *Dictionnaire de droit et de pratique*, II: 595.

71   *Dictionnaire de Trévoux*, V: 1042. For a virtually identical explanation of practice, see de Ferrière, *Dictionnaire de droit et de pratique*, II: 509–10.

72   De Ferrière, *Dictionnaire de droit et de pratique*, II: 591–92.

73   De Ferrière, *Dictionnaire de droit et de pratique*, I: 197.

74   To be clear, the accused had no right to counsel in Ancien Régime France. Advocates did not argue in criminal cases either, but unlike attorneys, they could file amicus briefs on behalf of the accused; Bell, *Lawyers and Citizens*, 30, note 48.

75   De Ferrière, *Dictionnaire de droit et de pratique*, II: 596.

76   Guyot, *Répertoire universel et raisonné*, XLVIII: 431.

77   De Ferrière, *Dictionnaire de droit et de pratique*, II: 596.

78   I borrow this term from C.W. Brooks, *Pettyfoggers and Vipers of the Commonwealth: The "Lower Branch" of the Legal Profession in Early Modern England* (New York: Cambridge University Press, 1986).

79   Hervé Leuwers, "La fin des procureurs: les incertitudes d'une recomposition professionnelle (1790–1791)," *Histoire, économie & société* 33, no. 3 (2014): 18–31.

80   Dickinson, *Justice et justiciables*, 84.

81   On this practice among écuyers and *chevaliers*, see Lorraine Gadoury, *La noblesse de Nouvelle-France: familles et alliances* (LaSalle, QC: Hurtubise, 1991), 18–19. Although *écuyer* translates roughly to esquire, esquire carried different connotations in early America, where nobility was despised.

82 Vachon, *The Administration of New France*, 78.

83 Bataillard and Nusse have made this argument of French Caribbean colonies in *Histoire des procureurs et des avoués*, 98.

84 De Ferrière, *Dictionnaire de droit et de pratique*, II: 591.

85 De Ferrière, *Dictionnaire de droit et de pratique*, II: 591.

86 *Dictionnaire de Trévoux*, V: 1116.

87 *Dictionnaire de Trévoux*, V: 1116; De Ferrière, *Dictionnaire de droit et de pratique*, II: 590.

88 De Ferrière, *Dictionnaire de droit et de pratique*, II: 590; *Dictionnaire de Trévoux*, V: 1116–17.

89 Benoît Grenier and Catherine Ferland, "'Quelque longue que soit l'absence': procurations et pouvoir féminin à Québec au XVIIIe siècle," *Clio: Femmes, Genre, Histoire* 37, no. 1 (2013): 199.

90 Grenier and Ferland, "'Quelque longue que soit l'absence': procurations et pouvoir féminin à Québec au XVIIIe siècle," 200–1.

91 Grenier and Ferland, "'Quelque longue que soit l'absence': procurations et pouvoir féminin à Québec au XVIIIe siècle," 200.

92 Grenier and Ferland, "'Quelque longue que soit l'absence': procurations et pouvoir féminin à Québec au XVIIIe siècle," 202.

93 Grenier and Ferland, "'Quelque longue que soit l'absence': procurations et pouvoir féminin à Québec au XVIIIe siècle," 214.

94 Grenier and Ferland, "'Quelque longue que soit l'absence': procurations et pouvoir féminin à Québec au XVIIIe siècle," 203–4.

95 De Ferrière, *Dictionnaire de droit et de pratique*, II: 590.

96 Guyot, *Répertoire universel et raisonné*, XLVI: 324.

97 *Dictionnaire de Trévoux*, V: 1041.

98 De Ferrière, *Dictionnaire de droit et de pratique*, II: 509; Guyot, *Répertoire universel et raisonné*, XLVI: 324.

99 De Ferrière, *Dictionnaire de droit et de pratique*, II: 509.

100 *Dictionnaire de Trévoux*, V: 1041.

101 *Dictionnaire de Trévoux*, V: 1116.

102 *Dictionnaire de Trévoux*, V: 1041; Guyot, *Répertoire universel et raisonné*, XLVI: 324 (citing the Ordinance of April 1667, Title 24, Articles 25 and 26).

103 Miranda Frances Spieler, "The Legal Structure of Colonial Rule during the French Revolution," *William and Mary Quarterly*, 3rd ser., 66, no. 2 (April 2009): 370.

104 Although not technically absent from the colony, advocates did not typically make oral arguments in the courts of New France. On the absence of advocates orally arguing in criminal trials, see Denise Beaugrand-Champagne, *Le procès de Marie-Josèphe-*

Angélique (Montréal: Libre Expression, 200), 57–66. On the absence of advocates making oral arguments in civil trials, see Dickinson, *Justice et justiciables*, 85; Vachon, *Administration of New France*, xxiv. Joseph-Edmond Roy identifies an exception: the barrister Jacques Touzé, who orally argued before the Superior Council in 1703: *L'ancien Barreau au Canada*, 21.

105 Initially known as the Sovereign Council, the colony's highest court was renamed the Superior Council in 1703.

106 Girard, Phillips, and Brown, *History of Law in Canada*, 269; Édouard Fabre-Surveyer, "Louis-Guillaume Verrier (1690–1758)," *Revue d'histoire de l'Amérique française* VI, no. 2 (1952–3): 159–76; Vachon, "Verrier, Louis-Guillaume," in *Dictionary of Canadian Biography*, vol. 3, University of Toronto/ Université Laval, 2003-. http://www.biographi.ca/en/bio/verrier_louis_guillaume_3E.html.

107 Julie Hardwick, *The Practice of Patriarchy: Gender and the Politics of Household Authority in Early Modern France* (University Park: Pennsylvania State University Press, 1998), 42.

108 Philip Hoffman, Gilles Postel-Vinay, and Jean-Laurent Rosenthal, "What do Notaries do? Overcoming Asymmetric Information on Financial Markets: The Case of Paris, 1751," *Journal of Institutional and Theoretical Economics*, 154, no. 3 (1998): 499–530. For the classic study on notaries in Canada, see Vachon, *Histoire du notariat canadien, 1621–1960*.

109 Hardwick, *The Practice of Patriarchy*, 19.

110 Girard, Phillips, and Brown, *A History of Law in Canada*, 268–69; Hardwick, *The Practice of Patriarchy*, ix.

111 Atlantic literature urges us to focus not on today's political boundaries, but on yesterday's. Challenging the notion that the vast Atlantic Ocean separated the colony from the metropole, Atlantic history instead shows how water connected people, goods, and ideas. See for example Bernard Bailyn, *Atlantic History: Concept and Contours* (Cambridge: Harvard University Press, 2005); Nicholas Canny and Philip Morgan, *The Oxford Handbook of the Atlantic World, c.1450–c.1850* (New York: Oxford University Press, 2011); Alison Games, "Atlantic History: Definitions, Challenges, and Opportunities," *American Historical Review* 111, no. 3 (2006): 741–57. The Atlantic turn has modified previous understandings of the early Canadian population. Allan Greer estimates that of 27,000 migrants, approximately two-thirds returned to France before the British conquest: *People of New France* (Toronto: University of Toronto Press, 1997), 12–13.

112 Examples of these various functions abound in the archives described above. For a power of attorney agreement, see Procuration de Damien Quatresols à François Rageot, praticien de la ville de Québec (2 July 1704), notaire L. Chambalon, Parchemin. For an example of a client deferring to a practitioner's legal expertise, see Procuration de Marie-Madeleine Landron à Jacques Nouette (3 March1742), notaire C.-H. Dulaurent, Parchemin, in which the widow Marie-Madeleine Landron empowered Jacques Nouette to act in her name in whatever way he judged appropriate, in order to prevent the sale of a house of which she owned one-seventh. For examples of practitioners representing clients in court, see Appel, Pierre Raymond, *comparant par Nouette, son procureur,*

contre Olivier Abel [emphasis added] (26 June 1741), P19114, S28, TP1, BAnQ. For practitioners appearing in court, see Appel, Geneviève de Ramezay, veuve de Louis-Henri Deschamps, contre François Foucher, conseiller du Roi et son procureur en la Juridiction de Montréal, *comparant par le sieur Nouette, praticien* [emphasis added] (23 October 1741), P19177, S28, TP1 and Appel, François Havy, comparant par le sieur Nouette, contre Marie-Louise Corbin, *comparant par le sieur Poirier, praticien* [emphasis added] (24 July 1741), P19135, S28, TP1, BAnQ. *Sieur* is an early modern French title meaning *Monsieur* or Mister. The early modern French verb *comparoir* or *comparoître* means to present oneself in court or before a notary in order to respond to a summons, or to send an attorney in one's stead. De Ferrière, *Dictionnaire de droit et de pratique*, I: 461–62.

113   Cause entre le sieur Louis Levrard . . . demandeur, comparant par le sieur Jacques Nouette, *praticien, leur procureur*, et dame Marie-Anne Tarieu de la Pérade (LaPérade), veuve de feu sieur de la Richardière, défenderesse, comparant par le sieur Poirier, *praticien, son procureur* [emphases added] (3 October 1743), P34, D84, SS1, S11, TL1, BAnQ; Cause entre la veuve de feu Pierre Joly, boulangère de Québec, demanderesse, comparante par le sieur Jean-Claude Panet, *praticien, son procureur*, et le sieur Jacques Nouette, praticien, défendeur [emphasis added] (14 October 1743), P39, D84, SS1, S11, TL1, BAnQ. In the latter document, the practitioner Jacques Nouette appears as a party to the dispute.

114   Dubé, "Making a Career Out of the Atlantic: Louisiana's Plume," 60.

115   Contrat de mariage, Jacques Parant (19 January 1748), notaire N. Duprac, Parchemin.

116   *Dictionnaire de Trévoux*, V: 1041; Guyot, *Répertoire universel et raisonné*, XLVI: 324 (citing the Ordinance of April 1667, Title 24, Articles 25 and 26).

117   Procès entre Charles Ruette d'Auteuil de Monceaux, et Jacques Nouette de la Poufellerie (Poufellerie) (7 March – 22 April 1743), D4933, S1, TL4, BAnQ. Jean-Baptiste Adhémar is also likely the person referred to in Compromis entre Pierre-Joseph Celoron de Bienville et ? Adhemar, notaire royal et ancien praticien, de la ville et juridiction de Montréal (5 September 1746), notaire F. Simonnet, Parchemin. While the archivist has left a question mark in front of Adhémar's last name, this could not be the then-deceased Antoine Adhémar, and is most probably the royal notary of Montréal, Jean-Baptiste Adhémar. Despite the slightly different spelling, Jacques Nouette is the subject of Édouard-Zotique Massicotte's article, "Nouette dit la Souffleterie [sic]," *Le Bulletin des recherches historiques* 21, no. 1 (1915): 23–25. The mistranscription of Poufellerie as Souffleterie is understandable, given the very similar appearance of early modern PS and SS. Comparing these letters in a document written by the same person, however, determines that this attorney-practitioner's last name actually was Nouette de la Poufellerie. For example in Mémoire des dépens à payer par Jean-Baptiste Larchevêque (1 October – 21 November 1740), D224, S30, TP1, BAnQ, the "P" in Poufellerie on page 3, line 25 certainly resembles the "P" in "Qu'il vous Plaise" on line 16. Similarly on page 1, compare the "P" in "Poufellerie" to the "S" in "Suplie [sic] humblement." For an excellent primer on deciphering handwriting in early Canada, see Marcel Lafortune, *Initiation à la paléographie franco-canadienne: les écritures des notaires aux XVIIe-XVIIIe siècles* (Montréal: Société de recherche historique archiv-histo, 1982).

118 Jugement rendu par Christophe-Hilarion Dulaurent, ancien praticien et notaire royal de la Prévôté de Québec (3 December 1750), D3012-32, TL5, BAnQ.

119 In "Problems of Precedence in Louis XIV's New France," in *Majesty in Canada: Essays on the Role of Royalty*, ed. Colin M. Coates (Toronto: Dundurn Group, 2006), Colin Coates argues that rank and precedence in entries, processions, and church seating were the essence of politics in a colony that was part of an absolutist polity.

120 Michel Verrette, "L'alphabétisation de la population de la ville de Québec de 1750 à 1849," *Revue d'histoire de l'Amérique française*, 39, no. 1 (1985): 68.

121 Gadoury, *La noblesse de Nouvelle-France*, 17.

122 Gadoury, *La noblesse de Nouvelle-France*.

123 Gadoury, *La noblesse de Nouvelle-France*, 18.

124 Gadoury, *La noblesse de Nouvelle-France*, 17.

125 Gadoury, *La noblesse de Nouvelle-France*, 19.

126 Contrat de mariage, Charles Decoste de Letencour, écuyer, fils de Jean-Baptiste Decoste de Letancour, écuyer et ancien praticien de la juridiction de Montréal et de Renée Marchand (7 January 1759), notaire F. Simonnet, Parchemin.

127 Contrat de mariage entre Pierre Parret [sic], praticien, de la ville de Québec et natif de la ville de Paris et Marie-Anne Trefflet dit Rautot (29 September 1754), notaire C. Barolet, Parchemin.

128 Contrat de mariage entre Jacques Bourdon, praticien, et Marie Menard (3 January 1672), notaire T. Frérot de Lechesnaye, Parchemin; Vente d'une terre par Jacques Menard à Jacques Bourdon, praticien (9 March 1673), notaire T. Frérot de Lechesnaye, Parchemin.

129 Langlois, "Les Antilles et la Nouvelle-France," 243 (citing a document from the Guadeloupe notarial office of Du Laurent dated 3 February 1751).

Poursuivre son mari en justice : femmes mariées et coutume de Paris devant la Cour du banc du roi de Montréal (1795-1830)

*Jean-Philippe Garneau**

Introduction

Dans une lettre écrite en janvier 1813, Rosalie Papineau, sœur du célèbre chef patriote, expose clairement le dilemme auquel faisaient face les femmes bas-canadiennes confrontées aux difficultés financières de leur mari :

> La pauvre Mme Saint-G.! [...] : voir un mari qu'elle aime courir à sa perte et les entraîner, elle et ses enfants, dans son malheur, ou bien être obligée d'en venir à des extrémités aussi humiliantes que l'est une action en séparation [de biens], selon moi, ça met le comble à ses maux[1]!

Ce court extrait est intéressant à plusieurs égards. Il situe d'abord la relation du couple dans ce que Bettina Bradbury appellerait une forme de *companionate patriarchy*[2]. Sous la plume de Rosalie, l'amour semble en effet lier encore la pauvre Mme Saint-G. à son mari, en dépit des difficultés économiques. Mais cet amour conjugal est tout de même clairement inscrit dans les rapports patriarcaux qui subordonnaient alors la femme à son époux. C'est bien le mari de Mme Saint-G. qui paraît entièrement responsable du malheur de sa femme et de ses enfants. En théorie, on le sait, la femme mariée ne pouvait ni s'obliger juridiquement ni poursuivre en justice sans le consentement de son époux. Aux yeux du droit, la direction des affaires du ménage demeurait une prérogative masculine et seul l'époux disposait d'une personnalité juridique pleine et entière. La coutume de Paris en exprimait l'idée en faisant du mari le « seigneur » de la communauté de biens des époux, le régime légal régissant la propriété conjugale au Bas-Canada. Même si ce régime se révélait plutôt avantageux pour la femme mariée (il lui attribuait la moitié des biens communs), le principe de la puissance maritale prévalait, que le couple ait vécu dans cette colonie ou dans une juridiction de *common law* à part entière.

Depuis plusieurs années cependant, nombre de travaux ont bien montré que les femmes mariées, avec ou sans consentement marital, pouvaient être des agentes économiques très actives malgré l'incapacité juridique dont elles faisaient l'objet. Particulièrement en matière de consommation, l'épouse savait engager tacitement la responsabilité de son conjoint, pour peu que les dépenses fussent jugées légitimes et raisonnables[3]. C'est probablement cette latitude accordée à l'épouse que Rosalie évoque un peu plus loin dans la même lettre qu'elle adressait à sa cousine. La jeune sœur de Louis-Joseph Papineau semble en effet mettre la faute des problèmes financiers du couple, non pas sur le mari, mais plutôt sur « les écarts » de Mme Saint-G. S'il faut en croire l'épistolière, celle-ci aurait même dû en rougir de honte :

> [. . .] il n'y a plus de ressource pour elle [Mme Saint-G.]. Quel triste sort! Quelle affligeante perspective lorsque l'illusion sera cessée! Quels remords ne l'accableront-ils pas, si elle est capable de rougir sur ses écarts! Et si, par malheur, elle ne l'était pas, quelle inquiétude ne doit pas nous donner une telle insouciance pour l'avenir! Dieu veuille en préserver sa famille! Son père et sa mère en mourraient de chagrin, j'en suis sûre[4].

De quels écarts, de quelle insouciance parlait Rosalie Papineau, sinon des dépenses que cette épouse aurait multipliées au point de conduire son mari à la ruine? Il n'a pas été possible d'identifier Mme Saint-G. avec certitude. Nous ne connaissons donc pas les raisons exactes de la déconfiture de son mari ni ne savons si une action en séparation de biens fut finalement intentée. Mais cette critique, qui ressemble fort au stéréotype de l'épouse dépensière, en dit long sur ce que pouvait penser une jeune femme de l'élite canadienne-française au début du XIXe siècle. Rosalie semble implicitement reconnaître l'autonomie des femmes mariées de la bourgeoisie en matière de consommation et, du même souffle, les soucis qu'une épouse « insouciante » pouvait causer à son mari[5]! En évoquant la possibilité d'un recours en séparation de biens, elle soulignait aussi que la justice demeurait une alternative pour ces épouses, aussi déshonorante cette solution fût-elle. Mais, du même coup, elle imposait à ses congénères une morale sévère qui semble bien avoir relevé, du moins en partie, de la position subordonnée de la femme durant le mariage.

Mais était-ce bien le cas? Qu'en était-il vraiment pour les épouses bas-canadiennes au début du XIXe siècle? Ce témoignage évocateur soulève évidemment plusieurs questions dont certaines ont été abondamment traitées dans l'historiographie. Pour la société préindustrielle, le rôle des femmes mariées dans l'économie domestique ne fait plus beaucoup de mystère, qu'il s'agisse d'économie informelle, de consommation ou encore du travail exercé conjointement avec le mari ou de façon indépendante[6]. Les travaux scientifiques ont également bien mis en évidence l'importance de la classe sociale et de la race (ou l'identité ethnoculturelle) pour expliquer la diversité de l'expérience des femmes. Face au patriarcat, qui imprégnait les institutions et les mentalités de multiples façons, les femmes n'étaient évidemment pas toutes égales. C'est d'ailleurs cette diversité d'expériences et les différents degrés de l'*empowerment* des femmes qui me semblent ressortir de l'historiographie plus récente. La difficulté demeure de savoir comment réconcilier l'*agency* des femmes mariées et la chape du patriarcat, comment contrebalancer l'autonomie individuelle et les contraintes sociojuridiques. C'est ce qui explique le succès de la notion de « négociation » qui inspire tant de travaux depuis quelque temps[7].

Gardant à l'esprit ces considérations, j'ai étudié plus spécifiquement le recours en séparation de biens qu'évoque Rosalie Papineau dans sa lettre.

Selon le droit français en vigueur au Bas-Canada, l'épouse pouvait exercer un certain contrôle sur la gestion maritale de l'avoir domestique. Une fois autorisée par le juge, la femme mariée avait en effet la possibilité de poursuivre son mari en justice en cas de mauvaise administration financière. Un jugement favorable lui octroyait alors le pouvoir de gérer elle-même les biens et les revenus qui lui appartenaient[8]. Sans équivalent en *common law*, une telle action en justice, uniquement réservée à l'épouse, avait de quoi paraître subversif aux yeux des élites masculines, même pour la France d'Ancien Régime[9]. Dans le contexte bas-canadien du début du XIXe siècle, cette option était susceptible de déconcerter davantage encore les maris d'origine britannique. Quelques-uns d'entre eux, les immigrants tout particulièrement, étaient peu au fait du droit civil français et des modalités de la propriété conjugale. Comme Evelyn Kolish et Bettina Bradbury l'ont déjà souligné, certains marchands britanniques étaient hostiles à l'univers juridique du droit civil d'origine française[10]. En plus de jeter l'opprobre sur le mari, voire sur la famille entière, la séparation de biens était susceptible d'inquiéter les créanciers du ménage anxieux de se faire payer. Or, comme on le verra, la pratique judiciaire montréalaise s'est chargée d'en faire un instrument le plus souvent au service des maris, sans pour autant bafouer le droit des créanciers. Avec l'aide d'un avocat, plus d'un chef de ménage en déconfiture a pu compter sur la nouvelle personnalité juridique de son épouse pour se sortir d'un mauvais pas économique. Dans tout ce brouhaha judiciaire, nombre de femmes mariées semblent avoir été sinon négligées, du moins bien mal conseillées.

Ce « détournement » apparent de la procédure en séparation de biens n'est pas entier, puisque certaines épouses ont tout de même bénéficié de ses avantages. Mais il permet de réfléchir sur les difficultés que ces dernières rencontraient pour lier propriété et pouvoir dans une colonie britannique où le droit civil français et les exigences masculines du marché ne faisaient pas bon ménage. Pour bien aiguiller la réflexion, il m'a semblé important d'étayer, dans un premier temps, le questionnement à la base de l'enquête. Puis, nous nous pencherons sur le recours censé protéger la propriété des femmes mariées en étudiant la pratique judiciaire montréalaise de 1795 à 1829.

Les femmes mariées et la propriété au regard du droit coutumier français

C'est sous l'angle de la propriété et du droit français que j'aimerais situer le problème de l'endettement des ménages pour les femmes mariées comme Mme Saint-G. Particulièrement sous la gouverne de maris défaillants ou fautifs, on sait que les femmes de cette époque subissaient parfois durement les inconvénients d'un patriarcat qui les plaçait en situation de vulnérabilité ou de dépendance économique. Pour les pays de *common law*, les études ayant abordé la genèse et l'impact des *Married Women's Property Acts* du XIXe siècle sont là pour en témoigner[11]. Il est vrai que, parmi les classes possédantes recourant à la technique du *trust*, des épouses se voyaient attribuer une propriété séparée, particulièrement à l'occasion d'un *marriage settlement*. Cette opération juridique leur conférait alors une certaine autonomie durant le mariage de même qu'après le décès de leur mari, le cas échéant[12]. Mais la marge de manœuvre ainsi acquise, du reste toute relative, ne concernait qu'une fraction des épouses et dépendait de la protection des tribunaux d'*Equity*. Dans les colonies, ces derniers n'étaient d'ailleurs pas toujours établis (ce qui fut le cas du Haut-Canada avant 1837)[13]. Au Bas-Canada, la situation ne se présentait pas de la même façon, comme on le sait. Rappelons que, sauf stipulation contraire à la coutume de Paris, les épouses avaient droit à la moitié des biens communs du ménage, présents et à venir, ce qui pouvait représenter une richesse non négligeable chez les marchands ou les artisans (les effets mobiliers étant considérés comme des biens communs). Elles disposaient également d'une hypothèque légale sur les biens propres de leur mari[14] afin que leur soient garantis, dès la célébration du mariage, certains droits comme le douaire ou les reprises matrimoniales (un concept juridique sur lequel nous reviendrons plus loin dans ce texte). Pour Bettina Bradbury, le droit parisien, repris par le Code civil du Bas-Canada, explique en bonne partie qu'il n'y ait pas eu au Québec de réforme juridique comparable à celle que connurent au XIXe siècle la plupart des juridictions de *common law*[15]. D'ailleurs, c'est en raison de ce droit français que Jan Noel avance que les femmes de la Nouvelle-France étaient en meilleure posture que leurs consœurs des autres colonies britanniques à la même époque (et même plus tard)[16]. On connaît cependant le désaccord que cette thèse a suscité. Pour Josette Brun, la pratique notariale des couples des villes de Québec et de Louisbourg démontre plutôt que la puissance maritale limitait sérieusement l'action des femmes mariées dans l'espace public, malgré les avantages matrimoniaux de la coutume de Paris[17].

Demeure donc toujours ouverte la question du pouvoir réel des femmes mariées sur la richesse que la coutume de Paris leur garantissait. Cet aspect est particulièrement crucial dans les situations d'insolvabilité qui plaçaient plus d'un ménage à la merci de créanciers impatients. Dans quelle mesure la communauté de biens et les autres dispositions du droit français protégeaient-elles l'avoir des femmes mariées, considérant l'incapacité juridique dont celles-ci faisaient l'objet? Quel *pouvoir* les épouses avaient-elles, *durant le mariage*, sur leur part de communauté de biens ou sur tout autre forme de propriété que le droit français leur reconnaissait (leur héritage en particulier, étant donné l'égalitarisme successoral de la coutume de Paris qui, à cet égard aussi, différait de la *common law* anglaise)? Quelle était par ailleurs l'attitude des maris censés incarner l'autorité domestique (en dépit de leurs difficultés économiques)?

Plusieurs auteurs ont noté très justement qu'une partie des réponses à ces questions dépendait de l'identité juridique de l'épouse. Les « marchandes publiques » disposaient par exemple d'une plus grande liberté d'action. Un peu comme pour la *feme-sole trader* en *common law*, ce statut permettait à la femme mariée de gérer son propre commerce de façon relativement autonome, quoique toujours sujette à la « puissance » de son mari[18]. De même, les futures épouses pouvaient choisir un régime de séparation de biens et disposer d'une autonomie semblable pour les biens qui leur étaient spécifiquement attribués au contrat de mariage. Mais pour déroger ainsi au régime légal de la communauté de biens, un tel contrat de mariage était absolument nécessaire et se devait d'être rédigé par un notaire préalablement à l'union. La belle étude que Bettina Bradbury a consacrée aux couples de la ville de Montréal indique que ce choix était surtout populaire chez les élites, particulièrement après 1840. S'apparentant à certains objectifs du *marriage settlement*, ce régime d'exception a d'abord eu la cote chez les époux d'origine britannique, avant de connaître une certaine popularité chez les classes supérieures de toute origine. Bettina Bradbury formule d'ailleurs l'hypothèse qu'un tel choix se voulait une forme de protection contre l'insolvabilité, fléau qui frappa plus durement la colonie à partir de 1837. Par rapport à l'ensemble de la population citadine toutefois, il faut comprendre que peu de futures épouses optèrent pour le régime de la séparation de biens, tout simplement parce que la pratique du contrat de mariage, seul moyen de déroger à la coutume de Paris, déclina au fil du temps. De telle sorte que le régime légal de la communauté de biens prévalait largement à Montréal chez les Canadiens français, tout comme chez bon nombre d'anglo-protestants ou de catholiques irlandais ne disposant pas d'un contrat de mariage[19].

Si l'identité juridique des femmes mariées nous est désormais bien connue, il n'en va pas de même du pouvoir qu'elles ont pu effectivement exercer durant le mariage en vertu des droits ou des privilèges conférés par le droit parisien. Il est vrai que documenter l'activité de cette majorité silencieuse n'est pas aisé. Particulièrement pour le problème du rapport des femmes à la propriété, on connaît généralement mieux les stratégies des veuves qui accédaient à la gouverne du ménage au décès de leur époux. C'est surtout pour cette phase de leur vie que l'impact réel de la communauté de biens est d'ailleurs évalué par les historiennes et les historiens. Au décès de leur mari, les femmes récupéraient en effet le pouvoir sur la moitié des biens communs, en plus de certains droits spécifiques comme le douaire. Certes, on sait que quelques femmes mariées se sont démarquées par leur implication civique ou leur dynamisme dans la sphère économique du marché[20]. Il est vrai aussi que l'absence du mari, soulignée par une historienne comme Jan Noel, permettait à certaines épouses de « sortir de l'ombre ». La correspondance entre mari et femme est riche d'enseignements à cet égard, mais elle est rare, parcellaire et réservée aux lettrées. Elle mériterait tout de même une analyse plus attentive des stratégies économiques et financières des épouses bas-canadiennes[21]. Du côté des sources juridiques, certaines études ont mis en lumière le recours à la procuration générale ou spéciale que le mari absent accordait à son épouse afin que celle-ci puisse agir en toute légalité, de façon plus ou moins étendue. Une telle pratique, centrée sur l'autorisation écrite plutôt que sur le mandat tacite, était courante dans les pays de droit civil. Mais elle existait également dans les juridictions de *common law*, dans une mesure plus difficile à évaluer cependant[22]. Dans le contexte québécois, l'analyse des procurations a offert une fenêtre d'observation sur l'activité de la femme mariée placée aux commandes du ménage ou de l'entreprise familiale[23].

Privilégiant les couples des classes possédantes, cet angle d'approche favorise évidemment la vision plus optimiste du *companionate marriage*. Mais le principe de la puissance maritale n'en demeure pas moins réaffirmé, la procuration étant par définition une délégation du pouvoir marital. Du reste, les actes notariés ne nous disent pas toujours dans quelle mesure ce pouvoir a été effectivement exercé par l'épouse esseulée[24]. Il en va de même pour les droits matrimoniaux définis au contrat de mariage, un document souvent utilisé en histoire de la famille.

Malgré leurs limites, les sources judiciaires apportent un éclairage précieux à cet égard. Bien connues des spécialistes, elles n'ont pourtant guère été mises à contribution dans la perspective envisagée ici, du moins pour le Québec préindustriel[25]. Il est vrai que plusieurs études se sont penchées sur l'intervention de la justice dans les conflits familiaux marqués par l'abus, la négligence ou l'abandon d'un mari. L'univers plus sombre ou plus âpre du conflit, très révélateur, éclaire particulièrement bien les situations difficiles des épouses tout comme certaines de leurs stratégies. Ce choix n'est pas sans conséquence cependant, puisque c'est la vision plus normative des gens de justice (et parfois des témoins) qui est alors mise en lumière. Certains de ces travaux ont ainsi souligné le double standard dont les femmes étaient l'objet, notamment pour les causes en séparation de corps. D'autres ont insisté sur l'attitude chevaleresque de la justice masculine qui, sous couvert d'assurer la « protection » des femmes maltraitées ou abandonnées, réaffirmait ainsi une vision patriarcale des rapports de genre[26]. L'activité des tribunaux ne se limite toutefois pas aux seuls dysfonctionnements du couple ou aux abus d'un mari. Le contentieux ordinaire de la justice civile, moins étudié, apporte aussi un éclairage particulièrement utile pour la question du pouvoir domestique. Ce volet est évidemment moins spectaculaire en raison de la nature des causes impliquées, très largement des réclamations pour dettes auxquelles s'ajoutaient certains procès concernant notamment des affaires de famille[27]. Dans les affaires de nature commerciale, les femmes mariées étaient somme toute peu présentes devant la justice civile et elles figuraient presque toujours aux côtés de leur mari, sauf pour quelques rares marchandes publiques, néanmoins très actives. C'est ce qui ressort d'une étude sur l'activité judiciaire en Nouvelle-Écosse au tournant des XVIIIe et XIXe siècles[28]. C'est également ce que j'ai observé pour le district de Montréal devant la juridiction supérieure de la Cour du banc du roi[29]. Toutefois, les femmes mariées agissaient aussi de leur propre chef dans les cas plus rares où elles poursuivaient leur mari. Or, à la lumière des dossiers judiciaires de la juridiction supérieure de Montréal, ces femmes s'adressaient aux juges le plus souvent pour obtenir une séparation de biens. C'est dire tout l'intérêt que cette procédure judiciaire revêt pour mieux comprendre les rapports de propriété entre époux. Souvent étudiée de concert avec la séparation de corps, la séparation de biens a fait l'objet d'une attention plutôt distraite jusqu'à maintenant. Lorsque cette dernière est considérée comme telle, les enjeux plus strictement économiques du recours se confondent souvent avec les problèmes conjugaux qui caractérisent l'action en séparation de corps[30]. Cela dit, quelques auteurs ont pris la mesure plus exacte du recours en séparation de biens dans le contexte de la France d'Ancien Régime[31]. Leurs travaux permettront de mieux situer l'expérience bas-canadienne. Cette société coloniale, on le sait, se distinguait par un pluralisme culturel croissant qui, en partie du moins, s'est aussi répercuté dans l'administration de la justice elle-même[32]. C'est attentif à ce contexte particulier que j'ai d'abord pris la mesure d'une action judiciaire réservée aux femmes mariées.

L'action en séparation de biens dans le district de Montréal, 1795-1829

Pour Rosalie Papineau, le recours en séparation de biens demeurait la pire des possibilités. C'est peut-être ce qui explique que, jusqu'en 1815 du moins, cette action ait été peu fréquente devant la Cour du banc du roi de Montréal. On compte à peine deux ou trois demandes par année pour l'ensemble d'un district dont la population atteignait environ 150 000 personnes à la fin de la guerre anglo-américaine. Durant les années 1820, en revanche, les difficultés économiques que traversait le Bas-Canada paraissent avoir fortement contribué à augmenter la fréquence du recours judiciaire. Oscillant autour d'une dizaine de procès par année au début de la décennie 1820, la courbe dépasse la vingtaine de litiges après 1825, ce qui représente une augmentation bien au-delà de la croissance de la population (graphique 9.1)[33]. Dans le district de Montréal, en quelque 35

Figure 9.1 Distribution annuelle du nombre d'actions en séparation pour le district de Montréal, 1795-1829

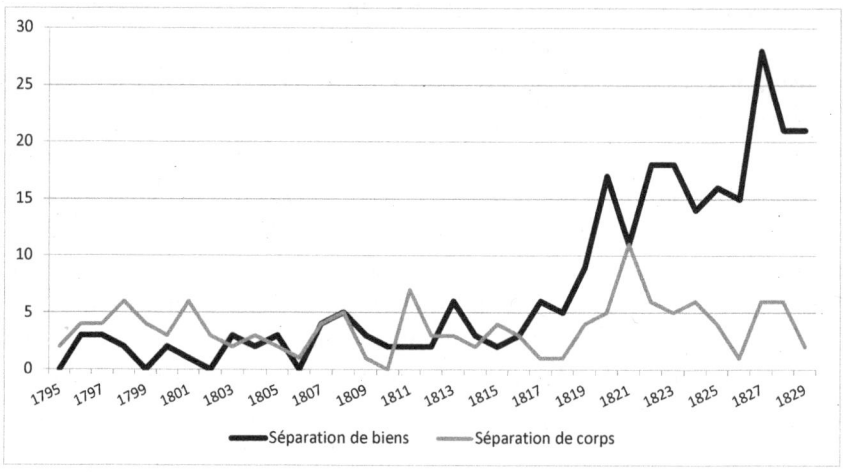

ans (soit de 1795 à 1829), 250 demandes ont été reçues au tribunal. Pour la période allant de 1680 à 1789, Laurence Croq a retrouvé une séparation de biens pour 140 couples de la bourgeoisie marchande parisienne, plus susceptibles d'avoir recours à cette procédure. Julie Hardwick, qui explore les registres de cours de la ville de Nantes entre 1598 et 1710, dénombre quant à elle 106 poursuites de cette nature[34]. La pratique bas-canadienne semble donc assez vigoureuse, surtout après 1815. Dans la très grande majorité des cas, les demandes en séparation de biens ont été reçues favorablement par les magistrats (voir tableau 9.1), à l'instar de ce qu'observe Hardwick pour le long XVIIe siècle[35].

Remarquons au passage que ce recours est nettement plus fréquent que la demande en séparation de corps, en France comme au Québec. Certes, les deux actions étaient parfois provoquées par des problèmes conjugaux de même nature, comme l'abandon ou la défaillance lourde du mari (alcoolisme, « débauche », prodigalité, etc.). Mais demander une séparation de biens ne nécessitait pas qu'il y ait eu conflit conjugal ni faute grave de l'époux. Ne mettant pas fin à la cohabitation d'un point de vue légal, le recours était également plus facile à obtenir. Il suffisait que l'épouse soit en danger de perdre ses « droits et avantages matrimoniaux » pour qu'elle puisse demander à la cour de mettre sa propriété à l'abri du mari et de ses créanciers. Dans la demande en séparation de biens que Marguerite Belecque dépose contre son mari en 1828, son avocat expose à la cour que ce dernier :

> [. . .] aurait mal administré les biens de la dite communauté [de biens]. Il aurait contracté diverses dettes, aurait fait de faux marchés, se serait exposé à des poursuites en conséquence desquelles ses meubles seraient sous saisie, et que par ces moyens les droits de la demanderesse tels que stipulés en son contrat de mariage, et nommément ce qu'elle y aurait apporté, seraient en péril[36].

Voilà, exprimée en détail, l'une des raisons donnant ouverture au recours selon les juristes de l'époque. Au tournant des années 1820, les avocats invoquent d'ailleurs plus volontiers les infortunes du mari (les poursuites ou les saisies dont il était l'objet) que les fautes de ce dernier, épargnant ainsi une partie de l'opprobre au chef de ménage. C'est peut-être ce qui explique aussi la plus grande fréquence du recours à partir de la fin des années 1810 (soit près de deux fois plus que la demande en séparation de corps). En raison du taux de succès élevé de la procédure (tableau 9.1), quelques couples ont emprunté cette voie plus facile pour régler les aspects matériels d'une véritable séparation de fait. Catherine Anger et Louis Cavilhe obtinrent une séparation de biens le 18 juin 1798 permettant d'homologuer le partage de leur communauté de biens. L'un des témoins au procès déclara cependant que le couple s'était entendu pour mettre fin à la cohabitation conjugale. Les époux s'en seraient tenus à une entente à l'amiable si le notaire ne leur avait pas conseillé d'obtenir auparavant une séparation de biens devant le tribunal[37]. Ce cas de figure demeure toutefois l'exception. Le plus souvent, les difficultés financières du mari justifiaient le recours des femmes mariées.

Clairement, les femmes n'ont pas toujours agi de leur propre initiative. La collusion entre les conjoints était manifeste, peut-être plus fréquente

Tableau 9.1 Issues des demandes en séparation de biens, 1795-1829

	NOMBRE DE PROCÈS
Abandon de la demande	8
Rejet de l'action	8
Jugement favorable	*182*
Mention d'un jugement non retrouvé	24
Cas inconnus	28
Total	250

Source: TL19, S4, SS11, CaM, BAnQ

à Montréal qu'ailleurs[38]. Seulement 18 des 250 demandes en séparation de biens ont été véritablement contestées par le mari. À aucun moment la contestation de ces hommes n'évoque les dépenses excessives que leur femme aurait accumulées pour expliquer leur ruine[39]. Dans les rares cas où l'époux se présentait en personne, celui-ci semblait satisfait de s'en « rapporter à justice », bel exemple de complicité ouverte ou, du moins, d'aveu d'impuissance du chef de ménage[40]. L'initiative du recours revenait peut-être même à l'avocat de l'épouse qui agissait aussi pour le compte du mari dans d'autres procès[41]. Les créanciers, quant à eux, n'intervenaient pratiquement jamais[42]. Peut-être parce que le tribunal veillait naturellement à leurs intérêts, comme nous allons le voir. Mais sans doute aussi parce que les femmes ne revendiquaient pas toujours des sommes très importantes, au surcroît difficiles à récupérer lorsque le mari était insolvable ou mal intentionné. Au terme du procès, certaines femmes n'obtenaient rien ou recevaient un pécule d'une valeur à peine supérieure aux frais judiciaires[43]. Examinons la situation de plus près.

L'avoir des épouses bas-canadiennes sous la plume des hommes de loi

Dans une très forte proportion, les demanderesses étaient mariées sous le régime de la communauté de biens (soit dans près de neuf cas connus sur dix). Le jugement favorable à la séparation avait pour effet de mettre un terme à ce régime de propriété entre les époux. Dans le meilleur des scénarios, la dissolution du régime permettait à la femme mariée de récupérer la moitié des biens communs. Cette *acceptation* de la communauté de biens n'était avantageuse que si les actifs demeuraient clairement supérieurs aux dettes. Si le bilan était déficitaire, la femme ne pouvait évidemment partager que les dettes. La coutume de Paris permettait alors à l'épouse de renoncer à la communauté de biens afin d'éviter d'être débitrice des créanciers du ménage. Cet avantage non négligeable ne mettait néanmoins pas beaucoup de beurre dans les épinards...

L'examen attentif des dossiers montre que nombre de femmes n'avaient sans doute pas d'autres choix que d'opter pour une *renonciation* à leur part de communauté. Seul un véritable bilan financier versé au dossier pourrait confirmer l'état d'insolvabilité du chef de ménage. Mais les demandes en séparation de biens n'offrent pas une telle comptabilité[44]. Les pièces au dossier signalent tout de même les nombreuses dettes du mari, les saisies et ventes judiciaires survenues, parfois une faillite récente, ce que des vérifications dans la banque de données Thémis I permettent à l'occasion de valider. Sur cette base, on peut penser que près d'une femme sur deux a dû faire face aux difficultés financières du « seigneur » de la communauté de biens (graphique 9.2).

Dans ces cas, l'épouse devait assurément renoncer à la communauté. En contrepartie, le droit français lui permettait de réclamer sa « dot », en particulier les biens qu'elle avait apportés au mariage (ou leur valeur). La très grande majorité des femmes mariées sous le régime de la communauté de biens optèrent pour cette solution (renonciation et restitution de la dot, plutôt qu'acceptation et partage de la communauté). En fait, ces femmes renoncèrent à leur part de communauté bien plus souvent que l'insolvabilité apparente de leur mari semble l'avoir justifié. Le tableau 9.2 montre qu'au moins deux épouses sur trois choisirent la renonciation, alors que les cas d'insolvabilité apparente du mari semblent n'avoir concerné qu'une

FIGURE 9.2 Difficultés financières des maris selon les dossiers en séparation de biens, 1795–1829

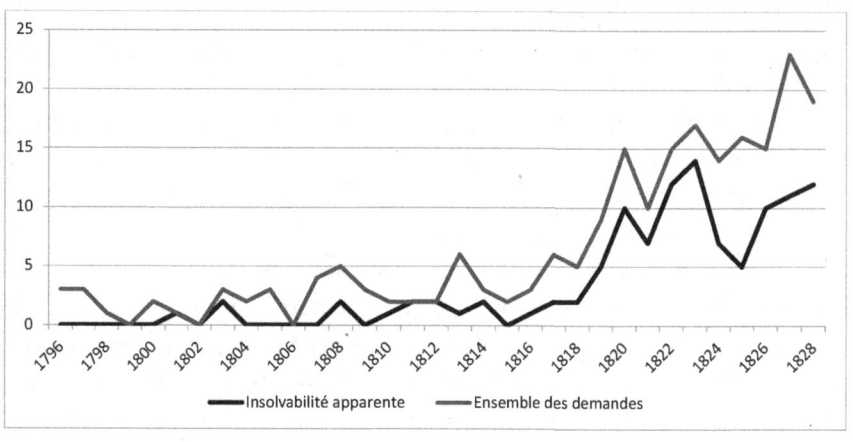

Source: TL19, S4, SS11, CaM, BAnQ

cause sur deux tout au plus (graphique 9.2)[45]. Les lacunes documentaires des dossiers judiciaires expliquent le fort taux de cas inconnus (28,4%). Mais l'histoire juridique permet de penser que, le plus souvent, la renonciation à la communauté de biens intervenait également dans ces cas[46]. C'est donc dire que pour une majorité écrasante de poursuivantes, leur droit à la moitié de la communauté de biens, si souvent invoqué dans l'historiographie, ne se matérialisa jamais. Seule restait la dot qui, contrairement à la part de communauté, était garantie par une hypothèque générale sur les biens propres du mari.

Encore fallait-il que l'épouse ait pris soin de faire rédiger un contrat de mariage dans lequel était inscrite une clause dite de *reprises*. Cette clause précisait les biens ou les sommes que la future aurait droit de réclamer advenant une renonciation à la communauté[47]. Or, faute de contrat de mariage, ou encore faute de clause de reprises adéquate, plusieurs de ces femmes ne purent réclamer leur dot, en tout ou en partie. Certaines d'entre elles ne possédaient probablement que quelques effets personnels au moment de l'union, au mieux un trousseau bien garni. C'est peut-être pourquoi plusieurs s'estimèrent satisfaites du seul prononcé de la séparation de biens, sans songer à réclamer quoi que ce soit. Il se peut également que les

TABLEAU 9.2 Option des épouses communes en biens après un jugement favorable connu, 1795-1829*

	AVEC CONTRAT DE MARIAGE	SANS CONTRAT DE MARIAGE	TOTAL
Renonciation	85	18	103
Acceptation	5	1	6
"Entente"**	0	2	2
Inconnu	34	10	44
Total	124	31	155

Source: TL19, S4, SS11, CaM, BAnQ
*Seulement 155 des 182 dossiers dont le jugement nous était connu indiquaient clairement que le couple était marié sous le régime de la communauté de biens.
** Certains dossiers parlent d'une entente entre les parties équivalant à un partage des biens du couple. Comme ces cas ne semblent pas suivre la norme juridique, ils ont été rangés dans une catégorie à part. Mais ils sont plutôt à verser du côté de l'acceptation de la communauté de biens.

TABLEAU 9.3 Décisions concernant les biens de l'épouse pour les jugements connus, 1795–1829

	NOMBRE DE PROCÈS
Jugement attribuant des biens à l'épouse	99
Jugement n'accordant aucun bien à l'épouse	29
Aucune demande de l'épouse	51
Dossier incomplet	3
Total	182

Source: TL19, S4, SS11, CaM, BAnQ

Tableau 9.4 Occupation socioprofessionnelle des maris, 1795-1829

	N	%
Écuyers, seigneurs et officiers civils	22	8,8%
Marchands et commerçants	85	34,0%
Professionnels	12	4,8%
Gens de métier	60	24,0%
Cultivateurs et *yeomen* ruraux	69	27,6%
Cas inconnus	2	0,8%
Total	250	

Source: TL19, S4, SS11, CaM, BAnQ

frais judiciaires additionnels pour déterminer la dot aient été jugés trop élevés, considérant la modicité des biens apportés par l'épouse[48]. Chose certaine, une forte proportion de femmes mariées (44%) n'obtenaient rien au terme du procès, soit que le jugement ne leur accordait aucun bien, soit qu'elles n'en revendiquaient tout simplement pas (tableau 9.3).

Précisons que ces couples n'appartenaient pourtant pas aux classes populaires. L'occupation du mari montre que les commerçants, les gens de métier et les professionnels étaient surreprésentés, même si les propriétaires ruraux formaient tout de même une bonne part du contingent (tableau 9.4).

On aurait donc pu s'attendre à ce que ces familles possédantes, particulièrement exposées aux rigueurs du marché, sachent faire bon usage des rouages du droit. Mais combien de femmes, combien d'hommes connaissaient le jeu subtil des reprises stipulées au contrat de mariage? Le problème était particulièrement criant pour les immigrants britanniques. Sur la cinquantaine d'épouses anglophones ayant demandé la séparation de biens, la majorité n'avait pas de contrat de mariage (30 sur les 52 cas connus). Faute d'un tel contrat, elles ne pouvaient donc espérer récupérer quoi que ce soit à titre de dot. À l'exception d'Isabella Campbell, ces femmes renoncèrent néanmoins au régime légal de la communauté de biens, ce qui les condamnait à ne pouvoir rien obtenir au terme du procès. Dans un cas, c'est le mari lui-même qui, après avoir autorisé sa femme à renoncer à la communauté de biens, signa l'acte de renonciation et le déposa en main propre au tribunal[49]! La renonciation, tout comme la séparation de biens, était pourtant un privilège réservé à la seule épouse. On l'a déjà souligné, la communauté de biens n'avait pas la cote chez bon nombre de maris britanniques. Plusieurs apprenaient trop tard qu'ils étaient soumis à ce régime faute de l'avoir exclu par contrat de mariage. Certains profitaient donc du recours pour mettre un terme à un régime légal qui pouvait octroyer à l'épouse la moitié de la fortune du ménage[50]. Même lorsque les conjoints ne s'étaient pas mariés au Bas-Canada, et n'étaient donc probablement pas régis par la communauté de biens, le jugement entérinait la renonciation de l'épouse[51].

Les Canadiennes (françaises) semblent avoir été plus avisées en la matière. Nombre d'entre elles signaient un contrat de mariage. Les rurales, surtout s'il s'agissait d'un second ou d'un troisième mariage, étaient les plus susceptibles de récupérer leur mise initiale, bien qu'on retrouve également de jeunes citadines dans le groupe. Sur les 99 femmes à qui le tribunal octroya des biens (en argent et/ou en nature), 88 étaient Canadiennes, dont 61 résidaient dans l'espace rural. Seules dix épouses portant un nom anglophone ou germanique furent dans la même situation, dont trois avaient épousé un Canadien. Si on ne tient compte que des cas où une somme d'argent précise fut allouée à l'épouse, la proportion de Canadiennes est encore plus écrasante (79/82). Un petit nombre se vit attribuer un avoir se chiffrant en centaines de livres auxquelles s'ajoutaient parfois des effets personnels et des immeubles. Isabella Campbell, la seule Britannique à avoir accepté la communauté de biens, récupéra la moitié d'une maison estimée à £700, en plus du mobilier, comme quoi le droit français pouvait à l'occasion bénéficier aussi aux anglophones[52]. Mais la médiane des sommes restituées se chiffrait plutôt à £97, certaines épouses n'obtenant que quelques livres.

On s'étonne de constater que seulement cinq Canadiennes ont accepté et partagé la communauté de biens après avoir fait procéder à un inventaire de l'avoir commun. Les autres renoncèrent à la communauté sans recourir à l'inventaire des biens domestiques qui aurait permis de prendre une décision véritablement éclairée. Du reste, certains avocats conseillaient très mal leur cliente et semblaient plutôt désireux de régler les affaires de l'époux d'une façon qui ne porte pas trop atteinte aux créanciers (des clients potentiels, faut-il le rappeler). Ainsi, Marguerite Gougeon se plaignit au tribunal que l'avocat qui la représentait en cour avait obtenu contre sa volonté la renonciation à la communauté de biens. Elle espérait pourtant l'accepter après en avoir fait dresser un inventaire. Alors que le mari ne s'était pas opposé à l'action de sa femme jusque-là, il en serait venu aux coups avec son épouse parce que celle-ci demandait au notaire de ne pas tenir compte de la renonciation déposée en cour contre sa volonté[53]. Il fallait une réelle détermination pour s'opposer à un mari têtu, et même violent, qui bénéficiait de la solidarité masculine des juges, des avocats et sans doute des créanciers.

Au terme d'une procédure coûteuse, l'épouse n'obtenait donc souvent que la seule capacité juridique sur les biens qu'elle pourrait acquérir ultérieurement. Pour celles qui faisaient commerce ou qui exerçaient déjà un métier, l'avantage n'était sans doute pas négligeable[54]. L'acquisition d'une personnalité juridique permettait pour bon nombre d'obtenir du crédit. Dès le jugement, les cordons de la bourse des parents et amis se déliaient sans risquer de voir ce nouvel apport être dilapidé par le mari ou englouti par sa faillite. Nul doute que cette embellie ne profitait pas qu'à l'épouse. Mais pour celles qui ne pouvaient plus compter sur leur mari, obtenir du crédit s'avérait essentiel. La séparation de biens avait également pour effet d'empêcher que le mari absent, une fois de retour à la maison, fasse main basse sur le fruit du travail et des économies de son épouse industrieuse[55]. Après avoir été abandonnée par son mari vingt ans plus tôt, Victoire Ritchot fit si bien en l'absence de son époux qu'elle décida d'agrandir la maison qu'elle possédait au village de Pointe-aux-Trembles, près de Montréal. Peu préoccupée par les formalités juridiques jusque-là, elle décida néanmoins d'obtenir une séparation de biens « [. . .] sur les observations qu'on lui auroit faites que son mari pouvoit rentrer dans la moitié des augmentations qu'elle pourroit faire, même en l'absence de son dit mari »[56].

Cela dit, pour bon nombre de femmes séparées de biens, l'acquisition d'une nouvelle personnalité juridique constituait surtout un paravent légal pour l'époux insolvable. Contrairement à Victoire Ritchot qui fit saisir en justice les biens de son mari absent, plusieurs de ces femmes n'apparaissent pour ainsi dire jamais dans les dossiers judiciaires postérieurs à la séparation de biens[57]. Parfois, certaines rachetaient une partie des biens domestiques vendus en justice, ce qui profitait à l'ensemble du ménage. D'autres, il est vrai, usaient pleinement de leur nouveau statut juridique. Quelques épouses remplacèrent en effet leur mari comme associée de l'entreprise en difficultés financières[58]. C'est le cas particulièrement de Marie-Claire Perrault, conjointe d'Austin Cuvillier. Appartenant à une famille de marchands, Marie-Claire n'agissait sans doute pas comme simple prête-nom dans la société d'encanteurs établie par son mari : très active devant les tribunaux, elle poursuivit bon an mal an de nombreux débiteurs sous le nom de « Marie-Claire Cuvillier & Compagnie »[59]. Une fois les difficultés financières passées cependant, elle céda formellement la place à son mari.

Conclusion

Ce dernier cas montre que l'action en séparation de biens pouvait devenir un outil précieux entre les mains d'un mari en déconfiture, pour peu que celui-ci ait été bien conseillé. Dotée d'une nouvelle personnalité juridique, l'épouse séparée de biens recouvrait le ménage d'une sorte de « voile corporatif ». Elle protégeait une partie de l'avoir familial et se trouvait mieux placée que son mari pour obtenir un crédit particulièrement nécessaire en ces moments de soudure financière. Bien connue des historiens et des historiennes, la collusion des époux pour frauder les créanciers était un stratagème généralement combattu par les tribunaux, avec plus ou moins de succès. Mais ici, il importe de souligner que cet usage marital d'un recours en principe réservé à l'épouse était pleinement légitimé par la Cour du banc du roi de Montréal, à une époque où la procédure de faillite et le droit des corporations n'existaient pas encore au Bas-Canada[60]. Peut-on parler de « détournement » du droit coutumier français ? Je ne le pense pas, pas entièrement du moins.

Tout d'abord, certaines femmes mariées plus fortunées que d'autres, mais également plus familières avec le droit français, profitaient pleinement de ce pouvoir et des possibilités qu'offrait la justice bas-canadienne. Toutes n'accédaient pas au cœur de la sphère masculine du marché comme Marie-Claire Perrault, mais plusieurs amélioraient vraisemblablement leur sort, même s'il est difficile de retracer leur parcours dans les sources disponibles[61]. Quelques épouses d'origine britannique, comme Isabella Campbell, semblent même avoir tiré leur épingle du jeu malgré tout. Mais ces dernières agissaient plus souvent en marge d'une justice civile appliquant un droit qui leur était mal connu, peut-être davantage que pour leurs consœurs canadiennes habituées aux démarches conjointes auprès du notaire ou du juge[62]. Cela dit, Victoire Ritchot a longtemps vécu en l'absence de son mari sans avoir senti le besoin de se rendre au palais de justice. Il est évident que l'économie dite informelle ne s'embarrassait pas beaucoup de poursuites en justice ni même de visites chez le notaire. Il ne fait pas de doute que ces activités « infrajuridiques » étaient néanmoins régulées par des usages tout de même infléchis par le droit en vigueur, toujours susceptible d'être mobilisé (comme le cas de Ritchot le montre bien). Bien plus que la honte évoquée par Rosalie Papineau, c'est la faible utilité ou accessibilité du recours judiciaire qui explique le petit nombre de demandes en séparation de biens soumises par les femmes mariées. Combien d'épouses (ou leur mari) n'ont pas jugé bon saisir le tribunal ou, peut-être comme la pauvre Mme Saint-G., n'ont pas osé recourir à l'action en séparation de biens? Combien n'ont tout simplement pas pu s'en prévaloir, faute de ressources suffisantes ou par ignorance?

D'ailleurs, la pratique judiciaire que j'ai étudiée ne fait pas beaucoup écho au témoignage de Rosalie Papineau. Certes, les femmes qui réclamèrent la séparation de biens semblent avoir été sans reproche. Certaines procédures soulignent leurs qualités et leur contribution indéfectible au bien-être familial, selon une formule qui visiblement se transmettait entre avocats. Mais la plupart des demandes ne s'embarrassaient pas de telles précautions stéréotypées. Il ne semble pas y avoir eu de *double standard* généralisé, sans doute parce que la demande en justice n'était pas souvent contestée par le mari. Le discours genré, auquel plusieurs études nous ont habitués, était manifestement moins pertinent dans les circonstances. De même, on ne retrouve pas ici, sous la plume des avocats, la vision chevaleresque justifiant ailleurs l'intervention du tribunal au nom de la protection de femmes mariées. Le portrait d'un sexe naturellement faible et sans défense n'est pas tellement présent dans les pièces judiciaires. Certes, quelques demandes exposaient la précarité de l'épouse négligée ou abandonnée, quitte à forcer le trait à l'occasion[63]. Mais, dans la très grande majorité de ces dossiers, on se souciait peu de décrire la situation, réelle ou imaginée, des femmes ou des enfants (on ne sait presque rien de ceux-ci). Ce qui ressort surtout, c'est la volonté de neutraliser le plus possible la charge subversive (à l'encontre de l'ordre patriarcal) ou déstabilisatrice (menaçant la sécurité contractuelle) d'un recours fondé sur le droit coutumier français. Déjà, l'accès difficile à ce savoir technique jouait au détriment de ceux et celles qui étaient peu familiers avec la tradition juridique française. Mais qui plus est, les aspects avantageux de ce droit (le régime de la communauté de biens ou les reprises de l'épouse) ont reçu la lecture la plus stricte que les juges et même les avocats pouvaient leur donner, sans doute à la satisfaction de l'élite marchande et masculine de Montréal.

C'est aussi en ce sens qu'il n'est pas vraiment possible de parler de « détournement » de la coutume de Paris. Les études sur la France d'Ancien Régime montrent que le recours en séparation de biens donnait également lieu à une collusion entre époux. Elles ont de même révélé l'existence d'un contrôle judiciaire qui, susceptible de devenir plus strict, conférait aux échanges économiques et au crédit une certaine stabilité. Il n'en demeure pas moins qu'à partir de la fin des années 1810, la pratique judiciaire montréalaise se transforme au rythme des difficultés économiques de la colonie. Les avocats canadiens, mais aussi leurs confrères d'origine britannique, s'entichent résolument de cette procédure en l'utilisant plus volontiers comme solution partielle à l'endettement de leurs clients. Dès lors, on observe une évaluation plus stricte des demandes en ce qui concerne la détermination de la dot de l'épouse (assimilée au seul apport décrit au contrat de mariage). Les notaires, chargés par la cour d'établir le montant des reprises, ne se montrent pas toujours très rigoureux dans leur appréciation. Mais les juges ne manquent pas de soustraire les sommes réclamées qui apparaissent sans justification à leurs yeux. Certains notaires plus stricts, comme Nicolas-Benjamin Doucet[64], sont visiblement sur la même longueur d'onde que le tribunal. Par ailleurs, plusieurs avocats ne jugent même pas utile de faire procéder à l'évaluation de la dot ou de la communauté de biens. Le stratagème apparaît clairement pour les maris qui souhaitaient visiblement mettre un terme au régime non désiré de la coutume de Paris, en forçant sa dissolution en justice. Pourtant, cet usage judiciaire était proscrit par les juristes : la dissolution devait se conclure par la restitution de la dot (le cas échéant) ou, plus rarement, par le partage de la communauté de biens. Cette étape de la liquidation du régime matrimonial était jugée essentielle pour rendre la séparation de biens pleinement effective[65].

Si, dans certains cas, des épouses ont pu jouir de l'application généreuse du droit, il semble cependant que leur marge de négociation se soit nettement rétrécie à mesure que le temps passait. De ce point de vue, les avantages de la coutume de Paris apparaissent somme toute assez limités pour les femmes durant le mariage, même pour celles qui se présentaient devant la justice pour sauver l'avoir que le droit français leur reconnaissait. Non seulement perdaient-elles pour la plupart leur portion de la communauté de biens, mais peu de femmes mariées arrivaient à récupérer une mise initiale au demeurant assez modeste. On a peut-être exagéré les différences entre le système de droit civil et de *common law*, en négligeant la pratique judiciaire tissée au jour le jour par des juges, mais aussi par des avocats qui, bien que d'horizons divers, partageaient une même conception patriarcale et capitaliste de l'ordre des choses.

NOTES

* Je tiens à remercier Martin Robert et Manuel Truffy pour la numérisation des sources judiciaires à la base de ce chapitre, ainsi que le Centre d'histoire des régulations sociales (UQAM) qui a rendu possible cette numérisation.

1. Rosalie Papineau à Perrine Viger (sa cousine), janvier 1813, dans *Rosalie Papineau-Dessaulles, Correspondance, 1805-1854*, édité par Georges Aubin et Renée Blanchet, Montréal, Varia, 2001, p. 37-38. Le contexte suggère que Rosalie Papineau fait référence à la séparation *de biens* et non à la séparation *de corps* qui implique la cessation de la cohabitation.

2. Bettina Bradbury, *Wife to Widow : Lives, Laws, and Politics in Nineteenth-Century Montreal*, Vancouver, UBC Press, 2011, p. 62-63.

3. On consultera notamment : Amy Louise Erickson, « Coverture and Capitalism », *History Workshop Journal* 59, n° 1 (2005), p. 1-16; Margot C. Finn, *The Character of Credit : Personal Debt in English Culture, 1740-1914*, Cambridge, Cambridge University Press, 2003; Craig Muldrew, « 'A Mutual Assent of Her Mind'? Women, Debt, Litigation and Contract in Early Modern England », *History Workshop Journal*, 55, n° 1, 2003, p. 47-71; Amy Louise Erickson, *Women and Property in Early Modern England*, London, Routledge, 1997.

4. Rosalie Papineau à Perrine Viger, janvier 1813, dans George Aubin et Renée Blanchet (dir.), *Rosalie Papineau-Dessaulles, Correspondance, 1805-1854*, Montréal, Varia, 2001, p. 38.

5. Voir entre autres Mary Beth Sievens, *Stray Wives : Marital Conflict in Early National New England*, New York, New York University Press, 2005.

6   Pour un exemple récent, voir Nancy Christie, « Women in the Formal and Informal Economies of Late Eighteenth-Century Quebec, 1763-1830 », *Gender and History*, 29, n° 1, 2017, p. 104-123.

7   Cette tendance s'observe dans de nombreux domaines de recherche dont les travaux placent le pouvoir et l'identité au cœur de leurs préoccupations. Pour les rapports de genre, voir par exemple Bettina Bradbury et Tamara Myers, (dir.), *Negotiating Identities in Nineteenth- and Twentieth-Century Montreal*, Vancouver, UBC Press, 2005.

8   Cette capacité juridique n'était pas entière cependant. La femme séparée de biens devait obtenir l'aval de son mari pour tout acte translatif de propriété (vente, hypothèque, etc.). Voir Robert-Joseph Pothier, *Traité de la puissance du mari*, Paris, Chasseriau, 1823, p. 6-7.

9   Julie Hardwick, « Seeking Separations : Gender, Marriages, and Household Economies in Early Modern France », *French Historical Studies*, 21, n° 1, 1998, 157-180. Voir plus généralement Julie Hardwick, *Family Business : Litigation and the Political Economies of Daily Life in Early Modern France*, Oxford, Oxford University Press, 2009.

10 Evelyn Kolish, *Nationalismes et conflits de droits : Le débat du droit privé au Québec (1760-1840)*, LaSalle, Québec, Éditions Hurtubise HMH Ltée, 1994; Bradbury, *Wife to Widow*.

11 Voir Lee Holcombe, *Wives and Property : Reform of the Married Women's Property Law in Nineteenth-Century England*, Toronto, University of Toronto Press, 1983; Norma Basch, *In the Eyes of the Law, Women, Marriage, and Property in Nineteenth Century New York*, Ithaca, NY, Cornell University Press, 1982; Lori Chambers, *Married Women and Property Law in Victorian Ontario*, Toronto, University of Toronto Press for the Osgoode Society, 1997.

12 Susan Staves, *Married Women's Separate Property in England, 1660-1833*, Cambridge, Massachusetts, Harvard University Press, 1990; Marylynn Salmon, *Women and the Law of Property in Early America*, Chapel Hill, University of North Carolina Press, 1986.

13 Chambers, *Married Women and Property Law in Victorian Ontario*, p. 17. Pour la Nouvelle-Écosse, où une *Court of Chancery* existait dès le XVIIIe siècle, Julian Gwyn n'a trouvé aucun recours devant cette juridiction avant 1802 : « Female Litigants Before the Civil Courts of Nova Scotia, 1749-1801 », *Histoire sociale/Social History*, 36, n° 72, 2003, p. 345. Voir aussi Philip Girard, « Married Women's Property, Chancery Abolition, and Insolvency Law : Law Reform in Nova Scotia, 1820-1867 », dans Philip Girard et Jim Phillips (dir.), *Essays in the History of Canadian Law*, vol. 3, *Nova Scotia* Toronto, University of Toronto Press for the Osgoode Society, 1990.

14 Les biens propres, ou biens de famille, sont les immeubles hérités d'un parent ou reçus en donation en ligne directe.

15 Bradbury, *Wife to Widow*, 86.

16 Jan Noel, *Along a River : The First French-Canadian Women*, Toronto, University of Toronto Press, 2013.

17   Josette Brun, *Vie et mort du couple en Nouvelle-France, Québec et Louisbourg au XVIIIe siècle*, Montréal, McGill-Queen's University Press, 2006.

18   Brian Young, « Getting Around Legal Incapacity : The Legal Status of Married Women in Trade in Mid-Nineteenth-Century Lower Canada », dans Peter Baskerville (dir.), *Canadian Papers in Business History*, vol. 1, Victoria, University of Victoria Public History Group, 1989, p. 1-16.

19   On se rapportera au second chapitre du livre de Bradbury, *Wife to Widow*.

20   Pour le Bas-Canada, Bradbury, *Wife to Widow*; Christie, « Women in Formal and Informal Economies ».

21   On trouvera des éléments de ces stratégies dans : Françoise Noël, *Family Life and Sociability in Upper and Lower Canada, 1780-1870*, Montréal, McGill-Queen's University Press, 2003; W. Peter Ward, *Courtship, Love, and Marriage in Nineteenth-Century English Canada*, Montréal, McGill-Queen's University Press, 1990 ; Jane Errington, *Wives and Mothers, Schoolmistresses and Scullery Maid s: Working Women in Upper Canada, 1790-1840*, Montréal, McGill-Queen's University Press, 2007.

22   Pour l'usage conjugal du *power of attorney*, voir Joanne Bailey, *Unquiet Lives : Marriage and Marriage Breakdown in England, 1660-1800*, Cambridge, Cambridge University Press, 2003, p. 98-99; Laurel Thatcher Ulrich, *Good Wives : Image and Reality in the Lives of Women in Northern New England, 1650-1750*, New York, Vintage, 1991.

23   Cela dit, peu de femmes mariées jouirent d'une telle procuration durant le régime français, si l'on excepte la dernière décennie troublée de la Nouvelle-France. Outre Brun, *Vie et mort du couple*, 31-34, voir Catherine Ferland et Benoît Grenier, « Les procuratrices à Québec au XVIIIe siècle : résultats préliminaires d'une enquête sur le pouvoir des femmes en Nouvelle-France », dans Catherine Ferland et Benoît Grenier (dir.), *Femmes, Culture et Pouvoir : Relectures de l'histoire au féminin, XVe -XXe siècles*, Québec, Presses de l'Université Laval, 2010, p. 127-144.

24   Nous ignorons tout de cette pratique au moment où Rosalie Papineau prenait la plume, mais quelques sondages pour les premières décennies du XIXe siècle indiquent qu'elle était peu développée.

25   Soulignons les recherches récentes de Thierry Nootens pour le premier tiers du XXe siècle, en particulier : *Genre, patrimoine et droit civil : les femmes mariées de la bourgeoisie québécoise en procès, 1900-1930*, Montréal, McGill-Queen's University Press, 2018.

26   Pour le Québec, on consultera notamment : Marie-Aimée Cliche, « L'infanticide dans la région de Québec (1660-1969) », *Revue d'histoire de l'Amérique française*, 44, n° 1, 1990, p. 31-59; Marie-Aimée Cliche, « Les procès en séparation de corps dans la région de Montréal 1795-1879 », *Revue d'histoire de l'Amérique française*, 49, n° 1, 1995, p. 3-33; Kathryn Harvey, « Amazons and Victims : Resisting Wife-Abuse in Working-Class Montreal, 1869-1879 », *Journal of the Canadian Historical Association/ Revue de la société historique du Canada*, 2, 1991, p. 131-148. Voir aussi Constance Backhouse, *Petticoats and Prejudice : Women and Law in Nineteenth-Century Canada*, Toronto, Women's Press, 1991; Carolyn Strange, « Wounded Womanhood and Dead Men : Chivalry and the Trials of Clara Ford and Carrie Davis », dans Franca Iacovetta et

Mariana Valverde (dir.), *Gender Conflicts : New Essays in Women's History*, Toronto, University of Toronto Press, 1992, p. 149-188; Chambers, *Married Women and Property Law in Victorian Ontario*.

27 Evelyn Kolish, « Some Aspects of Civil Litigation in Lower Canada, 1785-1825 : Towards the Use of Court Records for Canadian Social History », *Canadian Historical Review*, 70, n° 3, 1989, p. 337-365. Pour la Nouvelle-Écosse du XVIIIe siècle, voir James Muir, *Law, Debt, and Merchant Power : The Civil Courts of 18th Century Halifax*, Toronto, University of Toronto Press, 2016.

28 Gwyn, « Female Litigants Before the Civil Courts of Nova Scotia, 1749-1801 »; Julian Gwyn, « Women as Litigants before the Supreme Court of Nova Scotia, 1754-1830 », dans Philip Girard, Jim Phillips et Barry Cahill (dir.), *The Supreme Court of Nova Scotia, 1754–2004: From Imperial Bastion to Provincial Oracle*, Toronto: University of Toronto Press, 2004, p. 294-320; Muir, *Law, Debt, and Merchant Power*, p. 29-31.

29 Grâce à un index pour les années 1795-1829 (société Archiv-Histo, Thémis I), j'ai identifié les causes impliquant une femme devant la juridiction civile supérieure de la Cour du banc du roi de Montréal. Dans un second temps, j'ai vérifié dans les dossiers judiciaires l'état matrimonial de ces femmes pour les années 1796, 1805, 1816 et 1825 (Bibliothèque et Archives nationales du Québec (BAnQ), centre d'archives de Montréal (CaM), dossiers civils de la Cour du banc du roi, district de Montréal, juridiction supérieure, TL19, S4, SS11). Dans l'ensemble, on ne compte guère plus d'une femme pour dix justiciables, encore moins pour le XIXe siècle. Les femmes mariées représentent généralement un peu plus de la moitié du contingent féminin. Mais dans la très grande majorité des cas, ces épouses accompagnaient leur mari, agissant très rarement de leur propre chef. Elles ne semblent pas avoir représenté leur conjoint devant cette juridiction. Il se peut toutefois que le portrait soit légèrement différent devant la juridiction inférieure de la Cour du banc du roi. Malheureusement, les archives de cette dernière n'étaient pas encore disponibles au moment d'effectuer notre recherche.

30 Sylvie Savoie, « La rupture du couple en Nouvelle-France : les demandes de séparation aux XVIIe et XVIIIe siècles », *Canadian Woman Studies/Les cahiers de la femme*, 7, n° 4, 1986, p. 58-63; Sylvie Savoie, « Les couples séparés : les demandes de séparation aux 17e et 18e siècles », dans André Lachance (dir.), *Les marginaux, les exclus et l'autre au Canada aux 17e et 18e siècles*, Saint-Laurent, Québec, Fides, 1996, p. 245-282; Marie-Aimée Cliche, « Les procès en séparation de corps ».

31 Outre Hardwick, « Seeking Separations » et *Family Business*, voir : Laurence Croq, « La vie familiale à l'épreuve de la faillite : les séparations de biens dans la bourgeoisie marchande parisienne aux XVIIe-XVIIIe siècles », *Annales de démographie historique*, 2, 2009, p. 33-52. Je n'ai pas pu consulter l'étude de Marie Landelle, « *Les plaintes en séparation sont éternelles* », masters, École des Chartres, 2012.

32 Jean-Philippe Garneau, « Civil Law, Legal Practitioners, and Everyday Justice in the Decades Following the *Quebec Act* of 1774 », trad. du français par Steven Watt, dans Constance B. Backhouse et W. Wesley Pue (dir.), *The Promise and Perils of Law: Lawyers in Canadian History*, Toronto, Irwin Law Inc., 2009, p. 129-139.

33   Aux fins de ce chapitre, ont été systématiquement repérés tous les dossiers en séparation de biens du district de Montréal pour la période 1795-1829 inclusivement (TL19, S4, SS11, CaM, BAnQ). Ici encore, j'ai pu compter sur l'index de la société Archiv-Histo déjà cité. L'identification des procès ne s'est donc pas faite à partir des jugements colligés dans les registres conçus à cet effet. Notons aussi qu'aucune décision concernant un procès en séparation de biens n'a été publiée dans les très rares recueils de jurisprudence de la période (George Pyke, *Cases Argued and Determined in the Court of King's Bench, for the District of Quebec* [...], Montréal, 1811); George Okill Stuart, *Reports of Cases Argued and Determined in the Court of King's Bench and in the Provincial Court of Appeals of Lower Canada* [...], Québec, Neilson and Cowan, 1834.

34   Croq, « La vie familiale à l'épreuve de la faillite », p. 33; Hardwick, « Seeking Separations », p. 162.

35   Hardwick, « Seeking Separations », p. 163. La situation semble s'être resserrée au milieu du XVIIIe siècle toutefois, alors que les femmes mariées virent leurs demandes plus fréquemment déboutées par les magistrats parisiens : Croq, « La vie familiale à l'épreuve de la faillite », p. 39-40. Pour le district de Montréal, sur les 198 causes dont l'issue est connue avec certitude, seulement huit demandes ont été rejetées et huit abandonnées avant que le jugement de la cour n'intervienne (tableau 9.1). Dans 24 autres causes, mention est faite d'un jugement sans que celui-ci n'ait été retrouvé dans le dossier. Une recherche dans les registres de jugement aurait sans doute permis de retracer quelques décisions additionnelles, mais sans que le portrait d'ensemble ne soit vraiment modifié. Mentionnons que j'ai consulté les principales pièces déposées au dossier afin de reconstituer, autant que possible, le déroulement du procès jusqu'à son terme. D'habitude, les dossiers conservaient l'original des procédures judiciaires émanant des avocats, d'un expert ou du greffier de la cour. Les jugements appartenaient à cette dernière catégorie, mais plusieurs d'entre eux sont néanmoins absents.

36   Marguerite Belecque c Paul Rinville, octobre 1828, n° 1974, TL19, S4, SS11, CaM, BAnQ.

37   Catherine Anger c Louis Cavilhe, juin 1798, n° 50, TL19, S4, SS11, CaM, BAnQ.

38   Les femmes parisiennes du XVIIIe siècle semblent avoir disposé d'une véritable autonomie d'action. Il faut dire que plusieurs possédaient une fortune personnelle qu'elles tentaient de protéger de la faillite de leur mari : Croq, « La vie familiale à l'épreuve de la faillite ».

39   En Angleterre comme en Nouvelle-Angleterre, les maris ne se gênaient pas pour faire publier des avis dans les journaux dans le but de tarir le crédit que les marchands accordaient à leur conjointe : Joanne Bailey, « Favoured or Oppressed? Married Women, Property and 'Coverture' in England, 1660-1800 », *Continuity and Change*, 17, n° 3, 2002, p. 351-372; Sievens, *Stray Wives*. L'étude de cette pratique reste à faire pour le Bas-Canada. Voir cependant Nancy Christie et Michael Gauvreau, « Marital Conflict, Ethnicity, and Legal Hybridity in Postconquest Quebec », *Journal of Family History*, 41, n° 4, 2016, p. 430-450.

40   La défense rédigée par George Stanley ressemble davantage à une confession de jugement qu'à une contestation de la demande puisqu'il admet « *all and every allegations in the Plaintiff's* [l'épouse] *declaration to be true* » et qu'il soumet au tribunal « *whether the said Plantiff ought to have or obtain the conclusions of her said declaration* ».

Eliza-Margaret Mason c George Stanley, *plea*, février 1821, n° 1835, TL19, S4, SS11, CaM, BAnQ.

41 L'avocat John Boston représentait tant l'épouse que son mari dans les procès des années 1820 : Elizabeth Boston c John Sanford, avril 1823, n° 1803, TL19, S4, SS11, CaM, BAnQ; Lucile Lebrun c John Sanford, juin 1825, n° 620, TL19, S4, SS11, CaM, BAnQ. Durant l'année 1819, Jean-Roch Rolland défendit Jean-Baptiste Belly, poursuivi pour dettes, avant de déposer une demande en séparation de biens au nom de l'épouse de ce dernier : Marie-Angélique Heynemand c Jean-Baptiste Belly dit St Louis, février 1819, n° 739, TL19, S4, SS11, CaM, BAnQ.

42 Je n'ai trouvé qu'un seul cas où un créancier est intervenu avec succès pour contester une demande en séparation de biens en invoquant la fraude du mari. Ce créancier était un avocat ayant déjà représenté des femmes réclamant une séparation de biens. Geneviève Dumouchelle c Nicolas Boyer, François Bender intervenant, octobre 1829, n° 2142, TL19, S4, SS11, CaM, BAnQ.

43 Les frais judiciaires de l'action en séparation de biens étaient en principe supportés par le mari, ce qui alourdissait les dettes de ce dernier. Les frais étaient de l'ordre d'une dizaine de livres, parfois moins, mais souvent un peu plus. Marie-Louise Frégau obtint £11 dans le jugement lui accordant la séparation de biens, mais les frais de justice s'élevaient à un peu plus de £15. Marie-Louise Frégau c Michel Privé, avril 1827, n° 268, TL19, S4, SS11, CaM, BAnQ.

44 Trois dossiers indiquent qu'un tel exercice a été réalisé, mais *a posteriori*, devant notaire et à la demande du mari qui cherchait visiblement à favoriser son épouse au détriment des créanciers. Par exemple : Catherine Bérard c Pierre Demers, février 1828, n° 597, TL19, S4, SS11, CaM, BAnQ.

45 Près d'un tiers des renonciations retracées intervinrent avant le jugement déclarant la séparation de biens, ce qui constitue une aberration juridique. Pourtant, la Cour du banc du roi s'est prononcée en faveur de cette pratique incongrue en 1824. Voir McDonell c Atkinson (19 février 1824), James Reid Collection, *Court of King's Bench bound notes*, vol. 5, p. 27-31, MG24 B173, Bibliothèque et Archives du Canada.

46 Après répartition proportionnelle des 44 cas inconnus, le taux de renonciation s'élève à environ 85 % des couples mariés sous le régime de la communauté de biens.

47 Le terme utilisé le plus souvent est celui de reprises, plutôt que dot. La coutume de Paris n'appartient pas à l'univers du régime dotal qui prévalait surtout dans les pays de droit écrit. Le concept de la dot n'avait d'ailleurs pas la même signification en pays coutumier qu'en pays de droit écrit. Claude-Joseph de Ferrière, *Dictionnaire de droit et de pratique*, nouvelle édition, tome 1, Paris, Veuve Brunet, 1769.

48 Pour obtenir ses reprises, l'épouse devait produire un rapport notarié détaillant ses droits matrimoniaux, à la suite duquel un second jugement intervenait pour homologuer (ou non) les conclusions du notaire.

49 Elizabeth Bunker c Thomas McLeish, octobre 1820, n° 1712, TL19, S4, SS11, CaM, BAnQ.

50 En 1828, un couple a même déposé sa demande en séparation de biens le jour de la célébration du mariage! N'ayant pas fait de contrat de mariage, c'est le régime légal de

	la communauté de biens qui s'appliquait dès lors pour eux, une situation que seul le tribunal avait le pouvoir de changer. Plumea Patrick c Aaron Wheeler, octobre 1828, n° 1890, TL19, S4, SS11, CaM, BAnQ.
51	Le jugement traduit le doute sur cette question en parlant de la communauté de biens « *that might subsist between her and the said defendant* ». Elizabeth Harvie c Robert Armour, juin 1819, n° 353, TL19, S4, SS11, CaM, BAnQ. Cette question de droit international privé ne semble pas avoir été débattue devant la Cour du banc du roi, mais la recherche en ce sens reste à faire.
52	Isabella Campbell c Thomas Prior, octobre 1817, n° 815, TL19, S4, SS11, CaM, BAnQ.
53	Marguerite Gougeon (assistée de son père) c Jean-Baptiste Poirier, octobre 1820, n° 893, TL19, S4, SS11, CaM, BAnQ.
54	Mais ces femmes pouvaient très bien alors être reconnues marchandes publiques, sans devoir passer par une action en séparation de biens.
55	Au moins 24 cas concernent une épouse abandonnée ou délaissée par son mari, tandis que 50 autres dossiers témoignent d'une conduite maritale défaillante, sinon abusive.
56	Victoire Ritchot c Charles Ratté, octobre 1820, n° 1522, TL19, S4, SS11, CaM, BAnQ.
57	Une recherche dans les dossiers de la juridiction civile inférieure de la Cour du banc du roi, de même que dans les archives notariales, modifierait peut-être ce portrait obtenu à partir de l'index des dossiers de la juridiction civile supérieure de cette même Cour du banc du roi.
58	Outre le cas de Marie-Claire Perrault, voir : Eleanor Fraser c William Buchanan, octobre 1823, n° 1570, TL19, S4, SS11, CaM, BAnQ. Un autre cas semble permettre au mari insolvable de poursuivre une association autrement menacée. Les frères Cutter s'étant unis à deux sœurs, celles-ci reprirent le flambeau : Sophia Whittemore c Ezekiel Cutter, février 1828, n° 573, TL 19, S4, SS11, BAnQ.
59	Dans les nombreux procès qui s'échelonnent sur plusieurs années à partir de 1810, la nouvelle société s'affichait sans ambages sous la désignation de « Marie-Claire Perrault, encanteure, courtière et marchande publique, séparée quant aux biens de Austin Cuvillier, écuyer, son époux, de Montréal, et Jacques-Antoine Cartier, marchand et encanteur, de Montréal, faisant commerce sous le nom de Marie-Claire Cuvillier & Compagnie ».
60	Evelyn Kolish, « L'introduction de la faillite au Bas-Canada : conflit social ou national ? », *Revue d'histoire de l'Amérique française*, 40, n° 2, automne 1986, p. 215-238.
61	On retrouve devant les tribunaux un certain nombre de ces femmes ayant obtenu leur séparation de biens en justice. L'étude de leur histoire juridique reste à faire plus systématiquement, mais il est évident que celles qui disparaissent du radar des hommes de loi étaient de loin les plus nombreuses, ce qui nous laisse dans l'ignorance la plus complète de leur sort réel.
62	C'est l'impression assez nette qui ressort de la fréquentation des archives notariales et judiciaires de la région de Montréal pour cette période.
63	Voir à ce sujet Jean-Philippe Garneau, « Des femmes abandonnées par leur mari : récits judiciaires de l'absence conjugale dans la région de Montréal au début du 19e siècle »,

dans Emmanuelle Charpentier et Benoît Grenier (dir.), *Les Femmes face à l'absence de l'Antiquité à l'époque contemporaine : terre, mer, outre-mer (Europe-Amérique du Nord)*, Rennes, Presses Universitaires de Rennes, à paraître.

64 Rappelons que Nicolas-Benjamin Doucet est l'auteur d'un traité juridique expliquant en anglais les rudiments du droit civil français. Voir son *Fundamental Principles of the Laws of Canada*, Montréal, John Lovell, 1842.

65 Plusieurs auteurs comme Pothier rappellent que le jugement devait être exécuté sans fraude. Concrètement, cela signifie que le mari devait avoir restitué la dot à son épouse ou que, du moins, celle-ci ait entrepris des démarches en ce sens (l'estimation de sa dot étant vraisemblablement une étape de cette démarche). Voir Pothier, *Traité de la puissance du mari*, p. 324. Cette exigence ne figure pas dans le Code de procédure civile du Bas-Canada, au chapitre traitant du recours en séparation de biens (articles 972 à 984).

Getting Their Man: The NWMP as Accused in the Territorial Criminal Court in the Canadian North-West, 1876–1903

Shelley A.M. Gavigan[*]

Introduction: Low Law and the Meanings of Justice

Low law, found everywhere in the lives of poor and marginalized peoples, has long been relegated to muted insignificance by high law, the "most loudly articulated account of law."[1] High law and its high justice processes have long ruled—in the legal academy and in courthouse corridors, chambers and court rooms dusted by power, legal actors in judicial robes and barristers' gowns, and litigants with money and property at stake. One is hard pressed to find the faces or legal struggles of the poor in these places. Their sites of justice are invariably less august. Historians of low law courts and tribunals find justice that is unadorned, leaner, and usually meaner—more "No Frills" than "Whole Foods." In the current Canadian context, low justice can be found in small town curling rinks and Legion halls, in justice of the peace courts, and in windowless urban office buildings, where matters such as landlord and tenant and social assistance issues are adjudicated, sometimes presided over by legally trained adjudicators—often not—sometimes with lawyers—often not.

High law's chains and claims have been rattled as Canadian legal historians have begun to turn their attention to forms of low law and sites of low justice.[2] However, myriad methodological challenges await the historian of low law and justice. The people of low law, especially children, women, Indigenous prisoners, and even magistrates, were not people of wealth and have not left many words, letters, diaries, or newspaper articles. There are few official reports of their "small" cases. The records and documents are often thin and incomplete, where they exist at all. Historians who comb official records and government reports—police, immigration, hospital, asylum, Indian department records, treaty annuity pay lists, penitentiary registers, and so on— are thrilled when they catch a glimpse of someone's name, distressed when another's name simply drops off a page. Researchers often turn to newspaper accounts of legal proceedings because the original records have been lost or culled.[3] But even here, one often does not find extensive reports. Working with and between gaps and silences, and statistics "incomplete and interpretive as they are,"[4] legal historians piece together what we can, looking wide to find traces, mindful that the stories we tell are not pieces of a jigsaw puzzle, but rather interpretations of partial fragments of lives engaged, and often irreparably harmed, by low law and justice.

While "every day criminal justice"[5] or law "for the lower orders"[6] is self-evidently not high law, is low law best known only by what it is most not? Does it simply underscore the essence of high law and justice, and illustrate the legal and social distance from the Supreme Court down to the justice of the peace court or welfare tribunal? Recent historical work on low law rejects fixed or static notions of the meaning and sites of low law. In her work on local governance in Upper Canada/Ontario, Mary Stokes has widened the analytical frame of high law and low law, away from an exclusive focus on the "judicial" and a "restrictive vision of binary hierarchy."[7] In his study of petty justice in nineteenth-century New Brunswick, Paul Craven also argues that one should not think of low law simply as law for the lower orders, but as "an administrative, legislative, regulatory and judicial whole."[8] For Craven, "high" and "low" law sites—where the power and privilege associated with state, class, and gender are either expressed or experienced—are not silos as he demonstrates "considerable interplay" between them.[9] In his work on borderline crime, Bradley Miller similarly speaks of sites of "convergence" between high law and low law.[10] This advice to look at different contexts and to eschew bifurcation in favour of connections, convergence, and interplay is most assuredly sound.

In this chapter, I take up some of that advice. However, I am interested less in the lines or interplay between high and low justice, than in the lines and interplay between different forms of low law and justice, and in a different set of "lower order" accused persons. Through a study of a small set of nineteenth-century criminal cases from Western Canada involving members of the North-West Mounted Police (NWMP) accused of criminal and disciplinary offences, I study the relationship between two statutorily created and ostensibly legal regimes: criminal justice and police discipline.

To do this, I rely on two kinds of archival records housed in different archives. The first, and foremost, is comprised of two different sets of court records, housed at the Provincial Archives of Saskatchewan in Regina. These are court records pertaining to Hugh Richardson, who was appointed in 1876 as one of the first three stipendiary magistrates of the North-West Territories (NWT). Richardson, born in England but raised in what is now southern Ontario, was called to the Bar in Upper Canada in 1847 and practised law in Woodstock until his appointment as chief clerk of the Department of Justice. He received his commission as stipendiary magistrate for the NWT in 1876.[11] During his career, he also served in the militia, rising to the rank of lieutenant-colonel, a title by which he continued to be known in the NWT. Richardson and his family made their home in the territorial capital of Battleford from his arrival on 27 September 1877 until 1883 when the capital shifted to Regina. The three stipendiary magistrates served ex officio as members of the Council of the NWT. Richardson, who has been described as "the most influential member"[12] of the Council, played a leadership role in legislative drafting (territorial ordinances) and, later, as legal expert and advisor to the territorial government.[13]

During his time as stipendiary magistrate in the Saskatchewan District,[14] he frequently sat in Battleford (where court was held at the NWMP detachment), but he also travelled widely[15] to points as far west as Edmonton (387 km) and Fort Saskatchewan (400 km), and to the east, at Prince Albert (211 km) and Fort Carlton (150 km). His court records show that he also travelled to the far south east of the NWT (now southern Manitoba) to hear cases in Fort Ellice (611 km) and Shoal Lake (647 km). Even before he relocated to Regina, he travelled to the southern part of the NWT to hold court in Qu'Appelle (454 km) in 1881 and 1882. He was one of the first five judges appointed to the Supreme Court of the North-West Territories when it was created in 1886[16] and when the office of stipendiary magistrate was eliminated.

Hugh Richardson's court records, from his two different judicial positions in the NWT from 1876 until his retirement in 1903, yield fifteen members of the NWMP in the court records: twelve criminal accused persons, one police discipline accused, and two civil defendants.[17] My primary focus in this chapter is on the criminal and police discipline cases.

The second type of archival material from which I draw includes NWMP records and reports: the *Annual Reports of the Commissioner of the North-West Mounted Police*,[18] and the NWMP Personnel – Personnel Records, 1873–1904 that form part of the collection of Library and Archives Canada.[19] Initially, I turned to these two sets of NWMP records to see if they contained any additional information on the NWMP accused men I had found in the Richardson court files. The NWMP personnel records provide a bit more information about the men themselves and (less frequently) some additional information about the criminal charges. They also introduced me to the NWMP recruitment and termination process and to "defaulters' sheets" on which a member's disciplinary record was maintained. The NWMP used the language of "crimes" and "convictions" to describe these disciplinary offences and dispositions, although none were recorded as such in the NWMP's annual reporting of criminal case returns.

I also turned to the NWMP annual reports to see if the division superintendents or the commissioner himself included any reference to the criminal cases I had found in the court records. In the annual reports, I found a handful of other cases (which I discuss in the chapter) that engaged the criminal and police disciplinary processes. In combination, these two sources yield a broader range of accused men, including those charged with "crimes" against police discipline as well as desertion. From the annual reports, one finds that more constables and sub-constables were charged, punished, and imprisoned (sometimes for lengthier periods of time) for breaches of police discipline. As I will discuss below, five of the fourteen Mounted Police who appeared in Richardson's court as criminal accused (and whose NWMP personnel records have survived) had experienced police disciplinary processes and punishments for what the NWMP called disciplinary crimes.

In both legal contexts, the adjudicators before whom the accused police could find themselves were the most senior men in the NWMP, either their own superior officers (superintendents or inspectors) or the commissioner or assistant commissioner. These cases are interesting not least because the North-West Mounted Police force has long been synonymous with the face of law and justice in the early years of the NWT and regarded as essential to the colonial aspirations of the young Canadian state. Criminal prosecutions of members of the police and police discipline have not been at the forefront of legal historical research. And yet, they offer both an opportunity and a challenge to think through the lines, sites, and forms of law and justice, and the power relationship within and between "Mounted Police courts [and] the ordinary Courts of Law."[20] The questions they invite involve broad and narrow issues, including the meaning of legal and judicial process, and low law sites of justice and injustice. Did the police justices of the peace leave their "disciplinary" sensibilities at the door of the courtroom when they presided as justice of the peace in ordinary criminal matters? Was that even a reasonable prospect given that court sittings in the Territories were held in the police barracks? And yet, as I will demonstrate, the senior officers guarded the separate sphere of their disciplinary process; they could move back and forth with ease, but the quality of their internal justice was regarded as off limits.

Stokes's reminder of the analytical constraints imposed by "binary" categories is important here, because one might be too readily inclined to drop a heavy curtain between police disciplinary justice and (regular) criminal justice. But to do so would result in a study of only the "front of stage" parts of the unique and complex roles of the Mounted Police in the administration of justice in the NWT. The police disciplinary justice cases demonstrate instances of interrelationship and the importance of senior NWMP officers in both contexts. Tracking these cases allows one to see how interconnected these presumptively separate systems were. I am interested in revisiting the lines that define military/police and civil justice and, aided by the insights of historians Jeffrey McNairn and Greg Marquis, in demonstrating that the lines between these two sites of low law's justice were often messy and "blurred."[21]

In the next two sections, I introduce the legal framework of both regimes, before turning to cases of members of the Mounted Police who were prosecuted in one or both legal contexts. Despite the formally discrete processes, senior NWMP brass were, to say the least, significant and powerful actors in both. As I will show, these cases reveal the fluidity of their roles and their often close relationships with the stipendiary magistrate. More than a few procedural lapses occurred, and cases slipped back and forth between police discipline and criminal justice, often highlighting the tensions between the disciplinary priorities of the NWMP and the procedural safeguards of the criminal law process.

The Legal Framework of Criminal Justice in the North-West Territories

The acquisition of the territory of the western plains in 1870 had been a priority for the young Canadian state, one that eclipsed any process or consultation with the Indigenous peoples who lived there. However, the matter of the establishment of the institutions for the administration of justice also was not an immediate priority. The "inadequate legal system," described by Peter Ward as a renovated "hand-me-down judicial system" from the Hudson's Bay Company, was one in which the Lieutenant-Governor of the NWT was empowered to appoint a recorder and justices of the peace.[22] Six justices were appointed. Neither a legislative framework nor new institutions for the administration of justice were created until 1873, when John A. Macdonald's government "hastily"[23] introduced a trio of federal statutes to provide for the creation of the Department of the Interior (whose minister was to have control and management of the affairs of the NWT and to act as Superintendent General of Indian Affairs), for the administration of justice and the creation of the NWMP, and for the application of Canadian criminal legislation to the Territories.[24]

The most important Act introduced the office of stipendiary magistrate as the senior judicial position in the NWT, and created the North-West Mounted Police,[25] originally a force of three hundred men whose ranks rose and ebbed over the next three decades at the will of their political masters.[26] Although the police force was established almost immediately, the stipendiary magistrates were not appointed until 1876, when James Farquharson Macleod, Matthew Ryan, and Hugh Richardson received their commissions.

By the NWMP Act, 1873, a stipendiary magistrate was to be appointed "by commission" by the Governor General, to receive a yearly salary of $3,000 (as well as actual travel expenses), to hold office within the NWT "during pleasure," with the ability to perform magisterial and judicial functions of a justice of the peace or two justices of the peace.[27] The stipendiary magistrate was given summary jurisdiction to "hear and determine ... without the intervention of a jury," a wide range of offences, including larceny, assaults, sexual assaults on young girls, and obstruction and assault upon judicial and other officers in the execution of their duty, and to sentence convicted individuals to terms of imprisonment less than two years.[28]

The Manitoba Court of Queen's Bench was to play a role in respect of offences Parliament considered more serious: either a judge of that Court or two stipendiary magistrates sitting together were empowered to conduct trials without a jury for offences punishable by up to seven years imprisonment.[29] Only a Manitoba Queen's Bench judge had jurisdiction to try, before a jury, anyone charged with a capital offence.[30]

The North-West Territories Act, 1875[31] consolidated and amended the administrative institutions and legal framework of the Territories. The Lieutenant-Governor and Council were empowered to establish ordinances (local legislation for the Territories), which were to be laid before Parliament but no longer required its prior approval.[32]

The 1875 Act limited the summary jurisdiction of the NWT stipendiary magistrates through a cumbersome requirement that introduced a new supervisory role for the Manitoba Court of Queen's Bench: a judge of the Manitoba Court had jurisdiction to hear both criminal and civil claims, with a stipendiary magistrate sitting as an associate.[33] Given the expanse of the Territories and the difficult logistics of travel, this new requirement was an onerous impediment to access to justice and one that was immediately subject to criticism. In 1877, this requirement was abandoned, and the NWT stipendiary magistrates again had summary jurisdiction to adjudicate in criminal matters and, now, in civil matters as well.[34]

Beyond the judicial office of the stipendiary magistrate, the administration of justice was placed in the hands of the police. The NWMP Act, 1873 reposed in the NWMP extensive responsibility in relation to all aspects of criminal justice in the Territories. In addition to duties relating to preventing crime, preserving the peace, enforcing the laws and ordinances of the NWT, and apprehending alleged criminal offenders, the NWMP were to attend upon the stipendiary magistrate and justices of the peace, to execute their warrants, to escort prisoners and lunatics to their respective places of the confinement, and to confine sentenced prisoners in their guardrooms.[35]

Significantly, senior NWMP officers also had juridical authority. The men who served as NWMP commissioners and officers had been military men, many of them born in England. They brought to the NWMP and to the administration of justice in the NWT their military training and experience. However, only three (James Farquharson Macleod, William M. Herchmer, and Quebec-born Sévère Gagnon) had legal training and were qualified as barristers.[36]

By statute in 1873 and 1874, the commissioner (then George Arthur French, in charge of the whole force) was made, ex officio, first a justice of the peace and then a stipendiary magistrate. The office of assistant commissioner was created in 1874, and he and the superintendents (who would be in charge of each of the force's geographically dispersed divisions, as they were established), and potentially other officers appointed by the commissioner, were also made justices of the peace (ex officio) by virtue of these statutes.[37] In 1879, the assistant commissioner also became ex officio a stipendiary magistrate.[38] As suggested above, in these early years, stipendiary magistrates and justices of the peace had jurisdiction to conduct trials for less serious criminal and regulatory (ordinance) offences and to conduct preliminary criminal processes (committal hearings) for more serious offences, which would be tried by a more senior judge or magistrate. For a brief period (1875–1877), serious criminal and all civil matters were required to be tried by a Manitoba Queen's Bench judge, with a stipendiary magistrate sitting as an associate. But after 1877 and until 1886, when the judicial position of stipendiary magistrate was supplanted by the Supreme Court of the North-West Territories,[39] the stipendiary magistrates had jurisdiction to hear matters alone, or in serious or capital offence cases, with a justice of the peace as associate and a jury of six men.

In the NWT, the matters over which a justice of the peace, sitting alone or with another justice of the peace, had jurisdiction to preside ranged widely. Their jurisdiction included such matters as enforcing minor criminal statutes and the penal clauses of territorial ordinances; adjudicating on a person's sanity; issuing orders of alcohol interdiction; conducting marriages; and ordering veterinarians to inspect animals for sickness.[40] Presiding over committal hearings, justices of the peace received depositions of witnesses when serious offences were alleged and also committed accused persons for trial before stipendiary magistrates. Justices of the peace conducted summary trials in less serious criminal matters, sentencing those they convicted. The NWMP annual criminal case returns appended to the commissioners' annual reports reveal that the police justices presided over most of the criminal cases that came before justices of the peace,[41] including trials of accused persons they themselves had apprehended.[42] Then, as now, "low law/low justice" judicial officers carried the heaviest load.

When the five-member Supreme Court of the NWT came into being in 1886, with full civil and criminal jurisdiction, three stipendiary magistrates (Macleod, Richardson, and Quebec-born lawyer and jurist Charles-Borromée Rouleau, who had been appointed in 1883) became judges of the new court. The two new judges were Edward L. Wetmore and Thomas H. McGuire. The judges held office "during good behavior," a more secure form of judicial tenure that replaced their earlier "at pleasure" appointments as stipendiary magistrates and increased the bench's independence.

When, with the creation of the NWT Supreme Court, the position of stipendiary magistrate ceased to exist,[43] the commissioner (Lawrence W. Herchmer) and the assistant commissioner (Lawrence's brother William) continued to sit as justices of the peace.[44] Because no grand jury sat in the NWT, preliminary hearings would continue to be conducted by justices of the peace.[45] The capacity of the commissioner, assistant commissioner, and superintendents to continue to act as justices of the peace was formally clarified by statute in 1894.[46]

No image is more associated with Canadian law on the nineteenth-century plains than that of the NWMP. It would be an error in interpretation to suggest that the NWMP were anything less than the expression and embodiment of law and law enforcement in the NWT. However, they also represented a great deal more. They were representatives of the Queen and, as others have noted, the "eyes and ears of the government."[47] When no Indian Agent was appointed initially for the Treaty Seven region, it fell to the NWMP to attend to the First Nations in that territory.[48] They were responsible for delivering mail, patrolling the US/Canadian border, administering customs and quarantine, and providing supports and services to settlers and their communities. They kept an eye on European immigrant communities and a careful watch on the American Mormons thought to engage in polygamy. They policed the First Nations and provided relief to starving First Nations and Métis communities.[49] And so on. Whether one describes their role as "Agents of the National Policy,"[50] in which one can see the "first faint stirrings of the Canadian welfare state,"[51] and/or as an expression of colonial domination, and/or as the coercive and repressive arm of the young Canadian state, no historian of Western Canada denies their importance.[52]

THE NORTH WEST MOUNTED POLICE ACT: THE LEGAL REGULATION OF THE MEN OF THE NWMP

> The expressions made use of by [Acting Staff Constable] Marshall were to the effect that the prisoner in question [Henry Elliott] had been punished without any proof that he was guilty. He said it was an imitation of Capt. Frechette's mode of disposing of a case, "You are guilty! Prove yourself innocent."[53]

J.W. Little's statement above, in an 1878 case, recounts the assessment of the quality of police disciplinary justice by those on the receiving end. The roles of the NWMP in relation to the administration of justice and to government policy, including policies in relation to Indigenous peoples, have been well documented.[54] Less has been written about the role of the police in policing themselves, whether through the "conduct and discipline" process or through criminal prosecution of "delinquent" members who had offended Canadian criminal law.[55]

As well as playing important roles in the legal processes brought by civilians, the commissioner (and after 1875, also the assistant commissioner, inspectors commanding NWMP posts, and stipendiary magistrates[56]) had legal authority to investigate, judge, and punish members of the force for disciplinary offences. Notably, NWMP superintendents of the various divisions initially did not have this jurisdiction, although they were justices of the peace.[57] Thus, as of 1875, the commissioner and assistant commissioner, as ex officio stipendiary magistrates, were two of five of the senior judicial officers in the Territories and thus had jurisdiction over a wide range of criminal and police disciplinary offences. This combination of judicial and disciplinary power in the hands of individual NWMP officers produced jurisdictional confusion and unusual legal peril for the men of the force, peril that did not end even as a more regularized court system developed, as the NWMP managed to keep the courts at arm's length.

The Richardson court records yield twelve cases that came before him during his tenure as magistrate and later judge in which NWMP men were criminally prosecuted. The NWMP personnel records of these men add further information about them and about the disciplinary and/or dismissal proceedings several of them experienced. Their cases highlight the prominent role of the NWMP brass in both criminal justice and police justice. A review of their criminal cases and NWMP records, together with the annual reports of the NWMP commanding offices, opens a window onto another dimension of both criminal law and of the force itself in the NWT. The criminal and disciplinary processes, considered in relation to each other, demonstrate a perhaps unanticipated vulnerability of the members of the junior ranks of the police force to charges and imprisonment for myriad disciplinary crimes for which, as I will demonstrate, they had no recourse to appeal outside the force.

The original Act of 1873 had been silent with respect to internal governance of the rigidly hierarchical NWMP.[58] In fact, sixteen more years would pass before a complete set of written "Rules and Regulations" for the

North-West Mounted Police would be approved by Parliament.[59] RCMP historians William Beahen and Stan Horrall suggest that the influence of the Royal Irish Constabulary can be seen in the disciplinary procedures, but there were no provisions for forms of military punishment, such as "imprisonment, solitary confinement, punishment drills, flogging, [or] ... execution in time of war."[60]

Disciplinary crimes, as they were called, ranged from disobedience, insubordination, and drunkenness to desertion. A log of crimes and punishments was recorded in the "defaulters' books" for each division and on "defaulters' sheets" kept in individual members' personnel records. At the end of either disciplinary or criminal proceedings, NWMP offenders could find themselves in front of a discharge board of officers, facing dismissal.

In 1874, the NWMP's governing legislation, which came to be known as the "Police Act," was amended.[61] The statute's exhaustive section 22 listed no fewer than fifty offences for which a member of the force could be found in breach of discipline. This section cast a wide net, itemizing the expected forms of breach (disobedience, absenting oneself from duty, intoxication "however slight," misappropriation of funds, making false statements or certificates, insubordination, and mutiny) together with less precisely expressed forms of breaches, such as disgraceful or scandalous conduct. The section also made it a disciplinary offence for a member to use any of the necessaries belonging to any comrade without his consent, to be seen in a public house when not there on duty, and to borrow money from another member of the force of inferior rank, among others. The list was extensive. The commissioner himself had the discretion to dismiss, suspend, demote, or fine a member who was found to have committed a breach of discipline.

In 1875, Parliament scaled back the range of disciplinary offences to twenty-two, which ranged from immoral behaviour and intoxication to corruption, disobedience and insubordination, illegal or concealed possession of intoxicating liquor, and evincing partisan political support.[62] Imprisonment was added as an available form of punishment. On a written charge being preferred against a member, the commissioner, assistant commissioner, inspector commanding a post, or stipendiary magistrate was to cause that member to be brought before him. He was "then and there, *in a summary way*, to *investigate* the charge or charges, and *on oath if he thinks fit*, and if *proved to his satisfaction* . . . [to] *convict* the offender" (my emphasis); this was clearly an inquisitorial process, with a lower standard of proof. Upon conviction, the offending member was liable to a range of punishments, including a fine not exceeding one month's pay, imprisonment with hard labour, initially for a term not exceeding six months, or both a fine and imprisonment. The sentence imposed for a disciplinary "crime" was to be in addition to any punishment imposed for an offence under the law of the NWT. The consolidated "Police Act" of 1879 incorporated these changes.[63]

When the police legislation was revised in 1886, the disciplinary offences incorporated certain statutory changes made in 1882 and were enumerated as sub-sections (a) to (v) of section 18.[64] The 1882 changes increased the maximum sentence of imprisonment to twelve months (s. 18(2)). There were additional penalties for deserters (s. 24), and a dismissed or discharged member who neglected or refused to return his "clothing, arms, accoutrements and all property of the Crown in his possession" was also liable to be convicted of a summary conviction offence (s. 23). All sentences of imprisonment exceeding one month were to be reported to the commissioner, who could in his discretion reverse or mitigate the sentence. A sentence of imprisonment brought more than the pain of confinement: it packed a material punch as a member forfeited his pay during the period of imprisonment (s. 18(3)).

After 1886, under the leadership of a new commissioner, Lawrence W. Herchmer, the matter of conduct and discipline within the force took on great importance. Herchmer assumed command of a police force that had doubled its numbers in less than a year: by the end of 1885, the NWMP was comprised of 1,039 men, distributed across twelve divisions.[65] Prime Minister John A. Macdonald's appointment of Herchmer was controversial, as more than one senior NWMP officer in the force had thought he himself ought to have been elevated in place of Herchmer. The new commissioner had extensive history in the NWT but no history in the force. Herchmer became actively involved in discipline matters and developed a reputation as a "pitiless disciplinarian"; his approach to the scope of police discipline was broad and included using the disciplinary "code" to "punish men for actions that were really criminal in nature."[66]

Herchmer was aware of public concern and politicians' criticism of his expansive approach to the disciplinary process; he defended the importance of discipline over criminal justice:

> In the past men caught stealing, for example, have been charged with "disgraceful conduct" under the police regulations, which is what theft is considered to be. If we cannot continue to do this, it will be impossible to maintain discipline. In the civil courts they will be treated like civilians and punished like civilians with lenient sentences compared to those under the police regulation. What is more, there could be a delay of up to two months before their case would be heard. It is essential . . . that punishment is prompt if discipline is to succeed.[67]

In 1889, at Herchmer's instance, but largely penned by Superintendent R. Burton Deane,[68] an Order in Council established *Regulations and Orders for the Government and Guidance of the NWMP*.[69] Published in the form of a small handbook designed to fit in a uniform pocket, this was the force's first set of regulations, and every member was expected to know its provisions. Almost half of the regulations (twenty-one out of forty-three sections) were devoted to the description of the duties of each rank in the force (from commissioner down through twenty lower ranks to constable). These new Regulations bore an indelible stamp that marked an unflinching commitment to hierarchy, obedience, and discipline, and to the severe sanction of those in the lower ranks who challenged, disobeyed, or deserted. This won the NWMP no popularity contests within or without the ranks of the force, but once promulgated, the Regulations put all ranks on notice of their place in the hierarchy as well the consequences of their missteps.

The new Regulations reminded members of the force that the police were "a preventative as well as repressive force, and the prevention of crime [was] of even more importance than the punishment of criminals" (s. 1(2)). Every member was instructed "to receive the lawful commands of his superior officer with deference and respect" (s. 1(13)). Constables were directed that "obedience [was] the first quality required of them"—"the essence of discipline and the channel of advancement" (s. 25(4)). Constables were "always to appear properly dressed" and "gambling of any kind" was strictly forbidden (ss. 25(2) and (3)). The defaulters' records contain several entries in which the crime of being improperly dressed comprised the disciplinary breach.

Section 30, one of the longer sections in the 1889 Regulations, was devoted to "Offences and Punishments." It incorporated s. 18 of the NWMP Act, 1886 (i.e., "Police Act"), and subsection 3 explained that the explicitly specified offences were intended to include unspecified "minor offences and irregularities."

The disposition for "all first offences not of an aggravated nature" was to be one of "mild reproof and admonition" (s. 30(6)). Punishment was not to be resorted to until the offence was repeated. While imprisonment was clearly available as a form of punishment, the Regulations explicitly directed "both fine and imprisonment" only for drunkenness on duty (s. 30(13)). However, by implication, imprisonment was available for all cases that called for "severe punishment." If punishment involved a term of imprisonment, the imprisoned police found themselves in the same guardroom as (regular) prisoners awaiting trial or serving sentences for criminal convictions.[70]

When imprisonment was considered too severe, "confinement to barracks" was authorized for a period not to exceed twenty-eight days; this punishment could be accompanied by a fine (s. 30(7)). When confined to barracks, a member was required to perform all his regular duties, and, at the discretion of the commanding officer, he could be required to perform "duties of fatigue" (s. 30(8))—unspecified, but likely meaning "hard labour."

Drunkenness was described as an "unusually reprehensible offence in members of the force, and as such [was to be] severely dealt with" (s. 30(11)). Subsections 30(12) – (16) were devoted to the matter of drunkenness and the process to be followed in dealing with an intoxicated member (including the provision of a twenty-four-hour "sobering up" period before the member was brought before the commanding officer). Presumably the force's severity about alcohol was particularly intense because the NWT were "dry"—it was illegal to manufacture, possess, or import intoxicating liquor without a permit issued by the Lieutenant-Governor.[71]

As noted above, a detailed record in each defaulters' book and individual defaulter's sheet was to be kept. A review of one defaulters' book from the Eastend post in "B" Division (1880–82) in the southern region of the NWT reveals that over the period, thirty-one of fifty-six men across the ranks (sergeant, corporal, and constable) were found to have committed different forms of disciplinary crimes, ranging from the most minor (e.g., grumbling against an order of the sergeant-major; in this case, the grumbling was the constable's only recorded infraction, for which he was admonished) to more serious charges (some of them arguably criminal), such as "striking and using obscene threatening language" and breach of trust ("having appropriated to his own use [a] parcel addressed toward police with clerk [sic] which he had in his possession as troop orderly," for which the Commissioner reduced this corporal's rank to constable).[72]

The disciplinary offences entered in this defaulters' book include forms of disobedience and insubordination (nine entries); dereliction of duty, including absence without permission (fifteen, including six separate entries for one individual constable, with escalating sanctions culminating in seven days' imprisonment at hard labour); drunkenness (five, including three for "drunk on duty"); making false statements and/or statements which were harmful to the reputation of an officer or the force (three); and offences that were akin to criminal offences (six). Forms of sanction ranged from admonishment and severe reprimands to fines combined with confinement to barracks, loss of pay, and imprisonment in the cells.

It is difficult to assess with confidence, without knowing more about the particulars of each individual and each offence, whether the punishments were applied even-handedly. It does appear that being drunk on duty was regarded as a serious disciplinary breach (two men were reduced in rank and a third was fined one month's pay and confined to camp for three months). However, a constable whose offence was "being asleep in post" was sentenced to seven days in the cells and the loss of one month's pay, whereas another who made "false statements to civilians tending to leave a bad impression as to the workings of the force" and also falsely stated that "he could get illicit liquor at any time and had it every day with the exception of the last week" was fined only $5 and confined to barracks for one month.

It appears to have been possible to avoid police discipline, judging from the fact that twenty-five members of the Eastend post had no entries in the defaulters' book from 1879–82; however, it also appears that many of the men found themselves disciplined and sanctioned for some manner of disciplinary breach. It also bears noting that despite the force's concern with intoxication, the instances of drunkenness recorded in this defaulters' book were rare and severely punished.

The NWMP was not modest in its claims or vision for complete control of their process for dealing with what were, after all, legislatively prescribed disciplinary offences. Though based on federally enacted legislation, the force's brass brooked no oversight or intervention of legal counsel or the civil courts. Once the legislation was enacted, the "rule of law" had no further place in police discipline, as clearly "rule" trumped "law."

From time to time, the commissioner's annual report included recommendations for amendments to the "Police Act." In his 1885 report, Commissioner A.G. Irvine recommended that the Act be altered to provide explicitly that "an offender convicted under the penal clauses of the Police Act for an offence against police discipline shall not be subject to any writ of habeas corpus,[73] to ensure that no recourse to the civil courts to determine the validity of the internal process or the sentence imposed would be possible. Failing such a provision, Irvine insisted, "the interests of discipline will assuredly suffer."[74] He expanded upon his view of procedural safeguards and requisites—no lawyers, no courts:

> I have already had occasion to insist that a police prisoner has an appeal from a sentence *inflicted* by his commanding officer to myself, and through myself, if necessary, to the "Minister charged with the control and management of the Force," but that no other appeal is intended, or can be allowed. Further, that no legal counsel can be permitted in a question of police discipline.[75]

As noted above, this view was continued, and indeed reinforced, by Irvine's successor, Lawrence W. Herchmer, who maintained that the force's disciplinary jurisdiction had to encompass the right to deal with the criminal conduct of members through police discipline. For the NWMP brass, the

Act, its disciplinary offences, and its process for dealing with them were a comprehensive code, "based in law on amendments to the police act,"[76] but administered through the exclusive discretion of the senior officers. In 1886, however, in response to a sentence of twelve months at hard labour with "ball and chain" imposed on a deserter by Commissioner Herchmer (a form of punishment he favoured), Justice Edward Wetmore of the NWT Supreme Court observed that "there was no provision under the NWMP Act by which members could be sentenced to wear a ball and chain for infractions of the disciplinary code."[77] In other words, Herchmer had exceeded his jurisdiction in imposing a sentence that was not expressly authorized in the legislation.

Years later in his memoirs, Superintendent R. Burton Deane recalled a conversation with his friend, North-West Supreme Court Justice David Lynch Scott, about the discrete sphere of police "courts": "so long as I do not exceed my jurisdiction, you have no lawful right to interfere with me."[78] According to Deane, an initially incredulous Scott came to agree with him. Deane elaborated upon this issue in his 1899 annual report from the Macleod district:

> The Mounted Police Act having created a court and clothed it with authority, and having defined intoxication, however slight, and desertion or absence without leave, as two of the offences with which it has power to deal, it is not to be seriously contended that such a court exceeds its jurisdiction by proposing to deal with a deserter whenever he may chance to appear before it. . . .
>
> [T]he Northwest Mounted Police, if not a military body, are as nearly military as it is possible for an armed body of constabulary to be; that the statute by virtue of which they exist enjoins and provides for the maintenance of discipline, and that their regulations are essentially of a military character. *Their regulations* respecting the grant of an indulgence of a pass, and the form of pass itself, are adapted from those in vogue in the British Army, and *are purely matters affecting*

> the interior economy and discipline of the persons who are
> servants of the state, under the Mounted Police statute.[79]

Here Deane was defending one of his own actions earlier in 1892, when he cancelled a short leave that he had granted to a constable with only seven days remaining in his term of service. Before the end of his leave, the constable began to celebrate prematurely by drinking and expressing his dissatisfaction with the force—within earshot of Deane. Rather than having him taken into custody and charged with the offence of intoxication, Deane simply cancelled the man's leave and ordered him back to duty. The constable, believing he had already been discharged from the force but, clearly fearing punishment if he was wrong, fled the post. He retained a lawyer in Calgary to challenge Deane's action, and his counsel persuaded Justice Charles-Borromée Rouleau "to stay the hand of the police permanently."[80]

Deane maintained that his decision to cancel the pass fell within his unfettered jurisdiction. The "formidable legal argument for overturning Rouleau's judgment" that was presented on appeal to the full Supreme Court of the NWT had been prepared by Deane himself.[81] In setting aside Justice Rouleau's writ of prohibition, the full Court did not go so far as to endorse Deane's expansive notion of his jurisdiction; the Court simply found that the constable was still engaged as a member of the force when the incident occurred and thus still subject to Deane's authority. According to Beahen and Horrall, "[t]he question . . . of whether the disciplinary system of the NWMP was subject to the authority of the civil courts still remained unanswered."[82] However, the constable's initial success in the civil(ian) court and the perceived threat it posed to the authority of the NWMP had been received "like a knife at the jugular of Force discipline."[83] William Beahen quotes Commissioner Herchmer: "If the judges are to interfere in police discipline it will be the end of it, as every man will get a lawyer."[84]

The multiple roles assigned to the commanding officer under the NWMP legislation for matters of alleged disciplinary breaches—to investigate, to adjudicate, and to impose punishment – assumed amplified importance. These men had sweeping adjudicative authority in two legal contexts: as justices of the peace, they presided in "civilian" criminal court;

as commanding officers, they had the authority, indeed the responsibility, to preside over disciplinary "crimes" (which could include forms of criminal offences recast as disciplinary breaches) without being burdened by the requisite of the evidence being taken under oath, unless they saw fit. They had the power to impose sentences of imprisonment in both contexts. They likely wore their uniforms in both forms of proceedings, which would have been held in the police barracks.

Because they were both NWMP officers and either stipendiary magistrates or justices of the peace, the NWMP officers could adjudicate in two legal contexts—criminal justice and police justice—but they clearly preferred the expedited process and unfettered control they exercised in the disciplinary context. Senior men like Irvine, Herchmer, and Deane operated with an expansive notion of their jurisdiction. Confident that the "higher law" of police discipline permitted a regime of arbitrary justice, they freely and liberally "inflicted" (Irvine's word[85]) severe punishments upon men of the lower ranks.

It is difficult to assess how scrupulous the men who were both NWMP officers and justices of the peace were about the differences between their two roles. In Constable Arthur Miles Parken's personnel record, for instance, it is not clear how Superintendent Howe thought he was presiding at the 23 January 1894 hearing of a "charge" (the language of police discipline) that Parken did "steal take from and appropriate to his own use" a sum of money ($25.00), the property of another constable. The form of this hearing was identical to an earlier hearing of a breach of discipline charge brought against Parken by Superintendent Moffatt for "being drunk at the barracks" in August 1893, and for which he was fined $10.00. The record of the January 1894 proceeding reads as if it also was a disciplinary hearing under the NWMP Act even though Howe signed off as "JP" (and not as Superintendent, his NWMP rank); however, the last page of the record makes clear that Howe was conducting a preliminary (or committal) hearing into the criminal charge of larceny, as Parken was "committed for trial at the next court of competent jurisdiction."[86] Justice McGuire of the NWT Supreme Court subsequently sentenced Parken to six months' imprisonment at hard labour.[87]

It would not have been lost on the men under their command, such as Parken, that their superior officers were also justices of the peace. Their commanding officer was ex officio a justice of the peace for the NWT, but he was also, indeed first and foremost, their superior officer.

Another case from "C" division in Battleford offers yet another illustration: in addition to their dual judicial roles, commanding officers sometimes also acted as accusers or complainants in both discipline and criminal contexts. In late October 1894, Constable Frank Kiely was charged with three counts of theft of jewelry, a pocket book, and articles of clothing, involving three different informants (two of whom were members of the NWMP). Described by Superintendent Howe as his servant, Kiely was brought before Howe as a justice of the peace for committal on two of the criminal charges. Kiely also faced a third charge that alleged theft of Howe's pocket book from a locked drawer in his dressing room at his house. Another NWMP officer, Quebec-born and francophone Inspector Joseph Victor Bégin,[88] sitting as a justice of the peace, presided at the committal hearing on this charge. To all three criminal charges, Kiely indicated he wanted to plead guilty. When asked to elect whether to be tried summarily then and there by a (police) justice of the peace or to wait and be tried by a judge, Kiely appears not to have hesitated to elect to enter his plea on all three charges before a judge. On 15 June 1895 Kiely appeared before the NWT Supreme Court Justice Charles-Borromée Rouleau, who sentenced him to two months' imprisonment at hard labour.[89] Even though Kiely must have known that he would be held in custody in the NWMP guardhouse for several more months before being brought before a judge—in the end, he was held for almost seven months—he clearly did not want the police justices of the peace, including his commanding officer, determining his guilt and deciding his sentence.[90] The NWMP did not wait for the outcome in the criminal court to direct his dismissal from the force, which took effect on 1 December 1894.

The NWMP's legislation expressly contemplated that a member of the NWMP could be convicted and sentenced twice for the same misconduct.[91] This would prove to be Constable Robert Jones's unhappy experience in 1891.[92] Jones, a twenty-year-old recruit, was engaged as a constable on 28 February 1890 and posted to the division at Fort Macleod where he was put in charge of the saddle room; his duties included receiving the ration of oats and filling the horses' nose bags. On the morning of 5 February 1891, he was observed by the division's head teamster placing two bags of oats in a wagon owned by Thomas Craig, a rancher and former NWMP member. Apparently Craig had permission to haul away manure from the post and came every morning to do so; Superintendent S.B. Steele noted in his letter to the commissioner that the excuse offered was that "the oats were the sweepings of the saddle room."[93] Charged with larceny as a public servant, Jones was committed for trial and, on 17 February 1891, he was convicted by (former NWMP commissioner) Justice James Farquharson Macleod.[94] Macleod sentenced Jones, along with Craig, to six months' imprisonment at hard labour in the guardroom at Fort Macleod.[95] Following his sentencing, Jones was charged under the NWMP Act with a breach of discipline; he was convicted on 23 February 1891 and sentenced to twelve months' imprisonment at hard labour to run concurrently with Macleod's sentence. Dismissal at the end of his sentence was recommended. Almost immediately Superintendent Steele recommended to the commissioner a partial remission of the twelve-month sentence to match the six months imposed by Macleod; Steele did not dispute the sentence, but remarked, "as he is young the severe lesson he has already received may have weight with him and as it expires in the summer it gives him more chance of getting immediate employment."[96] Several months later, after the co-accused already had been released, the commissioner appears to have relented on the matter of remission. He authorized the matter to go to a Board of Officers[97] who, prior to the expiration of Jones's full "disciplinary" sentence, directed his dismissal for "bad conduct."[98]

For their part, many constables and sub-constables experienced "unfulfilled expectations and disenchantment:"[99] "I thought it was a Civil Force to fill the duty of a policeman. I found it more like soldiering. I am not cut out to be a soldier."[100] Others expressed disgust at "the unjust and arbitrary system of discipline" and punishment "often meted out according to the whim or humour of those in authority."[101] Beahen and Horrall also cite the case of a constable charged with insubordination, having refused to obey a corporal's order to "get on with his work," for which he was sentenced to seven days' imprisonment by his commanding officer; the constable apparently lost his temper and said, "Send me for the rest of my life. I won't do another stroke of work." The superintendent did not have jurisdiction to impose a life sentence and simply sentenced him to the longest sentence he could impose, a further twelve months, for mutinous language.[102]

Over the years, collective acts of protest and resistance known as "bucks" (as in "bucking the system") at the harsh conditions of life, work, and discipline in the Mounted Police force also occurred,[103] and many individual demonstrations of resistance, often "out of desperation,"[104] were expressed annually through desertion from the force.[105] Life and work under the conditions in the force, and the power that came with exclusive jurisdiction over police justice, were too much for many members who must have had a sense of injustice at police justice.

BLURRED LINES AND INTERSECTING FORMS: CRIMES AND CONDUCT, CRIMINAL AND DISCIPLINARY JUSTICE

One half of the NWMP men who appeared as accused persons in Hugh Richardson's court (including Richard C. Wyld, the sole disciplinary offender) had prior personal experience of a broader notion of "crimes" through disciplinary proceedings under the police legislation. They were liable to be charged, investigated, tried, and sanctioned within two legal regimes: one criminal, one disciplinary. From Richardson's court records over the entire period, an image emerges of a close, if occasionally contested, relationship between criminal offences and disciplinary offences as well as between the judiciary and the NWMP brass. The cases of NMWP accused men found in Richardson's records largely involved charges of theft, including theft of items of government property or belongings of other members of the NWMP (including a couple of commanding officers). Some prosecutions involved offences that were forms of breach of trust. In all but four cases, the accused police officers were convicted, either after a trial or by way of a guilty plea, and all the convicted men were sentenced to terms of imprisonment. While not all the personnel records for the NWMP that appeared before Richardson in the earlier period (1876–1885) are available, it appears that five of the seven men who were convicted and sentenced by Richardson in the NWT Supreme Court were dismissed from the force upon their conviction (or impending conviction). It is difficult to understand why the remaining two, George Robinson and

James Ford, whose cases I discuss below, were allowed to remain on the force, even for a brief period.

The cases found in Richardson's earlier magistrate's court records illustrate some of the intricacies, intimacies, and blurred lines between criminal and police justice. It must be acknowledged that in this first decade of the history of the NWT, including a newly created police force and administration of justice, the number of men responsible for law enforcement and the administration of justice was small. The relationship between Stipendiary Magistrate Richardson and the senior NWMP brass (especially in Battleford) appears to have been close. Settlements were far-flung, NWMP posts similarly few and far between. But, as far-flung as the posts and settlements were, the living conditions in the barracks (often little more than a couple of log cabins for quarters and a stable for horses and livestock) would have been stiflingly close. Battleford, where three of the four early cases below took place, had been chosen as the territorial capital in the fall of 1876. Even by territorial standards, Battleford was a new settlement. The year 1875 had "marked the beginning of a permanent settlement"; it was a "small settlement of construction workers, traders and Indians" then called Telegraph Flat.[106] Richardson and his family made their home in Battleford from his arrival on 27 September 1877, until 1883 when the territorial capital shifted to Regina.[107] The importance and standing of the Métis community in Battleford, when Richardson arrived in late September 1877, emerge early on in his court records; for instance, Métis men Peter Ballendine and Pierre Daigneault played prominent roles in the cases, including as litigants, witnesses, Cree interpreters, and jurors.

Regnier Brillon: Thief and Forgiving Friend

One of the earliest files in Richardson's stipendiary magistrate records involved the 1877 prosecution of Sub-Constable Regnier Brillon, stationed in Battleford, on three counts of theft of firearms from other members of the force.[108] Brillon's undoing was his effort to turn a profit by selling the guns to reasonably prominent members of the Battleford community, including James Mahoney, a local businessman, and Pierre Daignault, who would often serve as a Cree interpreter for the court.[109] The exact process followed in Brillon's case is not crystal clear. The preliminary hearing in Battleford, at which Superintendent James Walker, sitting as a justice of the peace, committed Brillon to stand trial, took place on 27 January 1877, eight months before Richardson arrived in the settlement. On 5 April 1877, Walker forwarded all the evidence to David Laird, Lieutenant-Governor of the NWT, with the following covering letter:

Sir,

I have the honour by direction of Lieut-Col Macleod to enclose you [sic] the evidence taken against Regnier Brillon for Theft, whom I committed to stand trial at the first competent court held in this district. I also convicted him on the 27th day of January last for "Disobedience of Orders and Desertion" to six months imprisonment which he is undergoing.

I also further convicted him for theft of public property to two months imprisonment or to pay the sum of One hundred and thirty dollars, value of the property stolen and costs. I do not know whether he intends to pay the money or undergo imprisonment. I will be greatly obliged if you would let me know about what date Brillon will be tried as the witnesses are under bond, to appear against him, and two of them want to go into Winnipeg on Business but are unable to do so not knowing when they will be required.

In the end, the witnesses were not required to testify. On 10 October 1877 (eight months after his committal for trial), Brillon entered guilty pleas to all three charges before the recently-arrived Richardson and was sentenced to two months' imprisonment at hard labour on each count, to be served in the guardroom of the police station at Battleford. Brillon would have been familiar with these cells, having served six months there already for disobedience and desertion, as Walker described, and two months for theft of public property. Disciplinary and criminal sentences were served in the intimate setting of the NWMP guardroom. One of the witnesses for the prosecution at Brillon's committal hearing was his colleague, Acting

Constable Norton H. Marshall. Brillon would only have been liberated from the NWMP cells for a couple of months when, in March 1878, he again found himself before Richardson. On this occasion, he was charged with a different criminal offence: of acting as an accessory to the theft of government property by NWMP constables Henry Elliott, Norton Marshall, and Patrick Balfe in the course of their desertion from the force.[110] On this occasion, Brillon walked away from court, as Richardson found there was not sufficient evidence to warrant committing Brillon and his co-accused for trial. This was perhaps a small measure of sweet revenge against the prosecutor, his former commanding officer, and quite possibly with no hard feelings toward Marshall, his former fellow constable who had testified against him in 1877.

Henry R. Elliott et al.: "Disgraceful Conduct"

On 2 March 1878, Stipendiary Magistrate Richardson himself preferred charges under the NWMP Amendment Act, 1875 against four members of the NWMP. On that date, he wrote to their commanding officer, Inspector James Walker of the Battleford Division, alleging that these four had committed certain offences and requesting that Walker have them brought before him "with the least possible delay."[111] The original complaint documents do not form part of the "Elliott" file in the Richardson court records, but three draft complaint documents convey that Richardson alleged that on 24 and 25 February 1878, all four members had been guilty of forms of "disgraceful conduct" within the meaning of the "Police Act."

The facts giving rise to the Richardson charges of disciplinary breaches derived from the romantic relationship between Henry R. Elliott, a sub-constable of the NWMP stationed at Battleford, and Richardson's daughter, Luders. Richardson forbade the relationship and forbade Elliott coming to their home (which he had occasion to do when he delivered the mail).[112] On 25 February 1878, Elliott went to the Richardson home, with three other constables, and "in spite of parental objection took the daughter away."[113] The result was an "elopement" wedding officiated by a local Presbyterian minister. Somehow, Luders' parents got her back to their home, which led to anguished correspondence from the groom, declaring he and their daughter loved each other and that they were now married. Richardson would have none of it.

He appears to have contemplated a criminal charge against Elliott and Acting Staff Constable Norton Marshall. The court file contains a draft, unsigned "Information and Complaint of Hugh Richardson," in Richardson's handwriting, in which he alleged that Elliott and Marshall,

> ... feloniously and fraudulently allured one Luders Richardson out the possession and against the will of this informant, her father, she the said Luders Richardson being under the age of twenty-one years and having a certain contingent interest in the real and personal estate of the informant, with intent [...] the said Luders Richardson to cause to be married to the said Elliott contrary to the statute in such case made and provided.[114]

This extravagant charge of "abduction of an heiress" seems not to have resulted in any criminal process and appears to have gone no further than Richardson's vexed and intemperate draft.[115] He turned to the police disciplinary process—perhaps because it was procedurally more expeditious.

Elliott's three colleagues (Marshall, Patrick J. Balfe, and "Davis"[116]) found themselves accused of scandalous conduct for assisting or supporting Elliott in the elopement and marriage and (with respect to Balfe and Davis) for neglect of their duty in failing to arrest Elliott and Marshall when, as Richardson alleged, they had unlawfully and forcibly entered the Richardson home. It is clear from the court file that Superintendent James Walker responded almost immediately to Richardson, expressing his "fullest sympathy in this unfortunate affair," and assuring Richardson that he would do what he could "to keep Elliott employed for a few days so that he may not give you any trouble."[117]

When he forwarded his disciplinary charges to the inspector, Richardson requested that Walker fix a time—"with the least possible delay"—and notify a list of men named by Richardson to attend to give evidence. The list included the minister who had performed the wedding, the legality of which Richardson impugned (he alleged that Elliott had misrepresented that Luders was of age and that the consent of her parents could not be obtained).[118] Again, Walker responded immediately, expressed his regret at Elliott's behaviour, assured Richardson that he had had Elliott and his friends confined to barracks as soon as they had returned home, and advised that he would "go into this case on Monday" and keep Richardson informed.

It appears that Richardson's complaints did not proceed. Together with a prisoner named Ducharme, who was serving a six-month sentence in the guardroom,[119] the four young constables fled the NWMP post on the night of 4 March 1878, taking with them horses, revolvers, saddles, and blankets.

Becoming "deserters," the four appear to have quickly made plans and arranged for provisions. Judging from the fact that two other men, David Hall and Regnier Brillon, were later charged with being accessories in the escape (for leaving word that they were heading out on a different trail, that is, acting as decoys), it seems that Elliott enjoyed the support of colleagues and friends.

Elliott and his colleagues had been caught in the crosshairs of a police disciplinary process in which they had little confidence. Richardson, the aggrieved father and stipendiary magistrate, clearly had the ear and the support of their commanding officer. Richardson, and not Superintendent Walker, appeared to be directing the disciplinary process. And so, with their previously unblemished records[120] about to be tarnished and an uncertain future with the force, the young men fled before the disciplinary process could continue, and thus became deserters and accused thieves. They headed south across the plain, reportedly in the direction of the Cypress Hills, possibly en route to the United States. Elliott's comrades, Marshall and Balfe, may have made their way across the US border; I have found no evidence that they ever appeared in criminal court facing criminal charges or in "police court" on the disciplinary breaches alleged by Richardson. Balfe's service record contains a cryptic note that he deserted on 5 March 1878.

Elliott apparently turned himself in at Fort Walsh some time in the summer of 1878. The court file contains a document that is identified as a "copy" of a "Warrant of Commitment" dated 26 August 1878 and signed by James F. Macleod in his capacity as stipendiary magistrate. The warrant stipulated that Elliott was charged with theft of "three horses and four saddles the property of the Government of Canada," and directed the police to convey him to Battleford and "safely to keep him until he shall be thence delivered by due course of law."[121] Elliott remained in custody in the guardroom at Battleford for three months, awaiting his trial. It is not clear whether the NWMP ever acted on Richardson's disciplinary charges, although this formed part of the theory of Elliott's defence in criminal court. Elliott was charged with "larceny of two horses, nine blankets, four saddles, three revolvers, one carbine, two halters and nine blankets, the property of Her Majesty, the prisoner at the time being a member of the Mounted Police." These charges arose from the night of the escape from the barracks. Elliott was tried before a jury of six men (including at least one Métis juror) at the police barracks in Battleford on 23 December 1878. His defence counsel was NWT lawyer Hayter Reed,[122] who later would be appointed Indian Agent at Battleford and rapidly rise through the Indian Department.[123] Superintendent Walker acted as prosecutor and served as the first witness for the prosecution. Hugh Richardson himself, together with a justice of the peace, W.J. Scott, presided at the trial of his forsaken son-in-law, whose alleged criminal actions flowed almost directly from Richardson's invocation of the NWMP disciplinary process.

The theory of the defence directly engaged the role played (or alleged to have been played) by the NWMP disciplinary process, implying that it had been improperly undertaken. The details of the trial come from an account in a local newspaper, the *Saskatchewan Herald*.[124] Through Reed's cross-examination of Walker, it appears that the defence strategy was organized along three lines: 1) that doubts could be raised about just what articles actually went missing from the NWMP barracks and stable, whose they were, and when they went missing; 2) that Elliott had been wrongfully imprisoned in March 1878 (on Richardson's complaints under the NWMP Act, 1875 and therefore "was justified in using any means to effect his escape"); and, (3) that while in custody, Elliott "had been undergoing punishment for the very offence for which he [was] now being tried, by direction of the officer commanding the station as being a justice of the peace."

Richardson ruled that the issue of wrongful imprisonment was irrelevant and overruled the question; Reed asked that his objection to this ruling be noted. However, to the question as to whether Elliott had been punished already for the same offence, Superintendent Walker is reported to have answered, "He has not, I am personally positive. . . . " However, here again, the press reported that "the Court overruled this because it would be an admission of the prisoner's guilt; secondly, he could not undergo punishment before conviction." It is difficult to gauge with confidence from the press report just what Richardson's ruling here meant. One might reasonably infer that Richardson was determined to stymie the defence.

Other members of the Battleford division testified, some agreeing with the defence counsel that Elliott's character was "always considered good." Reed is credited with making a strong address to the jury, and the newspaper, as Bowker also notes, reported that Richardson's charge to the jury was "strongly against the Prisoner."[125] The jury was not persuaded and quite possibly not impressed. After five minutes of deliberation, the jury returned with a verdict of not guilty. It was a clear rebuke to Richardson.

The *Saskatchewan Herald* closed its coverage of Elliott's trial with a brief reference to other charges he faced after this acquittal:

> On Thursday morning Elliott was brought up before the Stipendiary Magistrate on the remaining charges, namely stealing Major Walker's horse and aiding Descamps [sic] to escape.
>
> Major Walker asked for an enlargement, as he had discovered some further evidence too recently to be available for the last trial, but which could easily be obtained. As the roads were so bad he could not fix a definite time when he would be ready, and the magistrate released the prisoner on his own recognizances in [sic] $400 to appear when and where required on notice.[126]

There are no court documents relating to these two charges in Elliott's archived court file. Were they a last-ditch effort by Walker to find a way to convict Elliott of at least some offence? If so, even Richardson was not prepared to order that Elliott be held in custody for an indefinite time while the police organized the next round of charges.

However, Richardson was sufficiently distressed by the jury's verdict that he immediately wrote to the Deputy Minister of Justice with two questions arising out of Elliott's case. Richardson's letter to the Deputy Minister is not found in the court file, but the Deputy's response of 1 February 1879 references the magistrate's concerns. Richardson appears to have had second thoughts about his authority to release a prisoner on his own recognizance, as he had just done. Deputy Minister Zebulon A. Lash replied that while he had been unable to look into it, he "imagine[d], however, that you have power to do it." The second question is revealed in the Deputy Minister's reply: "I feel pretty sure . . . that you have no right to request a jury in a criminal case to answer certain fixed questions. They have a right to say guilty or not guilty without giving their reasons."[127] Despite this unhappy correspondence, the verdict stood.

The case had clearly excited local interest, not least because of Richardson's prominence in the NWT, the importance of the NWMP in Battleford, and possibly because of the thwarted young lovers. Luders was by this point likely long gone from the NWT, "safely" back with relatives in Ontario. It seems that in 1885, she married another man in New York City.[128]

Despite Elliott's legal victory and vindication by the Battleford jury, and the jury's clear rebuke of Richardson, it is unlikely that he felt he had cause to celebrate, perhaps only a sense of relief. His marriage thwarted and his career as a Mountie over, Henry R. Elliott's tumultuous relationship with different forms of justice appears to have ended here. I doubt that he would derive any comfort from the knowledge that his experience vividly supports the argument of this chapter: for Elliott, the relationship and lines between police discipline and criminal justice were messy and blurred. And unfair and personal.

Richard Wyld: "Mutinous Insubordination"

It is not clear how old Richard Wyld was when he signed on with the NWMP in 1877; his date of birth is listed as "unknown" in his personnel record.[129] He may have been twenty-two years of age, but some recruits were as young as eighteen.[130] Some parents— and the occasional magistrate—"saw service in the NWMP as a means for reforming the wayward habits of young men."[131] The recruits, who engaged for a term of three or five years, were almost invariably from central Canada, far from home and anything that resembled it. There were few comforts, little glamour, and limited outlets for a happy life for these young men, for whom even the consumption of alcohol was both a disciplinary and a territorial offence. Indeed, NWMP Superintendent Sam Steele acknowledged these difficult conditions in his assessment of the discipline and conduct of his men in his 1889 Report from Fort Macleod:

> I have much pleasure in reporting that the general conduct of the non-commissioned officersand [sic] constables is good.
>
> I am surprised that there is not more serious crime among the men, considering the temptations with which they are surrounded. There is hardly a respectable place of resort, such as they would be likely to visit, and none for amusement in the town. Another drawback is the fact that no recreation room worthy of the name is at this post. I ampleased [sic] to say that one is now in the course of construction. . . .
>
> The majority of men who get into trouble are new recruits who have little experience in the country.[132]

In 1877, Constable Richard Charles Wyld was one such recruit. On 5 June 1877, at Toronto, Wyld was engaged for a three-year term as a sub-constable of the NWMP and stationed at Battleford.[133] When Wyld applied to the force, the letters of reference sent to Minister of Justice Edward Blake were rather vague in respect of Wyld's own merits, but rather referenced his father and older brother (twenty-four-year-old Robert, a member of the NWMP since 1874, with an unblemished record[134]). Britton Bath Osler, a rising star in the Ontario legal profession (who would later be asked by the Dominion Government to assist in the prosecution of Louis Riel for treason), offered a one-sentence reference in which he pithily conveyed only that Richard Wyld was the son of a friend and expressed the belief that he was "a very fit and proper person for the position asked."[135]

Thus, supported by tepid letters that said little directly about him and nothing at all about his character, Richard Wyld was engaged by the NWMP and followed his older brother, Robert, into the force. They were both stationed at Battleford. One wonders whether Richard Wyld realized when he arrived in the NWT that he would never return to his old life in his hometown of Dundas, Ontario.

His brother Robert served two terms with the NWMP and was promoted twice over the course of his engagement, rising to the rank of corporal. At the end of his time in the NWMP, his character and conduct during his service was described as very good. Richard's experience, however, suggests a less perfect fit. During his three years on the force, he was charged with thirteen disciplinary offences by eight different superior officers (and in one occasion by Stipendiary Magistrate Richardson).

On 17 September 1877, three months after his engagement and shortly after his arrival in the Territories, the first entry on the defaulter's sheet in his personnel file was recorded. He was found to have been "absent from Roll Call" and "inattentive at drill"; for these first two offences, his character was listed as "good," and for punishment he was "admonished."[136] Two days later, he was brought up again on a charge, this time that he had engaged in "improper conduct while at drill." On this occasion, his character was described as "indifferent" and he was punished with two days confined to barracks and admonished. By the end of September 1877, he was serving seven days in the cells for inattention at drill, and on October 18, he was fined $5.00 (the equivalent of a week's pay) for insubordinate conduct towards a non-commissioned officer.

In March and May 1878, Wyld was sentenced twice by Assistant Commissioner Irvine to imprisonment of thirty days (on each occasion) in the cells at hard labour. On the first occasion he was accused of stealing cocoa milk out of the hospital; the second charge of breach of discipline was for drunkenness at Fort Walsh on 23 May 1878.

On 2 September 1878, Wyld was admonished by Sub-Inspector John French, interim commanding officer of "C" Division in Battleford, for another disciplinary breach "causing annoyance to Lt-Col Richardson"; once again the entry characterizing his character simply indicated "bad." Later that month, on September 25, Wyld found himself facing another disciplinary matter arising from his refusal to dig potatoes when ordered to do so.[137] One can perhaps imagine his surprise when he found himself in front of Richardson on the resulting charge of "mutinous insubordination" preferred against him by Sub-Inspector John French, and which French asked

Richardson to investigate. Wyld had had considerable experience with the disciplinary process and apparently regarded it as internal police business. He might well have wondered if Richardson would give him a fair hearing.

On a chilly September morning, French had ordered all available men at the post to go to the field and collect potatoes that were at risk of freezing. Some went, some seemed to take their time, while others, such as the cook, continued with their other work. French said that he found Wyld in the barracks "dressing his hair" and gave him five minutes to be out at the field. Some time later, Wyld was still at the barracks and, when pressed by French, apparently admitted that he had disobeyed French's order. He was placed under arrest and brought before Richardson on the disciplinary charge of mutinous insubordination. Given French's direct involvement and the likelihood that he would want to give evidence in the matter, he may have thought it best to have Richardson conduct the investigation. As well, French, as a sub-inspector, may not have been considered authorized to conduct this investigation, but that had not inhibited him from admonishing Wyld earlier in the month.

Richardson heard two witnesses in support of the charge and one witness for the defence. On the evidence, he convicted Wyld. However, he noted Wyld's objection to the process. Clearly, Wyld had enough prior experience with the NWMP discipline to know that the commanding officer ordinarily investigated the charge. Thus, at the close of the evidence, when Richardson asked Wyld if he had anything to say, Wyld "objected that [Richardson] had no legal right to interfere in police matters. After conviction, [he] stated he would appeal to the Commissioner." Richardson added:

> On both occasions I read the law to him. He professing ignorance at which I felt surprised and to his exception which while regretting I had to try the case could not stay sentence but must leave him to adopt his own course.[138]

Although French was not the investigator or adjudicator at this hearing, he was not shy about seeking to speak to the matter of sentence. He proposed to read out "Wyld's former character on the force," but here again Wyld objected. Acknowledging his past offences, Wyld argued that the commissioner "had forgiven him and had promised the record of [his past offences] should be erased." His record, of course, was not erased. However, Richardson noted that he disposed of the case without looking at or considering the record. He sentenced Wyld to one month of imprisonment at hard labour.

Leaving aside the negligible evidence of mutiny, Richardson's expression of regret at having to try the case is at best disappointing. The offence in section 22 of the NWMP Act 1873 was one of "mutinous *or* insubordinate conduct," not "mutinous insubordinate conduct." Wyld appears not to have raised an objection to the extravagant conflation in the charge against him. The evidentiary support for anything remotely resembling "mutinous" conduct was surely wanting, while a finding of "disobeying an order" and thus arguably for "insubordinate conduct" was possibly warranted on the facts. Perhaps the one-month sentence imposed by Richardson reflected a form of mitigation of penalty for the inflated charge that implied "mutiny" when resistance, and even flouting an order, might have been at play. Wyld, the "Fletcher Christian" of the Battleford post, had been slow to rescue potatoes from the frost. When, at the expiration of his term, Commissioner James Farquharson Macleod was required to indicate the quality of Wyld's conduct during his service, Macleod used an adjective frequently found in Wyld's service record: "bad"[139] and declined to find him entitled to a free land scrip. His NWMP service record notes that he died in 1906 in Wetaskiwin, Alberta.

Given the obvious lack of fit between Richard Wyld and the NWMP, one might surmise that the prospect of further disgracing his (successful) NWMP brother and the certainty of harsh punishment for desertion were all that kept him in the force until the end of his term. Richard Wyld was likely the last NWMP member, if not the only one, to have had a stipendiary magistrate who was not also an officer of the NWMP investigating and convicting him for a disciplinary breach. The niceties of legal analysis had no place in the disciplinary process, even when a legally trained jurist was given the reins for the process. The context itself was fertile ground, not for process, but for hard smacks. It was a process in which, as Acting Staff Constable Marshall had observed in 1878, the governing principle was, "You are guilty. Prove yourself innocent."

Walter Parkins's Intimidation

The rather opaque facts that gave rise, in 1885, to the invocation of the criminal process against Constable Walter Douglas Parkins are matched by the rather opaque nature of the legal process in the case. They do offer, nonetheless, another illustration of the porous line between "police justice" and "criminal justice," not least because of the position of the NWMP officer as justice of the peace.

On 16 May 1885, Robert McManus, a hotelkeeper at Troy,[140] apparently complained to a local justice of the peace that he had been threatened and intimidated by Parkins and another man. No formal criminal information was issued to initiate the proceedings—a critical misstep—but the file does contain a warrant issued by a lay justice of the peace, John W. Powers, commanding "all or any of the constables or peace officers in the District of Assiniboia . . . to apprehend" Parkins and the other man, and bring them before him to answer the charge and "to be dealt with according to law." On the basis of this warrant, Parkins was arrested. The court file contains correspondence indicating that McManus had accused Parkins of "assault, housebreaking, threatening language, etc."[141]

It appears that a local lawyer was consulted on the legality of the warrant for arrest, no information having been sworn before Powers. In a letter found in the court file, W.C. Hamilton, who often acted as crown prosecutor in the area, wrote to Superintendent Deane in reference to McManus's allegation, advising that he "had concluded on consultation with W Gordon a local JP to refer the matter to [Deane] as *a magistrate and commanding officer of the force* for investigation" (my emphasis).

On 20 May 1885, Deane wrote to Stipendiary Magistrate Hugh Richardson regarding an allegation of criminal intimidation against Constable Parkins that had been laid before a civilian justice of the peace. Deane's letter offers an exquisite synopsis of the complicated positions, dubious facts, and processes he was attempting to navigate:

> Sir,
>
> I have the honour to inform you that in pursuance of an information supposed to be laid by Mr. Robt McManus of

Troy, Constable Parkins, N.W.M. Police, was on the 16th inst arrested by Sergt Jones, 91st Batt. Militia, under the enclosed warrant issued and directed to him for execution by Mr. John W. Powers, JP at Troy.

After arrest the prisoner was handed over to Constable Farrell, NWM Police, and by him brought to the Police Headquarters. Notwithstanding the illegality of the warrant, I directed the prisoner to be re-escorted to Troy on Sunday night for trial before Mr. Power as a matter of police discipline; the following morning the prisoner was brought back to headquarters with a letter from Mr. Power, of which the enclosed is a copy. Constables Farrell and Pickering reported that no investigation had been held and that an order for the prisoner's discharge had not been made out.

Constable Parkins feels aggrieved that the criminal law should have been set in motion, and that he should not have been given the opportunity of answering the charge in question, and I therefore beg to request that you will be pleased to entrust me as to the proper course to be pursued, and I would submit for your consideration that the interests of the public, no less than the disciplinary interests of the Police force, would be best served if you consent to hear the case at Regina.

I have not thought it proper to institute an inquiry under the Police Act until the present charges shall have been conclusively disposed of.

Richardson's endorsement on the back of the warrant indicates how he disposed of the matter: "Trial for 26 May 85. Deft discharged Prosecutor not appearing."[142] The court file also contains a flurry of correspondence following the discharge. The hotelkeeper, McManus, complained bitterly that he had been unable to come to court due to a bad case of gout, and that he had sent word of this, together with a medical certificate, through another man who was to give the message to the police. By this point, Parkins had been released from custody, and the court file ends here.

Parkins's personnel record reveals a bit more of his story. He served almost eight years over two terms of engagement with the NWMP. His service record, while not unblemished, includes only four entries in the defaulter's sheet. The last entry in his personnel record indicates that he deserted from the Division at Maple Creek on 22 April 1888, prior to papers being drawn that would direct his transfer to "H" Division in Fort Saskatchewan. No mention of the saga of the McManus complaint in 1885 appears in his service record.[143]

The cases of Wyld, Elliott, and Parkins, in particular, demonstrate the significance and ramifications of police disciplinary processes for the young constables. Wyld was disciplined repeatedly but was never charged criminally, even though he was punished for "stealing" cocoa from the NWMP hospital; nevertheless, there can be no doubt about the misery he experienced. As for Elliott, there was a direct line—arguably a causal one—between Richardson's invocation of the disciplinary offence of "scandalous conduct" and Elliott's commanding officer's response to the escape and alleged thefts from the NWMP stable. For his part, Parkins found support from his commanding officer against the flawed invocation of the criminal law against him.

These three cases also demonstrate that far from being discrete forms of law—civil and military—the criminal and NWMP disciplinary processes were closely connected. The senior officers, and clearly even Richardson himself, moved easily between them. Not every irate father in the NWT could so easily command the ear of—and the process engaged by—a NWMP superintendent. When given the option, Frank Kiely did not hesitate to choose to enter his guilty plea in front of a (civilian) judge, rather than his commanding officer sitting as a justice of the peace. Henry Elliott did not have that choice in his criminal case: Superintendent Walker alleged that his own horse had disappeared as well on the night that Elliott and his colleagues took flight from the Battleford barracks; and, undoubtedly, Elliott preferred to be tried by anyone other than Walker or Richardson. Fortunately for Elliott, a jury of six sensible men in

Battleford acquitted him of larceny, a verdict that neither Richardson nor Walker would have preferred.

On Duty: Criminal Prosecutions for Theft, Fraud and Forgery ... on Duty

As we turn to the later period of Richardson's tenure on the territorial bench, it is important to note, yet again, the small number of cases in his court: nine criminal prosecutions of NWMP men between 1888–1901, yielding seven convictions.[144] It is also important to be attentive to the legal context of this set of records. On the NWT Supreme Court, Richardson was one of five judges on the bench. This raises methodological challenges, not least because it is distinctly possible that court records from the other judicial districts, if extant, may contain more cases involving NWMP accused. The legal process was also more formal in the Supreme Court and lawyers served as prosecutors (unlike the NWMP commanding officers in the earlier period).

The seven men whose cases I discuss in this section were charged criminally for misconduct either in the course of their duties or for conduct that brought discredit to the police force, including desertion. All the cases are forms of property offences, and theft figures prominently, but in half of these cases, the victims were the police themselves. Five men were charged with forms of theft, either of Her Majesty's property that they took with them upon discharge or desertion[145] or, often, from fellow members of the force.[146] Two men were charged with forgery or fraud perpetrated on members of the public.[147] The most egregious accusation of theft (really extortion) was against James Ford who abused his position as a member of the police to demand money from a Cree woman.[148]

Constable George Thomas Robinson's experience in 1888–89 demonstrates the dim view the NWMP took of police who used the privilege of their office to engage in criminal activity for personal gain. Robinson, an eighteen-year-old Torontonian, signed up on 27 June 1887 for a five-year term. One of his character references, written on letterhead of *The Globe – Toronto*, was signed by John Cameron who said he knew Robinson and believed him "to be a young man of steady habits, good character and one who knows to do what is right."[149]

In early September 1888, now stationed at Regina, Constable Robinson received a letter from his father, informing him that he had fallen ill and was an invalid. Apparently desperate to get back to Toronto, Robinson forged a telegram and a pass to return to Toronto, both bearing the name of Inspector John Cotton. Apparently, he obtained a lower fare because it appeared that he was travelling with the permission of the Inspector. Using the pass, Robinson then wrote to the Controller of the NWMP requesting a requisition to cover his fare to Toronto, which he asked to be deducted in installments from his pay. Once back in Toronto, he wrote again to the Controller asking for the same arrangement for his return travel at the end of October, after his furlough. However, Robinson appears to have secured other work in the East and did not return to Regina. A warrant for his arrest, dated 29 November 1888, was received in Toronto. After many procedural hurdles and possible misinformation as to his whereabouts, which made it difficult to effect service of the warrant for his arrest, he was finally located and the warrant was executed.

Robinson was returned to Regina in custody on 29 December 1888. An Officer's Board Hearing had been held in Robinson's absence earlier in December 1888; it had recommended that he be struck from the force for having "deserted on a pass in Eastern Canada." The Commissioner accepted this recommendation on 15 January 1889. The NWMP records indicate that Robinson was sentenced to twelve months' hard labour for desertion.

The NWMP records show that the forgery charge was dismissed for want of evidence. However, according to Richardson's records, on 6 February 1889 Robinson was committed for trial by Superintendent Sévère Gagnon JP, on an information sworn by Inspecting Superintendent John Cotton that asserted that Robinson had forged a telegram in Cotton's name and uttered the telegram with intent to defraud. On 4 March 1889, he entered a guilty plea before Richardson and was sentenced to fourteen days and time already served.

Then someone outside of the force, possibly John Cameron from *The Globe*, intervened on Robinson's behalf: a memorandum in his service file indicates that, at the request of the Governor General, the unexpired portion of Robinson's sentence for desertion was remitted to 31 October 1889. It appears that he was allowed to remain in the force. Upon his release,

Robinson was transferred to Maple Creek, where he said he tried to make a go of it. To no avail. Aggrieved at his treatment at the hands of the senior men of the force, the young man with friends in Toronto, and possibly other high places, is reported to have "re-deserted" on 17 March 1890.

Three cases from Regina demonstrate how the lower ranks in the NWMP also took care of their own interests. In 1894, two constables were charged with stealing from fellow members of the force. Constable John Martin was charged with stealing $1.00 from a pair of breeches in the barracks room at "Depot Division" in Regina, where all new NWMP recruits were sent to receive their training and where troublesome men from other districts were sent. Martin, thirty-six years of age, was a relatively recent but older recruit to the NWMP; he had served as a soldier for seven years before his engagement on 20 October 1893 with the police.[150] His career with the NWMP would be shorter: on two different occasions, 9 January 1894 and 13 July 1894, he was brought up before Superintendent Gagnon on two separate alcohol-related discipline offences.

Over Martin's time at Depot Division, others in the barracks had concluded that he was the stealthy thief who was lifting money from their clothes and boxes when no one was watching. They set up a sting operation: after they left a marked dollar bill in a pocket, Martin was caught trying to use it to buy a beer at the canteen. At the committal hearing on 17 August 1894 before Superintendent Gagnon in his capacity as justice of the peace, Martin said that he had found the dollar on a table in the room. Four days later, he entered a guilty plea before Justice Hugh Richardson who sentenced him to four months' imprisonment at hard labour. The day before Martin's appearance in criminal court, the NWMP dismissed him from the force. Once again, both processes worked together.

Constable Henry George Fisher, by contrast, was just twenty-one years of age when he signed on with the NWMP, but he too had a similarly short career in the force, scarcely long enough to find his way into the disciplinary process (although John Martin and Richard Wyld had managed this in short order). Perhaps it was the nature of his illicit activity that impelled him to keep a low profile, as he pilfered his way through the belongings of his fellow members over several months in 1894.[151] Although one of his character references in support of his application in April 1894 described him as a "steady reliable lad," his career was over by December of the same year, punctuated by a sentence of four months' imprisonment at hard labour for several counts of theft to which he pleaded guilty. The informal exhibit list of stolen property assembled by Sergeant Major Lewis Hooper contained thirteen items identified by a number of Fisher's colleagues: a fork, a cake of soap, a screwdriver, four pipes, several pieces of cutlery, a pair of drawers, and so on. As with Constable Martin, Constable Fisher was out of the force before he appeared in court: he was dismissed on 17 December 1894, in time to commence the sentence imposed by Richardson on 18 December.

One might have anticipated that the explicit breach of trust in the conduct of Constable Colin Lorne Campbell,[152] resulting in his 1899 conviction for theft, might have been reflected in a longer sentence than that imposed upon the pilferers, Martin and Fisher. Campbell worked in the canteen at the Regina barracks. The canteen was managed by a committee composed of members of the force. Campbell's regimental pay formed the largest part of his monthly income ($15.00), but he also received $10.00 per month as canteen pay. Since his duties included serving customers, he handled cash. During the month of April 1899, the corporal in charge of the canteen, to whom Campbell reported, was hospitalized. When Campbell was given responsibility for running the canteen, Staff Sergeant Reginald Spencer Knight noticed that something was amiss: the accounts were not in order. After an investigation, Constable Campbell was charged with theft of funds ($8.00). Unlike the other accused Mounties at the barracks, Campbell appeared before a Regina justice of the peace, William Trant, not one of the NWMP justices. Trant committed him for trial on the theft charge and, when he appeared before Richardson in the NWT Supreme Court on 5 May 1899, Campbell entered a guilty plea. Richardson sentenced him to two months' imprisonment at hard labour. On 5 June 1899, with an otherwise spotless discipline record in the force, Campbell was dismissed.

Finally, in the last case in this series, a NWMP member who had taken advantage of the trust and good will of a man who did business with the police similarly found himself convicted and imprisoned. In 1901, after a trial in the NWT Supreme Court, Constable James Cumines was criminally convicted by Richardson for obtaining money by false pretences. Cumines was sentenced on 19 April 1901 to three months at hard labour in the police guardroom.[153] Cumines had persuaded a Moose Jaw businessman, who knew and trusted Cumines, to endorse a cheque in his favour, on Cumines's assurance that he would be sending the endorsed cheque directly to Ottawa. It is not clear from the court file just why the Moose Jaw man did this. In any event, Cumines cashed the cheque himself. Cumines apparently had hoped against hope that his own paycheque would arrive in a timely way and he would be able to reimburse the man who had trusted him, before anyone else learned of it. With, again, an otherwise spotless discipline record, he was dismissed from the force in May before the completion of his sentence.[154]

Conclusion: O-cha-nah-kis and the Bad Cop, Redux

I conclude with a case that directly engages themes of colonialism and criminal justice, as well as the relationship between forms of low law and low justice. I have written elsewhere about this case as an instance illustrative of the relationship between Indigenous people and criminal law,[155] but it bears revisiting in the context of the relationship between the criminal and disciplinary processes involving police officers.

In early September 1889 a Cree woman named O-cha-nah-kis laid an information in Regina, charging NWMP Constable James Ford with stealing $12.00 from her.[156] Ford, a twenty-six-year-old Irish immigrant, had a well-documented record for intoxication and violence, having twice been imprisoned for both disciplinary and criminal alcohol-related offences.[157] James Ford had signed on with the NWMP in May 1885. In his application he indicated that he was twenty-two, single, in good health, and that his religious faith was Roman Catholic; a reference letter from a man who said he had employed Ford for the previous two years described him as a "sober, industrious and hard-working young man."[158] However, his NWMP service record tells a different story, even including correspondence from a woman claiming to be his wife. According to an early report, on Christmas Eve 1885, Ford was drunk at the NWMP barracks, discharged his rifle, and resisted the efforts of other policemen to subdue him. As a result, he was criminally convicted on 20 January 1885 by

Stipendiary Magistrate James Macleod and sentenced to three months' hard labour in Regina for "shooting at peace officers in the execution of their duty."[159] Other disciplinary infractions netted him, at different times, loss of pay as well as fourteen days in the guardroom. The defaulter's sheet in his personnel record indicates that in October 1886 he was again disciplined by his commanding office at Maple Creek for being drunk and causing a disturbance and, on this occasion, he was fined one month's wages and sentenced to six months' imprisonment at hard labour.

After completing his sentence the following spring, Ford was transferred to Depot Division in Regina with, as the commanding officer Superintendent Sévère Gagnon put it, "awkward men and bad characters" from other districts.[160] One can only infer that James Ford was one of the "bad characters" Gagnon had in mind.

It was here some months later that Ford accosted O-cha-nah-kis and her family. Ford had come to a Cree camp near Regina, kicking at tents and calling for a woman. He paid O-cha-nah-kis $1.00 for sexual connection. She said that he came back to her tent later that evening with two other police officers, demanding that she return money to him that he said he had lost in her blanket and intimidating her and her husband with a show of handcuffs. Frightened, she asked her husband to give over all their money, which he did.

This striking case is largely the story of O-cha-nah-kis's response to Ford's mistreatment. She complained to the NWMP that the policeman had extorted $12.00 from her and her family. He was charged with theft on an Information laid by Inspecting Superintendent John Cotton (only the commissioner and assistant commissioner were higher in rank to him). Although her identification of him at trial was a bit shaky, Ford was convicted by Justice Richardson for the theft of the $12.00 and sentenced to one hour in gaol.

Unlike Constables Jones, Constable Kiely, and other convicted police thieves, Ford was not dismissed for bad conduct. It will be recalled that in 1891 Constable Jones was sentenced to six months for larceny and, for his disciplinary offence, a concurrent twelve months, of which almost half was remitted. For lesser forms of bad conduct, other men had been sentenced to long terms of imprisonment in addition to disciplinary sentences. Despite Commissioner Herchmer's well-earned reputation and commitment to harsh treatment of "hard cases and repeat offenders," Ford's criminal conviction for theft from the Cree woman, together with his record of violence and misconduct in the force, appears to have triggered no further discipline charges. He was not dismissed from the force. Rather, and remarkably, he was allowed to buy his way out of the force. His application to be discharged, the second one he made in as many years, was granted in early November 1889; he was permitted to purchase his release for $50.00.[161] His NWMP service record is silent with respect to the conviction for theft of O-cha-nah-kis's money.

Ford's abuse of, and theft from, the Cree woman, including the extortion and threats that accompanied it, appear not to have weighed as grievously as Constable Kiely's thefts of Her Majesty's pistols or Superintendent Howe's pocket book. There is precious little to celebrate about the facts or even the outcome of Ford's case from Regina, offering as it does a graphic illustration of sexual exploitation of a First Nations woman, and cloaked as it is under the conviction for theft. But it also tells something of her and her response to it. O-cha-nah-kis complained to the police and to the Court. She stood up to the cop and, supported by one of the most senior officers in the force, she had him charged with stealing from her. Not a small thing. While the one hour in jail James Ford received as a sentence was insignificant, it may have been one hour longer than he ever thought he would spend there because of his behaviour towards O-cha-nah-kis. It was also the shortest sentence of imprisonment he received during the four years he served in the NWMP.

I have argued in this chapter that police discipline and criminal justice were not separate and discrete spheres; so much of the administration of justice in the Territories and the entirety of the administration of police justice was vested in the North-West Mounted Police. The multiple roles, including juridical and adjudicative, performed by senior police officers, most of whom had no legal training, shaped and informed the form and content of justice in the NWT. Far from being isolated silos, the cases of Mounted Police members accused on criminal and discipline charges shed light on how intimately interconnected these legal sites and institutional processes were. Clearly, the accused police constables had more to fear and worse to experience as they were marched along the blurred lines from the criminal court to police "court," where low justice could just as easily mean no justice at the hands of men who had boots in both places.

NOTES

* This chapter is based on papers presented at the Annual Meeting of the Canadian Historical Association, Ryerson University, Toronto, 29–31 May 2017 and at Canada's Legal Past: Future Directions, Canadian Legal History Conference, University of Calgary, 17–19 July 2017. Sincere thanks to Osgoode and Parkdale alumna Maryam Nisaa Khan for her research assistance, to Osgoode Hall Law Librarian Daniel Perlin for his research support and assistance, to Jodi-Ann Eskritt, Curator, RCMP Historical Collections Unit, Regina, Saskatchewan, to Karen Andrews for her comments (and endurance), to Lyndsay Campbell and Ted McCoy for the invitation to participate in the Calgary conference and to contribute to this collection, and to Lyndsay Campbell for her insightful advice and careful eye. The financial support received from Osgoode Hall Law School's Research Intensification Program for Senior Scholars is gratefully acknowledged.

1   Douglas Hay, "Time, Inequality and Law's Violence," in *Law's Violence*, ed. Austin Sarat and Thomas R. Kearns (Ann Arbor: University of Michigan Press, 1993), 167.

2   Donald Fyson, *Magistrates, Police and People: Everyday Criminal Justice in Quebec and Lower Canada, 1764–1837* (Toronto: University of Toronto Press and the Osgoode Society for Canadian Legal History, 2006); Amanda Glasbeek, *Feminized Justice: The Toronto Women's Court, 1913–34* (Vancouver: UBC Press, 2009); Shelley A.M. Gavigan, *Hunger, Horses and Government Men: Criminal Law on the Aboriginal Plains, 1870–1905* (Vancouver: UBC Press for the Osgoode Society, 2012); Paul Craven, *Petty Justice: Low Law and the Sessions System in Charlotte County, New Brunswick, 1785–1867* (Toronto: University of Toronto Press for the Osgoode Society, 2014); Mary Stokes, "Grand Juries and 'Proper Authorities': Low Law, Soft Law, and Local Governance in Canada/West/Ontario, 1850–1880," in *Essays in the History of Canadian Law*, vol. 11, *Quebec and the Canadas*, ed. G. Blaine Baker and Donald Fyson (Toronto: University of Toronto Press for the Osgoode Society, 2013); Bradley Miller, *Borderline Crime: Fugitive Criminals and the Challenge of the Border, 1819–1914* (Toronto: University of Toronto Press for the Osgoode Society for Canadian Legal History, 2016).

3   Craven, "Law and Ideology: The Toronto Police Court, 1850–80," in *Essays in the History of Canadian Law*, vol. 2, ed. David H. Flaherty (Toronto: University of Toronto Press for the Osgoode Society, 1982); Glasbeek, *Feminized Justice*.

4   Jeffrey L. McNairn, "'A Just and Obvious Distinction': The Meaning of Imprisonment for Debt and the Criminal Law in Upper Canada's Age of Reform," in Baker and Fyson, *Essays in the History of Canadian Law*, 204.

5   Fyson, *Magistrates, Police and People*.

6   Craven, "Law and Ideology"; Craven, *Petty Justice*, 7.

7   Stokes, "Grand Juries and 'Proper Authorities'," 538.

8   Craven, *Petty Justice*, 8.

9   Craven, *Petty Justice*, 10.

10 Miller, *Borderline Crime*, 53.

11 Thomas Flanagan, "Richardson, Hugh," in *Dictionary of Canadian Biography*, vol. 14, University of Toronto/Université Laval, 2003-, http://www.biographi.ca/en/bio/richardson_hugh_1826_1913_14E.html; Gavigan, *Hunger Horses and Government Men*, 42–44.

12 Lewis H. Thomas, *The Struggle for Responsible Government in the North-West Territories 1870–97*, 2nd ed. (Toronto: University of Toronto Press, 1978), 112.

13 For a fuller discussion of Richardson's role in Territorial governance and as a member of the judiciary of the NWT, see W.F. Bowker, "Stipendiary Magistrates and Supreme Court of the North-West Territories, 1876–1907," *Alberta Law Review* 26, no. 2 (1988): 245–86. See also Gavigan, *Hunger, Horses and Government Men*, 40.

14 Section 1(1) of *An Ordinance Respecting the Administration of Civil Justice*, no. 4 of 1878 stipulated the boundary of the Saskatchewan District:

> The "Saskatchewan District" shall comprise all of the Territories bounded on the west, south and west by Alaska and British Columbia; and on the southwest south and south east by the Red Deer River, the south branch of the River Saskatchewan and the River Saskatchewan from the junction of the two branches thereof, until the said river strikes the District of Keewatin; and on the east by Keewatin, and on the north by the northern boundary of the Territories.

This ordinance is printed in *Copies of Ordinances Passed by the Lieutenant-Governor and Council of the North-West Territories, on the 2nd August, 1878, and Laid before the Honorable the Senate and the House of Commons, in pursuance of the 3rd sub-section of the 7th Section of 40 Victoria, Chap. 7*, 3–20 (CSP 1879, vol. 9, no. 86), 3.

15 Bowker, "Stipendiary Magistrates," 267–68.

16 See Bowker, "Stipendiary Magistrates," 274; Gavigan, *Hunger, Horses and Government Men*, 40–41.

17 Six of these cases are found in the 282 files that make up "the first series" (1876–86) from the period when Richardson sat as a stipendiary magistrate: Provincial Archives of Saskatchewan (PAS), Department of the Attorney-General, Regina Judicial Centre, Court Records, 1st series 1878–86, files 1-282 [PAS, A-G (GR11-1) CR Regina, 1st series, 1876–1886]. Three files involve criminal charges, one involves NWMP discipline, and two involve NWMP men being sued civilly (with no disposition). I do not discuss the civil files here. In the later period (1887–1903), Richardson's records from the

Supreme Court of the NWT contain a further nine criminal prosecutions involving serving members of the North-West Mounted Police: PAS, CR-Regina, Coll. R1286. The numbers are modest and are surely imprecise; I am confident that further archival research into other court and NWMP records will yield even more cases.

18   These *Annual Reports* are found in the *Sessional Papers of the Dominion of Canada* (Ottawa: Hunter, Rose, 1868–1925) ["*CSP*"]. The reports from 1882–85 and 1886–87 have also been separately published in facsimile editions as The Commissioners of the Royal North-West Mounted Police, *Settlers and Rebels: Being the Official Reports to Parliament of the Activities of the Royal North-West Mounted Police Force from 1882–1885* (Toronto: Coles Publishing, 1973) and The Commissioners of the Royal North-West Mounted Police, *Law and Order: Being the Official Reports to Parliament of the Activities of the Royal North-West Mounted Police Force from 1886–1887* (Toronto: Coles Publishing, 1973).

19   Library and Archives Canada (LAC), Ottawa, R196-161-9-E (formerly RG 18-G), North West Mounted Police (NWMP) – Personnel Records, 1873–1904.

20   R. Burton Deane, *Mounted Police Life in Canada: A Record of Thirty-One Years' Service* (Toronto: Coles Publishing, 1975; first published 1916 by Cassell & Company), 132.

21   In his work on imprisonment for debt in Upper Canada, McNairn refers to what he characterizes as the "artificial cordoning off criminal from civil" and the "blurred lines" between them in practice and in cultural understandings of the two "sites": "'Just and Obvious Distinction,'" 198–99. Greg Marquis makes a similar point in "'A Machine of Oppression Under the Guise of Law': The Saint John Police Establishment, 1860–1880," *Acadiensis* 16 (1986): 59.

22   W. Peter Ward, "The Administration of Justice in the North-West Territories, 1870–1887," Master's thesis, University of Alberta, 1966, 14, 19.

23   Ward, "Administration of Justice," 20.

24   *An Act to Provide for the Establishment of "The Department of the Interior*," SC 1873, c 4; *An Act Respecting the Administration of Justice, and for the Establishment of a Police Force in the North West Territories*, SC 1873, c 35 [hereinafter NWMP Act, 1873]; *An Act Further to Amend the "Act to Make Further Provision for the Government of the North West Territories*," SC 1873, c 34. See Gavigan, *Hunger, Horses and Government Men*, 33–35. As to the third statute, the amended Act, SC 1871, c 16, simply provided for the appointment of a lieutenant-governor of the NWT, who could establish institutions of governance. As well as specifically extending criminal legislation to the NWT, the 1873 Act broadly empowered the Lieutenant-Governor and council "to make laws for the peace, order and good government of the North West Territories" (s 2) and to modify the law as necessary, subject to certain limitations.

25   NWMP Act, 1873. Section 13 of the Act specified that "persons" appointed to the Force were to be able to read and write either English or French, and be "of a sound constitution, able to ride, active and able-bodied, of good character, and between the ages of eighteen and forty years."

26   *An Act to Authorize the Augmentation of the North-West Mounted Police*, SC 1885, c 53. The force's numbers grew to one thousand in 1885, but by 1899 had dropped back to

just over five hundred members, reflecting the changed fortunes of the force under the Liberal government led by Prime Minister Wilfrid Laurier and Clifford Sifton, Minister of the Interior: William Beahen and Stan Horrall, *Red Coats on the Prairies: The North-West Mounted Police, 1886-1900* (Regina: Centax Books/PrintWest Publishing Services, 1998), 141–50.

27 NWMP Act, 1873, ss 1 and 2.

28 NWMP Act, 1873, s 3.

29 NWMP Act, 1873, s 4.

30 NWMP Act, 1873, s 5.

31 *An Act to Amend and Consolidate the Laws Respecting the North-West Territories*, SC 1875, c 49 [NWT Act, 1875].

32 NWT Act, 1875, s 7(8); however, an ordinance could be disallowed by the Governor General within two years of its passing.

33 NWT Act, 1875, s 64. See Gavigan, *Hunger, Horses and Government Men*, 39–40. The Act was declared in force on 7 October 1876, but immediately became the subject of criticism by outgoing Lieutenant-Governor Alexander Morris for its requirement that stipendiary magistrates sit with judges of the Manitoba Court of Queen's Bench: Ward, *Administration of Justice*, 47.

34 *An Act to Amend the "North-West Territories Act, 1875,"* SC 1877, c 7, s 7 (which repealed ss 62–64 of the 1875 Act and substituted the revised sections) and s 8 (which introduced a new s 71 by which the Stipendiary Magistrates received "jurisdiction, power and authority to hear and determine" in civil claims and disputes).

35 NWMP Act, 1873, s 19.

36 Beahen and Horrall, *Red Coats on the Prairies*, 156. William M. Herchmer, assistant commissioner (1886–1892) was also the brother of Lawrence W. Herchmer who was appointed commissioner in 1886. Unlike Lawrence, who had no previous experience in the NWMP, William had been an NWMP Superintendent since 1876. Despite the appearance of nepotism in his elevation to assistant commissioner, William Herchmer was said to be a popular figure in the NWMP and held the position until his death in 1892: R. C. Macleod, "HERCHMER, WILLIAM MACAULEY," in *Dictionary of Canadian Biography*, vol. 12, University of Toronto/Université Laval, 2003, accessed September 25, 2018, http://www.biographi.ca/ en/ bio/ herchmer_william_macauley_12E.html.

37 NWMP Act, 1873, ss 10 and 15; *An Act to Amend "An Act Respecting the Administration of Justice and for the Establishment of a Police Force in the North-West Territories,"* SC 1874, c 22, s 1 [NWMP Amendment Act, 1874].

38 *An Act to Amend and Consolidate as Amended the Several Enactments Respecting the North-West Mounted Police Force*, SC 1879, c 36, s 8 [NWMP Amendment Act, 1879]. See also R.C. Macleod and Heather Rollason, "'Restrain the Lawless Savages': Native Defendants in the Criminal Courts of the North-West Territories, 1878–1885," *Journal of Historical Sociology* 10, no. 2 (1997): 159.

39 *An Act Further to Amend the Law Respecting the North-West Territories*, SC 1886, c 25 [NWT Amendment Act, 1886].

40 For a review of the jurisdiction of NWT justices of the peace, see Thomas Reynolds, "Justices of the Peace in the NWT," Master's thesis, University of Regina, 1978, 10–22.

41 Reynolds, "Justices of the Peace in the NWT," 113–15; Macleod and Rollason, "Restrain the Lawless."

42 R.C. Macleod, *The North-West Mounted Police and Law Enforcement, 1873–1905* (Toronto: University of Toronto Press, 1976), 35.

43 NWT Amendment Act, 1886, ss 30–32. See also Thomas, *Struggle for Responsible Government*, 111.

44 While not the most active NWMP justice of the peace, Commissioner L.W. Herchmer, on 22 June 1889—as the NWMP criminal case returns indicate—along with Inspecting Superintendent Cotton, tried and convicted a man named Leach in Regina for vagrancy and imposed a fine of $2 with costs. The criminal returns from the Calgary district for 1889 contain three entries for (Assistant Commissioner) "W.M. Herchmer J.P." In a case on August 22, he tried two Cree men, Crow Collar and The Man That Moves for vagrancy; he dismissed the charges with a caution. See "Return of Criminal and Other Cases Tried in the North-West Territories, from 1st December, 1888, to 30th November, 1889," Appendix CC to "Annual Report of Commissioner L.W. Herchmer, North-West Mounted Police, 1889," in *Report of the Commissioner of the North-West Mounted Police Force 1889*, 163–88 (CSP 1890, vol. 10, no. 13), 166, 182.

45 NWT Amendment Act, 1886, ss 9, 28, 30–33, which came into force 18 February 1887; Bowker, "Stipendiary Magistrates," 269, 274–75, 277.

46 *The Mounted Police Act*, 1894, SC 1894, c 27, s 9 (also cited as the *Royal Northwest Mounted Police Act*, RSC 1906, c 91, s 12) [NWMP Act, 1894]. These judicial roles continued after the provinces of Saskatchewan and Alberta were created in 1905. Rather than diminish over time, these judicial roles of the RNWMP were extended in 1919 to provinces in the rest of Canada: *An Act to Amend the Royal Northwest Mounted Police Act*, SC 1919, c 69, s 7.

47 Beahen and Horrall, *Red Coats on the Prairies*, 23. See also Amanda Nettelbeck et al., *Fragile Settlements: Aboriginal Peoples, Law, and Resistance in South-West Australia and Prairie Canada* (Vancouver: UBC Press, 2016), 55.

48 Anthony Jacobus Looy, "The Indian Agent and His Role in the Administration of the North-West Superintendency, 1876–1893," PhD diss., Queen's University (Kingston), 1977, 57. After the signing of Treaty Six at Fort Carlton in 1876, NWMP Superintendent James Walker wrote, "For three years I was Acting Indian Agent for about one-third of the Indian population of the Territories. . . . In addition to my police duties, I was appointed 'Acting Indian Agent of Treaty Six'": James Walker, "My Life in the North-West Mounted Police," *Alberta Historical Review* 8 (1960): 10.

49 Beahen and Horrall, *Red Coats on the Prairies*, 14–22.

50 Macleod, *North-West Mounted Police*; R.C. Macleod, "Canadianizing the West: The North-West Mounted Police as Agents of the National Policy," in *Essays on Western*

History: In Honour of Lewis Gwynne Thomas, ed. Lewis H. Thomas (Edmonton: University of Alberta Press, 1976).

51 Carl Betke, "Pioneers and Police on the Canadian Prairies, 1885–1914," 32, quoted in Beahen and Horrall, *Red Coats on the Prairies*, 14.

52 Gavigan, *Hunger, Horses and Government Men*, 34–38; Nettelbeck et al., *Fragile Settlements*, 55–57.

53 J.W. Little, Written account of conversation between himself and "Marshall" [likely Acting Staff Constable Norton H. Marshall], 3 March 1878, likely referenced by defence counsel, Hayter Reed, in the trial of Henry R. Elliott (1878), file 26, AG CR-Regina, 1st series, 1876–86, PAS.

54 See e.g., Gavigan, *Hunger, Horses and Government Men*; Nettelbeck et al., *Fragile Settlements*, 53–59; Macleod, *North-West Mounted Police*; Macleod, "Canadianizing the West"; Walter Hildebrandt, *Views From Fort Battleford: Constructed Visions of an Anglo-Canadian West* (Regina: Canadian Plains Research Centre, 1994); John N. Jennings, "North-West Mounted Police and Indian Policy after the 1885 Rebellion," in *1885 and After: Native Society in Transition*, ed. F. Laurie Barron and James B. Waldron (Regina: Canadian Plains Research Center, 1986); William M. Baker, ed., *Mounted Police and Prairie Society, 1873-1919* (Regina: Canadian Plains Research Centre, 1998); Sarah Carter, *Aboriginal People and the Colonizers of Western Canada* (Toronto: University of Toronto Press, 1999); Beahen and Horrall, *Red Coats on the Prairies*.

55 For notable contributions, see Beahen and Horrall, *Red Coats on the Prairies*, 243–60; William Beahen, "For the Sake of Discipline: The Strange Case of Cst Basil Nettleship – Deserter," *RCMP Quarterly* 49, no. 3 (1984): 41–45; Anna Maria Mavromichalis, "Tar and Feathers: The Mounted Police and Frontier Justice," in Baker, *The Mounted Police and Prairie Society*.

56 *An Act further to Amend "An Act Respecting the Administration of Justice, and for the Establishment of a Police Force in the North-West Territories,"* SC 1875, c 50, s 1 [NWMP Amendment Act, 1875] (repealing and replacing s 22).

57 When the NWMP Act was revised in 1879, the NWMP brass maintained their jurisdiction as stipendiary magistrates and justices of the peace and could therefore exercise jurisdiction over civilians, but the list of officials who could address NWMP disciplinary offences was changed: non-NWMP stipendiary magistrates like Richardson lost this jurisdiction in favour of the "Superintendent commanding any Post, or such other Commissioned officer as is thereunto empowered by the Commissioner": NWMP Amendment Act, 1879, ss 8, 14.

58 The force, led by a commissioner and assistant commissioner, was organized by geographical divisions. In 1878, the force was distributed throughout the territories in divisions: "A" Fort Saskatchewan, "B" Fort Walsh, "C" Fort Macleod, "D" Shoal Lake & Prince Albert, and "E" Calgary & Battleford. By 1889 eleven divisions were distributed throughout the NWT (Divisions "A" to "K", with the twelfth, Headquarters/Depot Division, in Regina). Each division had a superintendent (the commanding officer), an inspector, and assorted less senior "non-commissioned" officers (e.g., staff sergeants and sergeants), as well as the lower ranks: corporals, constables, and sub-constables.

Given the vast territory for which a division was responsible, many divisions also had regional sub-posts in different locations.

59 Beahen and Horrall, *Red Coats on the Prairies*, 248.

60 Beahen and Horrall, *Red Coats on the Prairies*, 245.

61 NWMP Amendment Act, 1874.

62 NWMP Amendment Act, 1875, s 1, amending s 22. Beahen and Horrall, *Red Coats on the Prairies*, 245, note that the list of offences was "almost word for word from the 'Rules and Regulations' of the Royal Irish Constabulary."

63 NWMP Amendment Act, 1879.

64 *An Act Respecting the North-West Mounted Police Force*, RSC 1886, c 45, s 18 [NWMP Act, 1886], incorporating the provisions of *An Act to Amend 'An Act to Amend and Consolidate as Amended the Several Enactments Respecting the North-West Mounted Police Force*, SC 1882, c 29:

> Every member of the force, other than a commissioned officer, who is convicted of any of the following offences,
>
> (a) Disobeying the lawful command of or striking his superior;
>
> (b) Oppressive or tyrannical conduct towards his inferior;
>
> (c) Intoxication, however slight;
>
> (d) Having intoxicating liquor illegally in his possession, or concealed;
>
> (e) Directly or indirectly receiving any gratuity without the commissioner's sanction, or any bribe;
>
> (f) Wearing any party emblem;
>
> (g) Otherwise manifesting political partisanship;
>
> (h) Overholding any complaint;
>
> (i) Mutinous or insubordinate conduct;
>
> (j) Unduly overholding any allowance or any other public money intrusted [*sic*] to him;
>
> (k) Misapplying any money or goods levied under any warrant or taken from any prisoner;
>
> (l) Divulging any matter or thing which it is his duty to keep secret;
>
> (m) Making any anonymous complaint to the Government or the commissioner;
>
> (n) Communicating, without the commissioner's authority, either directly or indirectly, to the public press, any matter or thing touching the force;
>
> (o) Wilfully, or through negligence or connivance, allowing any prisoner to escape;
>
> (p) Using any cruel, harsh or unnecessary violence towards any prisoner or other person;
>
> (q) Leaving any post on which he has been placed as sentry or on other duty;
>
> (r) Deserting or absenting himself from his duties or quarters without leave;
>
> (s) Scandalous or infamous behavior;
>
> (t) Disgraceful, profane or grossly immoral conduct;

(u) Violating any standing order, rule or regulation, or any order, rule or regulation hereafter made; or –

(v) Any disorder or neglect to the prejudice of morality or discipline, although not specified in this Act or in any rule or regulation,

Shall be held to have committed a breach of discipline.

65   Beahen and Horrall, *Red Coats on the Prairies*, 11–12.

66   Beahen and Horrall, *Red Coats on the Prairies*, 249.

67   Beahen and Horrall, *Red Coats on the Prairies*, 249–50, quote a memorandum, dated 10 September 1887, from Commissioner Herchmer to NWMP Comptroller and Deputy Minister Frederick White.

68   Beahen and Horrall, *Red Coats on the Prairies*, 10.

69   Ottawa: Queen's Printer, 1889, Coll # NF/428 and 4085, RCMP Historical Collections Unit, Regina. These Regulations were the first adopted for the force: Beahen and Horrall, *Red Coats on the Prairies*, 248. I am grateful to Jodi-Ann Eskritt, Curator of the RCMP Historical Collections Unit, for her assistance in accessing this document and others from the Collection.

70   Beahen and Horrall, *Red Coats on the Prairies*, 256.

71   See *An Act to make further provision as to Duties of Customs in Manitoba and the North West Territories*, SC 1873, c 39, s 2 (pertaining to "[s]pirits or strong waters, or spirituous liquors of any kind") and *An Act to amend "An Act to make further provision as to Duties of Customs in Manitoba and the North West Territories," and further to restrain the importation or manufacture of Intoxicating Liquors into or in the North West Territories*, SC 1874, c 7, s 2 (extending the prohibition to include "wines, and fermented and compounded liquors and intoxicating drink of every kind"). These provisions were incorporated into the *North-West Territories Act, 1875*, SC 1875, c 49, s 74. See Gavigan, *Hunger, Horses and Government Men*, 131–32.

72   Defaulters Book, Coll #1943.10.1, RCMP Historical Collections Unit, Regina.

73   A writ of habeas corpus, obtained through a court application, required that a prisoner be brought before the court to determine the validity of his or her detention. For a discussion of the history of the writ in Canada, see Robert J. Sharpe, "Habeas Corpus in Canada," *Dalhousie Law Journal* 2, no. 2 (1975): 241–67.

74   A.G. Irvine, *Report of the Commissioner of the North-West Mounted Police Force 1885*, reproduced in *Settlers and Rebels: Being the Official Reports to Parliament of the Activities of the Royal North-West Mounted Police Force from 1882–1885* (Toronto: Coles Publishing, 1973, facsimile edition), 16.

75   Irvine, *Report of the Commissioner*, 16, emphasis added.

76   Beahen, "For the Sake of Discipline," 41.

77   Beahen and Horrall, *Red Coats on the Prairies*, 237. This came too late for another dissident NWMP member. Beahen and Horrall describe Commissioner Herchmer's "merciless treatment" of Constable John Henry Beggs through his escalating punishments imposed upon Beggs, as one of the leaders of the 1886 Edmonton

"buck": initially a bread and water diet for four days, leg irons for fourteen days, and two months wearing a ball and chain. Before the end of the two months, Herchmer sentenced Beggs to a further two months wearing a ball and chain; later he received two more months in leg irons, and still later two more months at hard labour. By the time of his release, he had served sixteen months in jail (*Red Coats on the Prairies*, 252–53).

78   Deane, *Mounted Police Life in Canada*, 135.

79   R. Burton Deane, "Annual Report of Superintendent R. B. Deane, Commanding Macleod District," Appendix B to "Annual Report of Commissioner L. W. Herchmer: North-West Mounted Police, 1899," in *Report of the North-West Mounted Police 1899*, 15–26 (*CSP* 1900, vol. 12, no. 15), 22, emphasis added. See also, Deane, *Mounted Police Life in Canada*, 137.

80   Beahen, "For the Sake of Discipline," 42.

81   Beahen and Horrall, *Red Coats on the Prairies*, 258; Deane, *Mounted Police Life in Canada*, 139; Beahen, "For the Sake of Discipline," 45.

82   Beahen and Horrall, *Red Coats on the Prairies*, 259.

83   Beahen, "For the Sake of Discipline," 45.

84   Beahen, "For the Sake of Discipline," 42–43.

85   Irvine, *Report of the Commissioner*, 16.

86   Arthur Miles Parken, Regimental Number 2863, North West Mounted Police (NWMP) - Personnel Records, 1873–1904, item no. 50582, vol. 10044, RG18, LAC (http://www.bac-lac.gc.ca/eng/discover/nwmp-personnel-records/Pages/item.aspx?IdNumber=50582&). See also his commanding officer's report concerning "Parker's criminal prosecution": Joseph Howe, "Annual Report of Superintendent Joseph Howe, Commanding "C" Division, 1894," Appendix G to "Annual Report of Commissioner L. W. Herchmer: North-West Mounted Police, 1894," in *Report of the Commissioner of the North-West Mounted Police Force 1894*, 119–31 (*CSP* 1895, vol. 9, no. 15), 119.

87   Parken (misspelled as "AM Parker") was sentenced to six months at hard labour for larceny by Judge Thomas H. McGuire on 16 March 1894. See the report of his conviction in "Return of Criminal and Other Cases tried in the North-West Territories, from 1st December 1893, to 30th November 1894," Appendix FF to "Annual Report of Commissioner L. W. Herchmer North-West Mounted Police, 1894," in *Report of the Commissioner of the North-West Mounted Police Force 1894*, 194–247 (*CSP* 1895, vol. 9, no. 15), 243.

88   Joseph Victor Bégin, Regimental Number O.68, North West Mounted Police (NWMP) – Personnel Records, 1873–1904, item no. 6765, vol. 10037, RG18, LAC (http://www.bac-lac.gc.ca/eng/discover/nwmp-personnel-records/Pages/item.aspx?IdNumber=6765&). Bégin's application and early correspondence to the NWMP were in French.

89   "Return of Criminal and Other Cases tried in the North-West Territories, from 1st December 1894 to 1st December 1895," Appendix FF to "Annual Report of Commissioner L. W. Herchmer," in *Report of the Commissioner of the NWMP 1895*, 194–246 (*CSP* 1896, vol. 11, no. 15), 223.

90 Frank Kiely, Regimental Number 2879, North West Mounted Police (NWMP) – Personnel Records, 1873–1904, item no. 39144, vol. 10044, RG18, LAC (http://www.bac-lac.gc.ca/eng/discover/nwmp-personnel-records/Pages/item.aspx?IdNumber=39144&). See also his commanding officer's report concerning Kiely's criminal prosecution: Howe, "Annual Report of Superintendent Joseph Howe, Commanding "C" Division, 1894," 119.

91 The Act provided that disciplinary punishment was to be "in addition to any punishment to which the offender is liable, in respect of such offence, under any law in force in the North-West Territories, or in any Province in which the offence is committed": NWMP Act, 1886, s 18(2).

92 Robert William Victor Jones, Regimental No. 2420, North West Mounted Police (NWMP) – Personnel Records, 1873–1904, item no. 38307, vol. 10043, RG18, LAC (http://www.bac-lac.gc.ca/eng/discover/nwmp-personnel-records/Pages/item.aspx?IdNumber=38307&). Superintendent. S.B. Steele, Commanding Officer, Division "B," reported on this case in his annual report of 30 November 1891: "Annual Report of Superintendent S. B. Steele, Commanding Macleod District, 1891." Appendix D to "Annual Report of Commissioner L. W. Herchmer North-West Mounted Police, 1891," in *Report of the Commissioner of the North-West Mounted Police Force*, 30–42 (*CSP* 1892, vol. 10, no. 15), 34.

93 Steele to Herchmer, 8 February 1891, in Robert William Victor Jones, personnel record.

94 For a study of Macleod's police and judicial career, see Roderick G. Martin, "Macleod at Law: A Judicial Biography of James Macleod, 1874–94," in *People and Place: Historical Influences on Legal Culture*, ed. Jonathan Swainger and Constance Backhouse (Vancouver: UBC Press, 2003), 37.

95 Warrant of conviction, in Robert William Victor Jones, personnel record.

96 Steele to Herchmer, 26 February 1891, in Jones, personnel record.

97 At the end of every member's term of engagement, a Board of Officers was convened to confirm the dates of his service, to determine any pay owing, and to record the quality of his conduct during his service (e.g., "good" or "bad").

98 Jones, personnel record.

99 Beahen and Horrall, *Red Coats on the Prairies*, 234.

100 Beahen and Horrall, *Red Coats on the Prairies*.

101 Constable Charles Dwight quoted by Beahen and Horrall, *Red Coats on the Prairies*, 248.

102 Constable Pat Power's case is described by Beahen and Horrall, *Red Coats on the Prairies*, 254.

103 Beahen and Horrall mention bucks by the sub-constables at Fort Macleod in 1874 and in Edmonton and Fort Saskatchewan in 1886 (*Red Coats on the Prairies*, 246, 251).

104 Beahen and Horrall, *Red Coats on the Prairies*, 234.

105   Penalties for desertion increased over the years. Beahen and Horrall estimate that between 1881 and 1885, five percent of the total force deserted annually (*Red Coats on the Prairies*, 233).

106   Arlean McPherson, *The Battlefords: A History* (Saskatoon: Modern Press, 1967), 36.

107   Flanagan, "Richardson, Hugh."

108   Regnier Brillon (1877), file 4, AG CR-Regina, 1st series, 1876–86, PAS. As with other NWMP members from the early days of the force, such as Henry R. Elliott, I have not been able to locate a digitized record of his personnel file at LAC.

109   Pierre Daignault also served on the six-man jury, in Battleford in December 1878, that acquitted Henry R. Elliott of the various larceny charges laid against him by Superintendent Walker arising out the escape from the NWMP barracks on 5 March 1878.

110   David B. Hall and Regnier Brillon (1878), file 49, AG CR-Regina, 1st series, 1876–86, PAS.

111   Richardson to Walker, 2 March 1878, in Henry R. Elliott case file, PAS. For a discussion of the "Richardson/Elliott affair," see also Bowker, "Stipendiary Magistrates," 262–64. I refer in passing to the case in Gavigan, *Hunger, Horses and Government Men*, 48–49.

112   Bowker, "Stipendiary Magistrates," 263.

113   Bowker, "Stipendiary Magistrates," 263.

114   Draft Information and Complaint of Hugh Richardson, unsigned and undated, in Henry R. Elliott case file, PAS.

115   I take a different view of this than does Bowker, who writes that Richardson forwarded "criminal charges" to Walker, making "three formal complaints" against the four men: "Stipendiary Magistrates," 264. The court file contains only a draft criminal information, not taken or issued by a justice of the peace.

116   This is the only reference to "Davis" in the Elliott court record; he was not named as one of the deserters who fled on March 4. In his draft complaint, Richardson did not include a first name for Davis or Balfe (but Balfe, on 3 March 1878, corresponded with Richardson, requesting a private meeting to settle the matter of defamation of his character); it is possible, but by no means certain, that he was Joseph Osborne Davis who had been stationed at Battleford between 1874–80. See Joseph Osborne Davis, Regimental Number 267, North West Mounted Police (NWMP) – Personnel Records, 1873–1904, item no. 26722, vol. 10038, RG18, LAC (http://www.bac-lac.gc.ca/eng/discover/nwmp-personnel-records/Pages/item.aspx?IdNumber=26722&).

117   Walker to Richardson, 25 February 1878, in Henry R. Elliott case file, PAS.

118   The validity of Richardson's view and the legal history of capacity and consent to marry at common law, and the regulation of the solemnization of marriage under the then *British North America Act*, are beyond the scope of this chapter. Later, on 2 August 1878, the North West Territorial Council passed *An Ordinance Respecting Marriage*, No. 9 of 1878, which, by s 8 gave the father of a person under the age of twenty-one the authority to consent to the marriage. See *Copies of Ordinances Passed by the Lieutenant-Governor and Council of the North-West Territories, on the 2nd August, 1878, and Laid*

before the Honorable the Senate and the House of Commons, in pursuance of the 3*rd* sub-section of the 7*th* Section of 40 Victoria, Chap. 7 (*CSP* 1879, vol. 9, no. 86, 22–25), 23. Given his legislative drafting experience, Richardson, an ex officio member of the Council, likely held the pen for this ordinance.

119 Deposition of Walker, at the hearing into the "accessory after the fact," charges against David Hall and Regnier Brillon later in March 1878: Hall and Brillon case file, PAS.

120 The brief personnel record of Patrick Balfe (one of Elliott's three comrades in the affair) simply records that he engaged with the NWMP in 1876 at the age of twenty-two, and he is listed as having deserted on 5 March 1878. The file does not contain a defaulter's sheet. Patrick J. Balfe, Regimental Number OS–507, North West Mounted Police (NWMP) – Personnel Records, 1873–1904, item no. 64834, vol. 10037, RG18, LAC (http://www.bac-lac.gc.ca/eng/discover/nwmp-personnel-records/Pages/item.aspx?IdNumber=64834&).

121 Henry R. Elliott case file, PAS.

122 Known principally for his career as a government bureaucrat, Reed was a lawyer and appeared as defence counsel before Richardson on at least one other criminal case before he became an Indian Agent: see Gavigan, *Hunger, Horses and Government Men*, 102–3, 231 notes 39 and 40.

123 Reed would go on to become Indian Commissioner and ultimately Deputy Superintendent of Indian Affairs. See Brian Titley, "Reed, Hayter," in *Dictionary of Canadian Biography*, vol. 16, University of Toronto/Université Laval, 2003–. http://www.biographi.ca/en/bio/reed_hayter_16E.html. See also Sarah Carter, *Lost Harvests: Prairie Indian Reserve Farmers and Government Policy* (Montreal and Kingston: McGill-Queen's University Press), 1990; Walter Hildebrandt, *Views from Fort Battleford: Constructed Visions of an Anglo-Canadian West* (Regina: Canadian Plains Research Centre, 1994).

124 "Henry R Elliott. Tried and Acquitted. A Full Report of the Case," *Saskatchewan Herald*, 30 December 1878, in Henry R. Elliot case file, PAS. In his evidence against Brillon and Hall at their trial on related charges earlier in the year, Walker gave the prisoner's name as Ducharme.

125 Bowker, "Stipendiary Magistrates," 265.

126 "Henry R Elliott. Tried and Acquitted. A Full Report of the Case," *Saskatchewan Herald*, 30 December 1878, in Henry R. Elliot case file, PAS.

127 Lash to Richardson, 1 February 1879, in Henry R. Elliott case file, PAS.

128 "New York, New York City Marriage Records, 1829–1940" in *FamilySearch* database (https://familysearch.org/ark:/61903/1:1:24SN-4TT : 10 February 2018), David Roger and L...Ders Richardson, 18 July 1885, citing Marriage, Manhattan, New York, New York, United States, New York City Municipal Archives, New York; FHL microfilm 1,570,465. Thanks are due to Lyndsay Campbell and to Theresa Ray, York University MA student for this bit of fact checking.

129 Richard Charles Wyld, Regimental Number 281, North West Mounted Police (NWMP) – Personnel Records, 1873–1904, item no. 64376, vol. 10038, RG18, LAC

(http://www.bac-lac.gc.ca/eng/discover/nwmp-personnel-records/Pages/item.aspx?IdNumber=64376&).

130   Beahen and Horrall, *Red Coats on the Prairies*, 171, 248.

131   Beahen and Horrall, *Red Coats on the Prairies*, 172.

132   S.B. Steele, "Annual Report of Superintendent Steele, Commanding Macleod District," Appendix F to "Annual Report of Commissioner L. W. Herchmer, North-West Mounted Police, 1889," in *Report of the Commissioner of the North-West Mounted Police Force 1889*, 54–75 (*CSP* 1890, vol. 10, no. 13), 55–56.

133   Richard Charles Wyld, personnel record.

134   Robert Wyld, Regimental Number 282, North West Mounted Police (NWMP) – Personnel Records, 1873–1904, item no. 64377, vol. 10038, RG18, LAC (http://www.bac-lac.gc.ca/eng/discover/nwmp-personnel-records/Pages/item.aspx?IdNumber=64377&).

135   Osler to Blake, 19 April 1877, in Richard Charles Wyld, personnel record.

136   Defaulter's sheet, in Richard Charles Wyld, personnel record.

137   Richard C. Wyld (1878), file 60, AG CR-Regina, 1st series, 1876–86, PAS.

138   Richard C. Wyld case file, PAS.

139   Certificate of Discharge, 2 September 1878. In Richard C. Wyld, personnel record.

140   Troy is now known as the town of Qu'Appelle (as distinct from Fort Qu'Appelle) in Saskatchewan, fifty kilometres east of Regina. In the spring of 1885, shortly before this alleged incident, Troy had been a temporary base for Major-General Frederick Middleton and his militia, before they headed north along the Carlton Trail to Batoche. See Macleod, *North-West-Mounted Police*, 103–4.

141   Walter Douglas Parkins (1885), file 276, AG CR-Regina, 1st series, 1876–86, PAS.

142   Walter Douglas Parkins case file, PAS.

143   Walter Douglas Parkins, Regimental Number 741, North West Mounted Police (NWMP) – Personnel Records, 1873–1904, item no. 50647, vol. 10039, RG18, LAC (https://www.bac-lac.gc.ca/eng/discover/nwmp-personnel-records/Pages/item.aspx?IdNumber=50647&).

144   The two acquittals derived from prosecutions in Regina in 1893 and 1896. Clement E. Hamilton was charged with the theft of items that went missing when he left the NMWP at the end of his term of service. Some of the items belonged to the superior officer for whom he had acted as a servant. Evidence was led that he had not done all his own packing and only discovered the items after a period of time, by which point everything was in quarantine due to diphtheria, and he was unable to retrieve them in a timely way: Clement E. Hamilton (1893), file 55, SCNWT (Criminal), Coll R1286, IR 19, PAS. See also his NWMP Personnel Record: Clement Edward Hamilton, Regimental Number 2521, North West Mounted Police (NWMP) – Personnel Records, 1873–1904, item no. 34252, vol. 10043, RG18, LAC (http://www.bac-lac.gc.ca/eng/discover/nwmp-personnel-records/Pages/item.aspx?IdNumber= 34252&). The other acquittal was that of Constable Stanley Hildyard on a charge of theft of a saddle and robes, following a fire at a stable and livery in Regina. According to the Regina *Leader*, at trial two other

men were convicted. The newspaper reported that Hildyard, represented by Regina lawyer Norman MacKenzie, gave an exculpatory explanatory statement that the trial judge accepted. The paper also noted that members of the community had expressed a sense of injustice at Hildyard's being charged in the first place: "Thieves Sentenced: Manseau and Henderson Go To Jail – The Policeman Very Properly Goes Free," *Leader* (Regina), 5 March 1896. Hildyard's defaulter's sheet has no entry for the criminal charge, but his record contains a letter from Superintendent A. B. Perry informing the commissioner of the charge, trial, and acquittal. Perry's letter suggests that in his view Hildyard was not entirely "free from blame" as he knew the property in question had been recovered from the fire. Stanley Hildyard (1896), file 119, SCNWT (Criminal), Coll R1286, IR 19, PAS; Stanley Hildyard, Regimental Number 2842, North West Mounted Police (NWMP) – Personnel Records, 1873–1904, item no. 35794, vol. 10044, RG18, LAC (http://www.bac-lac.gc.ca/eng/discover/nwmp-personnel-records/Pages/item.aspx?IdNumber=35794&).

145 See Sperry Bridon Storms (1894), file 43, SCNWT (Criminal), Coll R1286, IR 19, PAS. His NWMP personnel record is Sperry Storms, Regimental Number 2806, North West Mounted Police (NWMP) – Personnel Records, 1873–1904, item no. 58923, vol. 10044, RG18, LAC (http://www.bac-lac.gc.ca/eng/discover/nwmp-personnel-records/Pages/item.aspx?IdNumber=58923&). On 5 August 1892, Storms was sentenced by Superintendent Sévère Gagnon to six months at hard labour for desertion and, on 9 September 1892, by Judge Richardson to two months at hard labour for the theft of a pistol that he took with him when he deserted. He was discharged in April 1893, at the expiration of his sentence.

146 John Martin (1894), file 81, SCNWT (Criminal), R1286, PAS; Henry George Fisher (1894), file 92, SCNWT (Criminal), R1286, PAS; Colin Lorne Campbell (1899), file 200, SCNWT (Criminal), R1286, PAS.

147 George Thomas Robinson (1888–89), file 2, SCNWT (Criminal), R1286, PAS; James M. Cumines [or Cummines] (1900–1), file 242, SCNWT (Criminal), R1286, PAS.

148 James Ford (1889), file 11, SCNWT (Criminal), R1286, PAS.

149 George Thomas Robinson, Regimental Number 2174, North West Mounted Police (NWMP) – Personnel Records, 1873–1904, item no. 54238, vol. 10041, RG18, LAC (https://www.bac-lac.gc.ca/eng/discover/nwmp-personnel-records/Pages/item.aspx?IdNumber=54238&).

150 John Martin, Regimental Number 2952, North West Mounted Police (NWMP) – Personnel Records, 1873–1904, item no. 44446, vol. 10044, RG18, LAC (http://www.bac-lac.gc.ca/eng/discover/nwmp-personnel-records/Pages/item.aspx?IdNumber=44446&).

151 Harry George Fisher case file, PAS.

152 Colin Lorne Campbell case file, PAS.

153 James M. Cumines case file, PAS.

154 James MacGlashen Cumines, Regimental Number 3658, North West Mounted Police (NWMP) – Personnel Records, 1873–1904, item no. 26036, vol. 10046, RG18, LAC (http://www.bac-lac.gc.ca/eng/discover/nwmp-personnel-records/Pages/item.aspx?IdNumber=26036&).

155 Gavigan, *Hunger, Horses and Government Men*, 105–6.

156 James Ford (1889), file 11, SCNWT (Criminal), R1286, IR 19, PAS.

157 James Ford, Regimental Number 1348. North West Mounted Police (NWMP) – Personnel Records, 1873 – 1904, item no. 30646, vol. 10041, RG 18, LAC (http://www.bac-lac.gc.ca/eng/discover/nwmp-personnel-records/Pages/item.aspx?IdNumber=30646&).

158 James Conrick to unnamed addressee, 4 May 1885. In James Ford, personnel record, Conrick identified himself as the proprietor of the Dufferin Stables in Montreal.

159 See "Return of Criminal and Other Cases Tried in the North-West Territories, from 1st December, 1885, to 30th November, 1886," Appendix AA to "Annual Report of Commissioner L. W. Herchmer, North-West Mounted Police, 1886," in *Report of the Commissioner of the North-West Mounted Police Force 1886*, reproduced in *Law and Order: Being the Official Reports to Parliament of the Activities of the Royal North-West Mounted Police Force from 1886–1887* (Toronto: Coles Publishing, 1973), 115.

160 S. Gagnon, "Annual Report of Superintendent Gagnon, Commanding Depot Division, 1889," Appendix D to "Annual Report of Commissioner L. W. Herchmer, North-West Mounted Police, 1889," in *Report of the Commissioner of the North-West Mounted Police Force 1889*, 35–36 (*CSP* 1890, vol. 10, no. 13), 36; John Martin case file, PAS.

161 James Ford, personnel record.

SECTION III

WRITING LEGAL HISTORY: PAST, PRESENT, AND FUTURE

Sex Discrimination in Canadian Law: From Equal Citizenship to Human Rights Law

Dominique Clément

Introduction: Equality Deferred

For most of Canadian history the unequal treatment of Canada's female citizens was pervasive and entrenched in law. The law reflected common sense notions about gender and women's roles in public and private life. Male legislators created laws that restricted women's opportunities and choices, or imposed greater obligations on women. Nineteenth-century law often gave husbands control over their wives. Alternatively, some laws "privileged" women, such as protective labour laws that provided opportunities for women that did not exist for men. Such laws, however, were rooted in the belief that women were dependents, or defined women as mothers whose reproductive responsibilities needed to be regulated. In other words, these laws marginalized women in the workforce and reinforced unequal gender roles.

Most scholarship on women and the law in Canada is narrowly focused on a single jurisdiction or only addresses one form of law, such as criminal or family law.[1] Studies are also often concerned with a particular period in history, such as the late nineteenth century or the period following the

Charter of Rights and Freedoms.[2] These studies, while invaluable, fail to capture the broad scope of legal reform throughout Canadian history.[3] Moreover, they underestimate the extent of those legal disabilities that have historically been imposed on women in Canada by ignoring the multiple intersecting legal regimes that compound discrimination over time.

This chapter argues that there were three stages of legal reform in Canadian history that addressed sex discrimination in law: equal citizenship, formal legal equality, and human rights law.[4] Each stage of legal reform mirrored the evolution of the women's movement. The first wave of the women's movement, which gained prominence by the late nineteenth century, played a central role in lobbying for legal reforms that recognized fundamental rights of citizenship.[5] The most notable reform was the right to vote, but during this period there were also changes to the law on property, family, and work. Most of these reforms were designed to protect (i.e., regulate) women and children from abuse, rather than provide for equality under the law. Legal distinctions based on gender remained prevalent. The next stage of legal reform coincided with a second wave of mobilization within the women's movement during the mid-twentieth century.[6] These reforms were designed to achieve formal legal equality. By the 1980s most of the explicit legal distinctions based on gender were eliminated from statute law. Once again, however, these reforms had limits. They addressed only the most basic procedural forms of inequality. The last stage of legal reform—human rights law—signaled a shift towards substantive equality. Anti-discrimination statutes, in particular, became a powerful legal tool for women.

The country's complex legal system is a patchwork of municipal, provincial, territorial, and federal jurisdictions (including the common law and a civil code) divided between criminal, civil, and constitutional law. Nonetheless, it is possible to identify common trends over time. This chapter draws on a broad range of primary sources, including statutes and case law, as well as a comprehensive survey of the scholarship on women's legal history. Federal law and the provincial law of Ontario and British Columbia have been prominent for establishing key precedents in legal reform. To be sure, the country's federal system can make it difficult to identify common trends in legal reform. Women secured the right to vote in Manitoba in 1916, but not in Quebec until 1940. And yet the federal system can also foster unity. Ontario's pioneering human rights statute in 1961 became a model for every other jurisdiction. In this way, there was a shared experience in terms of how the law was gendered in Canada.

Equal Citizenship

Women in nineteenth-century Canada were, under the law, denied even the most basic rights. Women did, on occasion, vote before universal suffrage, usually if they were property owners. But they were gradually disenfranchised in the nineteenth century. Prince Edward Island, in 1832, was the first colony in British North America to prohibit women from voting, followed by New Brunswick (1836), the Canadas (1849), and Nova Scotia (1851).[7] Because they could not vote, women were unable to become legislators, coroners, magistrates, or judges: this is why not a single woman was appointed a judge, coroner, justice of the peace, police constable, or police magistrate in the nineteenth century. In 1905 a Supreme Court judge in New Brunswick, reflecting on the role of women in society, quoted a United States Supreme Court justice as saying that "[t]he paramount destiny and mission of women are to fulfil the noble and benign offices of wife and mother. This is the law of the Creator."[8]

Family law was explicitly patriarchal. Fathers determined their children's education and religion. A man could disinherit his wife; children were his sole property; a father could consent to have his twelve-year-old daughter married without his wife's consent; a husband could appoint a guardian for children under seven years old without the mother's consent (his wife's consent was not required after the child's seventh birthday unless children were sent "beyond the seas"); fathers inherited the estates of all children under twenty-one years old; and a father could even appoint a guardian in his will for children after his death, including *unborn* children. Custody battles often favoured the father in those uncommon circumstances when women left their husbands.[9] Only in extreme cases involving abuse would a judge have taken children from their father. Unsurprisingly, laws that dealt with marriage and divorce were premised on male dominance in the family. Nineteenth-century law in Upper and Lower Canada made it virtually impossible to divorce: the former required an Act of Parliament, and under the latter marriage was indissoluble until death.[10] Yet men had to prove only adultery on the part of their wives to secure a divorce, whereas a wife had to prove adultery as well as desertion without reason, extreme cruelty, incest, or bigamy. Judges often applied a cruel double standard, blaming wives for giving up too quickly if they left after one incident of abuse, or alternatively accusing battered wives of accepting or encouraging the abuse if they waited too long.[11] As an alternative to divorce, women could seek separation and damages. When women did secure a divorce, they often faced ostracism and poverty.[12]

Nineteenth-century common law denied women basic property rights (in Quebec, the Civil Code codified a community property regime). "Marriage," as one historian has described the legal reality for women under the common law in the nineteenth century, "meant civil death."[13] A woman lost her legal status when she married, and her husband was assumed to control her person. Women took their husbands' nationality and domicile when they married. Under the common law, a husband controlled his wife's earnings and could prohibit her from working for wages. Husbands could legally rape their wives, confine them, and mete out physical punishment or "discipline." Until the 1850s, the family farm belonged to the husband, including everything in the home. Canada's *Dominion Lands Act* of 1876 also banned women from homesteading, which was especially problematic for women in Western Canada where homesteading was common.[14] Without property, women could not hope to support themselves independent of their husbands. A lifetime of work on the farm did not ensure a woman any guarantee of ownership if her husband died. In fact, the land usually went to the son (leaving her dependent on her children) and widows could lose any claim to property if they remarried.[15] Married women had no control over property. Income and profits belonged to their husbands; they could not be sued, and they could not contract or sue another person in their name; their spouse's consent was required for them to start a business; and all personal property (including wages) was transferred to their husbands. In return, husbands were liable for their wives' debts and contracts.[16]

Minority women experienced discrimination as both women and minorities. British Columbia, for instance, went to extraordinary lengths to restrict immigration, and when Chinese women did manage to make it to the province, they were usually restricted to working in small restaurants, laundries, or fish canneries. Indigenous women worked in the province's canneries, although at lower pay and for fewer hours than men. Those few girls who did attend school were segregated based on race. Solicitation laws included particular provisions for Chinese and Indigenous peoples.[17] Chinese sex workers were banned under the 1885 head tax legislation, and in the 1880s Parliament passed a series of laws to impose harsher sentences and lower evidentiary standards for Indigenous sex workers.[18] Similarly, the 1880 federal *Indian Act* prohibited the owner of a house from allowing Indigenous sex workers on the premises and imposed harsher penalties for keepers of bawdy houses.[19] In 1869, Indigenous women were further banned from voting in band elections or holding political office.[20] African-Canadian women throughout Canada struggled to find jobs other than as domestics.[21] Retail sales work was not an option for most visible minority women. Jewish women found themselves unable to get hired at Eaton's or Woodward's. Women who did not come from Anglo-Celtic backgrounds might also find office work barred for them. In fact, white-collar work in general was usually off-limits to minority women, unless perhaps a segregated school needed to hire a black teacher.[22]

Some of the earliest legal reforms to recognize women's rights dealt with property, albeit they were never seriously designed to undermine male privilege (although they might protect women from husbands leaving the family destitute). New Brunswick (1851) and Ontario (1859) granted women, in certain cases, nominal control over their wages free from their husbands. In 1872, Ontario introduced the country's first *Married Women's Property Act*, which was later adopted with similar provisions by other provinces. It allowed women to hold and dispose of any property they brought to the marriage or acquired thereafter, including any profits deriving from the property, as well as acquire future property for themselves.[23] Any wages a wife earned *separately from her husband* belonged to her. At the same time, the law protected husbands from any debts arising from their wives' property before marriage, and immunized husbands from liability for any debts incurred from his wife's business or employment. In this way, the law "did not challenge the economic and social inequality central to nineteenth century marriage."[24] Moreover, women had few opportunities in the paid workforce. Explicit legal restrictions on women in occupations were admittedly rare, although British Columbia

(1877) and Ontario (1890) passed legislation preventing women from working in mines and regulated their work above ground (e.g., hours and meal breaks).[25] Professional associations refused to certify women, most notably law societies. Even when they did work, women invariably earned less for doing the same work as men, or they were often concentrated in the same occupations and paid less. Women were also routinely barred from higher education. McGill, for instance, did not admit women until 1857. By 1900, only 11 percent of university and college students were women.[26]

Similarly, laws designed to protect women and children workers, which were first introduced in Ontario and Quebec in the 1880s, were premised on the belief that "female workers needed greater protection than male workers because of their presumed physical frailty and moral vulnerability."[27] The need for protective labour legislation was routinely framed in terms of women's reproductive capabilities. These laws defined women as a dependent category of workers requiring state regulation.[28] In this way, although state legislation may have mitigated some of the harshest conditions in the workplace, it also restricted women's access to the paid labour force. Protective labour laws could also go to extremes. Between 1912 and 1919, Saskatchewan law banned "Chinese, Japanese or other Oriental persons" from employing white women.[29] Manitoba (1913), Ontario (1914), and British Columbia (1919) implemented similar measures.[30] Even more extraordinary was British Columbia's 1923 *Act for the Protection of Women and Girls in Certain Cases*. The law empowered a chief of municipal police, by the simple expedient of posting a certificate in his office, to prohibit any employer from providing lodging or hiring an "Indian" or white woman if the police deemed that it might undermine "the morals of such women and girls."[31]

Further legal reform was incremental. In 1855, the Province of Canada passed a statute for Canada West (Ontario) that allowed judges to grant women custody over children under twelve years old.[32] Women who had committed adultery, though, were automatically denied custody. Nineteenth-century courts rarely provided relief for women and children abandoned by the father. In the early 1900s, however, many provinces introduced legislation for deserted wives and children. In most cases, the law empowered a magistrate to order a husband to provide money to his wife for her basic necessities if he abandoned or severely beat her.[33] But women who had committed adultery could not sue for maintenance.

There were additional reforms to family law in the early twentieth century. Several provinces introduced legislation that allowed judges to remove children from abusive situations. In 1917, British Columbia was the first province to enact legislation that provided mothers with rights and obligations equal to fathers for the care, custody, and education of their children.[34] The province also set a Canadian precedent in 1921 with *An Act Concerning the Employment of Women before and after Childbirth*.[35] The law provided mothers modest financial support and prohibited employers from dismissing a woman because of her absence. Meanwhile, Ontario, Alberta, Saskatchewan, Manitoba, and British Columbia enacted legislation between 1916 and 1920 to support women raising young children (mothers' allowances). Still, many of these reforms continued to marginalize women. Mothers' allowances defined women as nurturers, mothers, and dependents. Benefits were usually discontinued when children turned sixteen years old.[36]

The women's movement was at the forefront of many of these campaigns for legal reform. The first wave of the movement, led by organizations such as the National Council of Women (including local and provincial councils), the Canadian Women's Suffrage Association, the *Fondation nationale Saint-Jean Baptiste*, and the Woman's Christian Temperance Union, mobilized women to campaign for the right to vote and reforms to property laws, among other issues.[37] And yet, by the early twentieth century, there was some hesitation among even the most prominent feminists in the country to demand full equality. In 1912, for example, several unions recommended to the Royal Commission on Labour Conditions that the government establish a minimum weekly wage of $6.50 for female workers. The Vancouver Local Council of Women in British Columbia, however, suggested the minimum wage be set at $5 "'to be fair to employers as well as the employee.'"[38] Similarly, while in the 1930s the Canadian Federation of Business and Professional Women's Clubs advocated against low salaries for women and passed resolutions against workplace discrimination based on marital status, by the late 1930s the organization hesitated to assert that equal treatment was a right. Rather, the organization framed the issue as financial need.[39] Moreover, women struggled to gain political influence by the mid-twentieth century because few women were elected to public office.

Nonetheless, the movement achieved a significant victory when women obtained the vote. Universal suffrage was first granted in 1916 in Manitoba. The franchise offered the opportunity for women to become more active in public life, although most provinces continued to ban women from serving on juries or allowed an exemption based on gender.[40] Women also gained access to additional professions. By 1926, only Quebec prohibited women from voting and practicing law. Organizations such as the *Ligue des droits de la femme* and *l'Alliance canadienne pour le vote des femmes du Québec* set the groundwork in the 1930s that ultimately secured women the right to vote in Quebec in 1940.[41] And although the Supreme Court of Canada affirmed in 1928 that women were not eligible to be senators, the Judicial Committee of the Privy Council overruled the decision and determined in 1929 that women were indeed "persons" as stated in the constitution.[42]

Criminal law, however, appeared immune from substantial reform during this period. Criminal law reflected an almost obsessive need to regulate women's sexuality. In 1892, for example, the *Criminal Code* prohibited an employer or coworker with any kind of directive power from seducing a female employee under his direction in any factory, mill, or workshop. In 1900 this prohibition was extended to shops and stores, and to all workplaces in 1920.[43] Chastity laws were introduced in the nineteenth century, and the practice of separately incarcerating female convicts became common by the 1870s. In 1910 the federal government also deemed it necessary to prohibit contact between female immigrants and male members of a ship's crew during passage.[44] It was also a crime, as of 1918, for a woman with a venereal disease to have sex or solicit sex with a member of the armed forces.[45]

In rape trials, which were rare in nineteenth-century Canada, judges and juries favoured women who fit a model of chastity. Women's sexual history was often a key issue at trial. Chastity was also an issue in seduction trials, which the federal Parliament criminalized in 1886. Previously, seduction had been a civil cause of action that permitted fathers to sue men who had "carnal knowledge" of their daughters. If the daughter was pregnant, and the man refused to marry her, the father would sue for the cost of maintaining the daughter and the child (essentially "asserting parental property interests in the sexual behaviour of their female offspring").[46] The law (except in Quebec) recognized only the father's right to sue, not that of the woman who had been seduced. When seduction was criminalized, a man who had sex with a girl between the ages of twelve and sixteen years old (the threshold was raised to twenty-one in 1887 if the male was over twenty-one) could be sent to jail for two years. Women under eighteen were also included if they were of previously chaste character and the act was committed under the promise of marriage.[47]

Criminal law on infanticide and abortion also targeted women. An 1892 amendment to the *Criminal Code* criminalized "failing to obtain reasonable assistance for childbirth." The crime carried the severe sentence of life in prison if a prosecutor could prove that a woman did not seek assistance so the child would die.[48] Procuring an abortion became a crime in British North America beginning in New Brunswick in 1810 and, soon after, the other colonies. Abortion trials were uncommon in the nineteenth century, but, when they did go to trial, the vast majority of accused women were found guilty. Doctors faced severe penalties, ranging from ten years to life in prison. Parliament went even further and, in 1892, banned the sale, distribution, and advertisement of any material relating to contraception or abortion.[49]

By the twentieth century the law touched on almost every aspect of women's lives: birth (infanticide), childhood (maintenance, child custody), work (labour laws, professions), courtship (seduction, marriage), sexual relations (rape, solicitation), marriage (property), parenting (maternity leave, abortion, adoption, legitimacy), divorce or separation (maintenance, child custody, pensions, desertion), and death (inheritance). Legal reforms during this period were designed to remove those legal distinctions that had created a separate and lesser form of citizenship for women such as voting, employment, or owning property. These reforms enabled women to better engage in public life. Yet the law continued to reinforce male privilege and patriarchal power, especially in the family.

Formal Legal Equality

Women born in mid-twentieth century Canada faced an inadequate and patronizing legal regime in property, labour, family, and criminal law. Alberta (1928) and British Columbia (1933) passed legislation to forcibly sterilize people who were mentally ill. In practice, the law disproportionately targeted women and Indigenous peoples.[50] That the state continued to define women in terms of rigid gender roles in the 1960s was exemplified in a 1966 publication of the federal Department of Citizenship and Immigration, which explained that "winter weather is a limiting factor [for Canadian women's political activity] as well as household duties and farm chores."[51]

After securing key victories around the right to vote and access to property among other issues, new campaigns emerged demanding full legal equality. A new wave of feminist activism, led in part by a generation of women coming of age in the 1950s and 1960s, reinvigorated the movement. Organizations such as the National Council of Women had been advocating on issues such as equal pay since the 1920s.[52] During the war, women's organizations successfully lobbied to raise the basic pay for servicewomen to 90 percent of the male rate. Twenty-one affiliates of the Young Women's Christian Association established Public Affairs committees in Ontario in 1950 to advocate for laws to ban sex discrimination. Margaret Hyndman, president of the Business and Professional Women's Clubs, led a delegation to Premier Leslie Frost in 1951 to demand equal pay legislation and a prohibition on sex discrimination in employment. Hyndman, a lawyer, helped draft the Ontario *Female Employees Fair Remuneration Act* (1952), which was the first equal pay statute in Canada. Business and Professional Women's Clubs committees outside Ontario also lobbied for equal pay laws.[53] Meanwhile, in Ottawa, the Business and Professional Women's Clubs and the National Council of Women convinced the federal Liberal government to implement equal pay legislation covering 70,000 women working in federal jurisdiction.[54] Women's Institutes were also active in lobbying for equal pay.[55]

A second stage of legal reforms sought to eliminate formal legal distinctions based on gender. Mothers' allowances had already been replaced with a more generous federal family allowances program in 1944. In 1951,

Ontario and Manitoba removed their bans against women serving on juries, which later spread to other jurisdictions.[56] New Brunswick (1964) and the federal government (1971) implemented policies for maternity leave.[57] Differential minimum wage laws were revoked in Alberta, Saskatchewan, Manitoba, Ontario, Quebec, and New Brunswick by 1970. In each jurisdiction women and men were given equal legal responsibility for maintaining their children, and both wives and husbands were eventually permitted to sue for alimony or maintenance.[58]

Women were no longer prohibited from voting or, in common law jurisdictions, from owning and controlling property if they were married.[59] By 1953, all references to race were removed from provincial electoral law and, in 1960, the federal government enfranchised Indigenous peoples. But the sudden disappearance of a legal prohibition did not diminish the legacy of generations of legal discrimination. The situation facing Indigenous women was especially bleak. The original *Indian Act* had given the Superintendent-General the power to "stop the payment of the annuity and interest money of any woman having no children who deserts her husband and lives immorally with another man." The 1884 *Indian Act* further specified that Indigenous widows had to be of "moral character" to inherit property. An especially contentious section was the provision that Indigenous women lost their status if they married a non-Indigenous man. The same did not apply to men. When women lost their status, they forfeited their right to live on Indigenous lands, own band property, inherit land or a house on a reserve, and to be buried on a reserve.[60] And they could not regain their status, and therefore return to their home, if their marriage dissolved or they divorced. The *Indian Act* was rife with such discriminatory provisions: women and their children were involuntarily enfranchised if their husband/father was enfranchised; married women's band membership was determined by their husband's band; illegitimate children of Indigenous men or non-Indigenous women were denied status; and children lost status when they reached the age of twenty-one if their mothers did not have status before they were married.[61]

Whereas Indigenous women continued to face widespread legal disabilities, there were several major reforms designed to remove distinctions based on gender in statute law. The 1968 federal *Divorce Act*, for instance, extended judicial divorce to jurisdictions where it had not been previously available and set consistent grounds for divorce across the country. Divorce was permitted on the basis of adultery, homosexuality, physical and mental cruelty, or marriage breakdown.[62] The law streamlined the process for applying for a divorce and reduced costs and delays, which had been a particular hardship for women. The divorce rate in Canada doubled in the first year following the *Divorce Act*, and most of those flocking to the courts were women.[63]

One of the most important developments during this period was the federal Royal Commission on the Status of Women (RCSW). The RCSW identified a plethora of discriminatory laws in its report published in 1970. Some of the more blatant forms of sex discrimination that were still rampant in several or all jurisdictions included prohibitions on enlisting in the Royal Canadian Mounted Police or serving in the military and attending military colleges; exemptions for serving on juries; separate policies for women who married non-citizens, such as refusing to automatically recognize their future children's Canadian citizenship; or requiring married women to have their husband's name on their passport. There were also many obscure provisions in statute law that discriminated against women: married women could not hold a legal domicile separate from their husbands; husbands were assumed to be the owner of a house under national housing loan regulations; federal prison legislation treated women differently in the punishment alternatives for different imputed offences and in the length of possible sentences; and the Canada Pension Plan had different entitlements for men and women, as did workers' compensation and unemployment insurance.

The RCSW's study of criminal law was especially revealing. By the 1970s the most common crimes for which women were convicted were theft; prostitution or keeping a bawdyhouse; abortion or attempted abortion; concealing the body of a child; and child neglect. Women were disproportionately convicted of narcotics, vagrancy, and attempted suicide, compared to other crimes.[64] The *Criminal Code* did not consider women capable of committing sexual offences except incest, buggery, indecent assault on another female, and gross indecency (the last was added in 1954). Women could not sexually assault or seduce men, or be charged for having illegal sex with a boy under a certain age. Only boys could seduce girls, and it was entirely based on age: if the boy was under eighteen years old or if the girl was older than eighteen it was not an offence. The basis of several offences continued to rest on a woman's "previously chaste character" up to twenty-one years old, while the burden was on the accused to prove otherwise. For instance, sexual intercourse with a girl under fourteen years old was criminal, but a man could be found innocent for having sex with a girl between fourteen and sixteen years old if he could show that she was not of previously chaste character.

The RCSW submitted 167 recommendations for legislative reform. The federal government responded with wide-ranging reforms, most notably the *Statute Law (Status of Women) Amendment Act, 1974*. The legislation amended ten federal statutes dealing with immigration, the military, unemployment insurance, pensions, elections, and the public service.[65] The *Criminal Code* was amended to recognize a spouse's (rather than a husband's) responsibility to provide necessities of life, and the *Citizenship Act* was changed to apply equally to men and women. Other legal reforms followed soon thereafter.[66] Women were permitted to enlist in the Royal Canadian Mounted Police beginning in 1974 and to enroll in military colleges after 1979. Vagrancy laws targeting prostitution were changed to solicitation in 1972. The law on solicitation applied equally to men and women although, in practice, women continued to be the primary targets for arrests. In 1983, Parliament repealed the section of the *Unemployment Insurance Act* that denied benefits to pregnant women.[67] In the same year, rape was removed from the *Criminal Code* and replaced with gender-neutral sexual assault provisions.[68] Marital rape became a crime. In 1986 Parliament passed the *Employment Equity Act* to enhance women and minorities' representation in any federally regulated industry with more than one hundred employees.[69]

There was further pressure for legal reform following Canada's ratification, in late 1981, of the United Nations *Convention on the Elimination of All Forms of Discrimination against Women*.[70] Provinces eliminated long-standing gendered language in statute law (from male to persons, or husband to spouse). Still, there were innumerable discriminatory statutes that managed to survive. In Newfoundland and Labrador, for example, women working in the civil service and at Memorial University were required to quit if they married (unless the Minister gave a special exemption); female civil servants received lower pensions, could not claim their pension until they were sixty-five years old (sixty for men), and could not receive compensation if they were injured on the job; women were prohibited from changing their name while married; unmarried girls (not boys) under sixteen years old were banned from employment without parental consent; married women's place of residence for elections was based on their husband's; the *Family Relief Act* implied that being an unmarried female was a disability; and the *Limitations of Actions Act* placed married women in the same category as persons of unsound mind.[71]

These statutory provisions were eliminated in the 1980s. By this time there was clearly a shift towards gender-neutral statute law. The law had undergone profound changes in eliminating formal legal discrimination against women. Yet formal legal equality as expressed in statute law was only the beginning. Discrimination remained a deeply embedded social practice.

Human Rights Law

While there were significant reforms to statute law throughout the twentieth century, widespread discriminatory practices remained embedded in state regulations. For example, several provinces denied social assistance to single women if there was evidence that they were living with a man. Such policies, which lasted into the 1980s, presumed that a sexual relationship implied an economic one.[72] Daycare (including the lack thereof), health care (including abortion), education (including textbooks), pensions, adoption, and many other policies were similarly gendered. Judge-made law could also be discriminatory. Women were routinely incarcerated for "immoral behaviour," which was often a pretext for using "incarceration as a means to regulate the sexual and moral behaviour of women perceived to be 'out of sexual control'."[73] Judges favoured men in property distribution during divorce proceedings. As late as 1975, the Supreme Court of Canada ruled that a lifetime of labour on a farm did not entitle a woman to a division of assets after divorce.[74]

Sex discrimination was also a pervasive social practice. Landlords refused to rent to single mothers; retailers refused to allow women to breastfeed on their premises; and gender stereotyping was commonplace in school textbooks. Employers justified lower wages for women on the basis of unsubstantiated beliefs: women were financially supported by men or they only needed to support themselves; they had a lower standard of living; they ate less; they should not spend money on luxuries such as alcohol or tobacco. Employers refused to hire women in certain professions and published advertisements for "male only" positions; women were ghettoized in low-paying professions or refused promotion; separate wage scales were often endorsed by unions; employers imposed job requirements such as height and weight minimums; and women were fired when they became pregnant, or married, or divorced. Sexual harassment, which the former editor of *Chatelaine* magazine described as "so common that it was rarely even talked about," appeared in the form of pin-ups or graffiti if not outright groping or propositions from male workers.[75] Workers' organizations were also exclusionary: unions routinely signed collective agreements that reinforced a gendered division of labour.

Beginning in the 1950s, the leading feminist organizations of the period, including the National Council of Women, Canadian Federation of Business and Professional Women's Clubs, and the Young Women's Christian Association (among others) began organizing campaigns calling for legislation that prohibited discrimination on the basis of sex. In 1953, for instance, a delegation from the Canadian Federation of Business and Professional Women's Clubs and the National Council of Women lobbied for a federal ban on sex discrimination as well as equal pay legislation.[76] The former complained that such legislation would "afford protection in matters of employment—hiring, promotion and pay—for Jews, Chinamen and Negros, but not for women."[77] Women's organizations also joined campaigns for provincial anti-discrimination legislation. These campaigns, which included large delegations from numerous community organizations, soon convinced the premier of Ontario to introduce the country's first comprehensive anti-discrimination statute in 1952—the *Fair Employment Practices Act*.[78] Within a year, women's organizations were presenting briefs before a Parliamentary committee demanding a similar statute for the federal government.[79]

Several jurisdictions introduced Fair Employment and Fair Accommodation Practices laws in the 1950s that prohibited discrimination in employment and housing.[80] These statutes were weak and poorly enforced. Moreover, none of them included sex and were restricted to race, religion, and ethnicity. The Canadian Federation of Business and Professional Women's Clubs' Vancouver Branch decried the federal government's failure to include sex in the 1953 *Canada Fair Employment Practices Act*.[81] Nonetheless, women's organizations were successful at least in campaigning for equal pay laws. Eight provinces introduced equal pay laws in the 1950s alongside the federal government's 1956 *Female Employees Equal Pay Act*.[82] And yet, as the president of British Columbia's Provincial Council of Women insisted in 1950, "equal opportunity and equal pay for men and women, regardless of sex, marital status, race, colour or creed, will not be firmly established unless vigorously promoted by education and legislation."[83]

There were some tentative reforms over the next few years that directly addressed the problem of sex discrimination. The federal government, for instance, banned sex discrimination in federal contracts beginning in 1953. Similarly, the federal *Bill of Rights* (1960) prohibited sex discrimination in employment. But the most significant development was the emergence of a new legal regime that began with Ontario's precedent-setting *Human Rights Code* in 1962. Although the statute did not include sex, Newfoundland and Labrador and British Columbia did include sex when they introduced their respective human rights statutes in 1969.[84] Within eight years every other jurisdiction would do the same.

Human rights legislation would become one of the most important legal innovations of the twentieth century. The Ontario model was copied in every jurisdiction. Human rights legislation prohibited discrimination in accommodation, employment, and services. Full-time human rights officers—civil servants working for the government—staffed the commission. Human rights officers were responsible for receiving and investigating complaints. If an individual had a legitimate complaint within the scope of the Code, the officer would first attempt conciliation between the two parties. If this failed, the Commission could recommend that the case be sent to an independent board of inquiry appointed by the minister of labour to force a settlement. Perhaps the most important innovation contained in human rights legislation, in addition to having the government absorb the entire cost of investigating the complaint, was that the commission would represent the complainant before the board of inquiry. Complainants thus did not have to shoulder the burden of investigating and litigating the complaint, which was one of the major obstacles to seeking remedy through the courts. Offenders might pay a fine, offer an apology, reinstate an employee, or agree to a negotiated settlement.[85]

Boards of inquiry were an innovative approach to human rights complaints. They were more accessible to the average person, partly because the proceedings were more informal than a court, but also because the human rights commissions helped complainants prepare and present their cases. Boards of inquiry contributed to changing employers' behaviour and constructing a culture of rights by raising the level of public debate and awareness. As one inquiry chairman noted, "its [the *Human Rights Code*] aim is to educate the public with respect to the need for tolerance as an essential weave in our social fabric."[86] Human rights law was premised on the belief that discrimination was not necessarily motivated by hatred or fear, but through misunderstandings, discomfort, or confusion. Formal inquiries offered an opportunity for people to re-assess their opinions and beliefs. Intent was not a factor in determining discrimination, so the accused did not need to be labelled a bigot or sexist to be found guilty. It was, perhaps, a subtle distinction, and yet a profound one that undoubtedly made it easier to conciliate conflicts. And if people refused to change, then boards of inquiry could force a settlement.

At the same time, human rights laws went beyond simply responding to explicit discriminatory acts. A key pillar of human rights law was education. Each commission had a mandate to educate the public about human rights. Moreover, human rights legislation provided a forum for addressing grievances outside the courts and established a process that favoured conciliation rather than confrontation. The goal was to promote tolerance. The primary mandate of human rights statutes was *prevention*; punishment was a last resort. The education mandate was an enduring legacy of human rights law.[87] In 1982, the Supreme Court of Canada ruled that human rights legislation was quasi-constitutional and held primacy over other laws.[88] Three years later, the court went further and affirmed that human rights law also prohibited systemic discrimination, such as the indirect effect of practices on classes of people.[89]

In this way, human rights law was unlike any previous legal reform. And although human rights law prohibited discrimination on numerous grounds, its most enduring impact was on sex discrimination. The largest number of complaints received by human rights commissions in almost every jurisdiction in Canada until the 1990s involved discrimination against women, especially in the workplace.[90] Boards of inquiry set legal precedents on a host of issues, from sexual harassment to arbitrary employment policies, and in doing so developed a corpus of human rights law. They became contested sites where a broad spectrum of people fought over the meaning of rights and equality. For example, in *Foster v. British Columbia Forest Products* (1979) and *Grafe v. Sechelt Building Supplies* (1979), boards of inquiry in British Columbia ruled that arbitrary height and weight requirements had the indirect effect of excluding women from employment.[91] There were also inquiries that ruled that firing a woman for being pregnant was sex discrimination (*H.W. v. Kroff*), as was denying a woman sick leave benefits because her illness was pregnancy-related (*Gibbs v. Bowman*).[92] Another inquiry awarded a woman damages in 1975 when a landlord refused to rent her a house because she was a single mother.[93] In 1984 an Ontario board of inquiry determined that sexual harassment was sex discrimination.[94] The Supreme Court of Canada would later confirm in 1989 that pregnancy and sexual harassment were forms of sex discrimination (and, in 1999, it extended the protection of human rights law to gays and lesbians).[95]

The women's movement played a critical role in the creation and enforcement of human rights law. Women's organizations engaged in a wide array of activities such as documenting cases of discrimination; producing surveys or conducting research on issues such as equal pay (e.g., listing specific employers' pay scales) to initiate inquiries; identifying large employers who were violating the legislation and mailing letters with a copy of the statute; sending volunteers to individual employers to discuss hiring and management practices (e.g., department stores that rarely hired women or factories with segregated job assignments); drawing the media's attention to deficiencies in the legislation, including delays and poorly-trained investigators; organizing and inviting investigators to conferences on human rights; lobbying government departments on policy issues (e.g., gender stereotyping in textbooks); promoting board of inquiry decisions through press releases and newsletters (a common critique was that the government did not publicize rulings); securing federal government funding to promote human rights in the province; and writing to the

Branch to support specific cases and to prod investigators to advance an inquiry.[96] In many ways, women's organizations were as important as the state in enforcing the law.

By the 1980s, human rights law in Canada had become overwhelmingly associated with gender. In 1976, British Columbia's Human Rights Branch compiled a survey of newspaper stories relating to human rights law. It examined even the smallest, most remote papers in the province as well as major papers across Canada. They found that, in every case, when the media wrote about human rights, they were most often writing about women's issues.[97] The largest number of complaints and boards of inquiry dealt with sex discrimination, and they were often successful: between 1956 and 1984, the success rate for sex discrimination complaints that reached boards of inquiry in Canada was 66.4 percent (and 75 percent for cases involving pregnancy).[98] Women used the law to extend its protections to women who were pregnant, unmarried, single mothers, or sexually harassed. Although financial penalties were often small and inconsequential, the process provided an affirmation of women's legitimate demands for equality.

The *Charter of Rights and Freedoms*, a constitutional amendment introduced in 1982, was the next step in securing equality under the law. Every government introduced omnibus legislation to remove the final vestiges of explicit discriminatory provisions in statute law (for instance, requiring married women to take their husband's name).[99] It was a testament to the transformative potential of the new constitution that governments needed several years to change their laws to ensure conformity with the equality section. In Ontario, the threat of a constitutional challenge forced the government to eliminate its notorious "man in the house" policy that denied welfare benefits to women who were living with a man.[100]

The *Charter*'s equality section transformed family law, criminal law, employment law, and a host of other statutes and policies.[101] One of the most symbolic decisions that exemplified the transformative potential of this new legal regime was handed down in December 2013. The Supreme Court of Canada declared that the country's solicitation laws were inconsistent with the *Charter of Rights and Freedoms*. The court ruled that the *Criminal Code* provisions restricting solicitation infringed on the "rights of prostitutes by depriving them of security of the person in a manner that is not in accordance with the principles of fundamental justice."[102] The *Bedford* decision symbolized a profound shift in Canadian law and the emergence of a new legal regime that could be used to challenge sex discrimination.

The Supreme Court of Canada has also redefined equality since the implementation of the *Charter*, from treating people equally and accommodating differences to ensuring equality in practice in order to remedy past disadvantages. Since the Supreme Court of Canada's 1999 *Law* decision, the equality section has been given a much broader interpretation.[103] The ruling provided judges with a litmus test for determining discrimination, which was defined as differential treatment based on an enumerated or analogous ground; whether or not differential treatment constitutes discrimination is, according to the court, based on contextual factors such as stereotyping, prejudice, vulnerability, or pre-existing disadvantages. Judges must now take into consideration how unspoken norms and practices produce inequality in the application of law. Such precedents recognized the need to go beyond formal legal inequality and address systemic inequality in the public and private realm.

Conclusion

Legal reform in Canada is a slow and imperfect process. The first stage of legal reform in Canada, which dealt with basic rights of citizenship such as voting or property rights, was premised on inequality and a concern with protecting (i.e., regulating) women. By the early twentieth century, the law continued to reinforce traditional gender roles in the family and the workplace. The second stage of legal reform was designed to guarantee formal legal equality. Explicitly discriminatory policies and laws, such as those prohibiting women from serving in the Royal Canadian Mounted Police or requiring them to adopt their husband's last name, were slowly eliminated over time. Yet even the guarantee of formal legal equality could not address the immense obstacles facing women in public and private life that were a product of centuries of legal discrimination.

Human rights law was an attempt to go beyond formal equality and address systemic discrimination. Rather than focus on punishing individual acts of discrimination, human rights statutes were designed to promote a culture of rights through conciliation and education. Boards of inquiry established key precedents and, in doing so, created new law. More importantly, human rights law constituted a new form of state practice. Human rights laws could not eliminate sexism, but they could endeavour to eliminate the public practice of sexism. The new human rights legal regime replaced a legal system that explicitly discriminated against women with a system that banned discrimination in the private and public spheres. At the same time, human rights law, as was the case with past legal reforms, was flawed. Human rights law applied to the private realm such as employment, services, and accommodation, but did nothing to address inequalities in other private spheres such as the family. The system was rife with delays, underfunded commissions and education programs, a propensity towards low monetary awards, as well as exemptions for philanthropic, charitable, religious, and educational institutions. Moreover, human rights law has done little to address broad social problems such as female job ghettos, underrepresentation in business and politics, or the feminization of poverty. It remains, as has been the case with all legal reforms in Canadian history, an imperfect solution.

NOTES

1   Constance Backhouse, *Carnal Crimes* (Toronto: University of Toronto Press, 2008); Bettina Bradbury, *Wife to Widow* (Toronto: University of Toronto Press, 2008); Joan Brockman, *Gender in the Legal Profession* (Vancouver: UBC Press, 2006); Lori Chambers, *Married Women and Property Law in Victorian Ontario* (Toronto: University of Toronto Press for the Osgoode Society, 1997); Lori Chambers, *Misconceptions: Unmarried Motherhood and the Ontario Children of Unmarried Parents Act, 1921–1969* (Toronto: University of Toronto Press, 2007); Lori Chambers, "Newborn Adoption: Birth Mothers, Genetic Fathers, and Reproductive Autonomy," *Canadian Journal of Family Law* 26, no. 2 (2010): 339–93; Chris Clarkson, *Domestic Reforms: Political Visions and Family Regulation in British Columbia, 1862–1940* (Vancouver: UBC Press, 2007); Ruth A. Frager and Carmela Patrias, "Human Rights Activists and the Question of Sex Discrimination in Postwar Ontario," *Canadian Historical Review* 93, no. 4 (2012): 583–610; Jean McKenzie Leiper, *Bar Codes: Women in the Legal Profession* (Vancouver: UBC Press, 2006); Isabelle Perreault, "'Sans honte et sans regret': les chemins de traverse entre le pénal et le psychiatrique dans les cas d'aliénation criminelle à Montréal, 1920–1950," *Canadian Bulletin of Medical History* 32, no. 1 (2015): 51–75; Joan Sangster, "Debating Maternity Rights: Pacific Western Airlines and Flight Attendants' Struggle to 'Fly Pregnant' in the 1970s," in *Work on Trial: Canadian Labour Law Struggles*, ed. Judy Fudge and Eric Tucker (Toronto: University of Toronto Press, 2010); Joan Sangster, *Through Feminist Eyes: Essays on*

Canadian Women's History (Edmonton: Athabasca University Press, 2011); Robert J. Sharpe and Patricia L. McMahon, *The Persons Case: The Origins and Legacy of the Fight for Legal Personhood* (Toronto: University of Toronto Press for the Osgoode Society, 2007); Wanda Wiegers, "Gender, Biology, and Third Party Custody Disputes," *Alberta Law Review* 47, no. 1 (2009): 1–36; Andrew Wingate, "Discrimination against Pregnant Employees in Canada, 1988–2000," Masters thesis, University of Windsor, 2000.

2 Constance Backhouse, *Petticoats and Prejudice* (Toronto: Women's Press, 1991); Gwen Brodsky, *Canadian Charter Equality Rights for Women* (Ottawa: Canadian Advisory Council on the Status of Women, 1989); Dorothy E. Chunn, Susan B. Boyd, and Hester Lessard, eds., *Reaction and Resistance: Feminism, Law, and Social Change* (Vancouver: UBC Press, 2007); Fay Faraday, Margaret Denike, and M. Kate Stephenson, eds., *Making Equality Rights Real: Securing Substantive Equality under the Charter* (Toronto: Irwin Law, 2006); Sue Findlay, "Feminist Struggles with the Canadian State: 1966–1988," *Resources for Feminist Research* 17, no. 3 (1988): 5–9; Judith Fingard and Janet Guildford, eds., *Mothers of the Municipality: Women, Work, and Social Policy in Post-1945 Halifax* (Toronto: University of Toronto Press, 2005); Amanda Glasbeek, *Feminized Justice: The Toronto Women's Court, 1913–1934* (Vancouver: UBC Press, 2009); Sherene H. Razack, *Canadian Feminism and the Law: The Women's Legal Education and Action Fund and the Pursuit of Equality*. (Toronto: Second Story Press, 1991).

3 For an example of how historians have attempted to offer a survey of the history of legal reform of women's rights, see Beverley Baines, "Law, Gender, Equality," in *Changing Patterns: Women in Canada*, 2nd ed., ed. Sandra Burt, Lorraine Code, and Lindsay Dorney (Toronto: McClelland and Stewart, 1993).

4 James Walker offers a comparable framework in his study of human rights law. However, Walker's study focuses on racial discrimination. Moreover, Walker's three stages—equal citizenship, protective shield, and remedial sword—address a very different legal regime. See James Walker, "The 'Jewish Phase' in the Movement for Racial Equality in Canada," *Canadian Ethnic Studies* 34, no. 1 (2002): 1–29.

5 Gail Brandt et al., *Canadian Women: A History* (Toronto: Nelson Education, 2011), 223–30.

6 Nancy Adamson, Linda Briskin, and Margaret McPhail, *Feminist Organizing for Change* (Toronto: University of Toronto Press, 1988); Naomi Black, "The Canadian Women's Movement: The Second Wave," in Burt, Code, and Dorney, *Changing Patterns*; Yolande Cohen, "Genre, religion et politiques sociales au Québec dans les années 1930: Les pensions aux mères," *Canadian Review of Social Policy* 56, no. 1 (2006): 87–112; Sangster, *Through Feminist Eyes*.

7 Women were further disenfranchised when provinces such as British Columbia banned people of Chinese (1874), Indigenous (1874), Japanese (1895), and East Indian (1907) descent as well as Doukhobours (1931), Hutterites (1947), and Mennonites (1947) from voting. Between 1885 and 1898, the federal government had its own criteria for voting eligibility. Women, however, were still denied the right to vote as were persons of Mongolian or Chinese descent. Moreover, between 1914 and 1946, women in Canada who married non-citizens lost their citizenship. For an overview on the history of suffrage, see Brandt et al., *Canadian Women*, 113–17.

8   Re Mabel P. French (1905), 37 NBR 359, 366.

9   Backhouse, *Petticoats and Prejudice*, 201.

10 Brandt et al., *Canadian Women*, 44–45.

11 The Maritimes provinces, in contrast, established divorce courts rather than requiring an act of the legislature.

12 The Maritime provinces did not apply the same double standard: women could apply for divorce on the basis of adultery alone, and divorce courts were established in New Brunswick (1758), Nova Scotia (1791), and Prince Edward Island (1833) to provide accessible venues for divorce.

13 Chambers, *Married Women and Property Law in Victorian Ontario*, 3.

14 Sarah Carter, "'Daughters of British Blood' or 'Hordes of Men of Alien Race' : The Homesteads-for-Women Campaign in Western Canada," *Great Plains Quarterly* 29, no. 1 (2009): 267–68. Parliament had earlier prohibited women, in 1872, from homesteading on their own unless they had children: Brandt et al., *Canadian Women*, 145.

15 Ruth A. Frager and Carmela Patrias, *Discounted Labour: Women Workers in Canada, 1870–1939* (Toronto: University of Toronto Press, 2005), 7–8.

16 Quebec's Civil Code was only somewhat less draconian. Women held property jointly with their husbands. Husbands were the acknowledged head of the household, but they had a legal obligation to support their wives and children, and husbands could not sell their wives' dower without their wives' permission. Quebec's Civil Code (1866) prohibited married women, however, from entering into contracts on their own or appearing before the courts; a wife could not engage in a profession separate from her husband or in commerce without his permission; and she could not discipline their children unless the father defaulted in his duty: Brandt et al., *Canadian Women*, 44–45, 103.

17 Amanda Glasbeek argues that in Toronto police targeted interracial couples, especially involving Chinese men. White women in relationships with Chinese men might be arrested for vagrancy for the purposes of "disciplining the young woman for her choice of lovers": *Feminized Justice*, 103.

18 Backhouse, *Petticoats and Prejudice*, 241.

19 Constance Backhouse, "Nineteenth-Century Canadian Prostitution Law: Reflection of a Discriminatory Society," *Histoire sociale/Social History* 18, no. 36 (1986): 420–22.

20 Sarah Nickel, "'I Am Not a Women's Libber although Sometimes I Sound Like One': Indigenous Feminism and Politicized Motherhood,'" *American Indian Quarterly* 41, no. 4 (Fall, 2017): 308.

21 Frager and Patrias, *Discounted Labour*, 44.

22 Frager and Patrias, *Discounted Labour*, 71–73.

23 *An Act to Extend the Rights of Property of Married Women*, SO 1871–72, c 16; *An Act to Extend the Rights of Property of Married Women*, SBC 1873, c 29.

24 Chambers, *Married Women and Property Law in Victorian Ontario*, 4. Ontario was the first jurisdiction to provide formal legal equality for wives in 1884. Over time other provinces would follow with similar legislation, although it was only in 1931 that Quebec granted greater control over property for married women: Backhouse, *Petticoats and Prejudice*, chapter 6.

25 Backhouse, *Petticoats and Prejudice*, 290-91.

26 Brandt et al., *Canadian Women*, 200-1.

27 Frager and Patrias, *Discounted Labour*, 105.

28 Frager and Patrias, *Discounted Labour*, 106.

29 *An Act to Prevent the Employment of Female Labour in Certain Capacities*, SS 1912, c 17.

30 *An Act to Amend the Municipal Act*, SBC 1919, c 63; *An Act to Prevent the Employment of Female Labour in Certain Capacities*, SM 1913, c 19; *An Act to Amend the Factory, Shop and Office Building Act*, SO 1914, c 40.

31 *An Act for the Protection of Women and Girls in Certain Cases*, SBC 1923, c 76, s 3.

32 *An Act to Amend the Law Relating to the Custody of Infants*, S Prov C 1855 (18 Vict) c 126.

33 *An Act Respecting the Maintenance of Wives Deserted by Their Husbands*, SBC 1901, c 18.

34 *An Act Respecting the Guardianship and Custody of Infants*, SBC 1917, c 27 [*Equal Guardianship Act*].

35 *An Act Respecting the Employment of Women Before and After Childbirth*, RSBC 1924, c 155.

36 Nancy Christie, *Engendering the State: Family, Work, and Welfare in Canada* (Toronto: University of Toronto Press, 2000); Margaret Hillyard Little, "'A Fit and Proper Person': The Moral Regulation of Single Mothers in Ontario, 1920-1940," in *Gendered Pasts: Historical Essays in Femininity and Masculinity in Canada*, ed. Kathryn McPherson, Cecilia Morgan, and Nancy Forestell (Toronto: Oxford University Press, 1999).

37 Yolande Cohen, "'Du féminin au féminisme'": l'exemple québécois," in *Histoire des femmes en Occident*, vol. 5: *Le XXe siècle*, ed. Georges Duby, Michelle Perrot, and Françoise Thébaud (Paris: Plon, 1992); Collectif Clio, *L'histoire des femmes au Québec depuis quatre siècles* (Montreal: Le Jour, 1992); Johanne Daigle, "Le siècle dans la tourmente du féminisme," *Globe* 3, no. 2 (2000): 65-86; Karine Hébert, "Une organisation maternaliste au Québec: la Fédération nationale Saint-Jean-Baptiste et la bataille pour le vote des femmes," *Revue d'histoire de l'Amérique française* 52, no. 3 (1999): 315-44; Michèle Jean, "Histoire des luttes féministes au Québec," *Possibles* 4, no. 1 (1979): 17-32; Diane Lamoureux, *Fragments et collages: Essai sur le féminisme québécois des années 70* (Montreal: Éditions du remue-ménage, 1986).

38 Marie Campbell, "Sexism in British Columbia Trade Unions, 1900-1920," in *In Her Own Right: Selected Essays on Women's History in B.C.*, ed. Barbara Latham and Cathy Kess (Victoria: Camosun College, 1980), 177.

39 Frager and Patrias, *Discounted Labour*, 82-83.

40 Alice Jane Jamieson and Emily Murphy became in 1916 the first female magistrates of the British Empire: see Mélanie Méthot, "Revoir Emily Murphy : première magistrat de police de tout l'Empire britannique," *Journal of Canadian Studies* 50, no. 1 (2016): 150-78.

41 Denyse Baillargeon, *To Be Equals in Our Own Country: Women and the Vote in Quebec* (Vancouver: UBC Press, 2019).

42 Robert J. Sharpe and Patricia L. McMahon, *The Persons Case : The Origins and Legacy of the Fight for Legal Personhood* (Toronto: University of Toronto Press for the Osgoode Society, 2007).

43 Walker, *"Race," Rights and the Law in the Supreme Court of Canada*, 82.

44 Sandra Burt, "The Changing Patterns of Public Policy," in Burt, Code, and Dorney, *Changing Patterns*, 214.

45 Robert A. Campbell, "Ladies and Escorts: Gender Segregation and Public Policy in British Columbia Beer Parlours, 1925 to 1945," *BC Studies* 105/6 (1995): 125.

46 Backhouse, *Petticoats and Prejudice*, 42, 56.

47 Backhouse, *Petticoats and Prejudice*, 74-75.

48 Backhouse, *Petticoats and Prejudice*, 133.

49 Glasbeek, *Feminized Justice*, 48-50.

50 Jana Grekul, "The Right to Consent? Eugenics in Alberta, 1928-1972," in *A History of Human Rights in Canada: Essential Issues*, ed. Janet Miron (Toronto: Canadian Scholars' Press, 2009).

51 As quoted in Prentice et al., *Canadian Women: A History*, *Canadian Women: A History*, 2nd ed. (Toronto: Harcourt Brace & Company, 1996), 400.

52 Josie Bannerman, Kathy Chopik, and Ann Zurbrigg, "Cheap at Half the Price: The History of the Fight for Equal Pay in BC," in *Not Just Pin Money: Selected Essays on the History of Women's Work in British Columbia*, ed. Barbara K. Latham and Roberta J. Pazdro (Victoria: Camosun College, 1984), 306.

53 Prentice et al., *Canadian Women*, 332-33.

54 Prentice et al., *Canadian Women*, 333. The Canadian Business and Professional Women's Clubs in British Columbia, Alberta, Ontario, and New Brunswick (and the federal executive) were among the most vocal critics of the 1953 federal Fair Employment Practices Act for not including sex.

55 Prentice et al., 334. Shirley Tillotson concludes that "had there been no pressure from women's groups, however, labour's interest in pay equity would not have led to legislation": Shirley Tillotson, "Human Rights Law as Prism: Women's Organizations, Unions, and Ontario's Female Employees Fair Remuneration Act, 1951," *Canadian Historical Review* 72, no. 4 (1991): 542.

56 Quebec retained a ban on jury duty until 1976, albeit "domestic obligations" remained a ground for exemption.

57 Maternity-leave provisions were added to the federal Canadian Labour (Standards) Code in 1970: Burt, "Changing Patterns of Public Policy," 222.

58 See e.g., *Family Relations Act*, SBC 1972, c 20.

59 Until 1954 women in Newfoundland could not vote before the age of twenty-five years old whereas men could vote at twenty-one.

60 Sally Weaver, "First Nations Women and Government Policy, 1970-92: Discrimination and Conflict," in Burt, Code, and Dorney, *Changing Patterns*, 93-94.

61 Weaver, "First Nations Women and Government Policy, 1970-92," 108-10. See also Indian and Northern Affairs Canada, *The Elimination of Sex Discrimination from the Indian Act* (Ottawa: Queen's Printer, 1982).

62 See sections 3 and 4 in *An Act Respecting Divorce*, SC 1968, c 24.

63 Brandt et al., *Canadian Women*, 485.

64 Between 1950 and 1966, women represented approximately 12.5 percent of all persons convicted of indictable offences, and rarely for violent crimes. There were twenty-nine convictions relating to women's child-bearing functions: Florence Bird et al., *Report of the Royal Commission on the Status of Women in Canada* (Ottawa: Information Canada, 1970), 366.

65 SC 1975, c 66.

66 For a useful overview of legal reforms based on the RCSW's recommendations, see Roger Gibbins and Robert Roach, *Building a Stronger Canada: Taking Action on Western Discontent* (Calgary: Canada West Foundation, 2004).

67 Baines, "Law, Gender, Equality," 261.

68 Judy Fudge, "The Effect of Entrenching a Bill of Rights Upon Political Discourse: Feminist Demands and Sexual Violence in Canada," *International Journal of the Sociology of Law* 17, no. 4 (1989): 451.

69 *An Act Respecting Employment Equity*, SC 1986, c 31 [*Employment Equity Act*].

70 United Nations General Assembly [UNGA], *Convention on the Elimination of All Forms of Discrimination against Women*. UN General Assembly, 34th Sess., 107th Plenary Meeting, UN Doc A/RES/34/180 (18 December 1979).

71 Fred Coates to Edward Maynard, Maynard (3 November 1976). Department of Justice Papers, file 7- 4-7-2, PRC #23, The Rooms Provincial Archives Division, St. John's, NL; Joseph Rousseau to the Executive Council, Memorandum (n.d.), History of the Human Rights Commission file, Newfoundland Human Rights Commission office files, St. John's, NL.

72 Canadian Civil Liberties Association, *Welfare Practices and Civil Liberties - A Canadian Survey* (Toronto: Canadian Civil Liberties Education Trust, 1975); Bruce Porter, "Twenty Years of Equality Rights: Reclaiming Expectations," *Windsor Y.B. Access Justice* 23, no. 1 (2005): 145-92.

73   Joan Sangster, "Incarcerating 'Bad Girls': The Regulation of Sexuality through the Female Refuges Act in Ontario, 1920–1945," *Journal of the History of Sexuality* 7, no. 2 (1996): 240.

74   *Murdoch v Murdoch*, [1975] 1 SCR 423.

75   Doris Anderson, *Rebel Daughter: An Autobiography* (Toronto: Key Porter Books, 1996), 89.

76   "Present Brief On Equal Pay, Equal Work," *Montreal Star,* 23 April 1953.

77   Cora Woloszyn to Don F. Brown (16 March 1953), Senate Committee on Industrial Relations, box 63, Acc.1987–88/146, RG14–20, LAC.

78   Walker, "The 'Jewish Phase' in the Movement for Racial Equality in Canada," 5–7. The first anti-discrimination law was in Ontario with the 1944 Racial Discrimination Act, which prohibited any signs or publications expressing racial or religious discrimination. Saskatchewan's 1947 Bill of Rights recognized a broad range of human rights, from fundamental freedoms, such as free speech, to non-discrimination in employment and services. But these laws were poorly enforced and they did not include sex discrimination.

79   List of organizations, 1952–53, Senate Committee on Industrial Relations, box 63, Acc.1987–88/146, RG14–20, LAC.

80   See, for example, *An Act to Promote Fair Employment Practices in Ontario*, SO 1951, c 24; *An Act to Promote Fair Accommodation Practices in Ontario*, SO 1954, c 28; *An Act to Prevent Discrimination in Employment because of Age*, SO 1966, c 3; *An Act Respecting the Legal Capacity of Married Women*, SQ 1964, c 66; *An Act to Amend the Fair Employment Practices Act*, SBC 1964, c 19 [*Fair Employment Practices Act Amendment Act*, 1964]; A Brief from the Association for Civil Liberties to the Premier of Ontario (1951), Jewish Labour Committee of Canada fonds, file 6, vol. 23, V75, MG28, LAC.

81   SC 1952–53, c 19; Margaret Campbell to A.F. Macdonald (20 February 1953), Senate Committee on Industrial Relations, box 63, Acc. 1987–88/146, RG14–20, LAC.

82   Legislation for equal pay was introduced for the first time in Ontario in 1949 by the Co-Operative Commonwealth Federation, but was defeated in the legislature: Dean Beeby, "Women in the Ontario C.C.F., 1940–1950," *Ontario History* 74, no. 4 (1982): 258–83. *An Act to Ensure Fair Remuneration to Female Employees*, SO 1951, c 26; *An Act to Ensure Fair Remuneration to Female Employees*, SS 1952, c 104 [*The Equal Pay Act, 1952*]; *An Act to Ensure Fair Remuneration to Female Employees*, SBC 1953 (2nd sess.), c 6 [*Equal Pay Act*]; *An Act to Ensure Equal Pay to Men and Women for Equal Work*, SNS 1956, c 5 [*Equal Pay Act*]; *An Act to Amend The Alberta Labour Act*, SA 1957, c 38; *The Equal Pay Act*, SPEI 1959, c 11; *An Act to Prevent Discrimination between the Sexes in the Payment of Wages for the Doing of Similar Work*, SM 1956, c 18 [*The Equal Pay Act*]; *Female Employees Fair Remuneration Act*, SNB 1960-61, c 7; *An Act to Promote Equal Pay for Female Employees*, SC 1956, c 38 [*Female Employees Equal Pay Act*]; Tillotson, "Human Rights Law as Prism," 535.

83   Fraudena G. ("Mrs. Rex") Eaton, Presidential Address, 1950, Provincial Council of Women, file 6, box 4, British Columbia Archives [BCA].

84 Dominique Clément, "Human Rights Law and Sexual Discrimination in British Columbia, 1953-1984," in *The West and Beyond*, ed. Sarah Carter, Alvin Finkel, and Peter Fortna (Edmonton: Athabasca University Press, 2010).

85 On human rights law in Canada, see R. Brian Howe and David Johnson, *Restraining Equality: Human Rights Commissions in Canada* (Toronto: University of Toronto Press, 2000).

86 Yvonne Bill v J.R. Trailer Sales, 1977, Vancouver Status of Women [VSW] fonds, file 46, vol. 2, University of British Columbia Rare Books and Special Collections [UBC RBSC].

87 Jim Gurnett, "Oral Histories," in *Alberta's Human Rights Story: The Search for Equality and Justice*, ed. Dominique Clément and Renée Vaugeois (Edmonton: John Humphrey Centre for Peace and Human Rights, 2012).

88 *Insurance Corporation of British Columbia v Heerspink*, [1982] 2 SCR 145; Day, *Reassessing Statutory Human Rights Legislation Thirty Years Later*.

89 *Ontario Human Rights Commission and O'Malley v Simpson-Sears Ltd.*, [1985] 2 SCR 536; *Bhinder v Canadian National Railway*, [1985] 2 SCR 561.

90 The exceptions were Ontario and Nova Scotia, where there were only slightly more complaints involving racial discrimination in some years. Even today, sex discrimination is still the basis for among the largest numbers of human rights claims in Canadian jurisdictions.

91 "Human Rights Board of Inquiry. Refusal to Hire: Jance Foster and BC Forest Products Limited," *Labour Research Bulletin* 7, no. 11 (November 1979): 52-53; *Grafe v Sechelt Building Supplies* (17 May 1979, BC Bd Inq); Joey Thompson, "Human Rights is B.S. to Company Man," *Kinesis* 8, no. 1 (1979): 3.

92 H.W. v Kroff (1976), VSW fonds, file 41, vol. 2, UBC RBSC; "Human Rights Code – Board of Inquiry Decision: Kerrance B. Gibbs v Robert J. Bowman," *Labour Research Bulletin* 7, no. 4 (April 1979): 51-52.

93 Norene Warren v F.A. Cleland & Son, and David Fowler (1975), British Columbia Human Rights Boards of Inquiry collection, file 2.21, Acc. 97-159, AR017, UVA.

94 *Bell v Ladas* (1980), 1 CHRR D/155 (ON Bd Inq).

95 *Brooks v Canada Safeway Ltd.*, [1989] 1 SCR 1219; *Janzen v Platy Enterprises*, [1989] 1 SCR 1252; *Vriend v Alberta*, [1998] 1 SCR 493.

96 Status of Women Action Group [SWAG], Report on discrimination in the retail trades (1972), AR119, file 32, vol. 3, British Columbia Archives [BCA]; SWAG report on the Human Rights Code (1981), British Columbia Department of Labour fonds, box 5, G84 079, BCA; Kathleen Ruff to Carol Pfeifer (15 December 1976), VSW fonds, file 2, vol. 10, UBC RBSC; Human rights policy (n.d.), British Columbia Federation of Women fonds, file 28, vol. 1, UBC RSBC; Linda Sproule-Jones to David Barrett (12 December 1973) and Linda Sproule-Jones to William Black (15 January 1974), both in Linda Sproule-Jones private collection; Victoria Human Rights Council Brief to the Human Rights Commission (1979), Dan Hill fonds, file 17, vol. 16, H155, MG31, LAC.

97 Newspaper index and outline (1974 to 1976), Acc. 1989-699-63, Ministry of the Attorney General, Human Rights Branch files.

98 P. Andiappan, M. Reavley, and S. Silver, "Discrimination against Pregnant Employees: An Analysis of Arbitration and Human Rights Tribunal Decisions in Canada," *Journal of Business Ethics* 9, no. 2 (1990): 146, 148.

99 Michael Mandel, *The Charter of Rights and the Legislation of Politics in Canada* (Toronto: Thompson Education Publishing, 1994), 399. A successful challenge under the *Charter of Rights and Freedoms* forced Yukon in 1985 to amend its laws prohibiting a married woman from changing her name, and in 1985 a married woman successfully challenged Ontario's vital statistics law that denied her the right to give her child her surname: Baines, "Law, Gender, Equality," 266–67.

100 Mary Gooderham, "Ontario Drops 'Spouse' Welfare Rule," *Globe and Mail*, 26 June 1987.

101 On the Charter of Rights and Freedoms and women's rights, see Faraday, Denike, and Stephenson, eds., *Making Equality Rights Real*.

102 *Canada (Attorney General) v Bedford*, 2013 SCC 72, [2013] 3 SCR 1101, 1104.

103 *Law v Canada (Minister of Employment and Immigration)* [1999] 1 SCR 497.

Legal-Historical Writing for the Canadian Prairies: Past, Present, Future

Louis A. Knafla

The legal history of the Canadian prairies is a relatively new area of modern historical studies compared to the richer origins in British, American, and central Canadian legal history. Indeed, the writing of Canadian legal history has lagged significantly behind that of Britain and the behemoth to the south. The initial impetus for legal-historical writing in Canada was provided by the Osgoode Society, but its early volumes were almost exclusively on Ontario and Quebec. Well-researched and written with a comparative focus, the subject matter caused one critic to see it masquerading as "Canadian" legal history, referring to it as "Losollah": the London Ontario School Of Lumber Law And History.[1] Legal-historical writing on the prairies coincided with a very early period in most of Canadian history where the sources were cases, statutes, and newspapers, and the account was chronological with little or no interpretative framework.[2] This coincided, perhaps, with Canada's alleged first legal historian, Ontario's prolific Justice William Renwick Riddell (1852–1945).[3] He was followed on the prairies by other law career writers such as Wilbur Bowker on lawyers, Roy St. George Stubbs on Rupert's Land, Lewis Thomas on constitutional history, and D. Colwyn Williams on the North-West Territories.[4] It was largely in the late 1960s that legal-historical writing for the prairie Canada region began, and from the late 1970s it has taken off; today, specialist studies abound. A problem is that there are few overarching themes, or stimulating interpretations, as one often finds in central/eastern Canadian, British, and American legal history.[5] The purpose of this chapter is to identify those areas and encourage the writers of the present future to go forth, flourish, and multiply.

Three groups comprised the Canadian prairies in the late nineteenth century: First Nations, the Dominion government and its institutions, and settlers. The major outside influences were the remnants of the Hudson's Bay Company's private law regime, the interface of British colonial and Canadian domestic influences, the challenge of Indigenous peoples who inhabited the plains on the south side of the border, and that country's westward movement of "manifest destiny." Entering the twentieth century, the region became influenced significantly by the advent of British and eastern Canadian financial interests which sought to exploit its natural resources—namely agriculture, mining, and forestry for Britain's colonial project.[6] Later, the discovery of rich oil and gas fields brought the region into the vortex of the world economy, which impacted the relations among First Nations, settlers, and new immigrants as much as the landscape on which they resided.

This chapter will explore the ways in which these external developments and influences have been interpreted by the academic community in terms of the major legal-historical issues in the law and society area. The somewhat "closed" economy of the late nineteenth century faced continuous outside social, commercial, and industrial influences related to empire and state-building that affected the social institutions of family, marriage, working conditions, and welfare in later generations. In addition, those socio-economic developments caused by the influences of global markets have led recently to an "anti-colonial" interpretation that challenges the "post-colonial" world which has formed the framework of most legal-historical studies of the region.[7] Given the multi-faceted nature of current research interests, the chapter will close with a comment on where we stand today compared to where we were at the turn of the past century.[8]

Much of the past historical writing on prairie Canada has been "internal" history, that is, studies of individual institutions, events, problems, and peoples within their individual settings with slight regard to external factors or influences. Many of such works began with MA theses or PhD dissertations, and worked their way into articles, book chapters, and monographs which retained this internal focus. This writing, and the research on which it was based, usually has been exemplary and badly needed for an area of the country which has often been in the backwaters of Canadian historiography. Since the early years of the twenty-first century, however, writers for this area have been turning increasingly to the wider world in order to gain a more informative perspective and comparative understanding of their subject matter. Such an understanding leads us beyond mere factual studies of individual persons, institutions, and events in the imperial context towards viewing and understanding settler and Indigenous peoples in a global environment, and the latter as participants in settler society and not merely antagonists. Indeed, if the legal-historical record of Indigenous peoples is to be fully revealed, we need to have more of their own studies.

With regards to prairie Canada, two books that appeared in 2005 reflected an impact upon an outward turn in its historiography—and, if not these two works in particular, others in which similar thinking took place in adjacent years.[9] Frederick Cooper's *Colonialism in Question*[10] and Chris Bayly's *Birth of the Modern World, 1780–1914*[11] highlighted the role of critical, interdisciplinary scholarship in post-colonial studies that did not see a flat version of European "modernity," but a version that had competing ideologies. Their work featured a historiographical change in purpose—to become familiar with the broader transnational and global connections which may have affected or influenced fundamentally the local or regional story. Bayly, in particular, argued that global uniformities developed in the course of the nineteenth century in the state, religion, politics, economies, and domestic domains which became manifest in post-colonial societies.

These views were enlarged by James Belich in his 2009 book *Replenishing the Earth*.[12] Reshuffling the map of the Anglo world, he saw a non-contiguous "British West" where the transfer of "things, thoughts, and people" flowed more easily within such regions than without. Explosive colonization was followed by overlapping periods of recolonization in the midst of Indigenous resistance. Hence, as in prairie Canada, a settler revolution took place against the resistance of Indigenous peoples which is best understood within this broader transcolonial context.

The perplexing role of liberalism in the subjugation of Indigenous peoples was raised to the forefront by P.G. McHugh in his magisterial work *Aboriginal Societies and the Common Law* in 2004, and his chapter "The Politics of Historiography and the Taxonomies of the Colonial Past" (2013).[13] Examining the uniform manner in which much English common law was applied to Indigenous peoples in Anglo settler societies, he highlights the role of Euro-American liberal ideology – recognizing that the humanitarian liberalism of the mid-nineteenth century Colonial Office and legal officials, such as the under-studied Saxe Bannister and the famous James Stephen—who has been recently examined as the archetype of nineteenth-century thinking on the rule of law—was short-lived.[14] Their view of bestowing rights to English law on Indigenous peoples was overwhelmed by officials on the ground who refused to recognize them as citizens of a British colony. This led to uneven development across such colonial societies.[15]

McHugh's insights highlight the "Anglo divergence" of settler colonialism by supporting both subjugation and its amelioration. This quasi-sovereignty led to fragmented geographical spaces in many British colonies which included the Anglo-Canadian prairies. It brought difficulties to colonial administrators as well as judges. With regards to recent historiography in the law and society area, John McLaren's significant 2011 book on colonial judges, *Dewigged, Bothered, and Bewildered*,[16] with its flow of judges and their controversies across the empire, makes for fascinating reading. What must be added for such external influences in prairie Canada, however, is the US borderlands which formed an equally close context. Also in 2011, Blanca Tovias published her study *Colonialism on the Prairies: Blackfoot Settlement and the Cultural Transformation*,[17] which details the threads of cross-country continuity that much future research and writing should follow.

These conflicting views led to a conundrum— the struggle between Liberty and Authority, in which liberty was a birthright of British settlers and authority gave them a contested absolute dominion over Indigenous people. Recently, a work that attempts to find a balance between these two forces within the multi-layered context of state sovereignty is Shelley

Gavigan's *Hunger, Horses and Government Men* (2012), which is examined more fully below.[18] Taken with my own recent coauthored work *Fragile Settlements: Aboriginal Peoples, Law, and Resistance in South-West Australia and Prairie Canada* in the long nineteenth century, the two books reveal through legal examples how that conundrum worked out in practice on the Canadian prairies.[19] They pit local Royal Canadian Mounted Police and civilian magistrates, who regarded Indigenous peoples as subjects of the British crown, against the Department of Indian Affairs and other government officials, who tried to implement a Dominion policy of control that bordered on extermination.

Also exploring relations between settlers and Indigenous peoples, Lauren Benton, in *A Search for Sovereignty* (2010), emphasizes the creation of spaces of uneven sovereignty throughout European colonial empires which led to concepts of "quasi-sovereignty."[20] Such concepts involve the influence of places, spaces, and ideas on where and how colonizers and Indigenous peoples had to carve out customary and legal positions to handle their particular problems in sharing the ground they inhabited. This is a rich theoretical approach for the study of places in prairie Canada, both geographical and spatial. The customary and legal complexities at issue led to pluralistic legal practices. Recognizing how such practices were developed in other Anglo settler societies would provide useful insights for prairie Canada, as well as showing how widespread was the very imperfect territorial sovereignty which most writers fear to acknowledge. Such questions of sovereignty impinge upon the livelihood of people who live on adjacent ground and concern the fabric of their existence. For example, a major element concerning human habitation on the desert-like conditions of prairie Canada was water. A study of the conflicts between Indigenous peoples and settlers over water rights on the Canadian prairies would enlighten us on their relationships as well as providing a useful context for such practices across the border.[21]

Sovereignty and jurisdiction are intimately related. Mark Finnane has done extensive work on the limits of jurisdiction in the Australian colonies which can be applied to prairie Canada. His 2010 chapter "Law, Governance and Indigenous Peoples in Colonized Australia" explores the ways in which settlers, striving for jurisdictional uniformity, have tried unsuccessfully to assert sovereignty and jurisdiction over Indigenous peoples.²² Too often, writers on prairie Canada have preferred to skate over such legal lumpiness. The goal here would be to study the problem of jurisdiction not only with respect to Indigenous peoples, but also to the non-Anglo immigrant settlers who have formed such a large part of prairie Canadian society. There have been individual studies for Icelanders and Ukrainians, for example, but a larger comparative canvas might reveal norms and an actual taxonomy that would better explain where individual non-Anglo groups fit—noting the distinctions between the "law ways" of the various legal authorities.²³

Thus what is a settler colonial state? According to Lorenzo Veracini, who has written numerous articles since 2006 and a major book in 2010 on this issue (*Settler Colonialism: A Theoretical Overview*), it is one where the settlers never went home.²⁴ He argues that such settlers were "inherently trans-national and transcultural." They faced a dialectic tension between the metropole and the settler colony, and their experience comprises a structure and not an event—as too many historians unfortunately define it. As Patrick Wolfe has emphasized in his study of settlers in the US, settler colonialism is different from colonialism as it foreshadows the marginalization and elimination of Indigenous peoples.²⁵ Considerable writing has been undertaken on Indigenous peoples and their interactions in individual settler colonial states, and how this has been interpreted by the courts. Drawing upon recent work, the time is appropriate for comparative studies of this matter for former British colonies.²⁶

Comparative studies may do well to be informed by the analysis of Edward Cavanagh, who argues that the Hudson's Bay Company exercised a particular kind of sovereignty in Rupert's Land. Using local alliances to cement its home ground, passing orders and regulations to shape intra-company operations, and eschewing both wars against rivals and the christianization of First Nations people, the local governors and chief factors aimed to stay out of the geo-political limelight. The HBC extended its governance over indentured labour and First Nations families closely connected to the forts for security and support, creating a welfare system that went against the preferences of the HBC's governing London Committee and endowed the HBC with a "formidable authority."²⁷ George Colpitts, in his exploration of the history of the bison hunts, *Pemmican Empire*, elaborates on this system, describing Indigenous people investing in these relationships in the interest of food security and the care of the elderly and infirm over long winters.[28] The HBC thus used the relations it forged with Indigenous peoples and outside organizations to devise a welfare regime that enhanced its unique form of sovereignty until, by the mid-nineteenth century, circumstances launched by settlers overtook these efforts.

For the law and society writer who sees law as the lens through which settler-colonial states can be studied, law must be de-centered from a doctrinal approach to include the study of other means by which settlers attempted to eliminate Indigenous peoples over the course of time through government agencies, policing, courts, the church, and local societies. In the end, we find that the evolving structure did not accomplish what it had originally set out to do (assimilation), because of conflicting interactions within and between those institutions and Indigenous resistance. Over time, the isopolitical relationship between the metropole and settler locales gave way to settler self-government and an accelerated subjugation of Indigenous peoples and non-British migrants. However, alongside this Anglo-Canadian legal system were the customary laws and practices of non-Anglo immigrant settlers and Indigenous peoples that formed a legal pluralist structure within which the factors of resistance and accommodation provided a moving platform of human interaction. It is the study of such factors that will bring the historiography of prairie Canada to a more robust stage and parallel the study of other Anglo-settler societies, while providing the means for more comparative legal-historical writing. Given the large body of specialized studies of an "internal" nature in prairie Canada, the doors are open for a wider and more meaningful interpretive canvas. But above all, this canvas must include Indigenous scholars exploring their customary laws and legal institutions within this pluralist paradigm,[29] lest we become bound to "white-settler scholarship."[30]

As the first part of this chapter has focussed on colonial settler society and relations with Indigenous peoples, the second part will address the historiography of a few other law and society subjects in prairie Canada with a relevant comparative eye. The region, from its settler period to the end of the twentieth century, has been in many instances a thorn in the side of imperial and dominion governments. Prairie Canada was seldom seen as integral to Confederation from its very beginning with the Riel Resistance of 1869, when Ontario militiamen tried to impose their will on the diverse peoples who occupied what became the province of Manitoba, until perhaps the National Energy Program of the 1980s which targeted revenues from the oil and gas industries centred in the West, a development that led to an ill-fated secession movement. While space necessarily is limited, I will touch on some of the major areas in which the historiography of law and society in prairie Canada could continue to flourish—including agriculture, civil society, business and labour, towns and cities, crime, policing, and the courts.

For the fur trade era itself, there is still work to be done on governance and the law leading up to the surrender of the Hudson's Bay Company Charter in 1870. Dale Gibson has contributed yet another detailed examination of the legal history of the Red River colony.[31] This follows Jack Bumsted's *Trials and Tribulations* and a number of articles and book chapters cited in Gibson's book.[32] What remains for the HBC era is the further study of legal relations and disputes among settler, Indigenous, and Métis peoples in the hinterlands of the region. The fur trade era was steeped in imperial and economic issues, and a recent article by David Smith delves into the parliamentary inquiry of 1749 that launched an attack on the HBC's trade monopoly and whether it operated for private corporate or public interest and good.[33] The issue is timeless and stretches into our current era. So too is the relationship between business and science. As Ted Binnema has explored in a fascinating work, the HBC assisted the royal navy with cartographic knowledge and used its monopoly to become a patron of science by convincing the Royal Society and government authorities to support its studies of geomagnetism, plant and animal biodistribution, geology, hydrography, ethnography, and craniometry, along with the collection of specimens and meterological data.[34]

The social and economic life of the prairies after the fur trade era was founded on agriculture, both arable and husbandry. This essentially rural society depended on small towns for forms of social engagement until Winnipeg, and then Regina, Calgary, and Edmonton rose to urban status. Thus, forms of municipal government and the rise and privatization of public utilities and of oligarchic and monopolistic forms of business organization were crucial to the region's development. We know that some small towns, such as Vulcan, were stopovers in the great westward movement, the average length of residence being perhaps five years.[35] As to how much mobility there was across the prairies, we still do not know, nor have we examined its ramifications for a settler society. Understanding mobility is an essential task for legal historiography because people carry their laws and customs with them from place to place.

As for local communities, what were the legal relations within and between town councils, municipal organizations, and public utilities when residency was of short duration? Was the tenure of councillors, magistrates, and legal officials similar, and did that situation affect governance in its wider sense? For example, it has been demonstrated that many towns and their local courts were keen to prosecute and convict persons of vagrancy who were targeted as "idle" and of "ill repute." When such cases were appealed to provincial superior courts, often the convictions were overturned.[36] We have a plethora of local histories, but to my knowledge no one has used them to garner the information that would provide answers and insight into these questions, and few of those histories delve into socio-legal matters. Some of the issues have been studied in states across the border, and it would be interesting to find the extent of commonalty. Since internal and external migration was the norm, did, or how did this factor affect the growth of monopolistic forms of transportation, power, and water which were so essential to an agrarian economy? Since there was conflict with each of those enterprises, how did government regulation and case law play out?

Twenty years ago, John Phillip Reid, writing about law on the Overland Trail, said that we can best understand a society from its civil behavioural patterns, and thus the role of the legal historian is to research property law, debtor-creditor relations, and common civil transactions.[37] While Reid's advice has been followed to some extent in the western United States, it has remained fallow in prairie Canada. Indeed, I wonder if it will ever happen. There appears to be an insufficient number of socio-legal historians today to mount such intensive studies. One of the most contentious areas of civil transaction, for example, concerns the law of dower. As we know, the province of Manitoba abolished it in 1885, the Northwest Territories in 1886, and the new provinces of Alberta and Saskatchewan in 1905. Since we have Margaret McCallum's study of the women's movement to restore dower and the origins of that legislation in 1917–1920,[38] it would be fascinating to examine the case law that developed in the three provinces over the course of the twentieth century and how dower has affected the development of family law since then.

Two other subjects common to civil transactions concern the business of business (bankruptcy law), and the business of labour (unions). For the former, we have the unique work of Thomas Telfer in his 2014 book *Ruin and Redemption: The Struggle for a Canadian Bankruptcy Law, 1867–1919*.[39] Using the rural and urban court records of Ontario, Telfer provides a thorough understanding of the legal structures involved in the regulation of debt and obligation while exploring the legal forms and changing public attitudes which were frequently contested. While we have a virtually complete run of civil files in Alberta and Manitoba with process books that identify the subject matter of the actions, such a study for the twentieth century would provide a kaleidoscope on the twists and turns of business history over challenging decades of economic rise and fall on the prairies.[40] This would include the emergence of the strange economics of Social Credit in the late 1930s, followed by the impact of the federal Natural Energy Program in 1980 that deceased the western provinces' share of oil and gas revenues and brought them into a nation-wide conflict that flirted with separation.

The study of the business of labour on the prairies has been somewhat moribund since the turn of this century. Apart from events of industrial strife, lockouts, and strikes, the non-union aspect of human labour has also been missing. An entry to the subject is that of the other side of labour, namely unemployment. Erik Strikwerda's fine study, *The Wages of Relief: Cities and the Unemployed in Prairie Canada, 1929–39*,[41] published in 2013, examines the crisis of unemployment in the three prairie cities of Edmonton, Saskatoon, and Winnipeg and brings us an interesting comparative study. Given the importance of the local perspective to regional history, such comparative studies for the second half of the century would rest on a vast array of sources and comprise a wonderful undertaking.

The writing of contemporary socio-legal history also applies to the fields of forestry and mining, which were major industries in prairie Canada throughout the course of the twentieth century. For south of the border, Gordon Bakken has written a study of the interaction of mining companies and local communities at the county and state court levels in the western states. Many of the cases involved the law of nuisance as ranchers and families took issue with the practices of mining companies.[42] A study of such cases in prairie Canada would provide an interesting introduction to settler and community acceptance of industrial practices. As we know, there was major litigation between citizens and the railway companies, as well as grain elevator and electric power conglomerates, as investors from Great Britain and Eastern Canada sought to install monopolistic and oligarchical structures upon the natural resources of the West.[43] On another level, such a study would also test the popular thesis of Jared Diamond on the entitlement values of the mining industry.[44] It would also be interesting to examine the differences between environmental practices by Indigenous and non-Indigenous peoples.[45]

The history of crime and criminal justice has been at the forefront of legal-historical writing on the prairies for decades, from the scholarly to the popular levels, and most often it has focussed on "violence" (interpersonal killing) and not necessarily the full panoply of criminality as reflected in the *Criminal Code* of Canada. The subject has been a major industry in the western United States, one which enables western Canadians to have a comparable focus. Taking homicide itself, Robert Dykstra has reset the terms of reference for its quantitative study. The conclusion is that any sampled population of less than 100,000 people, or at least 80,000, is too small for the analysis of its homicide rate to be meaningful.[46] Regarding "high violence," Dykstra suggests that a figure of about forty homicides per 100,000 people would provide a useful cut-off point for defining a society with a high level of violence. The general problem is that most studies of violence in the West are based on population levels of much less than 80,000, and modern figures reveal statistically that the smaller the population base the higher the rate of violence—which renders such figures meaningless. Why does this happen, and does it not then become impossible to study places (such as judicial districts) with populations below 80,000? What is useful, however, is the ratio of violence per capita based on socio-economic structures. Thus ranching communities in the western US, adjusted for population, had five times the killings of farming-urban ones, and two and a half times the rate in mining areas.[47] These distinctions are critical for a meaningful understanding of violent crime in its socio-economic context.

Compiling such data for the pre-modern era in the West is problematic due to factors such as reporting and randomness. The "academic" figures are also different from contemporary perceptions due to the press in the early period,[48] and the press and movies since the 1920s. It was, in fact, the "dime novel" which initiated the modern view that violent crime is rampant in our modern society. The statistical evidence for prairie Canada, however, is available thanks to the fact that policing and legal institutions were established at the outset. By Dykstra's methodology, the figures of forty-seven murders per year per 100,000 people for Manitoba, fifty-four for Saskatchewan, and thirty-nine for Alberta from 1870 to 1919 suggest that the rate of violent crime was high (over forty being the threshold).[49] With regard to the rural/urban areas, the figures are not far from the evidence of western states in the US where, for all criminal prosecutions, the rural area rate was four times that of the towns and cities. Moreover, for all indictable offences, the rate quadrupled from 1891 to 1931, confirming the public view.[50] Thus there are similarities in the western borderlands of both countries, but considerable research is needed to flesh out the evidence and its meaning on a topic of wide public interest.[51]

The history of crime relating to the convergence of settlers and Indigenous peoples on the prairies begins in the 1870s. Jeffrey Monaghan has dived into the correspondence of North-West Mounted Police (NWMP) officers who planned their patrol routes to gain knowledge of Indigenous peoples.[52] The Mounties focussed on distinguishing between good and bad individuals, and in doing so they contributed unknowingly to the anxiety of settlers whose calls for "law and order" established the colonial settler imagination and mentality. Settler leaders also used the "troubles" of the 1885 Rebellion, a Métis uprising in which most Indigenous people were not involved, in order to accelerate control over Indigenous communities and mobility.[53] Nonetheless, the records show that the Mounties went out of their way not to apprehend and remove individual Indigenous people who went beyond their reserves, or to arrest those who were cited by Department of Indian Affairs (DIA) officials. Instead, the Mounties, exercising their discretion to handle local conditions while maintaining a semblance of control over the Dominion policy for reserves, tended to allow individual chiefs to control and discipline their own men.[54] The role of the NWMP would diminish, however, with the rise of civilian governments and the establishment of reserves.

It was, in fact, the Conservative government of John A. Macdonald that established the first "industrial schools" for the Indigenous children of prairie Canada in 1883, even though such schools had failed in central Canada. Bypassing the protections of the Royal Proclamation of 1763, and the treaties of the 1880s, the expansion of these residential schools in the late nineteenth century brought the deaths of thousands of Indigenous children, and the injury and traumatization of thousands more as Ottawa's "cultural genocide" took root.[55] These schools appeared to fit the paradigm of Michel Foucault's art of "distribution" and his theory of "circulation": dividing or partitioning good and bad people so that the latter could be located, controlled, and disciplined.[56] For Foucault, schools were a place to control children through a regimented regime with surveillance, discipline, and punishment—a fitting description of Canada's residential schools' attempts to break Indigenous children away from their heritage.

When applied to prairie Canada in its formative years, the frontier with its settlers, buildings, and infrastructure could be seen as a geographical milieu where Indigenous peoples were seen as "subjectivities" which were thought to justify the imposition of settler colonial rule under "myths of liberal benevolence."[57] This was, out of interest, a hallmark of policing in European industrial cities.[58] Yet the police, whether the NWMP or the later RCMP, declined to use violence against Indigenous peoples in their general policing activities.[59] Since most of the complaints of Indigenous malevolence were unfounded or unsubstantiated, many patrols sent out to address complaints found no suspects, which probably gave rise to this seeming benevolence.[60] Instead, the Mounties, and later local police, turned most of their attention to European immigrants, who swelled the calendars of the criminal courts,[61] and Chinese immigrants in prairie towns[62]—subjects that await a full legal-historical study such as that of South-Asian immigrants in the US northwest.[63]

Shelley Gavigan's *Hunger, Horses and Government Men* addresses one of the most important public policy issues in Canada today: "What went wrong in Canadian Indian policy that led to the dismal poverty and high crime rates of most of today's reserves?"[64] Gavigan's book takes on the issue in a well-structured and clearly written analysis of the relationship between Plains First Nations and Canadian criminal law, in what is now Saskatchewan and Alberta. It is surprising that this is the first book-length legal history of the imposition of criminal law in the settlement era on the Indigenous peoples of the prairies. While we now have both histories and revisionist histories of the NWMP in the same period,[65] one hopes that this work marks the beginning of a rich discussion of the introduction of criminal law and the criminalization of First Nations people.

Moving from reserves to the settler countryside, recent writing by Warren Elofson and others has highlighted the early history of ranching on the prairies and the difficulties ranchers faced in eeking out a subsistence on a landscape they had never encountered before.[66] Several law and society issues have surfaced from such ranching history. These include the widespread theft of cattle by Anglo-Canadian thieves, who ranged back and forth across the border, and the inability of the NWMP or RCMP to investigate and bring them to justice. In the end, we have instances of rough justice and the NWMP's hiring of the Pinkerton Agency in Seattle, whose officials appeared much more adept in pursuing such criminal activity.[67] Indeed, the Canadian Pacific Railway also hired Pinkerton agents to investigate criminal activity on the rails. Thus a study of the Pinkertons on the Canadian prairies would not only be useful, but also make a very attractive study for a widely read book.

Rural farmers have fared worse in historical accounts of their socio-legal problems which ended up in the courts. It was the institutional practice of fencing that brought them into conflict with ranchers who, by contrast, had a wider view of an unencumbered landscape on the prairies and a strong preference for a cheap open range. Those issues, starting with fence law on the trans-Mississippi west,[68] and the land law under which they were litigated, have been examined in the prairies south of the border but not to the north. Although Canadian historian Allan Greer has set the framework for such a study, it has been developed only on the US northern frontier.[69]

Moving to the towns and urban life, it is also surprising that we have no solid history of crime in any of the prairie cities. The records are fully extant, both in terms of the official record and literary evidence. Historians across the common-law world, especially in England and the United States, have turned to criminal justice records in a quest for the history of crime in the growth of urban populations. In Canada, one could point to no finer example than Michael Boudreau's 2012 book on the early twentieth-century history of crime in Halifax, *City of Order*.[70] Boudreau, drawing upon that rich legacy, meshes the social and legal aspects and interrogates what we will call *law and crime*. Not only is it time for such studies to be undertaken for prairie cities,[71] but again there is a readership out there which would welcome such writing.

An important subject of crime and criminality concerns women. Here we have Lesley Erickson's superb 2011 book, *Westward Bound*.[72] Assessing the legal and literary evidence from 1886–1940, Erickson sets the framework for future studies into the second half of the twentieth century in which women's issues—and gender and family issues in general—become mainstream. There is still much, however, to be examined regarding women and the law in the earlier period, for which Robert J. Sharpe and Patricia L. McMahon's *Persons Case* is a hallmark of western Canadian historiography.[73] Other areas of research interest include temperance, eugenics, and vice.

Crime, of course, is only part of the law and society agenda. Equally important are the activities of the courts themselves. Thanks to the significant work of Dale Brawn, we have a thorough history of the Manitoba Court of Queen's Bench, as well as his historical study of the process of judicial appointment in Manitoba, *Paths to the Bench*, published in 2014.[74] Brawn's latter book is perhaps the most detailed analysis of court appointments in Canada. He has conducted an immense amount of research into the backgrounds of the judges, and he uses that data to shed significant light on trends in judicial appointments. A similar work on Alberta is in progress with a biographical history of its federally-appointed judges from 1886 to 2005.[75] Brawn's judicial history of a provincial high court has its equals in David Mittelstadt's in-depth history of the Alberta Court of Appeal, published the same year, as well as Jonathan Swainger's edited collection on the history of the Supreme Court of Alberta.[76] All three contributions follow in the footsteps of Philip Girard, Jim Phillips, and Barry Cahill's admirably edited book on the Nova Scotia Supreme Court.[77] In addition, we will soon have an equivalent work on Saskatchewan with Mittelstadt's current history of its Court of Appeal, which is nearing completion. We lack, however, that major tradition of lower-court historiography which has been developed so well in England and the US, as lower, provincially-appointed courts in Canada continue to receive less attention than they deserve.[78] A Canadian exception is Paul Craven's superb 2014 study of the sessions system in nineteenth-century New Brunswick, *Petty Justice*, which can serve as a model of researching the local courts in any prairie community.[79] An important older work for the prairies is Graham Price's massive thesis on the courts of the stipendiary magistrates of the Northwest Territories.[80]

While we have major studies of the courts, we have no studies of the juries before whom major cases were heard. In addition to juries themselves, we also need a study of the mixed anglophone-francophone juries (*de medietate*, that is, half and half) of the early period, and the role of women on later ones for which we have an admirable example south of the border.[81] Grand and petty (trial) juries, along with coroners' inquests—which formed the backbone of the criminal justice system—remain subjects in which we have a dearth of knowledge. Most of these legal records exist in major runs in the prairie provinces, and their archives wait for the researcher eager to explore them.[82]

An important "external" thesis has been explored recently by a young Canadian historian, Susan Dianne Brophy, of St Jerome's University in Waterloo. A graduate of York University's Department of Social and Political Thought, Brophy's 2013 article on "Freedom, Law and the Colonial Project" in *Law and Critique* uses Marxist-informed works on economic development that adopt an international scope to show that countries thrive "in an interconnected, evolving global landscape."[83] Her theory of UCD (Uneven and Combined Development) is taken from Trotsky's theory of gaps and disparities interrupting development to cause a new amalgam called "combined development"—a result of Eurocentric dialectic forces which, being "uneven," comprise a theory of law that challenges the legal pluralist approach.[84]

The UDC of capitalism and the law provides a way to analyze the connection between the local and the global, as well as between law and the economy. As the remnants of previous modes of production carry over and clash with new productive means, the laws of the past combine with new ones. Brophy's idea is that law and the state are not synonymous, but comprise a "state of exception."[85] Law has its own dialectic facets and is intrinsic, not tangential, to capitalism; its flexibility assists capitalism in negotiating its barriers. The effects of the rise of capitalism in post-colonial and post-industrial societies on their Indigenous peoples is an allied subject that deserves greater attention as we move into a more globalized digital world.[86]

Brophy, having written on Ukrainians and the colonial project,[87] UCD, and how the dialectical materialist logic is intrinsic to historical development itself, is currently in the process of completing a thematic history of the Hudson's Bay Company from the Proclamation of 1763 to the merger of 1821.[88] Her interest is to examine critically the fur traders and incoming settlers and their relations with Indigenous peoples over time. Brophy's recent and stimulating article "Reciprocity as Dispossession" suggests a framework for understanding the origins of Indigenous-settler relations in the nineteenth century.[89] The HBC and other trading companies exploited the labour of Indigenous peoples in various ways that have been "barely perceptible" to historians—an uneven and combined legal and economic transformation that became a major legacy of British-North American settler colonialism. Brophy argues that the distortion of customary labour by factors such as credit, debt, and the "truck" economy led to their fragmented and inconspicuous dispossession, which later facilitated the displacement of Indigenous populations on the prairies. With reference to Manitoba, the Dominion's purpose was to advance economically with the settlement of Ukrainians and the seclusion of Indigenous peoples on settled reserves in western Manitoba and elsewhere. Brophy's anti-colonial thesis will bring an interesting counter-argument to the received history of the HBC and the settlement of prairie Canada, all of which will be grist to the historian's mill.

Twelve years ago I wrote, in the concluding section of the introduction to *Laws and Societies in the Canadian Prairie West, 1670–1940*, that work on such various subjects as the law of intestacy, dower and divorce, family law in general, the end of riparian water rights, the privatization of public utilities, natural resources law, and consumer rights in the growth of a market economy—which were being researched and written about in the western United States—provided a rich background and context for the study of such subjects in prairie Canada.[90] To date, apart from family and natural resources law, most of these subjects critical to the study of law and society in the Canadian prairie provinces have not been undertaken in that comparative context, either within or without the region. It is, perhaps, the historian's conundrum that legal-historical writing often proceeds sloth-like—slow to adapt to the larger and ever-changing historiographical landscape. As witnesses in the common-law world have often said, after giving little satisfactory testimony to the interrogatories posed in court depositions, "I can say no more."[91]

NOTES

1 The leader was David H. Flaherty, who edited the Society's first two volumes, *Essays in the History of Canadian Law*, published by the University of Toronto Press in 1981 and 1982, whose contributors formed part of the initial cadre of professional legal historians. The critic was none other than myself, and the moniker appeared in Louis A. Knafla, Review of *Essays in the History of Canadian Law*, vol. 1, ed. David H. Flaherty, *American Journal of Legal History* 27, no. 4 (1983): 389–90.

2 See, for example, André Morel, "Canadian Legal History—Retrospect and Prospect," *Osgoode Hall Law Journal* 21, no. 2 (1983): 159–64.

3 Hilary Bates Neary, "William Renwick Riddell: Judge, Ontario Publicist and Man of Letters," *Law Society of Upper Canada Gazette* 11 (1977): 144–74.

4 For these and others, see the thorough bibliography on the early writing by Janice Dickin McGinnis, "Bibliography of the Legal History of Western Canada," in *Law & Justice in a New Land: Essays in Western Canadian Legal History*, ed. Louis A. Knafla (Toronto: Carswell, 1986). A later, select bibliography focussing on crime and criminal justice was Jim Phillips's "Crime and Punishment in the Dominion of the North," in *Crime History and Histories of Crime: Studies in the Historiography of Crime and Criminal Justice in Modern History*, ed. Clive Emsley and Louis A. Knafla (Westport: Greenwood Press, 1996).

5 The first overarching study for prairie Canada was Louis A. Knafla's, "From Oral to Written Memory: The Common Law Tradition in Western Canada," in Knafla, *Law & Justice in a New Land*, in which several conceptual themes were advanced.

6 For the legal intrigue of this early period, see Louis A. Knafla, "Richard 'Bonfire' Bennett: The Legal Practice of a Prairie Corporate Lawyer, 1898–1913," in *Essays in the History of Canadian Law*, vol. 4, *Beyond the Law: Lawyers and Business in Canada, 1830 to 1930*, ed. Carol Wilton (Toronto: Butterworths for the Osgoode Society, 1990).

7 The word "colonial" here refers to the French and British empires; "post-colonial" refers to a Canadian nation that grew out of those European controls and influences and became subject to global influences for which it was unprepared and struggled to accommodate. The term "anti-colonial" refers to the problems which arose out of those global influences.

8 For a larger historiographical landscape for the "West," see Benjamin H. Johnson and Andrew Graybill, *Bridging National Borders in North America: Transnational and*

Comparative Histories (Durham: North Carolina University Press, 2010); and for the colonial experience, Amanda Nettelbeck, Russell Smandych, Louis A. Knafla, and Robert Foster, *Fragile Settlements: Aboriginal Peoples, Law, and Resistance in South-West Australia and Prairie Canada* (Vancouver: UBC Press, 2016), 3–42.

9 It should be noted that advances in general historiography are not always reflected in writing at the local level, which often takes time for that work to "trickle down" and inform such writers.

10 Frederick Cooper, *Colonialism in Question: Theory, Knowledge, History* (Berkeley: University of California Press, 2005).

11 C. A. Bayly, *The Birth of the Modern World, 1780–1914: Global Connections and Comparisons* (Oxford: Blackwell, 2004).

12 James Belich, *Replenishing the Earth: The Settler Revolution and the Rise of the Anglo-World, 1783–1939* (Oxford: Oxford University Press, 2009).

13 P. G. McHugh, *Aboriginal Societies and the Common Law: A History of Sovereignty, Status, and Self-Determination* (Oxford: Oxford University Press, 2004) and "The Politics of Historiography and the Taxonomies of the Colonial Past: Law, History, and the Tribes," in *Making Legal History: Approaches and Methodology*, ed. Anthony Musson and Carolyn Stebbings (Cambridge: Cambridge University Press, 2013).

14 Keally McBride, *Mr Mothercountry: The Man Who Made the Rule of Law* (Oxford: Oxford University Press, 2016). See for Stephen and the colonies Russell Smandych, "Contemplating the Testimony of 'Others': James Stephen, the Colonial Office, and the Fate of Australian Aboriginal Evidence Acts, circa 1839–1849," *Australian Journal of Legal History* 10, no. 1–2 (2006): 97–143, and "Mapping Imperial Legal Connections: Toward a Comparative Historical Sociology of Colonial Law," *Adelaide Law Journal* 31, no. 2 (2010): 187–228.

15 The large and complex literature on this subject has been reviewed effectively by Russell Smandych in "Colonialism, Settler Colonialism, and Law: Settler Revolutions and the Dispossession of Indigenous Peoples through Law in the Long Nineteenth Century," *Settler Colonial Studies* 3, no. 1 (2013): 82–101.

16 John McLaren, *Dewigged, Bothered, and Bewildered: British Colonial Judges on Trial, 1800–1900* (Toronto: University of Toronto Press for the Osgoode Society, 2011).

17 Blanca Tovias, *Colonialism on the Prairies: Blackfoot Settlement and Cultural Transformation, 1870–1920* (Brighton: Sussex Academic Press, 2011).

18 Shelley A.M. Gavigan, *Hunger, Horses and Government Men: Criminal Law on the Aboriginal Plains, 1870–1905* (Vancouver: UBC Press for the Osgoode Society, 2012).

19 Nettelbeck et al., *Fragile Settlements*.

20 Lauren Benton, *A Search for Sovereignty: Law and Geography in European Empire, 1400–1900* (Cambridge: Cambridge University Press, 2010).

21 See Bonnie G. Colby, John E. Thorson, and Sarah Britton, eds., *Tribal Water Rights: Essays in Contemporary Law, Policy and Economics* (Tucson: University of Arizona Press, 2006). For a case study of the intersection of law and politics on this subject, see the major work of Norris Hundley, *Water and the West: The Colorado River*

Compact and the Politics of Water in the American West, 2nd ed. (Berkeley: University of California Press, 2009). See also Adele Perry, *Colonial Relations: The Douglas-Connolly Family and the Nineteenth-Century Imperial World* (New York: Cambridge University Press, 2015).

22   Mark Finnane, "The Limits of Jurisdiction: Law, Governance and Indigenous Peoples in Colonized Australia," in *Law and Politics in British Colonial Thought: Transpositions of Empire*, ed. Shaunnagh Dorsett and Ian Hunter (New York: Palgrave, 2010).

23   For the typology of this concept, see Louis A. Knafla,. "'Law-ways,' 'Law-jobs,' and the Documentary Heritage of the State," in *Law, Society, and the State: Essays in Modern Legal History*, ed. Louis A. Knafla and Susan W. S. Binnie (Toronto: University of Toronto Press, 1995).

24   See especially Lorenzo Veracini, "Settler Collective, Founding Violence and Disavowal: The Settler Colonial Situation," *Journal of Intercultural Studies* 29, no. 4 (2008): 363–79; "Introducing: Settler Colonial Studies," *Settler Colonial Studies* 1, no. 1 (2011): 1–12; "Isopolitics, Deep Colonizing, Settler Colonialism," *Interventions: International Journal of Postcolonial Studies* 13, no. 2 (2011): 171–89; and *Settler Colonialism: A Theoretical Overview* (London: Palgrave, 2010).

25   Patrick Wolfe, "Settler Colonialism and the Elimination of the Native," *Journal of Genocide Research* 8, no. 4 (2006): 387–409.

26   See, for example, Grace Li Xiu Woo, *Ghost Dancing with Colonialism: Decolonization and Indigenous Rights at the Supreme Court of Canada* (Vancouver: UBC Press, 2011) and Randi Dawn Gardner Hardin, "*Knight v Thompson*: The Eleventh Circuit's Perpetuation of Historical Practices of Colonization," *American Indian Law Review* 28, no. 2 (2013–2014): 579–98.

27   Edward Cavanagh, "A Company with Sovereignty and Subjects of Its Own? The Case of the Hudson's Bay Company, 1670–1763," *Canadian Journal of Law and Society/Revue canadienne droit et société* 26, no.1 (winter 2011): 37.

28   George Colpitts, *Pemmican Empire: Food, Trade, and the Last Bison Hunts in the North American Plains, 1780–1882* (New York: Cambridge University Press, 2015).

29   For example, the pioneering and stimulating work of John Borrows, from his *Recovering Canada: The Resurgence of Indigenous Law* (Toronto: University of Toronto Press, 2002) to *Drawing out Law: A Spirit's Guide* (Toronto: University of Toronto Press, 2010), *Canada's Indigenous Constitution* (Toronto: University of Toronto Press, 2010), and *Freedom and Indigenous Constitutionalism* (Toronto: University of Toronto Press, 2016).

30   Susan Dianne Brophy, "Reciprocity as Dispossession: A Dialectical Materialist Analysis of the Fur Trade," *Settler Colonial Studies* (1 March 2018): 2, https:doi.org/10.1080/2201 473X.2018.1432011.

31   Dale Gibson, *Law, Life and Government at Red River*, vol. I: *Settlement and Governance, 1812–1872* (Montreal: McGill-Queen's University Press, 2015).

32   J. M. Bumsted, *Trials and Tribulations: The Red River Settlement and the Emergence of Manitoba 1821–1870* (Winnipeg: Great Plains Publishers, 2003).

33 David Chan Smith, "The Hudson's Bay Company, Social Legitimacy, and the Political Economy of Eighteenth-Century Empire," *William and Mary Quarterly*, 3rd ser., 75, no. 1 (January 2018): 71-108.

34 Ted Binnema, *"Enlightened Zeal": The Hudson's Bay Company and Scientific Networks, 1670-1870* (Toronto: University of Toronto Press, 2014).

35 This is a theme of Paul Leonard Voisey's *Vulcan, The Making of a Prairie Community* (Toronto: University of Toronto Press, 1988).

36 These findings result from many research papers by students in my course on "Crime in Western Canada" at the University of Calgary over the 1990s.

37 John Philip Reid, *Law for the Elephant: Property and Social Behavior on the Overland Trail* (San Marino, CA: Huntington Library Press, 1996).

38 Margaret McCallum, "Prairie Women and the Struggle for a Dower Law, 1905-1920," *Prairie Forum* 18 (spring 1993): 19-34.

39 Thomas G. W. Telfer, *Ruin and Redemption: The Struggle for a Canadian Bankruptcy Law, 1867-1919* (Toronto: University of Toronto Press for the Osgoode Society, 2014).

40 See, for example, the extensive run of civil action files in Alberta, copies of which are available in the Provincial Archives of Alberta. See also Graham Parker, "The Alberta Legal History Project," *Now and Then* 1, no. 1 (1979): 7.

41 Erik Strikwerda, *The Wages of Relief: Cities and the Unemployed in Prairie Canada, 1929-39* (Edmonton: Athabasca University Press, 2013).

42 Gordon Morris Bakken, "Mining and Pollution in the West: The Limits of Law Protecting the Environment," *Western Legal History* 21, no. 2 (summer 2008): 209-36.

43 Knafla, "Richard 'Bonfire' Bennett."

44 Jared Diamond, *Collapse: How Societies Choose to Fail or Collapse* (New York: Viking, 2004).

45 Daren Ranco and Deane Suagee, "Tribal Sovereignty and the Problem of Difference in Environmental Regulation: Observations on 'Measured Separatism' in Indian Country," *Antipode* 39, no. 4 (September 2007): 691-707.

46 Robert R. Dykstra, "Quantifying the Wild West: The Problematic Statistics of Frontier Violence," *Western Historical Quarterly* 40, no. 3 (autumn 2009): 342-43. For example, the statistic for Detroit (central) in 2006 was 47.3, but for the county 11.3. What often occurs is that writers "cherry-pick" their area to match their thesis: Dykstra, 336.

47 See Randolph Roth, "Guns, Murder, and Probability: How Can We Decide Which Figures to Trust?" *Review in American History* 35, no. 2 (June 2007): 165-75. Dykstra has critiqued Roth's statistical models as exaggerated, but the referential comparisons are unaffected.

48 For example, the press in the Idaho Territory (1860-1890) reported an increasing rate of violent killings without any recorded evidence, thus contributing to the violent frontier thesis: Robert G. Waite, "Violent Crime on the Western Frontier: The Experience of the Idaho Territory, 1863-90," in *Violent Crimes in North America*, ed. Louis A. Knafla (Westport, CT: Praeger, 2003).

49   Louis A. Knafla, "Violence on the Western Frontier. A Historical Perspective," in *Violence in Canada. Sociopolitical Perspectives*, ed. Jeffrey Ian Ross (New Brunswick, NJ: Transaction Publishers, 200), 426-27. Using Dykstra's test, the population figures were too low in the later nineteenth century for a meaningful interpretation, but sufficiently high to be acceptable in the early twentieth.

50   Louis A. Knafla, "From Oral to Written Memory: The Common Law Tradition in Western Canada," in *Laws and Societies in the Canadian Prairie West, 1670-1940*, ed. Louis A. Knafla and Jonathan Swainger (Vancouver: UBC Press, 2005), 59-60. In the 1930s, however, crime rates in Calgary were almost doubled that of some rural prairie areas: Louis A. Knafla, "Introduction: Laws and Societies in the Anglo-Canadian North-West Frontier and Prairie Provinces, 1670-1940," in Knafla and Swainger, *Laws and Societies in the Canadian Prairie West, 1670-1940*, 27.

51   For a preliminary case study, see Harl L. Dalstrom, "Homicide on the Canada-U.S. Border," *Manitoba History* 73 (fall 2013): 9-18.

52   Jeffrey Monaghan, "Mounties in the Frontier: Circulations, Anxieties, and Myths of Settler Colonial Policing in Canada," *Journal of Canadian Studies/ Revue d'études canadiennes* 47, no. 1 (winter 2013): 122-48.

53   For the major trials of 1885, see the comprehensive study of Bill Waiser, "The White Man Governs: The 1885 Indian Trials," in *Canadian State Trials*, vol. 3, *Political Trials and Security Measures, 1840-1914*, ed. Barry Wright and Susan Binnie (Toronto: University of Toronto Press for the Osgoode Society, 2009).

54   The evidence is summarized in Nettelbeck et al., *Fragile Settlements*, 67-69, 113-20.

55   See Truth and Reconciliation Commission of Canada, *The Final Report of the Truth and Reconciliation Commission of Canada, vol. 1. Canada's Residential Schools. The History, Part 1: Origins to 1939*, a 962-page goldmine of evidence and sources for further research.

56   Michel Foucault, *Security, Territory, Population: Lectures at the Collège de France, 1977-1978*, ed. Arnold Davidson, Michel Senellart, Francois Ewald, and Alessandro Fontana, transl. Graham Burchell (New York: Picador, 2007). For a critical commentary see David Garland, "Foucault's Discipline and Punish: An Exposition and Critique," *American Bar Association* 11, no. 4 (October 1986): 847-80.

57   Monaghan, "Mounties in the Frontier," 125. Monaghan further argues that Commissioner L.W. Herchmer's patrols were organized along the lines conceptualized by Foucault to secure ever-widening space between Indigenous and settler peoples (p. 133). Patrick Wolfe asserts that this phenomenon led to settler calls for the elimination of Indigenous peoples: "Settler Colonialism and the Elimination of the Native."

58   For the European and colonial context, see Mark Neocleous, *Critique of Security* (Montreal: McGill-Queen's University Press, 2008). For the role of police in establishing liberal capitalism, see Randall Williams, "A State of Permanent Exception: The Birth of Modern Policing in Colonial Capitalism," *Interventions* 5, no. 3 (2003): 322-44.

59   Nettelbeck et al., *Fragile Settlements*, 62-75. This includes especially the troubled enforcement of the "pass" system: Nettelbeck et al., *Fragile Settlements*, 74-75, 117-18.

60 Ann Laura Stoler, *Along the Archival Grain: Epistemic Anxieties and Colonial Common Sense* (Princeton: Princeton University Press, 2009). For the continuing concept of benevolence afterwards, see Renisa Mawani, "Legalities of Nature: Law, Empire, and Wilderness Landscapes in Canada," *Social Identities* 13, no. 6 (2007): 715–34.

61 Nettelbeck et al., *Fragile Settlements*, 140–42. For comparative purposes, see Carolyn Moehling and Anne Morrison Pielh," Immigration, Crime and Incarceration in Early Twentieth-Century America," *Demography* 46, no. 4 (November 2009): 739–63.

62 Ken Leyton-Brown of the University of Regina is currently working on a history of Chinese immigrants and the law in early Saskatchewan history.

63 Nayan Shah, *Stranger Intimacy: Contesting Race, Sexuality and the Law in the North American West* (Berkeley: University of California Press, 2011).

64 Gavigan, *Hunger, Horses and Government Men*.

65 For a recent survey of this literature, see Nettelbeck et al., *Fragile Settlements*, 53–59.

66 Warren M. Elofson, *Cowboys, Gentlemen, and Cattle Thieves: Ranching on the Western Frontier* (Montreal: McGill-Queen's University Press, 2000) and *Frontier Cattle Ranching in the Land and Times of Charlie Russell* (Montreal: McGill-Queen's University Press, 2000).

67 Knafla, "From Oral to Written Memory," 65. This subject is still ripe for research and analysis.

68 Yasuhide Kawashima, "Farmers, Ranchers, and the Railroad: The Evolution of Fence Law in the Great Plains, 1865–1900," *Great Plains Quarterly* 30 (winter 2010): 21–36.

69 Allan Greer, "Commons and Enclosure in the Colonization of North America," *American Historical Review* 117, no. 2 (April 2012): 365–86; Lee J. Alston, Edwyna Harris, and Bernardo Mueller, "The Development of Property Rights on Frontiers: Endowments, Norms, and Politics," *Journal of Economic History* 72, no. 3 (September 2012): 741–70.

70 Michael Boudreau, *City of Order: Crime and Society in Halifax, 1918–35* (Vancouver: UBC Press, 2013).

71 An early attempt to write such a history for Calgary from local records is Thomas Thorner and Neil B. Watson, "Patterns of Prairie Crime: Calgary, 1870–1939," in *Crime and Criminal Justice in Europe and Canada*, 2nd ed., ed. Louis A. Knafla (Waterloo: Wilfred Laurier University Press, 1985).

72 Lesley Erickson, *Westward Bound: Sex, Violence, the Law, and the Making of a Settler Society* (Vancouver: UBC Press, 2011).

73 Robert J. Sharpe and Patricia L. McMahon, *The Persons Case: The Origins and Legacy of the Fight for Legal Personhood* (Toronto: University of Toronto Press for the Osgoode Society, 2007).

74 Dale Brawn, *The Court of Queen's Bench of Manitoba, 1870–1950: A Biographical History* (Toronto: University of Toronto Press for the Osgoode Society, 2006) and *Paths to the Bench: The Judicial Appointment Process in Manitoba, 1870–1950* (Vancouver: UBC Press, 2014).

75   Louis A. Knafla's *Lords and Ladies of a Western Bench, 1876-2005: A Biographical History of the Supreme and District Courts of Alberta, 1876-2005*, a two-volume work that will flesh out the judges' political, social, and cultural backgrounds in addition to their legal and judicial careers.

76   David Mittelstadt, *People Principles Progress: The Alberta Court of Appeal's First Century 1914 to 2014* (Calgary: Legal Archives Society of Alberta, 2014); Jonathan Swainger, ed., *The Alberta Supreme Court at 100: History and Authority* (Edmonton: University of Alberta Press for the Osgoode Society, 2007).

77   Philip Girard, Jim Phillips, and Barry Cahill, eds., *The Supreme Court of Nova Scotia, 1754-2004: From Imperial Bastion to Provincial Oracle* (Toronto: University of Toronto Press for the Osgoode Society, 2004).

78   See, for example, the books on the lower courts of the Midwest that have been authored by John R. Wunder: *Law and the Great Plains* and *Inferior Courts, Superior Justice: A History of the Justices of the Peace on the Northwest Frontier, 1853-1889* (Westport, CT: Greenwood Press, 1979, reprint, New York: Garland, 1999).

79   Paul Craven, *Petty Justice: Low Law and the Sessions System in Charlotte County, New Brunswick, 1785-1867* (Toronto: University of Toronto Press for the Osgoode Society, 2014).

80   Graham Price, "Remote Justice: The Stipendiary Magistrate's Court of the Northwest Territories (1905-1955)," LL.M. thesis, University of Manitoba, 1986.

81   Janolyn Lo Vecchio, "Western Women's Struggle to Serve on Juries, 1870-1954," *Western Legal History* 21, no. 1 (spring 2008): 25-54.

82   Thomas Thorner, "Sources for Legal History in the Archives of Saskatchewan and Alberta," in Canadian Society for Legal History, *Proceedings 1977*, ed. Louis A. Knafla (Toronto: Canadian Society for Legal History by the York University Law Library, 1977); Louis A. Knafla, "'Be It Remembered': Court Records and Research in the Canadian Provinces," *Archivaria* 18 (summer 1984): 105-23; and John P.S. McLaren, "Meeting the Challenges of Canadian Legal History: The Albertan Contribution," *Alberta Law Review* 32, no. 3 (1994): 423-35.

83   Susan Dianne Brophy, "Freedom, Law, and the Colonial Project," *Law and Critique* 24, no. 1 (2013): 39-61.

84   Susan Diane Brophy, "Legal Pluralism and its Explanatory Limits in Legal History," presentation at the Canadian Law and Society Association's Midwinter Conference, Waterloo, ON, 16 January 2016.

85   Susan Dianne Brophy, "Lawless Sovereignty: Challenging the State of Exception," *Journal of Social and Legal Studies* 18, no. 2 (2009): 199-220.

86   Caitlain Devereaux Lewis, "Policies of Inequity—A World Apart: A Comparison of the Policies Toward Indigenous Peoples of a Post-Colonial Developing Nation to those of a Post-Industrial Developed Nation," *American Indian Law Review* 37, no. 2 (2012/2013): 423-65.

87   Susan Dianne Brophy, "The Emancipatory Praxis of Ukrainian Canadians (1891-1919) and the Necessity of a Situated Critique," *Labour/Le Travail* 77 (May 2016): 151-79.

88 The provisional title is *Troublesome: The British North American Fur Trade and the Legacy of Dispossession, 1763–1821*. I wish to thank Dr. Brophy for sharing with me her table of contents and draft Preface.

89 Brophy, "Reciprocity as Dispossession."

90 Knafla, "Introduction: Laws and Societies in the Anglo-Canadian North-West Frontier and Prairie Provinces," 32–37.

91 For the origins of this response in the early modern era and an exploration of justices of the peace and witnesses, see Louis A. Knafla, "The Magistrate—and Humourous Magistrates—in Early Seventeenth-Century England," *Early Theatre* 14, no. 2 (2011): 183–207.

Bibliography

Primary Sources by Chapter

CHAPTER 1: Eric H. Reiter

Archives

BIBLIOTHÈQUE ET ARCHIVES NATIONALES DU QUÉBEC – VIEUX-MONTRÉAL ["BANQ, V-M"]

Andegrave dit Champagne v Andegrave dit Champagne et vir, [1893] No. 600 (Sup. Ct. Montreal), cont. 1987-05-007/2761, SSS1, SS2, S2, TP11.

Couillard v Jeannotte, [1889] No. 1912 (Sup. Ct. Montreal), cont. 1987-05-007/2301, SSS1, SS2, S2, TP11.

Mell v Middleton, [1902] No. 1880 (Sup. Ct. and Sup. Ct. Rev. Montreal), cont. 1987-05-007/2172, SSS1, SS2, S2, TP11.

Robert et ux v Barbeau, [1912] No. 2500 (Sup. Ct. Montreal), cont. 1987-10-014/1126, SSS1, SS2, S2, TP11.

Théoret v Letang, [1896] No. 1400 (Sup. Ct. Montreal), cont. 1987-05-007/2988, SSS1, SS2, S2, TP11.

Thomas v Robinson, [1904] No. 2540 (Sup. Ct. Montreal), cont. 1987-05-007/1829, SSS1, SS2, S2, TP11.

BIBLIOTHÈQUE ET ARCHIVES NATIONALES DU QUÉBEC – QUÉBEC ["BANQ, Q"]

Hamel v Buteau, [1906] No. 1700 (Sup. Ct. Quebec City), cont. 1960-01-353/1016, SSS1, SS2, S1, TP11.

BIBLIOTHÈQUE ET ARCHIVES NATIONALES DU QUÉBEC – TROIS-RIVIÈRES ["BANQ, T-R"]

Bellemare et ux v Bellemare, [1890] No. 216 (Sup. Ct. Trois-Rivières), cont. 1983-11-001/120, SSS1, SS2, S3, TP11.

Other

Statutes of Quebec (SQ) of 1871, 1884, and 1890, all printed by Charles François Langlois, Queen's Printer, in Quebec City.

Weir, R. Stanley, ed. *The Code of Civil Procedure of the Province of Quebec*. Montreal: C. Théoret, 1900, which contains the *Code of Civil Procedure (CCP)* and the *Rules of Practice of the Superior Court (Sup. Ct. Rules)*.

CHAPTER 2: Ted McCoy

Archives

Correctional Service of Canada fonds, RG 73, Library and Archives Canada, Ottawa (LAC)

Federal Records Centre, LAC, Burnaby

Federal Records Centre, LAC, Winnipeg

Kingston Penitentiary records, Héritage website, http://heritage.canadiana.ca/view/oocihm.lac_mikan_134807.

CHAPTER 3: Mélanie Méthot

Databases

Archives des notaires du Québec des origines à 1937. Bibliothèque et Archives nationales du Québec [BAnQ]. http://bibnum2.banq.qc.ca/bna/notaires/index.html.

Canadiana Online. canadiana.ca.

Censuses. Library and Archives Canada. http://www.bac-lac.gc.ca/eng/census/Pages/census.aspx.

FamilySearch. Church of Jesus Christ of Latter-day Saints. https://www.familysearch.org/.

Le fichier des prisonniers des prisons de Québec au 19e siècle. BAnQ. http://www.banq.qc.ca/archives/genealogie_histoire_familiale/ressources/bd/instr_prisons/prisonniers/index.html.

Peel's Prairie Provinces, University of Alberta Libraries. http://peel.library.ualberta.ca/newspapers/.

The Prosecution Project. https://prosecutionproject.griffith.edu.au/.

Registres de l'état civil du Québec des origines à 1915. BAnQ. http://bibnum2.banq.qc.ca/bna/ecivil/.

Ressources numériques. BAnQ. http://numerique.banq.qc.ca/ressources/details/RJQ.

Trove. National Library of Australia. https://trove.nla.gov.au/.

Other

An Act Respecting Offences against the Person, SC 1869, c 20, s 58, available on http://eco.canadiana.ca.

Prison registries 1870, #478, SS1, S1, E17, Centre d'archives de Montréal, BAnQ.

"A Romish Clergyman Lodged the Information." *Montreal Star*, 23 February 1870.

"Court of Queen's Bench – Crown Side." *Morning Chronicle* (Quebec), 28 April 1880.

"Court of Queen's Bench – Crown Side." *Morning Chronicle* (Quebec), 29 April 1880.

CHAPTER 4: Lyndsay Campbell

Pamphlets

Bacheler, Origen. *Review of the Trial of Origen Bacheler, Editor of the Anti-Universalist, for an Alleged Libel; And of the Report of that Trial*. Boston: Whitcomb & Page, 1829. Online Gale Primary Sources (The Making of Modern Law: Trials, 1600–1926).

A Correct Statement and Review of the Trial of Joseph T. Buckingham, for an Alledged [sic] Libel on the Rev. John N. Maffit, Before the Hon. Josiah Quincy, Judge of the Municipal Court, December 16, 1822. Boston: William S. Spear, 1822. Online: hathitrust.org.

An Exposure of the Misrepresentations Contained in a Professed Report of the Trial of Mr. John N. Maffitt, before a Council of Ministers of the Methodist Episcopal Church, Convened in Boston, December 26, 1822. Boston, 1832.

Greene, Samuel D. *Appeal of Samuel D. Greene, in Vindication of Himself against the False Swearing of Johnson Goodwill, a Morgan Conspirator, in the Case of Commonwealth v Moore & Sevey, Editors of the Masonic Mirror, for a Libel on Said Greene*. Boston, 1834. Online Gale Primary Sources (The Making of Modern Law: Trials, 1600–1926).

Howe, Joseph. *Trial for Libel, on the Magistrates of Halifax, the King v Joseph Howe, Before the Chief Justice and a Special Jury, Supreme Court Hilary Term*. Halifax, NS, 1835. Online: hathitrust.org.

Maffit's [sic] Trial; or, Buckingham Acquitted, on a Charge of Slander against the Character of John N. Maffit, Preacher in the Methodist Episcopal Society. New York: C.N. Baldwin, 1831.

Report of the Trial of Mr. John N. Maffitt, before a Council of Ministers, of the Methodist Episcopal Church. Convened in Boston, December 26, 1822. Boston: True & Greene, 1823. Online: hathitrust.org.

Trial of William J. Snelling for a Libel on the Honorable Benjamin Whitman, Senior Judge of the Police Court. Commonwealth v Snelling. Supreme Judicial Court of Massachusetts, December 27th, 1833. Before the Hon. Samuel Putnam, Justice. Boston, 1834. Online: Gale Primary Sources (Sabin Americana, 1500–1926).

A Vindication of Publick Justice and of Private Character, Against the Attacks of a "Council of Ministers" of the "Methodist Episcopal Church." Providence, RI: John Miller, 1823. Online: Gale Primary Sources (Sabin Americana, 1500–1926).

Whitman, John W. *Trial of the Commonwealth, versus Origen Bacheler, for a Libel on the Character of George B. Beals, Deceased, at the Municipal Court, Boston, March Term, A.D. 1829. Before Hon. P. O. Thacher, Judge.* Boston: John H. Belcher, 1829. http://lawcollections.library.cornell.edu/trial/catalog/sat:0105.

Newspaper articles

E.H.W., Untitled letter to the editor, *Boston Investigator*, 2 October 1835.

"Judge Whitman," *Boston Masonic Mirror*, 11 January 1834.

CHAPTER 5: Christopher Shorey

Archives

LIBRARY AND ARCHIVES CANADA, OTTAWA

Governor General Julian Byng to Secretary of State for the Colonies James Henry Thomas, October 16, 1924. Office of the Governor General of Canada fonds, file 192G, pt. 5a, vol. 103, G21, RG 7.

L.H. Davies to Governor General in Council, 25 May 1901. In "Claim of United States Government for compensation for seizure of schooner FREDERICK GERRING JR. - For breach of the fishery laws - From Marine Department," files 1901-320 and 1901-69, vol. 2306, RG13-A-2.

L.H. Davies to Governor General in Council, 21 June 1897. In Privy Council Office, "Seizure of fishing vessel FREDERICK GERRING JR., that same be released and returned to owners on payt [payment] of costs and copy of report be forwarded to Col Secy [Colonial Secretary] - Min M and F [Minister of Marine and Fisheries] 1897/06/21 recs," Privy Council Minutes, 28–30 June 1897, Series A-1-a, RG2 ["Privy Council Minutes"].

L.H. Davies to Wilfrid Laurier, 6 December 1897, Correspondence (December 20, 1897), C-752, vol. 59, MG26-G, LAC ["Davies Letter"].

C.J.B. Hurst to Edward Grey, 4 June 1914. In Foreign Office, Settlement of Questions between the United States, Canada and Newfoundland. Further Correspondence Part XV, 1914-15, Confidential Print: North America, FO 414/243, National Archives, UK.

William MacCoy to Mr. Cassels, 7 November 1896. In "Schooner Frederick Gerring Jr. v The Queen (1896)," file 1597, vol. 144, R927, RG125-A.

Treaties

Fisheries, Boundary, Restoration of Slaves, United States and United Kingdom, October 20, 1818, TS 112, 8 Stat 248 (entered into force October 20, 1818) ["Treaty of 1818"].

Statutes

An Act Respecting Fishing by Foreign Vessels, RSC 1886, c 94.

An Act to Enable His Majesty to Make Regulations with Respect to the Taking and Curing Fish on Certain Parts of the Coasts of Newfoundland, Labrador, and His Majesty's Other Possessions in North America, According to a Convention Made between His Majesty and the United States of America, 59 Geo. III (1819), c 38 (UK).

The Admiralty Act, 1891, SC 1891, c 29, s 3 ["*Admiralty Act*"].

An Act to Establish a Supreme Court, and a Court of Exchequer, for the Dominion of Canada, SC 1875, c 11.

The Immigration Act, SC 1910, c 27, s 38.

Cases

The "*Anna.*" In Christopher Robinson, *Reports of Cases Argued and Determined in the High Court of Admiralty; Commencing with the Judgments of the Right Hon. Sir William Scott, Michaelmas Term 1798*, vol. 5, 373–385d. London: A. Strahan, 1806. See also *The "Anna"* (1805), 165 ER 809 (High Ct Admiralty).

Buster v Newkirk, 20 Johns Rep 75 (1822).

Canada v Frederick Gerring, Jr. (The) (1896), 5 Ex CR 164 ["*Canada v Gerring*"].

Canada v Singh (1914), 6 WWR 1347, 20 BCR 243 (CA).

Canada v White, 2006 NLCA 71.

Carlson v Canada, [1914] 49 SCR 180.

Chon v Canada (Minister of National Revenue), 2008 TCC 622.

Desbois c R, 2016 QCCS 4265.

Frederick Gerring Jr. (The) v Canada (1897), 27 SCR 271 ["*Gerring v Canada*"].

John J Fallon (The) v Canada, [1917] 55 SCR 348.

Kwicksutaineuk/Ah-kwa-mish Tribes v Canada (Minister of Fisheries and Oceans), 2003 FCT 30.

Pierson v Post, 3 Cai R 175 (NY SC 1805).

R v Aleck, 2008 BCSC 1096.

R v Falconer, 2002 SKQB 174.

R v Johnson and Wilson (1987), 78 NBR (2d) 411, 198 APR 411 (NBPC).

R v Kelly, 2003 NBQB 148.

R v Krakowec (1931), [1932] SCR 134.

R v Gavin, 2009 PECA 23.

R v McKinnell Fishing Ltd, 2015 BCPC 205.

R v Morash (1994), 129 NSR (2d) 34 (NSCA).

R v Steer, 2013 BCPC 163.

R v Weir (1993), 110 Nfld & PEIR 121, 346 APR 121 (NLSCTD).

Newspaper accounts

"Claims Against Government: Some Famous Cases in Which Efforts Were Made to Get Damages from Uncle Sam." *Washington Post*, 10 September 1911, MS3 ["Some Famous Cases"].

"Richard Olney Dies; Veteran Statesman." *New York Times*, 10 April 1917.

"Tribunal Has Awarded $9,000 To Captain Morris." *Gloucester Daily Times*, 2 May 1914.

Other

Anderson, William P. "Annual Report of the Chief Engineer of the Department of Marine and Fisheries," in *Thirty-Sixth Annual Report of the Department of Marine and Fisheries 1900: Marine*, 35–77. In *Sessional Papers of the Dominion of Canada* [*CSP*] 1904, vol. 8, no. 21.

"Award in the Matter of the Frederick Gerring, Jr." *The American Journal of International Law* 8, no. 3 (1914): 655.

Blackstone, William. *Commentaries on the Laws of England*. 15th ed., edited by Edward Christian, 4 vols. London: A. Strahan, 1809.

Dawson, W. Bell. "Annual Report of the Chief Engineer of the Department of Marine and Fisheries," in *Thirty-Third Annual Report of the Department of Marine and Fisheries 1900: Marine*, 22–81. In *CSP* 1901, vol. 9, no. 21.

Girouard, Désiré. *Essai sur les lettres de change et les billets promissoires*. Montreal: J. Lovell, 1860.

Great Britain. *Arbitration of Outstanding Pecuniary Claims between Great Britain and the United States of America: The Frederick Gerring, Jr*. Ottawa: Government Printing Bureau, 1913 ["*British Memorial*"].

Holmes, Oliver Wendell, Jr. *The Common Law*. Boston: Little, Brown and Company, 1871.

Kent, James. *Commentaries on American Law*. Vol. 2. New York: O. Halsted, 1827.

Kent, James. *Commentaries on American Law*, new and revised edition, edited by William M. Lacy. Vol. 2. Philadelphia: Blackstone Publishing Co., 1889.

Mack, William, ed. *Cyclopedia of Law and Procedure*. Vol. 19. New York: American Law Book Company, 1905.

MacPhail, J.G. "Report of the Commissioner of Lights," Appendix 2 to "Report of the Deputy Minister of Marine and Fisheries." In *Forty-Eighth Annual Report of the Department of Marine and Fisheries for the Fiscal Year 1914–15: Marine*, 64–94. In *CSP* 1901, vol. 17, no. 21.

Morgan, Henry James, ed., *The Dominion Annual Register and Review for the Twentieth Year of the Canadian Union, 1886*. Montreal: Eusèbe Senécal & fils, Printers, 1887.

United States. *American and British Claims Arbitration: Frederick Gerring, Jr. Memorial of the United States in Support of the Claim*. Washington, G.P.O., 1913 ["*US Memorial*"].

Ziff, Bruce. "The Law of Capture, Newfoundland-Style," *University of Toronto Law Journal* 63, no. 1 (2013): 53–72.

CHAPTER 6: Angela Fernandez
Editions of Kent's and Blackstone's Commentaries

Blackstone, William. *Commentaries on the Laws of England*. Vol. 2. Oxford: Clarendon Press, 1766, http://avalon.yale.edu).gla.

Kent, James. *Commentaries on American Law*. Vol. 2. New York: O. Halsted, 1827.

Kent, James. *Commentaries on American Law*, 2nd ed. Vol. 2. New York: O. Halsted, 1832.

Kent, James. *Commentaries on American Law*, 5th ed. Vol. 2. New York: printed for the author, 1844.

Kent, James. *Commentaries on American Law*. 6th ed., 4 vols. New York: W. Kent, 1848.

Kent, James. *Commentaries on American Law*. 9th ed., 4 vols. Boston, MA: Little, Brown, 1858.

Kent, James. *Commentaries on American Law*, 10th ed., 4 vols. Boston, MA: Little, Brown, 1860.

Kent, James. *Commentaries on American Law*, 11th ed., edited by George F. Comstock, 4 vols. Boston, MA: Little, Brown, 1866.

Kent, James. *Commentaries on American Law*. 12th ed., edited by Oliver Wendell Holmes Jr., 4 vols. Boston, MA: Little, Brown, 1873.

Kent, James. *Commentaries on American Law*. 13th ed., edited by Charles M. Barnes, 4 vols. Boston: Little, Brown, 1884.

Kent, James. *Commentaries on American Law*, edited by William M. Lacy, 4 vols. Philadelphia: Blackstone Publishing Company, 1889.

Kent, James. *Commentaries on American Law*. 14th ed., edited by John M. Gould, 4 vols. Boston: Little, Brown, 1896.

Articles and advertising

"The Blackstone Text-Book Series." *Scottish Law Review and Sheriff Court Reports* 5, no. 58 (October 1889): 251–52.

"Book Notices." *Green Bag* 1, no. 9 (September 1889): 412.

"Book Notices." *Virginia Law Journal* 13, no. 7 (July 1889): 619.

"Book Reviews." *American Law Review* 23, no. 5 (September-October 1889): 850–51.

"Commentaries on American Law." *Canada Law Journal* 25, no. 14 (2 September 1889): 437.

"Copyright and Piracy." *Canada Law Journal* 24, no. 2 (1 February 1888): 35–36.

Kansas City Law Reporter 1, no. 7 (10 August 1888), advertising pages.

"Kent's Commentaries." *Copp's Land-Owner* 1, no. 11 (1 September 1889): 121.

"Kent's Commentaries." *Railway and Corporation Law Journal* 6 (24 August 1889): 160.

"Law. 12 vols. for $15." *Kansas City Law Reporter* 1, no. 7 (10 August 1888): vii.

"Law Books." *Canada Law Journal* 23, no. 8 (15 April 1887): 141.

"Law Books." *Cape Law Journal* 4, no. 3 (1887): 183–84.

"New Books." *Railway and Corporation Law Journal* 3 (7 January 1888): 24.

"New Books." *Railway and Corporation Law Journal* 6 (21 December 1889): 500.

"New Books and New Editions: Blackstone Publishing Company's Text-Book Series." *Albany Law Journal* 37, no. 20 (19 May 1888): 404.

"New Law Books." *Canada Law Journal* 23, no. 6 (15 March 1887): 116.

"New Publications." *American Law Record* 15, no. 10 (April 1887): 633–34.

"New Publications." *Legal News* 12, no. 41 (12 October 1889): 321.

"Notes." *Law Quarterly Review* 4, no. 2 (April 1888): 225.

"The Professor's Story: Chapter 1: The Brahmin Caste of New England." *Atlantic Monthly*, January 1, 1860, 91-93.

"Recent Publications." *Central Law Journal* 29, no. 15 (18 October 1889): 295–96.

Untitled, *Canada Law Journal* 23, no. 10 (15 May 1887): 181.

Untitled, *Law Journal*, 22 (12 November 1887): 597.

Untitled note, *Law Quarterly Review*, 4, no. 1 (January 1888): 121.

Other

Devereux, John C. *The Most Material Parts of Kent's Commentaries Reduced to Questions and Answers.* New York: Lewis & Blood, 1860.

Dickson, Frederick S. *An Analysis of Kent's Commentaries.* Philadelphia: Rees Welsh, 1875.

Drone, Eaton S. *A Treatise on the Law of Property in Intellectual Productions in Britain and the United States: Embracing Copyright in Works of Literature and Art, and Playright in Dramatic and Musical Compositions*. Boston: Little, Brown, 1879.

Frederick Gerring Jr. (The) v Canada (1897), 27 SCR 271.

Kinne, Asa. *The Most Important Parts of Kent's Commentaries Reduced to Questions and Answers*, 2nd edition. New York: W.E. Dean, 1840.

Ritchie, W.B.A. "Filed in the Registry of the Supreme Court: Respondents Factum: In the Supreme Court of Canada, 1896." In Great Britain, *Arbitration of Outstanding Pecuniary Claims Between Great Britain and the United States of America: The Frederick Gerring, Jr.*, Appendix, Annex 5, 25–34 (Ottawa: Government Printing Bureau, 1913).

Stewart, Alexander to James Kent (28 April 1847), reel 5, James Kent Papers, Library of Congress.

Thompson, Eben Francis. *The Student's Kent: An Abridgement of Kent's Commentaries on American Law*. Boston: Houghton, Mifflin, 1886.

Wheaton v Peters, 33 US (8 Pet) 591 (1834).

CHAPTER 7: Catharine MacMillan

Archives

NATIONAL ARCHIVES, KEW GARDENS, RICHMOND, SURREY, UNITED KINGDOM

Judicial Committee of the Privy Council, Minutes, PCAP 9.

Judicial Committee of the Privy Council, Printed Cases in Indian and Colonial Appeals and Printed Papers in Appeals, PCAP 6.

Other

Act for the Better Administration of Justice in His Majesty's Privy Council, 1833 (UK), 3 & 4 Wm IV, c 41.

Bentwich, Norman. *The Practice of the Privy Council in Judicial Matters in Appeals from Courts of Civil, Criminal and Admiralty Jurisdiction and in Appeals from Ecclesiastical and Prize Courts with the Statutes, Rules and Forms of Procedure*. London: Sweet & Maxwell, 1912.

British North America Act, 1867 (UK), 30–31 Vict c 3, now the *Constitution Act, 1867*.

Edwards v AG of Canada, [1930] AC 124 (JCPC).

Endowed Schools Act, 1873, 1873 (UK), 36 & 37 Vict, c 87.

Macpherson, William. *The Practice of the Judicial Committee of Her Majesty's Most Honorable Privy Council*. London: Henry Sweet, 1860.

Macpherson, William. *The Practice of the Judicial Committee of Her Majesty's Most Honorable Privy Council*, 2nd ed. London: Henry Sweet, 1873.

Macqueen, John. *A Practical Treatise on The Appellate Jurisdiction of the House of Lords and the Privy Council*. London: A. Maxwell & Son, 1842.

A Man [F.C. Burnand], "The Judicial Committee." *Punch*, 19 December 1868, 259.

Safford, Frank, and George Wheeler, *The Practice of the Privy Council in Judicial Matters in Appeals from Courts of Civil, Criminal and Admiralty Jurisdiction in the Colonies, Possessions, and Foreign Jurisdictions of the Crown, and in Appeals from Ecclesiastical and Prize Courts, Together with Practice as to Matters Heard upon Special Reference and Applications for the Prolongation of Patents; with Forms of Procedure and Precedents of Bills of Costs*. London: Sweet and Maxwell, 1901.

CHAPTER 8: Alexandra Havrylyshyn

Archives

BIBLIOTHÈQUE ET ARCHIVES NATIONALES DU QUÉBEC ["BANQ"]

Appel, François Havy, comparant par le sieur Nouette, contre Marie-Louise Corbin, comparant par le sieur Poirier, praticien, 24 July 1741, P19135, S28, TP1.

Appel, Geneviève de Ramezay, veuve de Louis-Henri Deschamps, contre François Foucher, conseiller du Roi et son procureur en la Juridiction de Montréal, comparant par le sieur Nouette, praticien, 23 October 1741, P19177, S28, TP1.

Appel, Pierre Raymond, comparant par Nouette, son procureur, contre Olivier Abel, 26 June 1741, P19114, S28, TP1.

Cause entre le sieur Louis Levrard ... demandeur, comparant par le sieur Jacques Nouette, praticien, leur procureur, et dame Marie-Anne Tarieu de la Pérade (LaPérade), veuve du feu sieur de la Richardière, défenderesse, comparant par le sieur Poirier, praticien, son procureur, 3 October 1743, P34, D84, SS1, S11, TL1.

Cause entre la veuve de feu Pierre Joly, boulangère de Québec, demanderesse, comparante par le sieur Jean-Claude Panet, praticien, son procureur, et le sieur Jacques Nouette, praticien, défendeur, 14 October 1743, P39, D84, SS1, S11, TL1.

Jugement rendu par Christophe-Hilarion Dulaurent, ancien praticien et notaire royal de la Prévôté de Québec, 3 December 1750, D3012-32, TL5.

Mémoire des dépens à payer par Jean-Baptiste Larchevêque, 1 October – 21 November 1740, D224, S30, TP1.

Procès entre Charles Ruette d'Auteuil de Monceaux, et Jacques Nouette de la Pouflerie, 7 March – 22 April 1743, D4933, S1, TL4.

PARCHEMIN (CREATED BY THE SOCIÉTÉ ARCHIV-HISTO)

Compromis entre Pierre-Joseph Celoron de Bienville et ? Adhemar, notaire royal et ancien praticien de la ville et juridiction de Montreal, 5 September 1746, notaire F. Simonnet.

Contrat de mariage, Charles Decoste de Letencour, écuyer, fils de Jean-Baptiste Decoste de Letancour, écuyer et ancien praticien de la juridiction de Montréal et de Renée Marchand, 7 January 1759, notaire F. Simonnet.

Contrat de mariage, Jacques Parant, 19 January 1748, notaire N. Duprac. Contrat de mariage entre Jacques Bourdon, praticien, et Marie Menard, 3 January 1672, notaire T. Frérot de Lechesnaye.

Contrat de mariage entre Pierre Parret, praticien, de la ville de Québec et natif de la ville de Paris et Marie-Anne Trefflet dit Rautot, 29 September 1754, notaire C. Barolet.

Procuration de Damien Quatresols à François Rageot, praticien, de la ville de Québec, 2 July 1704, notaire L. Chambalon.

Procuration de Marie-Madeleine Landron à Jacques Nouette, 13 March 1742, notaire C.-H. Dulaurent.

Vente d'une terre par Jacques Menard à Jacques Bourdon, praticien, 19 March 1673, notaire T. Frérot de Lechesnaye.

Other

Bouchel, Laurent. *La Bibliothèque ou Thrésor du droict français*. Paris: D. Langlois, 1615. https://catalogue.bnf.fr/ark:/12148/cb301374390

Brillon, Pierre Jacques. *Dictionnaire des arrests, ou Jurisprudence universelle des Parlemens de France, et autres tribunaux* [etc.]. Paris: G. Cavelier, 1711.

De Ferrière, Claude-Joseph. *Dictionnaire de droit et de pratique, contenant l'explication des termes de droit, d'ordonnances, de coutumes & de pratique*. 3rd ed. Paris: Chez Brunet, 1749.

Édits, ordonnances royaux, déclarations et arrêts du Conseil d'État du Roi concernant le Canada mis par ordre chronologique, et publiés par ordre de Son Excellence Sir Robert Shore Milnes, Baronet, Lieutenant Gouverneur de la province du Bas-Canada. Vol. 1. Québec, P.E. Desbarats, 1803.

Guyot, Joseph-Nicholas. *Répertoire universel et raisonné de jurisprudence civile, criminelle, canonique et bénéficiale*. Paris, 1775–83.

Dictionnaire universel françois et latin, contenant la signification et la définition tant des mots de l'une & de l'autre langue, avec leurs différens usages [etc.]. New ed. Nancy: Pierre Antoine, 1740, also entitled *Dictionnaire universel françois et latin, vulgairement appellé* Dictionnaire de Trevoux.

Imbert, Jean. *Les institutes de practique en matiere civile et criminelle* [etc.]. Paris: Jean Ruelle, 1547.

CHAPTER 9: Jean-Philippe Garneau

Archives

BIBLIOTHÈQUE ET ARCHIVES NATIONALES DU QUÉBEC, CENTRE D'ARCHIVES DE MONTRÉAL ["BANQ, CAM"]

Dossiers civils de la Cour du banc du roi, district de Montréal, juridiction supérieure, TL19, S4, SS11:

Catherine Anger c Louis Cavilhe, juin 1798, n° 50.

Marguerite Belecque c Paul Rinville, octobre 1828, n° 1974.

Catherine Bérard c Pierre Demers, février 1828, n° 597.

Elizabeth Boston c John Sanford, avril 1823, n° 1803.

Elizabeth Bunker c Thomas McLeish, octobre 1820, n° 1712.

Isabella Campbell c Thomas Prior, octobre 1817, n° 815.

Geneviève Dumouchelle c Nicolas Boyer, François Bender intervenant, octobre 1829, n° 2142.

Eleanor Fraser c William Buchanan, octobre 1823, n° 1570.

Marie-Louise Frégeau c Michel Privé, avril 1827, n° 268.

Marguerite Gougeon, assistée de son père, c Jean-Baptiste Poirier, octobre 1820, n° 893.

Elizabeth Harvie c Robert Armour, juin 1819, n° 353.

Marie-Angélique Heynemand c Jean-Baptiste Belly dit St Louis, février 1819, n° 739.

Lucile Lebrun c John Sanford, juin 1825, n° 620.

Eliza-Margaret Mason c George Stanley, février 1821, n° 1835.

Plumea Patrick c Aaron Wheeler, octobre 1828, n° 1890.

Victoire Ritchot c Charles Ratté, octobre 1820, n° 1522.

Sophia Whittemore c Ezekiel Cutter, février 1828, n° 573.

LIBRARY AND ARCHIVES CANADA ["LAC"] / BIBLIOTHÈQUE ET ARCHIVES DU CANADA ["BAC"], OTTAWA

McDonell c Atkinson (19 February 1824), James Reid collection, Court of King's Bench bound notes. Vol. 5, pp. 27–31, MG24 B173.

Other

De Ferrière, Claude-Joseph. *Dictionnaire de droit et de pratique*, new ed. Vol. 1. Paris: Veuve Brunet, 1769.

Doucet, Nicolas-Benjamin. *Fundamental Principles of the Laws of Canada*. Montréal: John Lovell, 1842.

Papineau-Dessaules, Rosalie to Perrine Viger, January 1813. In *Rosalie Papineau Dessaules, Correspondance, 1805–1854*, edited by Georges Aubin and Renée Blanchet, 37–38. Montréal: Varia, 2001.

Pothier, Robert-Joseph. *Traité de la puissance du mari*. Paris: Chasseriau, 1823.

Pyke, George. *Cases Argued and Determined in the Court of King's Bench, for the District of Quebec* […], Montreal, 1811.

Stuart, George Okill. *Reports of Cases Argued and Determined in the Court of King's Bench and in the Provincial Court of Appeals of Lower Canada* [...]. Quebec: Neilson and Cowan, 1834.

CHAPTER 10: Shelley A.M. Gavigan

Statutes

An Act to Make Further Provision for the Government of the North-West Territories, SC 1871, c 16.

An Act to Provide for the Establishment of "The Department of the Interior," SC 1873, c 4.

An Act Further to Amend the "Act to Make Further Provision for the Government of the Northwest Territories," SC 1873, c 34.

An Act Respecting the Administration of Justice, and for the Establishment of a Police Force in the North West Territories, SC 1873, c 35 [NWMP Act, 1873].

An Act to Amend "An Act Respecting the Administration of Justice and for the Establishment of a Police Force in the North-West Territories," SC 1874, c 22 [NWMP Amendment Act, 1874].

An Act to Amend and Consolidate the Laws Respecting the North-West Territories, SC 1875, c 49 [NWT Act, 1875].

An Act Further to Amend "An Act respecting the Administration of Justice, and for the Establishment of a Police Force in the North-West Territories," SC 1875, c 50 [NWMP Amendment Act, 1875].

An Act to Amend and Consolidate as Amended the Several Enactments Respecting the North-West Mounted Police Force, SC 1879, c 36 [NWMP Amendment Act, 1879].

An Act to Amend "An Act to Amend and Consolidate as Amended the Several Enactments Respecting the North-West Mounted Police Force," SC 1882, c 29.

An Act to Authorize the Augmentation of the North-West Mounted Police, SC 1885, c 53.

An Act Respecting the North-West Mounted Police Force, RSC 1886, c 45 [NWMP Act, 1886].

An Act Further to Amend the Law Respecting the North-West Territories, SC 1886, c 25 [NWT Amendment Act, 1886].

An Act to Amend and Consolidate the Acts Respecting the North-West Mounted Police, SC 1894, c 27 [short title *The Mounted Police Act, 1894*, per s 1, referred to here as NWMP Act, 1894]. This statute, as amended, is also cited as *Royal Northwest Mounted Police Act*, RSC 1906, c 91.

Archives

PROVINCIAL ARCHIVES OF SASKATCHEWAN ["PAS"] (HUGH RICHARDSON'S RECORDS)

DEPARTMENT OF THE ATTORNEY GENERAL, REGINA JUDICIAL CENTRE, COURT RECORDS, FIRST SERIES, 1878–86, FILES 1–282 [A-G (GR 11–1) CR-REGINA, 1ST SERIES, 1876–1886]

Regnier Brillon (1877), file 4.

Henry R. Elliott (1878), file 26.

David B. Hall and Regnier Brillon (1878), file 49.

Walter D. Parkins (1885), file 276.

Richard C. Wyld (1878), file 60.

SUPREME COURT OF THE NORTHWEST TERRITORIES (CRIMINAL) RECORDS, IR 19, R1286

Colin Lorne Campbell (1899), file 200.

James M. Cumines [or Cummines] (1900–1), file 242.

Henry George Fisher (1894), file 92.

James Ford (1889), file 11.

Clement E. Hamilton (1893), file 55.

Stanley Hildyard (1896), file 119.

John Martin (1894), file 81.

George Thomas Robinson (1888–89), file 2.

Sperry Bridom Storms (1894), file 43.

LIBRARY AND ARCHIVES CANADA [LAC], OTTAWA

NORTH WEST MOUNTED POLICE (NWMP) – PERSONNEL RECORDS, 1873–1904, RG18

Patrick J. Balfe, Regimental Number OS-507, item no. 64834, vol. 10037, http://www.bac-lac.gc.ca/eng/discover/nwmp-personnel-records/Pages/item.aspx?IdNumber=64834&).

Joseph Victor Bégin, Regimental Number O.68, item no. 6765, vol. 10037, http://www.bac-lac.gc.ca/eng/discover/nwmp-personnel-records/Pages/item.aspx?IdNumber=6765&.

James MacGlashen Cumines, Regimental Number 3658, item no. 26036, vol. 10046, http://www.bac-lac.gc.ca/eng/discover/nwmp-personnel-records/Pages/item.aspx?IdNumber=26036&.

Joseph Osborne Davis, Regimental Number 267, item no. 26722, vol. 10038, http://www.bac-lac.gc.ca/eng/discover/nwmp-personnel-records/Pages/item.aspx?IdNumber=26722&.

James Ford, Regimental Number 1348, item no. 30646, vol. 10041, http://www.bac-lac. gc.ca/eng/discover/nwmp-personnel-records/Pages/item.aspx?IdNumber=30646&.

Clement Edward Hamilton, Regimental Number 2521, item no. 34252, vol. 10043, http://www.bac-lac.gc.ca/eng/discover/nwmp-personnel-records/Pages/item. aspx?IdNumber=34252&.

Stanley Hildyard, Regimental Number 2842, item no. 35794, vol. 10044, http:// www.bac-lac.gc.ca/eng/discover/nwmp-personnel-records/Pages/item. aspx?IdNumber=35794&.

Frank Kiely, Regimental Number 2879, item no. 39144, vol. 10044, http://www.bac-lac. gc.ca/eng/discover/nwmp-personnel-records/Pages/item.aspx?IdNumber=39144&.

Robert William Victor Jones, Regimental Number 2420, item no. 38307, vol. 10043, http://www.bac-lac.gc.ca/eng/discover/nwmp-personnel-records/Pages/item. aspx?IdNumber=38307&.

John Martin, Regimental Number 2952, item no. 44446, vol. 10044, http://www.bac-lac. gc.ca/eng/discover/nwmp-personnel-records/Pages/item.aspx?IdNumber=44446&.

Arthur Miles Parken, Regimental Number 2863, item no. 50582, vol. 10044, http:// www.bac-lac.gc.ca/eng/discover/nwmp-personnel-records/Pages/item. aspx?IdNumber=50582&.

Walter Douglas Parkins, Regimental Number 741, item no. 50647, vol. 10039, https:// www.bac-lac.gc.ca/eng/discover/nwmp-personnel-records/Pages/item. aspx?IdNumber=50647&.

George Thomas Robinson, Regimental Number 2174, item no. 54238, vol. 10041, https://www.bac-lac.gc.ca/eng/discover/nwmp-personnel-records/Pages/item. aspx?IdNumber=54238&.

Sperry Storms, Regimental Number 2806, item no. 58923, vol. 10044, http://www.bac-lac. gc.ca/eng/discover/nwmp-personnel-records/Pages/item.aspx?IdNumber=58923&.

Richard Charles Wyld, Regimental Number 281, item no. 64376, vol. 10044, http:// www.bac-lac.gc.ca/eng/discover/nwmp-personnel-records/Pages/item. aspx?IdNumber=64376&.

Robert Wyld, Regimental Number 282, item no. 64377, vol. 10038, http://www.bac-lac. gc.ca/eng/discover/nwmp-personnel-records/Pages/item.aspx?IdNumber=64377&.

RCMP HISTORICAL COLLECTIONS UNIT, REGINA

Defaulters Book, Collection number 1943.10.1.

Regulations and Orders for the Governance and Guidance of the North-West Mounted Police, 1889. Ottawa: Queen's Printer, 1889, Collection numbers NF/428 and 4085.

Annual Reports of the North-West Mounted Police

THE COMMISSIONERS OF THE ROYAL NORTH-WEST MOUNTED POLICE. *LAW AND ORDER: BEING THE OFFICIAL REPORTS TO PARLIAMENT OF THE ACTIVITIES OF THE ROYAL NORTH-WEST MOUNTED POLICE FORCE FROM 1886-1887.* TORONTO: COLES PUBLISHING, 1973 (FACSIMILE ED.).

"Return of Criminal and Other Cases Tried in the North-West Territories, from 1st December 1885, to 30th November, 1886," Appendix AA to "Annual Report of Commissioner L. W. Herchmer, North-West Mounted Police, 1886." In *Report of the Commissioner of the North-West Mounted Police Force 1886.*

———. *SETTLERS AND REBELS: BEING THE OFFICIAL REPORTS TO PARLIAMENT OF THE ACTIVITIES OF THE ROYAL NORTH-WEST MOUNTED POLICE FORCE FROM 1882-1885.* TORONTO: COLES PUBLISHING, 1973 (FASCIMILE ED.).

A.G. Irvine, *Report of the Commissioner of the North-West Mounted Police Force 1885.*

SESSIONAL PAPERS OF THE DOMINION OF CANADA. OTTAWA: HUNTER, ROSE, 1868-1925 ["CSP"].

Deane, R. Burton. "Annual Report of Superintendent R. B. Deane, Commanding Macleod District," Appendix B to "Annual Report of Commissioner L. W. Herchmer: North-West Mounted Police, 1899." In *Report of the North-West Mounted Police 1899*, 15–26. CSP 1900, vol. 12, no. 15.

Gagnon, S. "Annual Report of Superintendent Gagnon, Commanding Depot Division, 1889," Appendix D to "Annual Report of Commissioner L. W. Herchmer, North-West Mounted Police, 1889." In *Report of the Commissioner of the North-West Mounted Police Force 1889*, 35–36. CSP 1890, vol. 10, no. 13.

Howe, Joseph. "Annual Report of Superintendent Joseph Howe, Commanding "C" Division, 1894," Appendix G to "Annual Report of Commissioner L. W. Herchmer: North-West Mounted Police, 1894." In *Report of the Commissioner of the North-West Mounted Police Force 1894*, 119–31. CSP 1895, vol. 9, no. 15.

An Ordinance Respecting the Administration of Civil Justice, No. 4 of 1878. In *Copies of Ordinances Passed by the Lieutenant-Governor and Council of the North-West Territories, on the 2nd August, 1878, and Laid before the Honorable the Senate and the House of Commons, in pursuance of the 3rd sub-section of the 7th Section of 40 Victoria, Chap. 7.* CSP 1879, vol. 9, no. 86, 3–20.

An Ordinance Respecting Marriage, No. 9 of 1878. In *Copies of Ordinances Passed by the Lieutenant-Governor and Council of the North-West Territories, on the 2nd August, 1878, and Laid before the Honorable the Senate and the House of Commons, in pursuance of the 3rd sub-section of the 7th Section of 40 Victoria, Chap. 7.* CSP 1879, vol. 9, no. 86, 22–25.

"Return of Criminal and Other Cases Tried in the North-West Territories, from 1st December, 1888, to 30th November, 1889," Appendix CC to "Annual Report of Commissioner L.W. Herchmer, North-West Mounted Police, 1889." In *Report of the Commissioner of the North-West Mounted Police Force 1889*, 163–88. CSP 1890, vol. 10, no. 13.

"Return of Criminal and Other Cases tried in the North-West Territories, from 1st December 1893, to 30th November 1894," Appendix FF to "Annual Report of Commissioner L. W. Herchmer North-West Mounted Police, 1894." In *Report of the Commissioner of the North-West Mounted Police Force 1894*, 194–247. CSP 1895, vol. 9, no. 15.

"Return of Criminal and Other Cases Tried in the North-West Territories, from 1st December 1894 to 1st December 1895," Appendix FF to "Annual Report of Commissioner L. W. Herchmer: North-West Mounted Police, 1895." In *Report of the Commissioner of the North-West Mounted Police Force 1895*, 194–246. CSP 1896, vol. 11, no. 15.

Steele, S.B. "Annual Report of Superintendent Steele, Commanding Macleod District," Appendix F to "Annual Report of Commissioner L. W. Herchmer, North-West Mounted Police, 1889." In *Report of the Commissioner of the North-West Mounted Police Force 1889*, 54–75. CSP 1890, vol. 10, no. 13.

Steele, S.B. "Annual Report of Superintendent S. B. Steele, Commanding Macleod District, 1891," Appendix D to "Annual Report of Commissioner L. W. Herchmer." In *Report of the Commissioner of the North-West Mounted Police Force*, 30–42. CSP 1892, vol. 10, no. 15.

Other

Deane, R. Burton. *Mounted Police Life in Canada: A Record of Thirty-One Years' Service*. Toronto: Coles Publishing, 1975; orig. pub'd New York: Cassell & Company Ltd, 1916.

Walker, James. "My Life in the North-West Mounted Police." *Alberta Historical Review* 8 (1960): 1–14.

CHAPTER 11: Dominique Clément

Cases

Bell v Ladas (1980), 1 CHRR D/155 (ON Bd Inq).

Bhinder v Canadian National Railway, [1985] 2 SCR 561.

Brooks v Canada Safeway Ltd., [1989] 1 SCR 1219.

Canada (Attorney General) v Bedford, 2013 SCC 72, [2013] 3 SCR 1101.

Grafe v Sechelt Building Supplies (May 17, 1979), BC Bd Inq (unreported).

Insurance Corporation of British Columbia v Heerspink, [1982] 2 SCR 145.

Janzen v Platy Enterprises, [1989] 1 SCR 1252.

Law v Canada (Minister of Employment and Immigration), [1999] 1 SCR 497.

Murdoch v Murdoch, [1975] 1 SCR 423.

Ontario Human Rights Commission and O'Malley v Simpson-Sears, [1985] 2 SCR 536.

Re. Mabel P. French (1905), 37 NBR 359 (SC)

Vriend v Alberta, [1998] 1 SCR 493.

Statutes

An Act to Amend the Law Relating to the Custody of Infants, S Prov C 1855 (18 Viet) c 126.

An Act to Extend the Rights of Property of Married Women, SO 1871–72, c 16.

An Act to Extend the Rights of Property of Married Women, SBC 1873, c 29.

An Act Respecting the Maintenance of Wives Deserted by Their Husbands, SBC 1901, c 18 [*Deserted Wives' Maintenance Act*, 1901].

An Act to Prevent the Employment of Female Labour in Certain Capacities, SS 1912, c 17.

An Act to Prevent the Employment of Female Labour in Certain Capacities, SM 1913, c 19.

An Act to Amend the Factory, Shop and Office Building Act, SO 1914, c 40.

An Act Respecting the Guardianship and Custody of Infants, SBC 1917, c 27 [*Equal Guardianship Act*].

An Act to Amend the Municipal Act, SBC 1919, c 63.

An Act for the Protection of Women and Girls in Certain Cases, SBC 1923, c 76, s 3.

An Act Respecting the Employment of Women before and after Childbirth, RSBC 1924, c 155 [*Maternity Protection Act*].

An Act to Ensure Fair Remuneration to Female Employees, SO 1951, c 26.

An Act to Promote Fair Employment Practices in Ontario, SO 1951, c 24.

An Act to Ensure Fair Remuneration to Female Employees, SS 1952, c 104 [*The Equal Pay Act, 1952*].

An Act to Prevent Discrimination in Regard to Employment and Membership in Trade Unions by Reason of Race, National Origin, Colour or Religion, SC 1952–53, c 19 [*Canada Fair Employment Practices Act*].

An Act to Ensure Fair Remuneration to Female Employees, SBC 1953 (2nd sess), c 6 [*Equal Pay Act*].

An Act to Promote Fair Accommodation Practices in Ontario, SO 1954, c 28.

An Act to Ensure Equal Pay to Men and Women for Equal Work, SNS 1956, c 5 [*Equal Pay Act*].

An Act to Prevent Discrimination between the Sexes in the Payment of Wages for the Doing of Similar Work, SM 1956, c 18 [*The Equal Pay Act*].

An Act to Promote Equal Pay for Female Employees, SC 1956, c 38 [short title *Female Employees Equal Pay Act*].

An Act to Amend The Alberta Labour Act, SA 1957, c 38.

Female Employees Fair Remuneration Act, SNB 1960–61, c 7.

The Equal Pay Act, SPEI 1959, c 11.

An Act to Amend the Fair Employment Practices Act, SBC 1964, c 19 [*Fair Employment Practices Act Amendment Act, 1964*].

An Act Respecting the Legal Capacity of Married Women, SQ 1964, c 66.

An Act to Prevent Discrimination in Employment because of Age, SO 1966, c 3.

An Act Respecting Divorce, SC 1968, c 24.

Family Relations Act, SBC 1972, c 20.

An Act to Amend Certain Statutes to Provide Equality of Status Thereunder for Male and Female Persons, SC 1975, c 66 [*Statute Law (Status of Women) Amendment Act, 1974*].

An Act Respecting Employment Equity, SC 1986, c 31 [*Employment Equity Act*].

Archives

BRITISH COLUMBIA ARCHIVES [BCA]

Eaton, Fraudena G. ("Mrs. Rex"). Presidential Address, 1950, Provincial Council of Women of British Columbia, file 6, box 4, PR–1124.

Status of Women Action Group [SWAG], Report on discrimination in the retail trades (1972), AR119, file 32, vol. 3.

SWAG report on the Human Rights Code (1981), British Columbia Department of Labour fonds, box 5, G84 079.

LIBRARY AND ARCHIVES CANADA [LAC], OTTAWA

A Brief from the Association for Civil Liberties to the Premier of Ontario (1951), Jewish Labour Committee of Canada fonds, file 6, vol. 23, MG28–V75.

Campbell, Margaret to A.F. Macdonald (20 February 1953), Senate Committee on Industrial Relations, box 63, Acc. 1987–88/146, RG14–20.

List of organizations, 1952–1953, Senate Committee on Industrial Relations, box 63, Acc. 1987–88/146, RG14–20.

Woloszyn, Cora to Don F. Brown (16 March 1953), Senate Committee on Industrial Relations, box 63, Acc.1987–88/146, RG14–20.

Victoria Human Rights Council Brief to the Human Rights Commission (1979), Dan Hill fonds, file 17, vol. 16, H155, MG31.

THE ROOMS PROVINCIAL ARCHIVES DIVISION, ST. JOHN'S, NL

Coates, Fred to Edward Maynard (3 November 1976). Department of Justice Papers, file 7-4-7-2, PRC #23.

UNIVERSITY OF VICTORIA ARCHIVES [UVA]

BRITISH COLUMBIA HUMAN RIGHTS BOARD OF INQUIRY COLLECTION, AR017:

Norene Warren v F.A. Cleland & Son, and David Fowler (1975), file 2.21, Acc. 97–159.

UNIVERSITY OF BRITISH COLUMBIA RARE BOOKS AND SPECIAL COLLECTIONS [UBC RBSC]

VANCOUVER STATUS OF WOMEN FONDS [VSW] ARC-1582]:

Yvonne Bill v J.R. Trailer Sales, 1977, vol. 2, file 46.

Ruff, Kathleen to Carol Pfeifer (15 December 1976), file 2, vol. 10.

H.W. v Kroff (1976), file 41, vol. 2.

BRITISH COLUMBIA FEDERATION OF WOMEN FONDS:

Human rights policy (n.d.), file 28, vol. 1.

Newspapers

Gooderham, Mary. "Ontario Drops 'Spouse' Welfare Rule," *Globe and Mail*, 26 June 1987.

"Present Brief On Equal Pay, Equal Work," *Montreal Star*, 23 April 1953.

Other

Anderson, Doris. *Rebel Daughter: An Autobiography*. Toronto: Key Porter Books, 1996.

Bird, Florence et al., *Report of the Royal Commission on the Status of Women in Canada*. Ottawa: Information Canada, 1970.

"Human Rights Board of Inquiry. Refusal to Hire: Jance Foster and BC Forest Products Limited." *Labour Research Bulletin* 7, no. 11 (November 1979): 52–53.

"Human Rights Code – Board of Inquiry Decision: Kerrance B. Gibbs v Robert J. Bowman." *Labour Research Bulletin* 7, no. 4 (April 1979): 51–52.

Indian and Northern Affairs Canada, *The Elimination of Sex Discrimination from the Indian Act*. Ottawa: Queen's Printer, 1982.

Newspaper index and outline (1974 to 1976), Acc. 1989-699-63, British Columbia, Ministry of the Attorney General, Human Rights Branch files.

Rousseau, Joseph to the Executive Council. Memorandum (n.d). History of the Human Rights Commission file, Newfoundland Human Rights Commission office files, St. John's, NL.

Sproule-Jones, Linda to David Barrett (12 December 1973), Linda Sproule-Jones private collection.

Sproule-Jones, Linda to William Black (15 January 1974), Linda Sproule-Jones private collection.

Thompson, Joey. "Human Rights is B.S. to Company Man," *Kinesis* 8, no. 1 (June 1979): 3.

United Nations General Assembly [UNGA], *Convention on the Elimination of All Forms of Discrimination against Women*. UN General Assembly, 34th Sess, 107th Plenary Meeting, UN Doc A/RES/34/180 (18 December 1979).

CHAPTER 12: Louis A. Knafla

Copies of Alberta civil action files are available in the Provincial Archives of Alberta.

Secondary Source Bibliography

"About Trove." Trove. National Library of Australia. https://trove.nla.gov.au/general/about.

Adamson, Nancy, Linda Briskin, and Margaret McPhail. *Feminist Organizing for Change: TheContemporary Women's Movement in Canada*. Toronto: University of Toronto Press, 1988.

Alston, Lee J., Edwyna Harris, and Bernardo Mueller. "The Development of Property Rights on Frontiers: Endowments, Norms, and Politics." *Journal of Economic History* 72, no. 3 (September 2012): 741–70.

Anderson, Chandler P. "American and British Claims Arbitration Tribunal." *American Journal of International Law* 15, no. 2 (April 1921): 266–68.

Anderson, Doris. *Rebel Daughter: An Autobiography*. Toronto: Key Porter Books, 1996.

Andiappan, P., M. Reavley, and S. Silver. "Discrimination Against Pregnant Employees: An Analysis of Arbitration and Human Rights Tribunal Decisions in Canada." *Journal of Business Ethics* 9, no. 2 (1990): 143–49.

Atwood, Margaret. "In Search of Alias Grace: On Writing Canadian Historical Fiction." *American Historical Review* 103, no. 5 (December 1998): 1503–16.

Backhouse, Constance. *Carnal Crimes: Sexual Assault Law in Canada, 1900–1975*. Toronto: University of Toronto Press, 2008.

———. "Nineteenth-Century Canadian Prostitution Law: Reflection of a Discriminatory Society." *Histoire sociale/ Social History* 18, no. 36 (1986): 387–423.

———. *Petticoats and Prejudice: Women and Law in Nineteenth-Century Canada*. Toronto: Women's Press, 1991.

Baillargeon, Denyse. *To Be Equals in Our Own Country: Women and the Vote in Quebec*. Vancouver: UBC Press, 2019.

Bailey, Joanne. "Favoured or Oppressed? Married Women, Property and 'Coverture' in England, 1660–1800." *Continuity and Change* 17, no. 3 (2002): 351–72.

———. *Unquiet Lives: Marriage and Marriage Breakdown in England, 1660–1800*. Cambridge: Cambridge University Press, 2003.

Bailyn, Bernard. *Atlantic History: Concept and Contours*. Cambridge: Harvard University Press, 2005.

Baines, Beverley. "Law, Gender, Equality." In Burt, *Changing Patterns*, 243–73.

Baker, G. Blaine. "The Reconstruction of Upper Canadian Legal Thought in the Late-Victorian Empire." *Law and History Review* 3, no. 2 (1985): 219–92.

Baker, G. Blaine, and Donald Fyson, eds. *Essays in the History of Canadian Law.* Vol. 11, *Quebec and the Canadas.* Toronto: University of Toronto Press for the Osgoode Society, 2013.

Baker, William M., ed. *The Mounted Police and Prairie Society, 1873–1919.* Regina: Canadian Plains Research Centre, 1998.

Bakken, Gordon Morris. "Mining and Pollution in the West: The Limits of Law Protecting the Environment." *Western Legal History* 21, no. 2 (summer 2008): 209–36.

Bale, Gordon, and E. Bruce Mellett. "Ritchie, Sir William Johnston." In *Dictionary of Canadian Biography*, vol. 12, University of Toronto/Université Laval, 2003-, http://www.biographi.ca/en/bio/ritchie_william_johnston_12E.html.

Bannerman, Josie, Kathy Chopik, and Ann Zurbrigg. "Cheap at Half the Price: The History of the Fight for Equal Pay in British Columbia." In *Not Just Pin Money: Selected Essays on the History of Women's Work in British Columbia*, edited by Barbara K. Latham and Roberta J. Pazdro, 297-313. Victoria: Camosun College, 1984.

Barbiche, Bernard. *Les institutions de la monarchie française à l'époque moderne (XVIe-XVIIIe siècle).* Coll. Quadrige. Paris: Presses universitaires de France, 2012.

Basch, Norma. *In the Eyes of the Law, Women, Marriage, and Property in Nineteenth Century New York.* Ithaca, NY: Cornell University Press, 1982.

Bataillard, Charles, and Ernest Nusse. *Histoire des procureurs et des avoués, 1483–1816.* Vol. 2. Paris: Librairie Hachette et Cie, 1882.

Bayly, C. A. *The Birth of the Modern World, 1780–1914: Global Connections and Comparisons.* Oxford: Blackwell, 2004.

Beahen, William. "For the Sake of Discipline: The Strange Case of Cst Basil Nettleship – Deserter." *RCMP Quarterly* 49, no. 3 (1984): 41–45.

Beahen, William, and Stan Horrall. *Red Coats on the Prairies: The North-West Mounted Police, 1886–1900.* Regina: Centax Books/PrintWest Publishing Services, 1998.

Beaugrand-Champagne, Denyse. *Le procès de Marie-Josèphe-Angélique.* Montreal: Libre Expression, 2004.

Beattie, J.M. *Attitudes Towards Crime and Punishment in Upper Canada, 1830–1850: A Documentary Study.* Toronto: University of Toronto Centre of Criminology, 1977.

Beeby, Dean. "Women in the Ontario C. C. F., 1940–1950." *Ontario History* 74, no. 4 (1982): 258–83.

Belich, James. *Replenishing the Earth: The Settler Revolution and the Rise of the Anglo-World, 1783–1939.* Oxford: Oxford University Press, 2009.

Bell, David A. *Lawyers and Citizens: The Making of a Political Elite in Old Regime France.* New York: Oxford University Press, 1994.

Bellomo, Manlio. *The Common Legal Past of Europe: 1000–1800.* Translated by Lydia G. Cochrane. Washington, D.C.: Catholic University of America Press, 1995.

Benton, Lauren. *A Search for Sovereignty: Law and Geography in European Empire, 1400–1900*. Cambridge: Cambridge University Press, 2010.

Betke, Carl. "Pioneers and Police on the Canadian Prairies, 1885–1914." *Historical Papers*, 15, no. 1 (1980): 9–32. Reprinted in Baker, *The Mounted Police and Prairie Society*, 209–29.

Bien, David. "Les offices, les corps et le crédit d'état: l'utilisation des privilèges sous l'Ancien Régime." *Annales: Histoire, Sciences Sociales* 43, no. 2 (March-April 1988): 379–404.

Binnema, Ted. *"Enlightened Zeal": The Hudson's Bay Company and Scientific Networks, 1670–1870*. Toronto: University of Toronto Press, 2014.

Black, Naomi. "The Canadian Women's Movement: The Second Wave." In Burt, *Changing Patterns*, 151–76.

Borrows, John. *Canada's Indigenous Constitution*. Toronto: University of Toronto Press, 2010.

———. *Drawing out Law: A Spirit's Guide*. Toronto: University of Toronto Press, 2010.

———. *Freedom and Indigenous Constitutionalism*. Toronto: University of Toronto Press, 2016.

———. *Recovering Canada: The Resurgence of Indigenous Law*. Toronto: University Press, 2002.

Boudreau, Michael. *City of Order: Crime and Society in Halifax, 1918–35*. Vancouver: UBC Press, 2013.

Bowker, W.F. "Stipendiary Magistrates and Supreme Court of the North-West Territories, 1876–1907." *Alberta Law Review* 26, no. 2 (1988): 245–86.

Bracha, Oren. "Commentary on the Copyright Act 1831." In Arts and Humanities Research Council, *Primary Sources on Copyright (1450–1900)*. http://www.copyrighthistory.org/cam/tools/request/showRecord?id=commentary_us_1831.

Bradbury, Bettina. *Wife to Widow: Lives, Laws, and Politics in Nineteenth-Century Montreal*. Vancouver: UBC Press, 2011.

Bradbury, Bettina, and Tamara Myers, eds. *Negotiating Identities in Nineteenth- and Twentieth-Century Montreal*. Vancouver: UBC Press, 2005.

Brandt, Gail Cuthbert, Naomi Black, Paula Bourne, and Magda Fahrni. *Canadian Women: A History*. Toronto: Nelson Education, 2011.

Brawn, Dale. *The Court of Queen's Bench of Manitoba, 1870–1950: A Biographical History*. Toronto: University of Toronto Press for the Osgoode Society, 2006.

———. *Paths to the Bench: The Judicial Appointment Process in Manitoba, 1870–1950*. Vancouver: UBC Press, 2014.

Brisson, Jean-Maurice. *La formation d'un droit mixte: l'évolution de la procédure civile de 1774–1867*. Montreal: Thémis, 1986.

Brockman, Joan. *Gender in the Legal Profession: Fitting in or Breaking the Mould.* Vancouver: UBC Press, 2006.

Brodsky, Gwen. *Canadian Charter Equality Rights for Women: One Step Forward or Two Steps Back?* Ottawa: Canadian Advisory Council on the Status of Women, 1989.

Brooks, C.W. *Pettyfoggers and Vipers of the Commonwealth: The "Lower Branch" of the Legal Profession in Early Modern England.* New York: Cambridge University Press, 1986.

Brophy, Susan Dianne. "The Emancipatory Praxis of Ukrainian Canadians (1891–1919) and the Necessity of a Situated Critique." *Labour/Le Travail* 77 (May 2016): 151–79.

———. "Freedom, Law, and the Colonial Project." *Law and Critique* 24, no. 1 (2013): 39–61.

———. "Lawless Sovereignty: Challenging the State of Exception." *Journal of Social and Legal Studies* 18, no. 2 (2009): 199–220.

———. "Legal Pluralism and its Explanatory Limits in Legal History." Presentation at the Canadian Law and Society Association's Midwinter Conference, Waterloo, 16 January 2016.

———. "Reciprocity as Dispossession: A Dialectical Materialist Analysis of the Fur Trade." *Settler Colonial Studies* (1 March 2018): 1–19. https://doi.org/10.1080/2201473X.2018.1432011.

Brun, Josette. *Vie et mort du couple en Nouvelle-France, Québec et Louisbourg au XVIIIe siècle.* Montréal: McGill-Queen's University Press, 2006.

Bumsted, J.M. *Trials and Tribulations: The Red River Settlement and the Emergence of Manitoba 1811–1870.* Winnipeg: Great Plains Publishers, 2003.

Burt, Sandra, ed. *Changing Patterns: Women in Canada.* 2nd ed. Toronto: McClelland and Stewart, 1993.

———. "The Changing Patterns of Public Policy." In Burt, *Changing* Patterns, 212–42.

Burton, Antoinette, ed. *Archive Stories: Facts, Fictions and the Writing of History.* Durham, N.C.: Duke University Press, 2005.

Cairns, John W. "Blackstone, an English Institutist: Legal Literature and the Rise of the Nation State." *Oxford Journal of Legal Studies* 4, no. 3 (1984): 318–60.

Campbell, Marie. "Sexism in British Columbia Trade Unions, 1900-1920." In *In Her Own Right: Selected Essays on Women's History in B.C.*, ed. Barbara Latham and Cathy Kess (Victoria: Camosun College, 1980).

Campbell, Robert A. "Ladies and Escorts: Gender Segregation and Public Policy in British Columbia Beer Parlours, 1925 to 1945." *BC Studies* 105/6 (1995): 119–38.

Canadian Civil Liberties Association. *Welfare Practices and Civil Liberties: A Canadian Survey.* Toronto: Canadian Civil Liberties Education Trust, 1975.

Canny Nicholas, and Philip Morgan. *The Oxford Handbook of the Atlantic World, c.1450–c.1850.* New York: Oxford University Press, 2011.

Carter, Sarah. *Aboriginal People and the Colonizers of Western Canada to 1900.* Toronto: University of Toronto Press, 1999.

———. "'Daughters of British Blood' or 'Hordes of Men of Alien Race': The Homesteads-for-Women Campaign in Western Canada." *Great Plains Quarterly* 29, no. 1 (2009): 267–86.

———. *Lost Harvests: Prairie Indian Reserve Farmers and Government Policy.* Montreal and Kingston: McGill-Queen's University Press, 1990.

Cavanagh, Edward. "A Company with Sovereignty and Subjects of Its Own? The Case of the Hudson's Bay Company, 1670–1763." *Canadian Journal of Law and Society/ Revue Canadienne Droit et Soci*été 26, no. 1 (winter 2011): 25–50.

Chambers, Lori. *Married Women and Property Law in Victorian Ontario.* Toronto: University of Toronto Press for the Osgoode Society, 1997.

———. *Misconceptions: Unmarried Motherhood and the Ontario Children of Unmarried Parents Act, 1921–1969.* Toronto: University of Toronto Press, 2007.

———. "Newborn Adoption: Birth Mothers, Genetic Fathers, and Reproductive Autonomy." *Canadian Journal of Family Law* 26, no. 2 (2010): 339–93.

Christie, Nancy. *Engendering the State: Family, Work, and Welfare in Canada.* Toronto: University of Toronto Press, 2000.

———. "Women in the Formal and Informal Economies of Late Eighteenth-Century Quebec, 1763–1830." *Gender and History* 29, no. 1 (2017): 104–23.

Christie Nancy, and Michael Gauvreau. "Marital Conflict, Ethnicity, and Legal Hybridity in Postconquest Quebec." *Journal of Family History* 41, no. 4 (2016): 430–50.

Chunn, Dorothy E., Susan B. Boyd, and Hester Lessard, eds. *Reaction and Resistance: Feminism, Law, and Social Change.* Vancouver: UBC Press, 2007.

Clarkson, Chris. *Domestic Reforms: Political Visions and Family Regulation in British Columbia, 1862–1940.* Vancouver: UBC Press, 2007.

Clément, Dominique. "Human Rights Law and Sexual Discrimination in British Columbia, 1953–1984." In *The West and Beyond,* edited by Sarah Carter, Alvin Finkel, and Peter Fortna, 297–325. Edmonton: Athabasca University Press, 2010.

Cliche, Marie-Aimée. "L'infanticide dans la région de Québec (1660–1969)." *Revue d'histoire de l'Amérique française* 44, no. 1 (1990): 31–59.

———. "Les procès en séparation de corps dans la région de Montréal 1795–1879." *Revue d'histoire de l'Amérique française* 49, no. 1 (1995): 3–33.

Coates, Colin M. "Problems of Precedence in Louis XIV's New France." In *Majesty in Canada: Essays on the Role of Royalty,* edited by Colin M. Coates, 181–95. Toronto: Dundurn Group, 2006.

Cohen, Yolande. "Du féminin au féminisme: l'exemple québécois." In *Histoire des femmes en Occident.* Vol. 5: *Le XXe siècle,* edited by Georges Duby, Michelle Perrot, and Françoise Thébaud. Paris: Plon, 1992.

———. "Genre, religion et politiques sociales au Québec dans les années 1930: Les pensions aux mères." *Canadian Review of Social Policy* 56, no. 1 (2006): 87-112.

Colby, Bonnie G., John E. Thorson, and Sarah Britton, eds. *Tribal Water Rights: Essays in Contemporary Law, Policy and Economics.* Tucson: University of Arizona Press, 2006.

Collectif Clio. *L'histoire des femmes au Québec depuis quatre siècles.* Montreal: Le Jour, 1992.

Colpitts, George. *Pemmican Empire: Food, Trade, and the Last Bison Hunts in the North American Plains, 1780-1882.* New York: Cambridge University Press, 2015.

Coombe, Rosemary J. "Contesting the Self: Negotiating Subjectivities in Nineteenth-Century Ontario Defamation Trials." *Studies in Law, Politics and Society* 11 (1991): 3-40.

Cooper, Frederick. *Colonialism in Question: Theory, Knowledge, History.* Berkeley: University of California Press, 2005.

Craven, Paul. "Law and Ideology: The Toronto Police Court, 1850-80." In Flaherty, *Essays in the History of Canadian Law.* Vol. 2, 248-307.

———. *Petty Justice: Low Law and the Sessions System in Charlotte County, New Brunswick, 1785-1867.* Toronto: University of Toronto Press for the Osgoode Society, 2014.

Creese, Gillian. "The Politics of Dependence: Women, Work and Unemployment in the Vancouver Labour Movement Before World War II." In *British Columbia Reconsidered: Essays on Women,* edited by Gillian Creese and Veronica Strong-Boag, 364-90. Vancouver: Press Gang Publishers, 1992.

Crête, Raymonde, Sylvio Normand, and Thomas Copeland. "Law Reporting in Nineteenth-Century Quebec." *Journal of Legal History* 16 (1995): 147-71.

Croq, Laurence. "La vie familiale à l'épreuve de la faillite: les séparations de biens dans la bourgeoisie marchande parisienne aux XVIIe-XVIIIe siècles." *Annales de démographie historique* 2 (2009): 33-52.

Daigle, Johanne. "Le siècle dans la tourmente du féminisme." *Globe* 3, no. 2 (2000): 65-86.

Dalstrom, Harl L. "Homicide on the Canada-U.S. Border." *Manitoba History* 73 (fall 2013): 9-18.

Danzig, Richard. *The Capability Problem in Contract Law: Further Readings on Well-Known Cases.* Mineola, NY: Foundation Press, 1978.

Dauchy, Serge, and Véronique Demars-Sion. *La justice dans le Nord: trois siècles d'histoire, 1667-1967.* Lille: Centre d'histoire judiciaire, 2001.

Day, Shelagh. *Reassessing Statutory Human Rights Legislation Thirty Years Later: Affirmative Action and Equality Concepts.* Ottawa: Human Rights Research and Education Centre, 1995.

Delia, Luigi. "L'encyclopédisme du *Dictionnaire de droit et de pratique* de Ferrière." In *Les Encyclopédies: Construction et circulation du savoir de l'Antiquité à Wikipédia*, edited by Martine Groult, 329–43. Paris: L'Harmattan, 2011.

Descimon, Robert. "Les auxiliaires de justice du Châtelet de Paris: aperçus sur l'économie du monde des offices ministériels (XVIe-XVIIIe siècle)." In Dolan, *Entre justice et justiciables*, 301–25.

Diamond, Jared. *Collapse: How Societies Choose to Fail or Collapse*. New York: Viking, 2004.

Dicey, A.V. *Lectures Introductory to the Study of the Law of the Constitution*. London: Macmillan and Co., 1885.

Dickin McGinnis, Janice. "Bibliography of the Legal History of Western Canada." In Knafla, *Law & Justice in a New Land*, 333–54.

Dickinson, John Alexander. *Justice et justiciables: la procédure civile à la Prévôté de Québec, 1667–1759*. Québec: Les Presses de l'Université Laval, 1982.

Dolan, Claire, ed. *Entre justice et justiciables: les auxiliaires de justice du Moyen Âge au XXe siècle*, Québec: Presses de l'Université Laval, 2005.

———. *Les procureurs du Midi sous l'Ancien Régime*. Rennes: Presses universitaires de Rennes, 2012.

———. "Regards croisés sur les auxiliaires de justice, du Moyen Âge au XXe siècle." In Dolan, *Entre justice et justiciables*, 15–32.

Doyle, William. *Venality: The Sale of Offices in Eighteenth-Century France*. New York: Oxford University Press, 1996.

Dubé, Alexandre. "Making a Career out of the Atlantic: Louisiana's Plume." In *Louisiana: Crossroads of the Atlantic World*, edited by Cécile Vidal, 44–67. Philadelphia: University of Pennsylvania Press, 2014.

Drummond, Forrest. "Supplement to List of American and British Law Book Dealers and Publishers." *Law Library Journal* 34, no. 6 (1941): 340–42.

Dykstra, Robert R. "Quantifying the Wild West: The Problematic Statistics of Frontier Violence." *Western Historical Quarterly* 40, no. 3 (autumn 2009): 321–47.

Eccles, William. *Essays on New France*. Toronto: Oxford University Press, 1987.

———. *The French in North America 1500–1783*. East Lansing: Michigan State University Press, 2000.

———. *The Government of New France*. Ottawa: Canadian Historical Association, 1971.

Edwards, Laura F. *The People and their Peace: Legal Culture and the Transformation of Inequality in the Post-Revolutionary South*. Chapel Hill, NC: University of North Carolina Press, 2009.

Elofson, Warren M. *Cowboys, Gentlemen, and Cattle Thieves: Ranching on the Western Frontier*. Montreal: McGill-Queen's University Press, 2000.

———. *Frontier Cattle Ranching in the Land and Times of Charlie Russell.* Montreal: McGill-Queen's University Press, 2004.

Erickson, Amy Louise. "Coverture and Capitalism." *History Workshop Journal* 59, no. 1 (2005): 1–16.

———. *Women and Property in Early Modern England.* London: Routledge, 1997.

Erickson, Lesley. *Westward Bound: Sex, Violence, the Law, and the Making of a Settler Society.* Vancouver: UBC Press, 2011.

Errington, Jane. *Emigrant Worlds and Transatlantic Communities: Migration to Upper Canada in the First Half of the Nineteenth Century.* Montréal, McGill-Queen's University Press, 2007.

———. *Wives and Mothers, Schoolmistresses and Scullery Maids: Working Women in Upper Canada, 1790–1840.* Montreal: McGill-Queen's University Press, 1995.

Fabre-Surveyer, Edouard. "Louis-Guillaume Verrier (1690–1758)." *Revue d'histoire de l'Amérique française* VI, no. 2 (1952–53): 159–76.

Faraday, Fay, Margaret Denike, and M. Kate Stephenson, eds. *Making Equality Rights Real: Securing Substantive Equality under the Charter.* Toronto: Irwin Law, 2006.

Ferland, Catherine, and Benoît Grenier. "Les procuratrices à Québec au XVIIIe siècle: résultats préliminaires d'une enquête sur le pouvoir des femmes en Nouvelle-France." In *Femmes, Culture et Pouvoir: Relectures de l'histoire au féminin, XVe–XXe siècles,* edited by Catherine Ferland and Benoît Grenier, 127–44. Québec, Presses de l'Université Laval, 2010.

Fernandez, Angela. "The Lost Record of *Pierson v Post,* the Famous Fox Case." *Law and History Review* 27, no. 1 (2009): 149–78.

———. *Pierson v Post, The Hunt for the Fox: Law and Professionalization in American Legal Culture.* New York: Cambridge University Press, 2018.

Findlay, Sue. "Feminist Struggles with the Canadian State: 1966–1988." *Resources for Feminist Research* 17, no. 3 (1988): 5–9.

Fingard, Judith, and Janet Guildford, eds. *Mothers of the Municipality: Women, Work, and Social Policy in Post-1945 Halifax.* Toronto: University of Toronto Press, 2005.

Finn, Margot C. *The Character of Credit: Personal Debt in English Culture, 1740–1914.* Cambridge: Cambridge University Press, 2003.

Finnane, Mark. "The Limits of Jurisdiction: Law, Governance and Indigenous Peoples in Colonized Australia." In *Law and Politics in British Colonial Thought: Transpositions of Empire,* edited by Shaunnagh Dorsett and Ian Hunter, 149–68. New York: Palgrave, 2010.

Flaherty, David H., ed. *Essays in the History of Canadian Law.* Vol. 1. Toronto: University of Toronto Press for the Osgoode Society, 1981.

———, ed. *Essays in the History of Canadian Law.* Vol. 2. Toronto: University of Toronto Press for the Osgoode Society, 1982.

———. "Writing Canadian Legal History: An Introduction." In Flaherty, ed. *Essays in the History of Canadian Law*. Vol. 1, 3–42.

Flanagan, Thomas. "Francisco de Vitoria and the Meaning of Aboriginal Rights." In *Papers Presented at the 1987 Canadian Law in History Conference*. Vol. 2, 125–60.

———. "Richardson, Hugh." In *Dictionary of Canadian Biography*, vol. 14, University of Toronto/Université Laval, 2003-, http://www.biographi.ca/en/bio/richardson_hugh_1826_1913_14E.html.

Foucault, Michel. *Security, Territory, Population: Lectures at the Collège de France, 1977-1978*. Edited by Arnold Davidson, Michel Senellart, Francois Ewald, and Alessandro Fontana. Translated by Graham Burchell. New York: Picador, 2007.

Frager, Ruth A., and Carmela Patrias. *Discounted Labour: Women Workers in Canada, 1870–1939*. Toronto: University of Toronto Press, 2005.

———. "Human Rights Activists and the Question of Sex Discrimination in Postwar Ontario." *Canadian Historical Review* 93, no. 4 (2012): 583–610.

Fudge, Judy. "The Effect of Entrenching a Bill of Rights upon Political Discourse: Feminist Demands and Sexual Violence in Canada." *International Journal of the Sociology of Law* 17, no. 4 (1989): 445–63.

Fyson, Donald. "À la recherche de l'histoire dans les bibliothèques numériques: les leçons de *Notre mémoire en ligne*." *Érudit* 59, no. 1–2 (été/automne 2005): 95–113.

———. "Judicial Auxiliaries Across Legal Regimes: From New France to Lower Canada." In Dolan, *Entre justice et justiciables*, 383–403.

———. *Magistrates, Police and People: Everyday Criminal Justice in Quebec and Lower Canada, 1764–1837*. Toronto: University of Toronto Press and the Osgoode Society, 2006.

———. "Searching for Canada's Past: A Historian's Take on Early Canadiana Online." *Facsimile* 27 (2005): 29–38.

Gadoury, Lorraine. *La noblesse de Nouvelle-France: familles et alliances*. LaSalle, QC: Hurtubise, 1991.

Games, Allison. "Atlantic History: Definitions, Challenges, and Opportunities." *American Historical Review* 111, no. 3 (2006): 741–57.

Garland, David. "Foucault's Discipline and Punish: an Exposition and Critique." *American Bar Association* 11, no. 4 (October 1986): 847–80.

Garneau, Jean-Philippe. "Appartenance ethnique, culture juridique et représentation devant la justice civile de Québec à la fin du XVIIIe siècle." In Dolan, *Entre justice et justiciables*, 405–24.

———. "Civil Law, Legal Practitioners, and Everyday Justice in the Decades Following the Quebec Act of 1774." Translated by Steven Watt. In *The Promise and Perils of Law: Lawyers in Canadian History*, edited by Constance B. Backhouse and W. Wesley Pue, 129–39. Toronto: Irwin Law, 2009.

———. "Des femmes abandonnées par leur mari: récits judiciaires de l'absence conjugale dans la région de Montréal au début du 19ᵉ siècle." In *Les Femmes face à l'absence de l'Antiquité à l'époque contemporaine: terre, mer, outre-mer (Europe-Amérique du Nord)*, edited by Emmanuelle Charpentier et Benoît Grenier. Rennes: Presses Universitaires de Rennes, forthcoming.

———. "Devenir porte-parole durant l'ère des révolutions: le lent et (parfois) difficile parcours des avocats du Québec colonial." *Criminocorpus: revue hypermédia* (novembre 2016). http://journals.openedition.org/criminocorpus/3391.

Gavigan, Shelley A.M. *Hunger, Horses and Government Men: Criminal Law on the Aboriginal Plains, 1870–1905*. Vancouver: UBC Press for the Osgoode Society, 2012.

Gibbins, Roger, and Robert Roach. *Building a Stronger Canada: Taking Action on Western Discontent* (Calgary: Canada West Foundation, 2004).

Gibson, Dale. *Law, Life and Government at Red River*. Vol. 1, *Settlement and Governance, 1812–1872*. Montreal: McGill-Queen's University Press for the Osgoode Society, 2015.

Giesey, Ralph E. "Rules of Inheritance and Strategies of Mobility in Prerevolutionary France." *American Historical Review* 82, no. 2 (April 1977): 271–89.

Gilles, David. "Le notariat canadien face à la Conquête anglaise: l'exemple des Panet." In *Les praticiens du droit du Moyen Âge à l'époque contemporaine: Approches prosopographiques (Belgique, Canada, France, Italie, Prusse)*, edited by Vincent Bernaudeau, 189–207. Rennes: Presses universitaires de Rennes, 2014.

Girard, Philip. "Married Women's Property, Chancery Abolition, and Insolvency Law: Law Reform in Nova Scotia, 1820–1867." In *Essays in the History of Canadian Law*. Vol. 3, *Nova Scotia*, edited by Philip Girard and Jim Phillips, 80–127. Toronto: University of Toronto Press for the Osgoode Society, 1990.

———. "Newcombe, Edmund Leslie." In *Dictionary of Canadian Biography*, vol. 16, University of Toronto/Université Laval, 2003–, http://www.biographi.ca/en/bio/newcombe_edmund_leslie_16E.html.

———. "'Of Institutes and Treatises': Blackstone's *Commentaries*, Kent's *Commentaries* and Murdoch's *Epitome of the Laws of Nova-Scotia*." In *Law Books in Action: Essays on the Anglo-American Legal Treatise*, edited by Angela Fernandez and Markus D. Dubber, 43–62. Oxford: Hart Publishing, 2012.

———. "Ritchie, William Bruce Almon." In *Dictionary of Canadian Biography*, vol. 14, University of Toronto/Université Laval, 2003–, http://www.biographi.ca/en/bio/ritchie_william_bruce_almon_14E.html.

Girard, Philip, Jim Phillips, and Barry Cahill, eds. *The Supreme Court of Nova Scotia, 1754–2004: From Imperial Bastion to Provincial Oracle*. Toronto: University of Toronto Press for the Osgoode Society, 2004.

Girard, Philip, Jim Phillips, and R. Blake Brown. *A History of Law in Canada*. Vol. 1: *Beginnings to 1866*. Toronto: University of Toronto Press, 2018.

Glasbeek, Amanda. *Feminized Justice: The Toronto Women's Court, 1913–1934.* Vancouver: UBC Press, 2009.

Gossage, Peter. "Familles, droit et justice au Québec, 1840–1920: aperçu global et bilan provisoire." Paper presented at the Séminaire CIÉQ-CERHIO, Angers, France, 19–20 May 2016.

Grendi, Edoardo. "Micro-analisi e storia sociale." *Quaderni storici* 35 (1977): 506–20.

Grenier, Benoît, and Catherine Ferland. "'Quelque longue que soit l'absence': procurations et pouvoir féminin à Québec au XVIIIe siècle." *Clio: Femmes, Genre, Histoire* 37, no. 1 (2013): 197–225.

Greer, Allan. "Commons and Enclosure in the Colonization of North America." *American Historical Review* 117, no. 2 (April 2012): 365–86.

———. *The People of New France.* Toronto: University of Toronto Press, 1997.

Grekul, Jana. "The Right to Consent?: Eugenics in Alberta, 1928–1972." In *A History of Human Rights in Canada: Essential Issues,* edited by Janet Miron, 135–53. Toronto: Canadian Scholars' Press, 2009.

Gurnett, Jim. "Oral Histories." In *Alberta's Human Rights Story: The Search for Equality and Justice,* edited by Dominique Clément and Renée Vaugeois, 41–58. Edmonton: John Humphrey Centre for Peace and Human Rights, 2012.

Gwyn, Julian. "Female Litigants Before the Civil Courts of Nova Scotia, 1749–1801." *Histoire sociale/Social History* 36, no. 72 (2003): 311–46.

———. "Women as Litigants before the Supreme Court of Nova Scotia, 1754–1801." In *The Supreme Court of Nova Scotia, 1754–2004: From Imperial Bastion to Provincial Oracle,* edited by Philip Girard, Jim Phillips, and Barry Cahill, 294–320. Toronto: University of Toronto Press, 2004.

Hardin, Randi Dawn Gardner. "*Knight v Thompson*: The Eleventh Circuit's Perpetuation of Historical Practices of Colonization." *American Indian Law Review* 38, no. 2 (2013–2014): 579–98.

Hardwick, Julie. *Family Business: Litigation and the Political Economies of Daily Life in Early Modern France.* Oxford: Oxford University Press, 2009.

———. *The Practice of Patriarchy: Gender and the Politics of Household Authority in Early Modern France.* University Park: Pennsylvania State University Press, 1998.

———. "Seeking Separations: Gender, Marriages, and Household Economies in Early Modern France." *French Historical Studies* 21, no. 1 (1998): 157–80.

Harvey, Kathryn. "Amazons and Victims: Resisting Wife-Abuse in Working-Class Montreal, 1869–1879." *Journal of the Canadian Historical Association/ Revue de la société historique du Canada* 2 (1991): 131–48.

Hay, Douglas. "Time, Inequality and Law's Violence." In *Law's Violence,* edited by Austin Sarat and Thomas R. Kearns, 141–73. Ann Arbor: University of Michigan Press, 1993.

Hay, Douglas, Peter Linebaugh, John G. Rule, E.P. Thompson, and Carl Winslow. *Albion's Fatal Tree: Crime and Society in Eighteenth-Century England*. London: Allen Lane, 1975.

Hébert, Karine. "Une organisation maternaliste au Québec: la Fédération nationale Saint-Jean-Baptiste et la bataille pour le vote des femmes." *Revue d'histoire de l'Amérique française* 52, no. 3 (1999): 315–44.

Hildebrandt, Walter. *Views from Fort Battleford: Constructed Visions of an Anglo-Canadian West*. Regina: Canadian Plains Research Centre, 1994.

Hoeflich, M.H. *Legal Publishing in Antebellum America*. New York: Cambridge University Press, 2010.

Hoffman, Philip, Gilles Postel-Vinay, and Jean-Laurent Rosenthal. "What do Notaries do? Overcoming Assymetric Information on Financial Markets: The Case of Paris, 1751." *Journal of Institutional and Theoretical Economics*, 154, no. 3 (1998): 499–530.

Holcombe, Lee. *Wives and Property: Reform of the Married Women's Property Law in Nineteenth-Century England*. Toronto: University of Toronto Press, 1983.

Horrall, S.W. "Herchmer, Lawrence William." In *Dictionary of Canadian Biography*, vol. 14, University of Toronto/Université Laval, 2003-, http://www.biographi.ca/en/bio/herchmer_lawrence_william_14E.html

Horton, Donald J. "Hocquart, Gilles." In *Dictionary of Canadian Biography*, vol. 4, University of Toronto/Université Laval, 2003-, http://www.biographi.ca/en/bio/hocquart_gilles_4E.html.

Howe, Mark DeWolfe. *Justice Oliver Wendell Holmes. Vol. 2: The Proving Years, 1870-1882*. Cambridge MA: Belknap Press of Harvard University Press, 1963.

Howe, R. Brian, and David Johnson. *Restraining Equality: Human Rights Commissions in Canada*. Toronto: University of Toronto Press, 2000.

Howell, P.A. *The Judicial Committee of the Privy Council 1833-1876: Its Origins, Structure and Development*. Cambridge: Cambridge University Press 1979.

Hubert, Ollivier. "Injures verbales et langage de l'honneur en Nouvelle-France." In *Une histoire de la politesse au Québec: normes et déviances, XVIIe-XXe siècles*, edited by Laurent Turcot and Thierry Nootens, 35–68. Quebec City: Septentrion, 2015.

Hundley, Norris. *Water and the West: The Colorado River Compact and the Politics of Water in the American West*. 2nd ed. Berkeley: University of California Press, 2009.

Jean, Michèle. "Histoire des luttes féministes au Québec." *Possibles* 4, no. 1 (1979): 17–32.

Jennings, John N. "The North-West Mounted Police and Indian Policy after the 1885 Rebellion." In *1885 and After: Native Society in Transition*, edited by F. Laurie Barron and James B. Waldron, 225–39. Regina: Canadian Plains Research Center, 1986.

Johnson, Benjamin H., and Andrew Graybill, eds. *Bridging National Borders in North America: Transnational and Comparative Histories*. Durham: North Carolina University Press, 2010.

Kary, Joseph. "The Constitutionalization of Quebec Libel Law, 1848–2004." *Osgoode Hall Law Journal* 42 (2004): 229–70.

Kawashima, Yasuhide. "Farmers, Ranchers, and the Railroad: The Evolution of Fence Law in the Great Plains, 1865–1900." *Great Plains Quarterly* 30 (winter 2010): 21–36.

Kelley, Donald R. "Gaius Noster: Substructures of Western Social Thought." *American Historical Review* 84, no. 3 (1979): 619–48.

Kim, Marie Seong-Hak. "Civil Law and Civil War: Michel de l'Hôpital and the Ideals of Legal Unification in Sixteenth-Century France." *Law and History Review* 28, no. 3 (2010): 791–826.

King, Andrew J. "Constructing Gender: Sexual Slander in Nineteenth-Century America." *Law and History Review* 13 (1995): 63–110.

Knafla, Louis A. "'Be It Remembered': Court Records and Research in the Canadian Provinces." *Archivaria* 18 (summer 1984): 105–23.

———. "From Oral to Written Memory: The Common Law Tradition in Western Canada." In Knafla, ed. *Law & Justice in a New Land*, 31–77.

———. "Introduction. Laws and Societies in the Anglo-Canadian North-West Frontier and Prairie Provinces, 1670–1940." In *Laws and Societies in the Canadian Prairie West, 1670–1940*, edited by Louis A. Knafla and Jonathan Swainger, 1–54. Vancouver: UBC Press, 2005.

———, ed. *Law & Justice in a New Land: Essays in Western Canadian Legal History*. Toronto: Carswell, 1986.

———. "'Law-ways,' 'Law-jobs,' and the Documentary Heritage of the State." In *Law, Society, and the State: Essays in Modern Legal History*, edited by Louis A. Knafla and Susan W. S. Binnie, 443–64. Toronto: University of Toronto Press, 1995.

———. "The Magistrate – and Humourous Magistrates – in Early-Seventeenth Century England." *Early Theatre* 14, no. 2 (2011): 183–207.

———. Preface. In Canadian Society for Legal History. *Proceedings 1977*, edited by Louis A. Knafla, i–ii. Toronto: Canadian Society for Legal History by the York University Law Library, 1977.

———. Review of *Essays in the History of Canadian Law*. Vol. 1, edited by David H. Flaherty, *American Journal of Legal History*, 27, no. 4 (1983): 389–90.

———. "Richard 'Bonfire' Bennett: The Legal Practice of a Prairie Corporate Lawyer, 1898 to 1913." In *Essays in the History of Canadian Law*. Vol. 4, *Beyond the Law: Lawyers and Business in Canada, 1830 to 1930*, edited by Carol Wilton, 320–76. Toronto: Butterworths for the Osgoode Society, 1990.

———. "Violence on the Western Frontier. A Historical Perspective." In *Violence in Canada. Sociopolitical Perspectives*, edited by Jeffrey Ian Ross, 10–39. New Brunswick, NJ: Transaction Publishers, 2004.

Kolish, Evelyn. *Guide des archives judiciaires*. Quebec: Bibliothèque et Archives nationales; revised and online ed., 2017. http://www.banq.qc.ca/documents/ressources_en_ligne/instr_rech_archivistique/garchjud_fr.pdf.

———. "L'introduction de la faillite au Bas-Canada: conflit social ou national?" *Revue d'histoire de l'Amérique française* 40, no. 2 (automne 1986): 215–38.

———. *Nationalismes et conflits de droit: le débat du droit privé au Québec (1760–1840)*. LaSalle: Éditions Hurtubise HMH Ltée, 1994.

———. "Some Aspects of Civil Litigation in Lower Canada, 1785–1825: Towards the Use of Court Records for Canadian Social History." *Canadian Historical Review* 70, no. 3 (1989): 337–65.

Lachance, André. "Une étude de mentalité: les injures verbales au Canada au XVIIIe siècle (1712–1748)." *Revue d'histoire de l'Amérique française* 31 (1977): 229–38.

Lafortune, Marcel. *Initiation à la paléographie franco-canadienne: les écritures des notaires aux XVIIe–XVIIIe siècles*. Montreal: Société de recherche historique archiv-histo, 1982.

Lamoureux, Diane. *Fragments et collages: essai sur le féminisme québécois des années 70*. Montreal: Éditions du remue-ménage, 1986.

Landelle, Marie. "'Les plaintes en séparation sont éternelles': la séparation de biens dans la haute société parisienne au milieu du XVIIIe siècle (1730–1761)." Master's thesis, École des Chartes, 2012.

Langlois, Michel. "Les Antilles et la Nouvelle-France." *L'Ancêtre*, 31, no. 4 (spring 2005): 239–43.

Lavallée, Louis. "La vie et la pratique d'un notaire rural sous le régime français: le cas de Guillaume Barette, notaire à La Prairie entre 1709–1744." *Revue d'histoire de l'Amérique française* 47, no. 4 (1994): 499–519.

Leiper, Jean McKenzie. *Bar Codes: Women in the Legal Profession*. Vancouver: UBC Press, 2006.

Leuwers, Hervé. "La fin des procureurs: les incertitudes d'une recomposition professionnelle (1790–1791)." *Histoire, économie & société* 33, no. 3 (2014): 18–31.

———. *L'invention du barreau français, 1660–1830: la construction nationale d'un groupe professionnel*. Paris: École des hautes études en sciences sociales, 2006.

Lewis, Caitlain Devereaux. "Policies of Inequality – a World Apart: A Comparison of the Policies Toward Indigenous Peoples of a Post-Colonial Developing Nation to those of a Post-Industrial Developed Nation." *American Indian Law Review* 37, no. 2 (2012–13): 423–65.

Little, Margaret Hillyard. "'A Fit and Proper Person': The Moral Regulation of Single Mothers in Ontario, 1920–1940." In *Gendered Pasts: Historical Essays in Femininity and Masculinity in Canada*, edited by Kathryn McPherson, Cecilia Morgan, and Nancy Forestell, 123–38. Toronto: Oxford University Press, 1999.

Lo Vecchio, Janolyn. "Western Women's Struggle to Serve on Juries, 1870–1954." *Western Legal History* 21, no. 1 (spring 2008): 25–54.

Looy, Anthony Jacobus. "The Indian Agent and His Role in the Administration of the North-West Superintendency, 1876–1893." PhD diss., Queen's University Kingston, 1977.

Macleod, R.C. "Canadianizing the West: The North-West Mounted Police as Agents of the National Policy." In *Essays on Western History: In Honour of Lewis Gwynne Thomas*, edited by Lewis H. Thomas, 101–10. Edmonton: University of Alberta Press, 1976.

———. "Herchmer, William Macauley." In *Dictionary of Canadian Biography*, vol. 12, University of Toronto/Université Laval, 2003-. http://www.biographi.ca/en/bio/herchmer_william_macauley_12E.html.

———. *The North-West Mounted Police and Law Enforcement, 1873–1905*. Toronto: University of Toronto Press, 1976.

Macleod, R.C., and Heather Rollason. "'Restrain the Lawless Savages': Native Defendants in the Criminal Courts of the North-West Territories, 1878–1885." *Journal of Historical Sociology* 10, no. 2 (1997): 157–83.

MacMillan, Catharine. "Canadian Cases before the Judicial Committee of the Privy Council." Institute of Advanced Legal Studies, School of Advanced Study, University of London. http://ials.sas.ac.uk/sites/default/files/files/IALS%20Digital/Digitisation%20projects/JCPC/Canadian_Constitutional_Cases_Comment.pdf.

———. "The Mystery of Privity: *Grand Trunk Railway Company of Canada* v *Robinson* (1915)." *University of Toronto Law Journal* 65, no. 2 (2015): 1–36.

Mance, Jonathan, and Jacob Turner. *Privy Council Practice*. Oxford: Oxford University Press, 2017.

Mandel, Michael. *The Charter of Rights and the Legislation of Politics in Canada*. Toronto: Thompson Education Publishing, 1994.

Marquis, Greg. "Doing Justice to 'British Justice': Law, Ideology and Canadian Historiography." In *Papers Presented at the 1987 Canadian Law in History*. Vol. 1, 20–57. Also published as Greg Marquis, "Doing Justice to 'British Justice': Law, Ideology and Canadian Historiography." In *Canadian Perspectives on Law and Society: Issues in Legal History*, edited by W. Wesley Pue and Barry Wright, 43–69. Ottawa: Carleton University Press, 1988.

———. "'A Machine of Oppression Under the Guise of Law': The Saint John Police Establishment, 1860–1880." *Acadiensis* 16 (1986): 58–77.

Martin, Roderick G. "Macleod at Law: A Judicial Biography of James Farquharson Macleod, 1874–94." In *People and Place: Historical Influences on Legal Culture*, edited by Jonathan Swainger and Constance Backhouse, 37–59. Vancouver: UBC Press, 2003.

Massicotte, Édouard-Zotique. "Nouette dit la Souffleterie." *Le Bulletin des recherches historiques* 21, no. 1 (1915): 23–25.

Mavromichalis, Anna Marie. "Tar and Feathers: The Mounted Police and Frontier Justice." In Baker, *The Mounted Police and Prairie Society*, 109–16.

Mawani, Renisa. "Legalities of Nature: Law, Empire, and Wilderness Landscapes in Canada." *Social Identities* 13, no. 6 (2007): 715–34.

Maza, Sarah. *Private Lives and Public Affairs: The Causes Célèbres of Prerevolutionary France*. Berkeley: University of California Press, 1993.

McBride, Keally. *Mr Mothercountry: The Man Who Made the Rule of Law*. Oxford: Oxford University Press, 2016.

McCallum, Margaret. "Prairie Women and the Struggle for a Dower Law, 1905–1920." *Prairie Forum* 18 (spring 1993): 19–34.

McHugh, P.G. *Aboriginal Societies and the Common Law: A History of Sovereignty, Status, and Self-Determination*. Oxford: Oxford University Press, 2004.

———. "The Politics of Historiography and the Taxonomies of the Colonial Past: Law, History, and the Tribes." In *Making Legal History: Approaches and Methodology*, edited by Anthony Musson and Carolyn Stebbings, 164–95. Cambridge: Cambridge University Press, 2013.

McLaren, John P.S. *Dewigged, Bothered, and Bewildered: British Colonial Judges on Trial, 1800–1900*. Toronto: University of Toronto Press for the Osgoode Society, 2011.

———. "Meeting the Challenges of Canadian Legal History: The Albertan Contribution." *Alberta Law Review* 32, no. 3 (1994): 423–35.

McNairn, Jeffrey L. "'A Just and Obvious Distinction': The Meaning of Imprisonment for Debt and the Criminal Law in Upper Canada's Age of Reform." In Baker and Fyson, *Essays in the History of Canadian Law*. Vol. 11, 187–234.

McNamara, Martha. *From Tavern to Courthouse: Architecture and Ritual in American Law*. Baltimore: Johns Hopkins University Press, 2004.

McPherson, Arlean. *The Battlefords: A History*. Saskatoon: Modern Press, 1967.

Menand, Louis. *The Metaphysical Club: A Story of Ideas in America*. New York: Farrar, Straus and Giroux, 2002.

Méthot, Mélanie. "Finding the Ordinary in the Extraordinary: Marriage Norms and Bigamy in Canada." In *Marriage, Law and Modernity: Global Histories*, edited by Julia Moses, 187–203. London: Bloomsbury Academic, 2017.

———. "Revoir Emily Murphy: première magistrate de police de tout l'Empire britannique." *Journal of Canadian Studies* 50, no. 1 (2016): 150–78.

Miller, Bradley. *Borderline Crime: Fugitive Criminals and the Challenge of the Border, 1819–1914*. Toronto: University of Toronto Press for the Osgoode Society, 2016.

Mittelstadt, David. *People Principles Progress: The Alberta Court of Appeal's First Century, 1914 to 2014*. Calgary: Legal Archives Society of Alberta, 2014.

Moehling, Carolyn, and Anne Morrison Pielh. "Immigration, Crime and Incarceration in Early Twentieth-Century America." *Demography* 46, no. 4 (November 2009): 739–63.

Monaghan, Jeffrey. "Mounties in the Frontier: Circulations, Anxieties, and Myths of Settler Colonial Policing in Canada." *Journal of Canadian Studies/ Revue d'études canadiennes* 47, no. 1 (winter 2013): 122–48.

Morel, André. "Canadian Legal History – Retrospect and Prospect." *Osgoode Hall Law Journal*, 21, no. 2 (1983): 159–64.

Muir, James. *Law, Debt, and Merchant Power: The Civil Courts of 18th Century Halifax.* Toronto: University of Toronto Press, 2016.

Muldrew, Craig. "'A Mutual Assent of her Mind?' Women, Debt, Litigation and Contract in Early Modern England." *History Workshop Journal* 55, no. 1 (2003): 47–71.

Nagle, Jean. *Un orgueil français: la vénalité des offices sous l'Ancien Régime.* Paris: Odile Jacob, 2008.

Neary, Hilary Bates. "William Renwick Riddell: Judge, Ontario Publicist and Man of Letters." *Law Society of Upper Canada Gazette,* 11 (1977): 144–74.

Neocleous, Mark. *Critique of Security.* Montreal: McGill-Queen's University Press, 2008.

Nettelbeck, Amanda, Russell Smandych, Louis A. Knafla, and Robert Foster. *Fragile Settlements: Aboriginal Peoples, Law, and Resistance in South-West Australia and Prairie Canada.* Vancouver: UBC Press, 2016.

Nickel, Sarah A. "'I Am Not a Women's Libber although Sometimes I Sound Like One': Indigenous Feminism and Politicized Motherhood." *American Indian Quarterly* 41, no. 4 (Fall, 2017): 299-335.

Nicol, Janet Mary. "'Not to Be Bought, Nor for Sale." *Labour/Le Travail* 78 (fall 2016): 219–36.

Noël, Françoise. *Family Life and Sociability in Upper and Lower Canada, 1780–1870: A View from Diaries and Family Correspondence.* Montreal: McGill-Queen's University Press, 2003.

Noel, Jan. *Along a River: The First French-Canadian Women.* Toronto: University of Toronto Press, 2013.

Nootens, Thierry. *Genre, patrimoine et droit civil: les femmes mariées de la bourgeoisie québécoise en procès, 1900-1930.* Montreal: McGill-Queen's University Press, 2018.

Oliver, Peter. *"Terror to Evil-Doers: Prisons and Punishment in Nineteenth-Century Ontario.* Toronto: University of Toronto Press, 1998.

Olson, Sherry, and Patricia A. Thornton. *Peopling the North American City: Montreal 1840–1900.* Montreal: McGill-Queen's University Press, 2011.

"On the Case: Explorations in Social History: A Roundtable Discussion." *Canadian Historical Review* 81, no. 2 (2000): 271–301.

Papers Presented at the 1987 Canadian Law in History Conference Held at Carleton University, Ottawa, June 8–10, 1987. 3 vols. Ottawa: Carleton University, 1987.

Parker, Graham. "The Alberta Legal History Project." *Now and Then* 1, no. 1 (1979): 7.

Payne, Brian. *Fishing a Borderless Sea: Environmental Territorialism in the North Atlantic, 1818–1910.* East Lansing: Michigan State University Press, 2010.

Perreault, Isabelle. "'Sans honte et sans regret': les chemins de traverse entre le pénal et le psychiatrique dans les cas d'aliénation criminelle à Montréal, 1920–1950." *Canadian Bulletin of Medical History* 32, no. 1 (2015): 51–75.

Perry, Adele. *Colonial Relations: The Douglas-Connolly Family and the Nineteenth-Century Imperial World.* New York: Cambridge University Press, 2015.

Phillips, Jim. "Crime and Punishment in the Dominion of the North." In *Crime History and Histories of Crime: Studies in the Historiography of Crime and Criminal Justice in Modern History*, edited by Clive Emsley and Louis A. Knafla, 163–99. Westport: Greenwood Press, 1996.

Porter, Bruce. "Twenty years of Equality Rights: Reclaiming Expectations." *Windsor Y.B. Access Justice* 23, no. 1 (2005): 145–92.

Prentice, Allison, Paula Bourne, Gail Cuthbert Brandt, Beth Light, Wendy Mitchison, and Naomi Black. *Canadian Women: A History.* 2nd ed. Toronto: Harcourt Brace & Company, 1996.

Price, Graham. "Remote Justice: The Stipendiary Magistrate's Court of the Northwest Territories (1905–1955)." LL.M. thesis, University of Manitoba, 1986.

Pruitt, Lisa R. "'On the Chastity of Women All Property in the World Depends': Injury from Sexual Slander in the Nineteenth Century." *Indiana Law Journal* 78 (2003): 965–1018.

Pue, W. Wesley, "Locating Hurst." *Law & History Review* 18, no. 1 (2000): 187–95.

Quemada, Bernard. *Les Dictionnaires du français moderne, 1539–1863.* Paris: Didier, 1968.

Ranco, Daren, and Dean Suagee. "Tribal Sovereignty and the Problem of Difference in Environmental Regulation: Observations on 'Measured Separatism' in Indian Country." *Antipode* 39, no. 4 (September 2007): 691–707.

Raymond, Michel. "Le mot du président de l'association Astrid et maire de la ville de Trévoux." In Turcan, *Quand le* Dictionnaire de Trévoux *rayonne*, 5–6.

Razack, Sherene H. *Canadian Feminism and the Law: The Women's Legal Education and Action Fund and the Pursuit of Equality.* Toronto: Second Story Press, 1991.

Reid, John Philip. *Law for the Elephant: Property and Social Behaviour on the Overland Trail.* San Marino: Huntington Library Press, 1996.

Remer, Rosalind. *Printers and Men of Capital: Philadelphia Book Publishers in the New Republic.* Philadelphia: University of Pennsylvania Press, 1996.

Reynolds, Thomas. "Justices of the Peace in the NWT: 1870–1905." Master's thesis, University of Regina, 1978.

Roth, Randolph. "W, Murder, and Probability: How Can We Decide which Figures to Trust?" *Reviews in American History* 35, no. 2 (June 2007): 165–75.

Roy, Joseph-Edmond. *L'ancien barreau au Canada.* Montréal: C. Théoret, 1897.

Salmon, Marylynn. *Women and the Law of Property in Early America.* Chapel Hill: University of North Carolina Press, 1986.

Sangster, Joan. "Debating Maternity Rights: Pacific Western Airlines and Flight Attendants' Struggle to 'Fly Pregnant' in the 1970s." In *Work on Trial: Canadian Labour Law Struggles*, edited by Judy Fudge and Eric Tucker, 281–314. Toronto: University of Toronto Press, 2010.

———. "Incarcerating 'Bad Girls': The Regulation of Sexuality through the Female Refuges Act in Ontario, 1920–1945." *Journal of the History of Sexuality* 7, no. 2 (1996): 239–75.

———. *Through Feminist Eyes: Essays on Canadian Women's History*. Edmonton: Athabasca University Press, 2011.

Savoie, Sylvie. "Les couples séparés: les demandes de séparation aux 17e et 18e siècles." In *Les marginaux, les exclus et l'autre au Canada aux 17e et 18e siècles*, edited by André Lachance, 245–82. Saint-Laurent, Quebec: Fides, 1996.

———. "La rupture du couple en Nouvelle-France: les demandes de séparation aux XVIIe et XVIIIe siècles." *Canadian Woman Studies/Les cahiers de la femme* 7, no. 4 (1986): 58–63.

Shah, Nayan. *Stranger Intimacy: Contesting Race, Sexuality and the Law in the North American West*. Berkeley: University of California Press, 2011.

Sharpe, Robert J. "Habeas Corpus in Canada." *Dalhousie Law Journal* 2, no. 2 (1975): 241–67.

Sharpe, Robert J., and Patricia L. McMahon. *The Persons Case: The Origins and Legacy of the Fight for Legal Personhood*. Toronto: University of Toronto Press for the Osgoode Society, 2007.

Shortt, Adam, and Arthur G. Doughty, eds. *Documents Relating to the Constitutional History of Canada, 1759–1791*. Ottawa: Dawson, 1907.

Sievens, Mary Beth. *Stray Wives: Marital Conflict in Early National New England*. New York: New York University Press, 2005.

Smandych, Russell. "Colonialism, Settler Colonialism, and Law: Settler Revolutions and the Dispossession of Indigenous Peoples through Law in the Long Nineteenth Century." *Settler Colonial Studies* 3, no. 1 (2013): 82–101.

———. "Contemplating the Testimony of 'Others': James Stephen, the Colonial Office, and the Fate of Australian Aboriginal Evidence Acts, circa 1839–1849." *Australian Journal of Legal History* 10, no. 1–2 (2006): 97–143.

———. "Mapping Imperial Legal Connections: Toward a Comparative Historical Sociology of Colonial Law." *Adelaide Law Journal* 31, no. 2 (2010): 187–228.

Smith, David Chan. "The Hudson's Bay Company, Social Legitimacy, and the Political Economy of Eighteenth-Century Empire." *William and Mary Quarterly*, 3rd ser., 75, no. 1 (January 2018): 71–108.

Smith, Michael Lawrence. "Girouard, Désiré." In *Dictionary of Canadian Biography*, vol. 14, University of Toronto/Université Laval, 2003-, http://www.biographi.ca/en/bio/girouard_desire_14E.html.

Solberg, Thorvald. "Copyright Law Reform." *Yale Law Journal* 35, no. 1 (1925): 48–75.

Spieler, Miranda Frances. "The Legal Structure of Colonial Rule during the French Revolution." *William and Mary Quarterly*, 3rd ser., 66, no. 2 (April 2009): 365–408.

Spoo, Robert E. "Courtesy Paratexts, Informal Publishing Norms and the Copyright Vacuum in Nineteenth Century America." *Stanford Law Review* 69, no. 3 (2017): 637–710.

Staves, Susan. *Married Women's Separate Property in England, 1660–1833*. Cambridge, Massachusetts: Harvard University Press, 1990.

Steedman, Carolyn. *Dust: The Archive and Cultural History*. New Brunswick, N.J.: Rutgers University Press, 2002.

Stokes, Mary. "Grand Juries and 'Proper Authorities': Low Law, Soft Law, and Local Governance in Canada/West/Ontario, 1850–1880." In Baker and Fyson, *Essays in the History of Canadian Law*. Vol. 11, 538–70.

Stoler, Ann Laura. *Along the Archival Grain: Epistemic Anxieties and Colonial Common Sense*. Princeton: Princeton University Press, 2009.

Stone, Arthur. "The Admiralty Court in Colonial Nova Scotia." *Dalhousie Law Journal* 17, no. 2 (1994): 363–429.

Strange, Carolyn. "Stories of Their Lives: The Historian and the Capital Case File." In *On the Case: Explorations in Social History*, edited by Franca Iacovetta and Wendy Mitchinson, 25–48. Toronto: University of Toronto Press, 1998.

———. "Wounded Womanhood and Dead Men: Chivalry and the Trials of Clara Ford and Carrie Davis." In *Gender Conflicts: New Essays in Women's History*, edited by Franca Iacovetta and Mariana Valverde, 149–88. Toronto: University of Toronto Press, 1992.

Strikwerda, Erik. *The Wages of Relief: Cities and the Unemployed in Prairie Canada, 1929–39*. Edmonton: Athabasca University Press, 2013.

Sugarman, David. "Reassessing Hurst: A Transatlantic Perspective." *Law & History Review* 18, no. 1 (2000): 215–21.

Swainger, Jonathan, ed. *The Alberta Supreme Court at 100: History and Authority*. Edmonton: University of Alberta Press for the Osgoode Society, 2007.

———. "Prologue: Louis Knafla and Canadian Legal History." In Swainger and Backhouse, *People and Place*, vii–xix.

Swainger, Jonathan, and Constance Backhouse, eds. *People and Place: Historical Influences on Legal Culture*. Vancouver: UBC Press, 2003.

Swinfen, D.B. *Imperial Appeal: The Debate on the Appeal to the Privy Council, 1833–1986*. Manchester: Manchester University Press, 1987.

Swygert, Michael I., and Jon W. Bruce. "The Historical Origins, Founding, and Early Development of Student-Edited Law Reviews." *Hastings Law Journal* 36, no. 5 (1985): 739–91.

Telfer, Thomas G.W. *Ruin and Redemption: The Struggle for a Canadian Bankruptcy Law, 1867–1919*. Toronto: University of Toronto Press for the Osgoode Society, 2014.

Thireau, Jean-Louis. *Introduction historique au droit*. 3rd ed. Paris: Flammarion, 2009.

Thomas, Gordon. *Fast and Able: Life Stories of Great Gloucester Fishing Vessels*, 50th anniversary ed. Beverly, MA: Commonwealth Editions, 2002.

Thomas, Lewis H. *The Struggle for Responsible Government in the North-West Territories 1870–97*. 2nd ed. Toronto: University of Toronto Press, 1978.

Thompson, E.P. *Whigs and Hunters: The Origin of the Black Act*. London: Allen Lane, 1975.

Thorner, Thomas. "Sources for Legal History in the Archives of Saskatchewan and Alberta." In Canadian Society for Legal History. *Proceedings 1977*, edited by Louis A. Knafla, 76–88. Toronto: Canadian Society for Legal History by the York University Law Library, 1977.

Thorner, Thomas, and Neil B. Watson. "Patterns of Prairie Crime: Calgary, 1870–1939." In *Crime and Criminal Justice in Europe and Canada*, 2nd ed., edited by Louis A. Knafla, 219–56. Waterloo: Wilfrid Laurier University Press, 1985.

Tillotson, Shirley. "Human Rights Law as Prism: Women's Organizations, Unions, and Ontario's Female Employees Fair Remuneration Act, 1951." *Canadian Historical Review* 72, no. 4 (1991): 532–57.

Titley, Brian. "Reed, Hayter." In *Dictionary of Canadian Biography*, vol. 16, University of Toronto/Université Laval, 2003–, http://www.biographi.ca/en/bio/reed_hayter_16E.html.

Tomlins, Christopher. "The Many Legalities of Colonization: A Manifesto of Destiny for Early American Legal History." In *The Many Legalities of Early America*, edited by Christopher L. Tomlins and Bruce H. Mann, 1–20. Chapel Hill: University of North Carolina Press for the Omohundro Institute of Early American History and Culture, 2001.

Tovias, Blanca. *Colonialism on the Prairies. Blackfoot Settlement and Cultural Transformation, 1870–1920*. Brighton: Sussex Academic Press, 2011.

Truth and Reconciliation Commission of Canada, *The Final Report of the Truth and Reconciliation Commission of Canada*. Vol. 1, *Canada's Residential Schools: The History, Part 1: Origins to 1939*. Montreal: McGill-Queen's University Press, 2015.

Turcan, Isabelle. "Les panneaux de l'exposition 'Trésors de la Principauté de Dombes' à Trévoux du 18 au 25 septembre 2004." In Turcan, *Quand le* Dictionnaire de Trévoux *rayonne*, 69–84.

———, ed. *Quand le* Dictionnaire de Trévoux *rayonne sur l'Europe des Lumières*. Paris: Harmattan, 2009.

Ulrich, Laurel Thatcher. *Good Wives: Image and Reality in the Lives of Women in Northern New England, 1650–1750*. New York: Vintage, 1991.

Ursel, Jane. "The State and the Maintenance of Patriarchy: A Case Study of Family, Labour and Welfare Legislation in Canada." In *Gender and Society: Creating a Canadian Women's Sociology*, edited by Arlene Tigar McLaren, 108–45. Toronto: Copp Clark Pitman, 1988. Reprinted in *Papers Presented at the 1987 Canadian Law in History Conference*. Vol. 1, 155–75.

Vachon, André. *The Administration of New France, 1627–1760*. Toronto: University of Toronto Press, 1970. http://admin.biographi.ca/en/special.php?project_id=49&p=16.

———. *Histoire du notariat canadien, 1621–1960*. Québec: Presses de l'Université Laval, 1962.

Vachon, Claude. "Verrier, Louis-Guillaume." In *Dictionary of Canadian Biography*, vol. 3, University of Toronto/ Université Laval, 2003-, http://www.biographi.ca/en/bio/verrier_louis_guillaume_3E.html.

Valverde, Mariana. "On the Case: Explorations in Social History: A Roundtable Discussion." *Canadian Historical Review* 81 (2000): 266–92.

Veilleux, Christine. *Aux origines du barreau Québécois, 1779–1849*. Sillery, PQ: Septentrion, 1997.

Veracini, Lorenzo. "Introducing: Settler Colonial Studies." *Settler Colonial Studies* 1, no. 1 (2011): 1–12.

———. "Isopolitics, Deep Colonizing, Settler Colonialism." *Interventions: International Journal of Postcolonial Studies* 13, no. 2 (2011): 171–89.

———. "Settler Collective, Founding Violence and Disavowal: The Settler Colonial Situation." *Journal of Intercultural Studies* 29, no. 4 (2008): 363–79.

———. *Settler Colonialism: A Theoretical Overview*. London: Palgrave, 2010.

Verrette, Michel. "L'alphabétisation de la population de la ville de Québec de 1750 à 1849." *Revue d'histoire de l'Amérique française* 39, no. 1 (1985): 51–76.

Voisey, Paul Leonard. *Vulcan, The Making of a Prairie Community*. Toronto: University of Toronto Press, 1988.

Von Schulte, Johann Friedrich. "Guyot, Joseph-Nicolas." In *Die Geschichte der Quellen und Literatur des canonischen Rechts von Gratian bis auf die Gegenwart*. Vol. 3, 650. Graz: Akademische Druck- und Verlagsanstalt, 1956, originally published in 1875.

Waddams, S.M. *Sexual Slander in Nineteenth-Century England: Defamation in the Ecclesiastical Courts, 1815–1855*. Toronto: University of Toronto Press, 2000.

Waiser, Bill. "The White Man Governs: The 1885 Indian Trials." In *Canadian State Trials*. Vol. 3, *Political Trials and Security Measures, 1840–1914*, edited by Barry Wright and Susan Binnie, 451–63. Toronto: University of Toronto Press for the Osgoode Society, 2009.

Waite, Robert G. "Violent Crime on the Western Frontier: The Experience of the Idaho Territory, 1863–90." In *Violent Crimes in North America*, edited by Louis A. Knafla, 53–74. Westport: Praeger, 2003.

Walker, James. "The 'Jewish Phase' in the Movement for Racial Equality in Canada." *Canadian Ethnic Studies* 34, no. 1 (2002): 1–29.

———. *"Race," Rights and the Law in the Supreme Court of Canada: Historical Case Studies*. Toronto: Wilfrid Laurier University Press, 1997.

Ward, W. Peter. "The Administration of Justice in the North-West Territories, 1870–1887." Master's thesis, University of Alberta, 1966.

———. *Courtship, Love, and Marriage in Nineteenth-Century English Canada*. Montreal and Kingston: McGill-Queen's University Press, 1990.

Watson, Alan. *Slave Law in the Americas*. Athens: University of Georgia Press, 1989.

Weaver, Sally. "First Nations Women and Government Policy, 1970–92: Discrimination and Conflict." In Burt, *Changing Patterns*, 92–150.

Webster's Ninth New Collegiate Dictionary. Springfield, MA: Merriam-Webster, 1986.

Wieacker, Franz. *A History of Private Law in Europe with Particular Reference to Germany*. Translated by Tony Weir. New York: Oxford University Press, 1995.

Wiegers, Wanda. "Gender, Biology, and Third Party Custody Disputes." *Alberta Law Review* 47, no. 1 (2009): 1–36.

Williams, David R. "Native Land Claims – Rule of History or Rule of Law?" In *Papers Presented at the 1987 Canadian Law in History Conference*. Vol. 2, 407–48.

Williams, Randall. "A State of Permanent Exception: The Birth of Modern Policing in Colonial Capitalism." *Interventions* 5, no. 3 (2003): 322–44.

Wilson, S. Craig. "Blackstock, George Tate." In *Dictionary of Canadian Biography*, vol. 15, University of Toronto/Université Laval, 2003-, http://www.biographi.ca/en/bio/blackstock_george_tate_15E.html

Wingate, Andrew. "Discrimination Against Pregnant Employees in Canada, 1988–2000." Master's thesis, University of Windsor, 2000.

Wionet, Chantal. "L'Esprit des langues dans le *Dictionnaire universel de Trévoux* (1704–1771)." *Dix-huitième siècle* 38 (2006): 283–302.

Wolf, Edwin, II. *The Book Culture of a Colonial American City*. Oxford: Clarendon Press, 1988.

Wolfe, Patrick. "Settler Colonialism and the Elimination of the Native." *Journal of Genocide Research* 8, no. 4 (2006): 387–409.

Woo, Grace Li Xiu. *Ghost Dancing with Colonialism: Decolonization and Indigenous Rights at the Supreme Court of Canada*. Vancouver: UBC Press, 2011.

Wunder, John R. *Inferior Courts, Superior Justice: A History of the Justices of the Peace on the Northwest Frontier, 1853–1889*. Westport, CT: Greenwood Press, 1979. Reprint, New York: Garland, 1999.

———. *Law and the Great Plains*. Westport, CT: Greenwood Press, 1996.

Young, Brian. "Getting Around Legal Incapacity: The Legal Status of Married Women in Trade in Mid-Nineteenth-Century Lower Canada." In *Canadian Papers in Business History*. Vol. 1, edited by Peter Baskerville, 1–16. Victoria, BC: University of Victoria Public History Group, 1989.

Zemon Davis, Natalie. *Fiction in the Archives: Pardon Tales and Their Tellers in Sixteenth-Century France*. Stanford: Stanford University Press, 1987.

Contributors

NICK AUSTIN was, at time of writing, a third-year Juris Doctor student at the University of Calgary. His primary areas of interest include intellectual property and internet law. Prior to law school, Nick completed his Bachelor of Fine Arts degree at the Alberta College of Art and Design, and still enjoys drawing and painting in his spare time.

LYNDSAY CAMPBELL is an Associate Professor cross-appointed between the Faculty of Law and the Department of History in the Faculty of Arts at the University of Calgary. Her research is largely about expression (especially libel law), race, constitutionalism, and the relationship between law and social norms between 1790 and 1914 in Canada and the British-American Atlantic. With Tony Freyer, she co-edited *Freedom's Conditions in the U.S.-Canadian Borderlands in the Age of Emancipation* (2011).

DOMINIQUE CLÉMENT is a Professor in the Department of Sociology at the University of Alberta and a member of the Royal Society of Canada (CNSAS). He is the author of *Canada's Rights Revolution*, *Equality Deferred*, *Human Rights in Canada*, and *Debating Rights Inflation*. Clément has been a Visiting Scholar in Australia, China, and the United Kingdom. His websites, HistoryOfRights.ca and statefunding.ca, serve as research and teaching portals on the study of human rights and social movements in Canada.

ANGELA FERNANDEZ teaches at the Faculty of Law at the University of Toronto and is cross-appointed in the Department of History. She has recently published *Pierson v. Post, the Hunt for the Fox: Law and Professionalization in American Legal Culture* (2018). Other recent publications include "Legal History as the History of Legal Texts," in the

Oxford Handbook of Legal History (2018), and "American Treatise Writers and the Nineteenth-Century Debate on Marriage with a Deceased Wife's Sister in the Transatlantic Context," in the *American Journal of Legal History* (2019). She is also penning a concurring dissent in *Pierson v. Post* in *Feminist Judgments: Rewritten Property Opinions*, edited by Eloisa C. Rodriguez-Dod & Elena Maria Marty-Nelson (forthcoming with Cambridge University Press). She is a contributing editor to the Legal History section of JOTWELL ("Journal of Things We Like (Lots)") and is the Book Review Editor (Americas) for the *Law and History Review*.

JEAN-PHILIPPE GARNEAU is a Professor of History at Université du Québec à Montréal where he teaches Quebec history. His research interests centre on the social and cultural history of law during the British Regime in Quebec/Lower Canada. His recent publications have focused on courts and the legal professions. He co-edited *Justice et espaces publics en Occident, du Moyen-Âge à nos jours*, Québec, Presses de l'Université du Québec, 2014.

SHELLEY A.M. GAVIGAN is Professor Emerita and Senior Scholar at Osgoode Hall Law School, York University, in Toronto. A member of the Osgoode faculty for thirty-one years, she served twice as Osgoode's Associate Dean and four terms as Academic Director of Osgoode's Intensive Program in Poverty Law at Parkdale Community Legal Services. She began her legal career as a lawyer in community legal clinics in Saskatchewan. With graduate degrees in Law and in Criminology, her scholarship is significantly interdisciplinary, located primarily in legal history, socio-legal studies, feminist legal studies, and social justice. Author of *Hunger, Horses and Government Men: Criminal Law on the Aboriginal Plains, 1870–1905* (UBC Press for the Osgoode Society, 2012), her research, involving the court records of nineteenth-century North West Territories, continues, as does her work on "historicizing criminalization" of Canada's Indigenous peoples.

ALEXANDRA HAVRYLYSHYN (JD-Ph.D.) is a postdoctoral research fellow at the Robbins Collection in Religious and Civil Law, at the University of California, Berkeley School of Law. She is currently preparing a book on black women, free soil suits, and the civil law. Her work on slavery and judges is forthcoming in *California Legal History*. She thanks the Social Sciences and Humanities Research Council, as well as the Edward Hildebrand Fellowship Fund, whose support made archival research possible for her article in this volume.

LOUIS A. KNAFLA, Professor Emeritus of History at the University of Calgary, is a legal historian whose career is focused on early modern England and Western Canada. His major project on *Kent at Law 1602* continues with Volume 6 on the courts of Wards and Liveries, published in 2017, and Volume 7 on Admiralty and Exchequer Bills, which is in progress. His co-authored book on *Fragile Settlements: Aboriginal Peoples, Law and Resistance in Prairie Canada and South-West Australia* was published in 2016. He is currently completing a two-volume biographical history of the federally appointed judges of Alberta 1886–2005. Enjoying a life of gardening, hiking, golfing, and fishing in the Kootenays, he serves as President of the Creston Historical and Museum Society and as a volunteer for the Creston Valley Wildlife Management Area.

CATHARINE MACMILLAN is a Professor of Private Law at the Dickson Poon School of Law, King's College London. Her research focuses on legal history in the common law world from 1750-1950 and contemporary private law. She has written widely on the historical development of private law, legal institutions, and individuals.

TED MCCOY is an Assistant Professor in Sociology at the University of Calgary, where he teaches Law & Society. He has written about penitentiary history in Canada's nineteenth century. He is currently researching a history of marginality and mass-incarceration in Canada.

MÉLANIE MÉTHOT is an Associate Professor of History at the Augustana Campus of the University of Alberta. She has developed expertise in legal history, particularly on bigamy in Canada and Australia. She is also researching and publishing on the administration of justice in Alberta. Méthot has a special interest in the scholarship of teaching and learning: she founded ACURIT (Augustana Conference on Undergraduate

Research and Innovative Teaching) and regularly presents papers and seminars in this field, both in Canada and internationally.

ERIC H. REITER is an Associate Professor in the Department of History at Concordia University, Montreal, where he teaches legal history and is director of the law and society program. He is also a retired member of the Quebec Bar. His research focuses on the history of Quebec civil law and the legal history of emotions.

CHRISTOPHER SHOREY currently has a broad commercial litigation practice with a focus on bankruptcy and insolvency law with Lerners LLP in Toronto. In his previous career, he spent several years crewing on traditionally rigged sailing ships, where he developed a love of the sea and all things nautical.

Index

1885 Uprising, 34, 282

Aberdeen, *The* (ship), 51-52, 54, 55, 57, 59, 71
abortion, 249, 252, 254
Act Respecting Fishing by Foreign Vessels, 52
admiralty, 6, 51-52, 55-56, 68
  cases. *See Anna, The; Gerring, Canada v*
  Judicial Committee of the Privy Council, 105
  procedure, 57
advocates. *See* lawyers
African-descended people, 245, 255
agriculture, 278, 284
Alberta, 6, 228n46, 247, 250, 251, 279, 280, 282, 284, 285
aléas du marché, 159
alienation of affection, 17
American Antiquarian Society, 46
anglophones, au Québec, 152, 164-65, 167-68
animals. *See* property
Anna, The (ship), 68
Annual Reports of the Commissioner of the North-West Mounted Police, 182, 183, 189
arbitration, 52, 69
archival case files, 12-17, 25-26
archives. *See also* Bibliography
  American Antiquarian Society, 46
  Bibliothèque et Archives nationales du Québec (BAnQ), 12-13, 38-39, 41, 128
  British Library, 109
  Burnaby (BC), 33
  Google Books, 46
  Hathi Trust, 46
  Institute for Advanced Legal Studies (UK), 109
  Library and Archives Canada (LAC), 33-34, 38, 53, 182
  Manitoba, 33
  National Archives (UK), 108-9
  prisons, 31-36
  Provincial Archives of Saskatchewan, 181, 189, 201
  Quebec, 12-16, 38-39, 128-30, 161
  as text, 7, 12
Aristotle, 84
Association canadienne droit et société, 3
attorneys. *See* lawyers
Atwood, Margaret, 34

Austin, Nick, ix-x
Australia, 37-39, 110, 275
authorship. *See* copyright
autonomie (des femmes), 153, 154, 157, 160, 167, 174
avocats, 115-17, 120-24, 133, 139n5, 159-70. *See also* lawyers
avoués. *See under* lawyers

Bacheler, Origen, 49
Backhouse, Constance, 8n14
Bakken, Gordon, 280
Balfe, Patrick, 10, 205, 206
Ballendine, Peter, 202
bankruptcy, 280
Bannister, Saxe, 271
banques de données. *See* databases
Barnes, Charles, 89
barristers. *See* lawyers
Battleford (NWT), 181, 199-217
Bayly, Chris, 273
Beahen, William, 190, 197, 200
Beattie, J.M. (John M.), 31-32
Bedford, Canada (AG) v, 259-60
Bégin, Joseph Victor, 199
Belecque, Marguerite, 159
Belich, James, 273
Bell, David G., 5, 8n14
Benton, Lauren, 275
bias, 48-49
Bibliothèque et Archives nationales du Québec (BAnQ), 12-13, 38-39, 41, 128
Bibliothéque [sic] ou Thrésor du droict français, 118
biens communs, 150, 153, 161
bigamy, 6, 37-43
Big Bear (Chief), 34-35
Binnema, Ted, 278
Blackstone Publishing Company, 86-92, 94. *See also* Text Book Series
Blackstone, William, 84. *See also Commentaries on the Laws of England*
Blake, Edward, 210
Borden, Robert, 57, 85
border (Canada-U.S.), 206, 284
Bouchel, Laurent, 118
Boucher d'Argis, Antoine-Gaspard, 119-20

347

Boudreau, Michael, 8n14, 285
Bowker, Wilbur, 208, 271
Bradbury, Bettina, 149, 152-55
Brawn, Dale, 285
Briggs, Jacqueline, 5
Brillon, Pierre Jacques, 118
Brillon, Regnier, 202-4, 206
Britain, 51-53, 56, 65-71, 115, 278. *See also* colonialism
    copyright protection of authors, 94
    influences, 2, 86-87, 103, 196-97, 242, 272, 273-75, 281, 287
    legal commentators, 87, 103
    legal historiography, 1, 271-72
    in Quebec, 115, 117-18
britanniques (Québec), 152, 154-55, 164-65, 167-69
British Columbia, 242, 244-47, 250, 262n7
"British justice," 3
Brophy, Susan Dianne, 286-87
Brougham, Henry, 104-5
Brown, George, 33-34
Brown, R. Blake, 8n14
Brun, Josette, 154
Buck, Andrew, 8n14
Buckingham, Joseph T., 46
bucks. *See under* North-West Mounted Police
Bumsted, Jack, 278
Buster v Newkirk, 62, 81n145

Cahill, Barry, 285
Calgary, 197, 278, 292n50. *See also* University of Calgary
Campbell, Colin Lorne, 220
Campbell, Isabella, 164-65, 167
Campbell, Lyndsay, x, 1-8, 39, 45-40
Canada
    Census of. *See under* databases
    colonialism on prairies, 183-84, 272-78
    Department of the Interior, 184
    federalism, 242-43
    independence of, 53, 66, 69-71
    Indian Affairs, 184, 235, 275, 282
    legal publishers, 86, 93
    Privy Council of, 66
Canadian Charter of Rights and Freedoms, 241-42, 259-60
Canadian Law and Society Association, 3
Canadian Pacific Railway, 284
Canadiana Online. *See under* databases
capital cases, 12, 187

capitalism, 286-87. *See also* colonialism
Carleton University. *See under* conferences
Carswell & Co., 86
case files *(dossiers)*, 12-17, 25-26, 38, 42n3, 161, 166
Catholicism. *See* Roman Catholics
Cavanagh, Edward, 276
censorship, 122
Chamberlain, Erika, 8n14
Chambers, Lori, 8n14
Chatterjee, Nandini, 110
chevalier. *Voir/See* knight
children, 18, 19-20, 48, 88, 134t, 180, 242, 243, 244, 246-47, 249, 251, 252-53, 283
Chinese, 244-46, 255, 263n17, 283
Choate, Joseph, 67-68
citizenship. *See* children; Indigenous people; women
civil jurisdiction, 185-87
civil law (Quebec). *See/Voir droit civil de Québec*; bigamy; family: defamation and
civil procedure. *See under* procedure
Clément, Dominique, x, 7, 8n14, 241-69
Code civil du Bas-Canada, 153. *Voir aussi droit civil de Québec*
Coke Upon Littleton, 84
colonialism, 184, 272-78, 282-84, 286-87. *See also* Indigenous people; judges; North-West Mounted Police; North-West Territories; post-colonial scholarship; sovereignty
Colpitts, George, 276
Commentaries on American Law (James Kent), 61-64, 71, 72, 83-100
Commentaries on the Laws of England (William Blackstone), 62, 84
Common Law, The (Oliver Wendell Holmes), 62
communauté de biens, 150, 154-55, 159-70. *Voir aussi/See also droits des femmes mariées*; *séparation de biens*; women (*femmes*)
companionate patriarchy, 149
Comstock, George, 88-89
conferences
    Carleton University (1987), 3-4
    Université Laval (1977), 1-3
    University of Calgary (2017), ix, 4-5, 7
connaissance des droit, 165-69. *Voir aussi* legal knowledge
Convention Respecting Fisheries, Boundary, and Restoration of Slaves. *See* Treaty of 1818
constitutional law, 259-60
continuous process, fishing as, 61. *See also* fishing

contraception, 249
contrat de mariage, 154-56, 159, 161-65, 169
Cooper, Frederick, 273
copyright, 87-90
court clerks (*greffiers*), 131, 134-38
courts. *See also* judges; juries
   Alberta civil records, 280
   Alberta Court of Appeal, 285
   Alberta Supreme Court, 285
   Cour du banc du roi (Québec King's Bench), 7, 13, 149, 156-71
   Exchequer Court of Canada, 56
   free speech in (France), 122
   Halifax Court of Commissioners, 48
   High Court of Admiralty, 68
   histories of, 285-86
   human rights boards, 256-59
   Judicial Committee of the Privy Council, 103-10, 24
   justices of the peace, 179-80, 183, 184-89, 197-99, 202-3, 207, 214, 216, 219, 220, 229n57, 243. *See also* North-West Territories
   Manitoba civil records, 280
   Manitoba Queen's Bench, 185-87, 285
   New Brunswick Courts of Sessions, 286
   New Brunswick Supreme Court, 243
   North-West Territories recorder, 184
   North-West Territories Supreme Court, 182, 187, 189, 196-97, 217
   Nova Scotia Court of Vice-Admiralty, 56
   Nova Scotia Supreme Court, 285
   Quebec civil, 27n8
   Quebec King's Bench (*Cour du banc du roi*), 7, 13, 149, 156-71
   Quebec Provost Court, 117, 120
   Quebec Superior Court, 13
   Saskatchewan Court of Appeal, 285
   Sovereign Council, 116-18. *See also* Superior Council
   stipendiary magistrates. *See* North-West Territories
   Superior Council, 128. *See also* Sovereign Council
   Supreme Court of Canada, 51, 56, 59-61, 71-72, 85, 103, 248, 254, 257-59
   United States Supreme Court, 243
coutume de Paris, 150, 153-55, 161, 169-70, 175
Craven, Paul, 180-81, 286
créanciers, 152, 154, 160-61, 165-67, 175n42

Cree
   1885 Uprising leaders, 34-35
   Big Bear (Chief), 34-35
   instigating proceedings, 217, 221-23
   interpreters, 202
   O-cha-nah-kis, 217, 221-23
   Poundmaker (Chief), 34-35
   vagrancy charges against, 228n44
criminal jurisdiction, 185-89
criminal law. *See also* criminal libel; homicide; Indigenous people; North-West Mounted Police; women
   police discipline and, 181, 188-224
   prairie historiography of, 281
   presumption of innocence, 188, 213
   records, 284-85
   vagrancy, 228n44, 252-53, 263n17, 279
criminal libel, 45-48
criminal procedure. *See under* procedure.
   See also North-West Mounted Police: disciplinary proceedings
Croq, Laurence, 158
Cumines, James, 220-21
Cuvillier, Austin, 167

Daignault, Pierre, 202, 234n109
databases (*banques de données*)
   Appeals to the Privy Council from the American Colonies, 110, 113n26
   British and Irish Legal Information Institute (BAILII), 110-11
   Canadiana Online, 38
   Census of Canada, 41
   decisions of the Superior Courts of New South Wales, 1788-1899, 110, 113n25
   Early Alberta Newspapers Collection, 47
   FamilySearch, 41-42
   Gale Primary Sources, 46
   Globe and Mail online, 47
   Internet Archive (archive.org), 46
   Making of Modern Law, 46
   Nineteenth Century US Newspapers, 47
   Paper of Record, 47
   Parchemin, 129-30
   Peel's Prairie Provinces, 37-38
   Pistard, 128, 130
   Privy Council Appeals Data, Anglo-Indian Legal History, 110, 113n24
   Privy Council Papers (UK), 110
   Programme de recherche en démographie historique (PRDH), 129-30, 132

Themis I, 161
TROVE, 42n1
Worldcat, 46-47
Dauchy, Serge, 8n13
Davies, Louis Henry, 65-68, 71
Deane, R. Burton, 192, 196, 197-98, 214
de Bauval, Henri Basnage, 119
de Ferrière, Claude-Joseph, 118-27
debt, 3, 48, 126, 244, 245, 279-80, 287. *See also/Voir aussi endettement*; property (*propriété*); *séparation de biens*
defamation. *See also* libel
   claims, 23-25
   damages, 20-24
   evidence, 15
   family and, 11-26
   goals of, 23-25
   honour and, 17-18, 20-24
   honourable retractions of, 20
   intra-family vs. extra-family, 19-20, 23-24
   procedure, 12, 15, 18-19, 21-23
   in Quebec, 7, 11-26
   temporal length of proceedings, 22-25
defaulters' books. *See under* North-West Mounted Police.
defaulters' sheets. *See under* North-West Mounted Police
desertion. *See* North-West Mounted Police.
Diamond, Jered, 281
Dicey, A.V. (Albert Venn), 103
dictionaries. *See* legal dictionaries
Dictionnaire de droit et de pratique. See under legal dictionaries
Dictionnaire de Trévoux. See under legal dictionaries
Dictionnaire des arrests, ou Jurisprudence des Parlemens de France, et autres tribunaux, 118
Dictionnaire universel françois et latin, Le. See under legal dictionaries
digitalization, 37-38
diplomacy, 64-72
discretion. *See also* North-West Mounted Police
   executive clemency, 59, 66
   Indigenous people and, 282
   police discipline, 190-200
   punishment, 33-34
discrimination, 241-69
divorce, 243-44, 246-47, 250-51
Dolan, Claire, 123, 142n36
Doren, Daniel (Captain), 51, 54

Dorsett, Shaunnagh, 5
dossiers, 157, 161-62, 166. *See also* case files
dot (*reprises*), 153, 161-64, 169, 175n47, 177n65.
   Voir aussi dower (*douaire*); property (*propriété*); *séparation de biens*; women
Doucet, Nicolas-Benjamin, 169
dower (*douaire*), 153, 155, 263n16, 279-80, 287. *Voir aussi dot*; property (*propriété*); *séparation de biens*; women
droit civil de Québec (Québec civil law), 152, 154-55, 161, 167-70
droits des femmes mariées, 149-77. *Voir aussi* women (*femmes*)
Drone, Eaton, 89-90
drunkenness, 20, 47-48. *See also* North-West Mounted Police; North-West Territories
Durand, Mortimer, 69
Dykstra, Robert, 281-82

Early Canadiana Online. *See* databases: Canadiana Online
ecclesiastical cases, 105-6
economy, 272, 278-81, 284, 286-87. *Voir aussi aléas du marché*; labour
écuyer. Voir/see esquire
editions. *See* copyright
Edmonton, 182, 278, 280
education, 56-57, 254, 256-58, 260-61
Elliott, Henry, 188, 204-9, 216-17
endettement, 153, 169. *See also* debt
enfranchisement. *See under* Indigenous people; voting
equal citizenship. *See under* women
equality, 241-69
   formal, 250-54
   substantive, 242
Erickson, Lesley, 285
esquire (*écuyer*), 125, 132, 164t9.4
evidence
   admiralty, 57
   bigamy, 40
   cohabitation, 254
   forgery, 218
   Judicial Committee of the Privy Council, 107
   Massachusetts, 48, 49
   North-West Mounted Police discipline, 198, 203-4, 205, 208, 212-13, 218, 236n114
   Quebec civil cases, 15, 20-21
séparation de biens, 168-69
executive clemency. *See under* discretion

family
  bigamy prosecutions and, 38-42
  defamation and, 11-26
  defining, 18
  divorce and, 243-44
  parenting, 48
  paternal authority, 204-5, 243-44, 248-49
  procuration (power of attorney) and, 125-26
  records respecting, 11-29, 107, 129
  séparation de biens, 151-71
family defamation (defined), 17-18
farming. *See* agriculture
fautes (du mari débiteur), 159
femmes. See women
femmes d'affaires, 154, 156, 166-67
Fernandez, Angela, x, 6, 8n14, 77n75, 83-100
Finnane, Mark, 42n1, 275
First Nations, 34-35, 188, 202, 217, 221-23, 228n44, 272, 276, 283-84. *See also* Indigenous people; Cree
Fisher, Henry George, 219-20
Fisher Rare Books Library, 46
fish (when captured), 52, 58-61, 85
fishing
  case. *See Gerring, Canada v*
  definition, 52, 58-64, 95
  purse seines, 54-55, 58-61, 85
Fitzpatrick, Charles, 40-41
Flaherty, David H., 2, 4, 6
Flanagan, Thomas, 4
Ford, James, 202, 221-23
formal equality. *See* equality
fox hunting case. *See Pierson v Post*
Frederick Gerring, Jr., The (ship), 6, 51-81
freedom of the press, 48
freedom of religion, 49
French, George Arthur, 186
French inheritance, 2, 63, 115, 124-26, 129-30
French, John, 211-13
Furetière, Antoine (Abbot), 119
Fyson, Donald, 8n13, 38

Gagnon, Sévère, 186, 218, 219, 222
Gaius, 84
gaols. *See under* penitentiaries
Garneau, Jean-Philippe, x, 7, 8n13, 149-77
Gavigan, Shelley, ix, 6-7, 8n14, 32, 121, 179-238, 274-75, 283-84
Gerring, Canada v, 6, 51-81, 83, 85, 95
Gibson, Dale, 278
Girard, Philip, 8n14, 85, 285

Girouard, Désiré. *See under* judges
Gjertsen, Claire, 8n14
Google Books. *See* archives
Gossage, Peter, 8n13
Gougeon, Marguerite, 166
grand juries, 187-88. *See also* juries
Great Britain. *See* Britain.
Greene, Samuel, 45
Greer, Allan, 146n118, 284
greffiers. See court clerks
Gull Ledge, 51, 55, 57-58, 67
Guyot, Joseph-Nicolas, 120-21, 123-24, 127
Gwynne, John. *See under* judges

habeas corpus, 195, 231n73
Halifax, 48, 51, 55, 67, 93, 285
Hamill, Sarah, 8n14
Hamilton, Robert, 5
Hardwick, Julie, 158
Harris, Douglas C., 8n14
Harvard University, 56-57, 62, 85, 110
Hathi Trust, 46.
Havrylyshyn, Alexandra, ix, 6, 115-48
Hay, Douglas, 2, 3
Hay, John, 68-69
Herchmer, Lawrence W., 187, 191-92, 195-98, 222-23, 227n36, 228n44
Herchmer, William M., 186, 187, 227n36, 228n44
high law, 121, 124, 179-81
historiography, 31-32, 115-18, 132-33, 271-88. *See also* legal history
Hoeflich, Michael, 92
Holloway, Ian, 8n14
Holmes, Oliver Wendell Jr., 62, 81n145, 85, 89-94, 98n54, 100n77
homesteading, 244
homicide, 281-82
honour. *See under* defamation
Horrall, Stan, 190, 197, 200
Howe, Joseph, 48
Hudson's Bay Company, 184, 272, 276, 278, 287
human rights legislation, 242, 254-62
Hurst, Willard, 2
huissiers. See process-servers
Hyndman, Margaret, 250

Imbert, Jean, 118
immigrants, 75n39, 116-17, 152, 164, 188, 221, 244-45, 248, 272, 276, 277, 283
Indian agents, 188, 207, 228n48

Indian appeals to Judicial Committee of the Privy Council, 104-6
Indigenous people. *See also* colonialism; Cree; Hudson's Bay Company; Indian agents; legal pluralism; Métis; sovereignty
    1885 Uprising, 34, 282
    Canadian colonialism and, 184, 272-78, 282-84, 287
    citizenship, 274-75
    criminal law and, 283-84
    enfranchisement, 251
    First Nations, 34-35, 188, 202, 217, 221-23, 228n44, 246, 272, 276-78, 283-84
    histories of, 273
    Hudson's Bay Company and, 276-78, 287.
    incarceration of Poundmaker and Big Bear, 34-35
    Indian status, 251
    legal scholarship, 277
    liberalism and, 274-75
    Métis, 188, 202, 207, 278, 282
    North-West Mounted Police and, 184, 188-89, 282-83
    North-West Rebellion, 34, 282
    resistance, 273-74, 277-78. *See also* 1885 Uprising; Riel, Louis
    settler colonialism and, 276-77
    sterilization, 250
    subjecthood, 275
    vagrancy charges, 228n14
    women, 217, 221-23, 244-45, 246, 251, 254
innocence (presumption of), 188, 213
institutes, 84, 95n6, 95n7, 118
Institutes de practique en matiere civile et criminelle, 118
intellectual property, 87-90
interlibrary loan, 47
"internal" history, 272-73
Irvine, A.G., 195, 198, 211

Japanese, 246
Jews, 245, 255
Jones, Robert, 199-200, 222-23
judges. *See also* courts
    careers, 274, 285
    Girouard, Désiré, 52-53, 60-63
    Gwynne, John, 60
    Holmes, Oliver Wendell Jr., 62, 81n145, 85, 89-94, 98n54, 100n77
    Kent, James, 81n145, 83-85, 88-89, 94. *See also Commentaries on American Law*

King, George Edwin, 60-61, 63
Macleod, James Farquharson, 185-86, 187, 200, 203, 206, 213, 222
McDonald, James, 51, 52, 56-60, 63, 64
McGuire, Thomas H., 187, 198
Richardson, Hugh, 181-83, 185, 187, 189, 201-21, 310
Riddell, William Renwick, 271
Rouleau, Charles-Borromée, 187, 197, 199
Ryan, Matthew, 185
Scott, David Lynch, 196
Sedgewick, Robert, 60-61, 63
Stewart, Alexander, 83
Strong, Henry, 60
tenure of office, 187
travelling, 117, 174
Wetmore, Edward L., 187, 196
women, 243
Judicial Committee of the Privy Council. *See also under* courts
    records of, 6, 108-11
juries, 43, 48, 94, 207-9, 216-17, 248, 251-52, 256n56, 286
jurisdiction
    criminal. *See* criminal jurisdiction
    disciplinary. *See* North-West Mounted Police
    Indigenous people, 275-76. *See also* colonialism; sovereignty; North-West Territories
    international waters. *See* three-mile limit
justices of the peace. *See under* North-West Territories. *See also* judges

Kent, James, 81n145, 83-85, 88-89, 94. *See also Commentaries on American Law*
Kent, William, 85, 88-89
Kiely, Frank, 199, 216, 222-23
King, George Edwin. *See under* judges
Kingston Penitentiary. *See under* penitentiaries
Knafla, Louis A., x, 1-3, 7, 8n14, 271-95
knight (*chevalier*), 125, 132
Knopff, Rainer, 3
Knowlton, Charles (Captain), 51, 55, 57, 59
Kolish, Evelyn, 152
Komagatu Maru, The (ship), 75n39
Kostal, Rande, 8n14

labour
    fishing, 54-55
    fur trade era, 276-78, 287

hard. *See* North-West Mounted Police:
   punishment
Hudson's Bay Company, 276-77, 287
Indigenous people, 287
intellectual property and, 88-90
mobility, 278-79
prairies and, 276-77, 280-81, 287. *See also*
   North-West Mounted Police
prisoners, 43n9, 193
property and, 58-59
women, 3-4, 241, 244-47, 249, 250, 252-56,
   258
Lacy, William M., 87, 90-92
Laperrière, Marie-Neige, 8n13
Laurier, Wilfrid, 66, 69
Laval University. *See* conferences: *Université Laval*
lawyers. *See also* notaries; *procuration*
   in admiralty court, 56
   advocates (*avocats*), 115-17, 120-24, 133, 139n5, 159-70
   attorneys (*procureurs*), 116-17, 120-38
   avoués, 124
   barristers (*avocats*), 121-23, 127-28, 139n5
   career paths, 85, 130-31
   definitions, 115-16
   France, 120-27
   as historians, 271
   Lacy, William M., 87, 90-92
   in libel cases, 48
   MacCoy, William F., 56-58
   merit and, 125
   mobility of, 129, 132-33
   police disciplinary proceedings and, 195-97, 214
   practitioners (*praticiens*), 116-18, 120, 125-26, 130-38
   purchasing venal office, 121-22
   Quebec (New France), 115-18, 127-33
   reputation of, 117
   Ritchie, W.B.A. (William Bruce Almon), 56-57, 58, 62-63, 75n39, 83, 85, 93
   social status of, 120-23, 127, 131-32
   women, 246, 248. *See also procuratrices*
legal dictionaries, 118-27
   Dictionnaire de droit et de pratique, 119-20, 123-24, 126-27
   Dictionnaire de Trévoux, 119-20, 127
   Dictionnaire des arrests, ou Jurisprudence des Parlemens de France, et autres tribunaux, 118

Dictionnaire universel françois et latin, Le. See Dictionnaire de Trévoux
Répertoire universel et raisonné de jurisprudence civile, criminelle, canonique et bénéficiale, 120, 124, 127
legal education, 56-57, 84, 86-87, 115-17, 119-21, 123
legal history. *See also* historiography
   Canadian, 1-5
   feminism and, 3-4
   gender and, 3-4
   Marxism and, 4
   social history and, 3
   western Canadian, 271-88
   Wisconsin School, 2
legal knowledge (*connaissance des droits*), 62-63, 83-100, 106, 118-27, 165-69
legal pluralism, 275-77. *See also* colonialism; sovereignty
legal precedent, 71-72
legal publishing, 85-95, 96n24, 99n71, 106, 107
legal treatises, 86, 87, 89, 95n7, 96n9, 106, 110
lexicographers, 118, 121-24, 126-27, 130-31. *See also* legal dictionaries
libel, x, 13, 45-48. *See also* defamation
liberalism, 274, 283
Library and Archives Canada (LAC). *See under* archives
Little, Brown (publishers), 85, 89-92, 94
Little, J.W., 188
Lodge, Henry Cabot, 69-70
London (ON), 271
London (UK), 59, 68, 103-4, 108-11
low law, 179-84, 187, 221
Lower Canada. *See.*Quebec
Lozier, Jean-François, 5

MacCoy, William F. *See under* lawyers
Macdonald, John A., 184, 191, 283
Macleod, James Farquharson. *See under* judges
MacMillan, Catharine, x, 6, 8n14, 103-13
Maffitt (Maffit), John, 46
Manitoba, 182, 242, 246, 247, 248, 251, 278, 279, 280, 282, 285, 287
marchandes publiques, 154, 156
Marks, Grace, 34
Marquis, Greg, 3, 8n14, 184
marriage (*mariage*). *See also/Voir aussi* bigamy; divorce; family; *séparation de biens*; *séparation de corps*; women
   contrat de mariage, 154-56, 161-65, 169

elopement, 204-9
parental consent, 234n118, 243
records, 41, 129, 132
seduction, 248-49
settlements, 153-54
validity, 204-5, 234n118
married women's rights. *See* women
Marshall, Norton, 203-6, 213
Martin, John, 219-20
Massachusetts, 45-50, 54, 62, 67, 69, 93
McCallum, Margaret, 279
McCoy, Ted, x, 1-8, 31-36
McDonald, James. *See under* judges
McGuire, Thomas H. *See under* judges
McHugh, P.G., 274
McLaren, John P.S., 3, 8n14, 274
McMahon, Patricia L., 285
McManus, Robert, 214-15
McNairn, Jeffrey L., 8n14, 184
Méthot, Mélanie, x, 1-8, 37-43
Métis. *See also* Indigenous people
   1885 Uprising, 282
   Ballendine, Peter, 202
   in Battleford (NWT), 202
   Daignault, Pierre, 202
   historical writing, 278
   jurors, 207
   North-West Mounted Police and, 188
   North-West Rebellion, 282
   Riel, Louis, 210
microforms, 47
Miller, Bradley, 8n14, 181
minorities, 48, 152, 154-55, 164-65, 167-69, 244-46, 251, 253, 255, 262n7, 276-77, 283, 287.
   See also Indigenous people
Mittelstadt, David, 285
Monaghan, Jeffrey, 282
Montreal, x, 11, 13, 20-23, 38, 131, 149-70. *Voir aussi* Université de Montréal
Moody, William, 67-68
Morin, Michel, 8n13
Mormons. *See under* North-West Mounted Police
Morris, Edward (Captain), 51-52, 54, 56-57, 59-60, 65-68, 71, 73
Muir, James, 8n14
mythology-building, ix

natural resources, 272, 275, 280-81. *See also* fish
New Brunswick, 67, 115, 180, 243, 245, 249, 251, 263n12, 286

New France. *See* Quebec
New York, 45, 52, 62, 93, 209
Newfoundland and Labrador, 74n17, 253, 256, 266n59
newspapers, 38-40, 45-50, 52, 54, 105-6, 217
nobility, 131-32
Noel, Jan, 153, 155
Nootens, Thierry, 8n13
North-West Mounted Police
   as accused, 179-238
   bucks, 201, 231n77
   Canadian colonial aspirations and, 183-84
   cattle theft, 284
   commissioners, 186
   criminal proceedings against, 6, 189-224
   defaulters' books, 190, 194-95
   defaulters' sheets, 182, 190, 194, 216
   desertion, 182, 190-91, 196, 201, 203-04, 206, 213, 217-19, 234n105
   disciplinary jurisdiction, 195-98, 229n57
   disciplinary offences, 190-96, 230n64
   disciplinary proceedings, 181-84, 189-224
   drunkenness, 190, 193-95, 198, 211, 221-22
   force size, 191
   geographical divisions, 229n58
   habeas corpus, 195, 231n73
   Indigenous people and, 184, 188-89, 283
   innocence, presumption of, 188, 213
   insubordination, 190, 194, 200, 209-13
   justice, 183-84
   living conditions, 202
   military nature, 196-97, 200
   Mormons and, 188
   organization, 229n58
   prohibition of alcohol, 190, 193, 209-10, 219, 221, 230n64
   punishment, 190-96, 198-201, 203, 207-9, 213, 218-20, 222-23, 231n77
   ranks, 186-89, 211, 229n58
   records, 181-82
   recreation, 210
   recruits, 209-10
   Royal Irish Constabulary and, 190
   rules and regulations, 189-93, 196-97
   theft and, 192, 199, 201-04, 206-09, 216-17, 219-20, 222-23, 236n144, 237n145, 284
North-West Rebellion, 34, 282. *See also* Riel, Louis
North-West Territories. *See also* Cree, First Nations, Métis, Indigenous people

Council, 181
dower, 279
francophones. *See* Bégin, Joseph Victor;
    judges: Rouleau, Charles-Borromée
justices of the peace, 179-80, 183-89, 197-99,
    202-03, 207, 214, 216, 219-20, 229n57,
    243
legal pluralism, 275-76
Lieutenant-Governor, 203
ordinances, 181, 185
prohibition of alcohol in, 193
recorder, 184
Saskatchewan district, 181, 225n14
settlers, 276
stipendiary magistrates, 181, 184-87, 202,
    206, 214, 222, 229n57, 286
Supreme Court, 182, 187, 189, 196-97, 217
notaries (*notaires*), 128-30, 134-38, 159, 166,
    168-69
Nova Scotia, 6, 48, 51, 54-56, 67, 72f, 74n17, 83,
    85, 96n22, 115, 243, 263n12, 268n90, 285
nuisance, 280-81

O'Byrne, Nicole, 5, 8n14
O-cha-nah-kis, 217, 221-23
Oliver, Peter, 32
Ontario, 31-32, 180, 181, 209, 210, 211, 242-47,
    250-51, 255, 256, 259, 269n99, 271, 277, 280
Osgoode Society for Canadian Legal History,
    2, 271
Osgoode, William, ix

Pacione, Darren, 8n13
Painter, Genevieve, 5
pamphlets, 45-50
Papineau, Louis-Joseph, 150
Papineau, Rosalie, 149-51, 157, 168
Parken, Arthur Miles, 198
Parker, Stephan, 8n14
Parkins, Walter Douglas, 214-16
Parmar, Pooja, 8n14
patriarcat (patriarchy), 150-51, 153, 156, 161, 166,
    169-70
Pauncefote, Julian, 65-66
Pearlston, Karen, 8n14
penitentiaries
    gaols vs., 36, 43n9
    histories of, 31-32
    Kingston Penitentiary, x, 31-34
    Manitoba, 33, 34
    New Westminster, 33
    North-West Rebellion and, 34
    Ontario, 31-32
    prisoners, 34-35
Perrault, Marie-Claire, 167
Persons Case, 107, 248, 285
Philadelphia, 87, 92, 93
Phillips, Jim, 8n14, 285
Pierson v Post, ix, 52-53, 61-64, 71-72
Pike, Sarah P., 5
Pinkerton Agency, 284
piracy (in publishing), 87, 93, 97n32
pleadings, 15, 107
police. *See also* North-West Mounted Police
    approaches, 283
    criminal justice and, 188-224
    immigrants, 283
politics
    interaction with law, 52-53, 64-72
    post-colonial scholarship, 273-78, 282-84, 287
Poundmaker (Chief), 34-35
power of attorney (*procuration*), 125-26, 130,
    155-56
Powers, John W., 214-15
practitioners. *See under* lawyers.
Prairies
    Confederation and, 277-78
    historiography of, 7, 271-89
    water, 275, 279, 287
praticiens. *See under* lawyers
precedent (legal), 71-72
preliminary hearings, 187-88
Presbyterians, 204-05
Price, Graham, 8n14, 286
priests, 38-40
Prince Edward Island, 115, 243, 263n12
prison records, 6, 31-36
prisons (provincial), 36n1. *See also* penitentiaries
prisoners, 34-36. *See also* North-West Mounted
    Police
procedure
    admiralty, 57
    civil, 12, 15, 18-19, 21-23, 48-49, 128
    criminal, 39, 48, 187-88, 198, 202-3, 205-9,
        214-15
    Judicial Committee of the Privy Council,
        106-7
process-servers (*huissiers*), 131, 134-38
procuration (power of attorney), 125-26, 130,
    155-56
procuratrices, 126
procureurs. *See under* lawyers

prohibition of alcohol. *See under* North-West Mounted Police; North-West Territories. *See also* drunkenness
property (*propriété*). *See also Buster v Newkirk*; *Pierson v Post*; *State v Shaw*
- biens communs, 150, 153, 161
- Blackstone, 84-85
- dot (*reprises*), 153, 161-64, 169, 175n47, 177n65. *Voir aussi* dower (*douaire*); séparation de biens
- dower (*douaire*), 153, 155, 263n16, 279-80, 287. *Voir aussi dot*; séparation de biens
- endettement des ménages, 153, 169
- fish, 52, 58-64, 72, 85, 95
- intellectual, 87-90
- Kent, 84-85. *See also Commentaries on American Law*; Kent, James
- married women (*femmes mariées*), 149-70, 244-45, 247, 251, 254
- nuisance, 280-81
- open range, 284
- qualified property, 84-85
- reprises. *Voir dot*
- séparation de biens, 151-71. *Voir aussi dot*; dower (*douaire*)
- venal offices (France), 121-22, 124-25
- wild animals, 52-53, 62-64, 84-85, 95. *See also* property: fish
prostitution. *See* women: sex work
publishing. *See* legal publishing
Pue, W. Wesley, 4
puissance d'agir (des femmes), 150-51, 156. *Voir aussi procuratrices*
punishment. *See also* North-West Mounted Police; penitentiaries; women
- abortion, 249
- human rights remedies, 257, 259, 260-61
- seduction, 249
- women (discrimination in), 252
Quebec (*Bas-Canada*, New France). *See also* archives; courts
- defamation in, 11-26
- divorce in, 243-44
- juries, 265n56
- lawyers in, 6, 115-48
- origines britanniques en, 152, 154-55, 164-65, 167, 169
- Sovereign Council, 116-17, 124
racialized minorities, 35, 48, 244-46, 251, 255, 263n17, 283. *See also* Indigenous people

Red River colony, 278
Reed, Hayter, 207
Regina, 182, 202, 215, 218-23, 278
Reid, John Phillip, 279
Reiter, Eric, 7, 8n13, 11
religion, 46, 49, 119, 129, 204, 221, 243, 255-56, 261, 267n78, 273, 276
renonciation, 161-66
Répertoire universel et raisonné de jurisprudence civile, criminelle, canonique et bénéficiale. *See under* legal dictionaries
reprises. *Voir dot*
Richardson, Hugh. *See under* judges
Richardson, Luders, 204-5, 209
Riddell, William Renwick, 271
Riel, Louis, 210, 277-78. *See also* 1885 Uprising
Risk, R.C.B., 2, 6
Ritchie, W.B.A. (William Bruce Almon). *See under* lawyers
Ritchot, Victoire, 166, 168
Robinson, George Thomas, 201, 217-18
Roman Catholics, 119, 129, 155, 221
Root, Elihu, 69
Rouleau, Charles-Borromée. *See under* judges
Royal Canadian Mounted Police, 252-53, 275. *See also* North-West Mounted Police
Royal Commission on the Status of Women (RCSW). *See under* women
Ryan, Matthew. *See under* judges

Saskatchewan, 6, 246, 247, 251, 267n78, 279, 282, 284, 285-86
Saskatchewan district, 181, 225n14
Saskatoon, 280
schooner. *See* fishing schooner
Scott, David Lynch. *See under* judges
Sedgewick, Robert. *See under* judges
sentencing. *See* punishment
séparation de biens, 151-71. *Voir aussi/See also dot*; dower (*douaire*); property (*propriété*); women
séparation de corps, 156-58
separation from bed and board, 17
Sessional Papers of the Dominion of Canada, 32
settlement (of cases), 70-71
settler colonialism, 276, 287. *See also* colonialism
sex discrimination, 241-69. *See also* women
sexual orientation (discrimination on the basis of), 258
Sharpe, Robert J., 285
Sherman, John, 65-66

ships, 73n3. *See also* Aberdeen, *The*; Anna, *The*; Frederick Gerring, Jr., *The*; Komagata Maru, *The*
Shorey, Christopher, ix, 6, 8n14, 51-81
Simon, Robert, 119
slander. *See* defamation. *See also* libel
Smith, Charlotte, 110
Smith, David, 278
Smith, Henry, 33-34
Snelling, William J., 47
Société de recherche historique Archiv-Histo, 129
Souciet, Etienne, 119
sources, 6. *See also* Bibliography
Sovereign Council, 116-18
sovereignty, 275. *See also* colonialism; *Frederick Gerring, Jr., The*; Hudson's Bay Company; post-colonial scholarship
Spieler, Miranda, 127
State v Shaw, 64
Steele, Samuel B., 200, 210
sterilization, 250
Stewart, Alexander. *See under* judges
stipendiary magistrates. *See under* North-West Territories
Stokes, Mary, 8n14, 180, 183
Strange, Carolyn, 8n14, 12, 38
Strikwerda, Erik, 280
Strong, Henry. *See under* judges
Stubbs, Roy St. George, 271
Superior Council, 128. *See also* Sovereign Council
Supreme Court of Canada. *See under* courts
Swainger, Jonathan, 8n14, 285

taxation, 131-32
Telfer, Thomas, 280
témoins. *See* witnesses
Text Book Series, 85, 90-92, 94. *See also* Blackstone Publishing Company
theft, 21-22, 64, 76n58, 185, 192, 198-204, 206-09, 211, 216-17, 219-20, 221-23, 236n144, 237n145, 252, 284
three-mile limit, 51, 55-57, 59, 65, 67-68
Thomas, Lewis, 271
Thompson, E.P. (Edward Palmer), 2, 3
Toronto, 210, 217-19
Toronto Public Library, 46
Tovias, Blanca, 274
treatises. *See* legal treatises
Treaty of 1818 (Britain-U.S.), 51, 64, 67-68
Treaty of Paris 1763, 115

UBC Press Law and Society Series, 4
Ukrainians, 276, 287
United Kingdom. *See* Britain
United States
   government, 52, 65-71
   influences, 2, 53, 61-71, 83-84, 87-88, 92-93, 272, 274
   legal publishers, 85-95
Université de Montréal, 129
Université Laval. *See under/Voir sous* conferences
University of Calgary. *See under* conferences
University of Toronto, 31, 46
Upper Canada. *See* Ontario
urbanization, 128, 278, 281-82, 284-854
Ursel, Jane, 3-4

Valverde, Mariana, 25
venal offices, 121-22, 124-25
Veracini, Lorenzo, 276
Verrier, Louis-Guillaume, 127-28
violence, 33, 221-23, 230n64, 244, 246-47, 252, 280-83
voting, 242-43, 245, 247-51, 260, 262n7, 266n59

Walker, Barrington, 8n14
Walker, James (NWMP), 202-3, 206-8, 216-17
Ward, Peter, 184
welfare. *See* women: benefits
Wetmore, Edward L. *See under* judges
Wheaton v Peters, 88, 90, 94
Whitman, Benjamin, 47, 48
wild animals. *See under* property
Williams, D. Colwyn, 271
Williams, David R., 4
Winnipeg, 203, 278, 280
witnesses (*témoins*), 15, 48-49, 159, 203, 214-16
women (*femmes*). *See also* bigamy; divorce; family; marriage; *séparation de corps*
   abandoned (*abandonnées*), 166, 168, 246
   abduction of heiress, 205
   abortion, 249, 252
   activism of, 7
   African-descended, 245
   alimony. *See* divorce
   anglophoniques (au Québec). *Voir origines britanniques*
   autonomie des, 153-54, 157, 160, 167, 174
   benefits (federal and provincial), 247, 249, 250, 252, 253-54, 259
   children and, 48, 246-47
   Chinese, 244-46

citizenship, 243-50, 252
communauté de biens, 150, 154-55, 159-70
connaissance de ses droits, 165-69
contraception, 249
contracts, 244-45. *Voir aussi* women: *femmes d'affaires*
Convention on the Elimination of All Forms of Discrimination against Women, 253
criminal law, 248-49, 252-54, 259-60, 285
custody, 246
debts, 244-45. *Voir aussi* women: *femmes d'affaires*
discrimination, 241-69
divorce, 243-44, 246-47, 250-51
dot (*reprises*), 153, 161-64, 169, 175n47, 177n65. *Voir aussi* dower (*douaire*), property (*propriété*), *séparation de biens*
dower (*douaire*), 153, 155, 263n16, 279-80, 287. *Voir aussi dot*; property (*propriété*); *séparation de biens*
droits des femmes mariées, 150, 152-53, 159, 165-66. *Voir aussi* women: married
education, 246
elopement, 204-09
employment, 241-56, 258
equal citizenship, 242-50, 260
equal pay, 250, 256
equality, 7, 241-69
femmes d'affaires, 154, 156, 166-67
formal equality, 250-54
historiography of rights, 241-69
homesteading, 244
human rights, 254-61
imprisonment, 35-36
Indigenous, 217, 221-23, 244-46, 251, 254
Japanese, 246
Jewish, 245
juries, 248, 250, 252, 265n56, 286
lawyers, 246, 248. *Voir aussi procuratrices*
lesbians, 258
maintenance. *See* divorce
"man in the house" (policy), 254, 259
marchandes publiques, 154, 156
married (*mariées*), 7, 126, 149-70, 221, 241, 243-45, 250-54. *See also droits des femmes mariées*
military service, 252-53
minimum wage, 247, 251

names, 252, 254
newspapers and pamphlets, 6, 37-43, 48
O-cha-nah-kis, 217, 221-23
organizations, 247, 250, 255, 256, 258-59
origines britanniques au Québec, 152, 154-55, 164-65, 167-69
Persons Case, 107, 248, 285
pregnancy, 253, 255, 258, 259. *See also* abortion
procuratrices, 126
professionals, 246, 248. *Voir aussi procuratrices*
property of (*propriéte de*), 149-70, 244, 245, 247, 251, 254
prostitution. *See* sex work
protective legislation, 242, 244-46
public office-holding, 243, 247-48
puissance d'agir, 150-51, 156. *Voir aussi procuratrices*
racialized minorities, 244-45, 251. *See also* Indigenous people
rape, 244, 248, 253
in Royal Canadian Mounted Police, 252-53
Royal Commission on the Status of Women (RCSW), 252-53
seduction, 248, 252-53
as senators, 248
sentencing, 252
séparation de biens, 151-54, 156-71. *Voir aussi dot*; dower (*douaire*); property (*propriété*)
sex work, 217, 221-23, 245, 253, 259-60
sexual harassment, 258-59
solicitation, 245, 249, 253, 259-60
"spouse in the house" rule. *See* women: "man in the house"
sterilization, 250
subordination, 151, 154, 156, 241-61
substantive equality, 242, 254-62
vagrancy, 252, 253, 263n17
veuves, 155. *See also* women: widows
violence against, 244, 246-47, 252
voting, 242-43, 245, 247-51, 260, 262n7, 266n59
widows, 244. *Voir aussi* women: *veuves*
Wyld, Richard Charles, 201, 209-13, 216, 219

Young, Brian, 8n13